MILITARY STRATEGY, JOINT OPERATIONS, AND AIRPOWER

Other Titles of Interest from Georgetown University Press

Arms Control for the Third Nuclear Age: Between Disarmament and Armageddon
David A. Cooper

China's Strategic Arsenal: Worldview, Doctrine, and Systems
James M. Smith and Paul J. Bolt, Editors

Diplomacy and the Future of World Order
Chester A. Crocker, Fen Osler Hampson, and Pamela Aall, Editors

Geospatial Intelligence: Origins and Evolution
Robert M. Clark

The National Security Enterprise: Navigating the Labyrinth, Second Edition
Roger Z. George and Harvey Rishikof, Editors

Reconsidering the American Way of War: US Military Practice from the Revolution to Afghanistan
Antulio J. Echevarria II

Russian Cyber Operations: Coding the Boundaries of Conflict
Scott Jasper

US Foreign Policy and Defense Strategy: The Evolution of an Incidental Superpower
Derek S. Reveron, Nikolas K. Gvosdev, and Mackubin Thomas Owens

War and the Art of Governance: Consolidating Combat Success into Political Victory
Nadia Schadlow

MILITARY STRATEGY, JOINT OPERATIONS, AND AIRPOWER

AN INTRODUCTION

SECOND EDITION

Ryan Burke
Michael Fowler
Jahara Matisek
Editors

Georgetown University Press / Washington, DC

Library of Congress Cataloging-in-Publication Data

Names: Burke, Ryan, editor. | Fowler, Michael W., 1971– editor. | Matisek, Jahara, 1983– editor.
Title: Military strategy, joint operations, and airpower : an introduction / Ryan Burke, Michael Fowler, Jahara Matisek, editors.
Description: Second edition. | Washington, DC : Georgetown University Press, 2022. | Includes bibliographical references and index.
Identifiers: LCCN 2021037937 (print) | LCCN 2021037938 (ebook) | ISBN 9781647122508 (paperback) | ISBN 9781647122492 (hardcover) | ISBN 9781647122515 (ebook)
Subjects: LCSH: United States. Air Force. | Air power. | Air warfare. | Strategy. | Unified operations (Military science)
Classification: LCC UG630 .M533 2022 (print) | LCC UG630 (ebook) | DDC 358.4—dc23
LC record available at https://lccn.loc.gov/2021037937
LC ebook record available at https://lccn.loc.gov/2021037938

♾ This paper meets the requirements of ANSI/NISO Z39.48-1992 (Permanence of Paper).

23 22 9 8 7 6 5 4 3 2 First printing

Printed in the United States of America

Cover design by TG Design

CONTENTS

ILLUSTRATIONS

FIGURES

LEARNING BOXES

TABLES

PREFACE

SOME PERSPECTIVES ON PLANNING AND EXECUTING WARFARE

Welcome to the second edition of *Military Strategy, Joint Operations, and Airpower*. This book is about warfare, plain and simple. It is about applying military force against an adversary in order to make it do what we want. In this book, you will learn how we plan and execute military operations in order to accomplish national objectives. We do this through strategy.

STRATEGY AND STRATEGIC THINKING

This preface is a brief introduction to military strategy. My desired end state (DES)—in this case, what I want you to know and think when you're done reading this—is for you to have a broad understanding of what strategy is and why thinking strategically is critical to our national security. I want you to be motivated to learn about military strategy, and I sincerely hope that you find the topics in this work to be approachable, meaningful, and deeply applicable to your understanding, and perhaps your execution, of military strategy

So, let's get started. Your first question: Why is this concept of military strategy (and strategic thinking in general) important to me?

Well, two reasons: First, if you're engaging in this text, exploring these topics, you are likely on a chosen trajectory to enter a strategic profession (military or civilian) defending our nation and its interests, leading people, operating weapon systems, orchestrating warfare, and managing violence. Or perhaps you are actively engaged in this already. Thank you. This book is designed to introduce you to, or perhaps refresh for you, the fundamentals of military strategy, with an emphasis on airpower employment in a joint operating environment. These are the primary tools in your kit. These concepts constitute the foundation for whatever professional specialty in which you currently operate or strive to enter. This is how we plan and win wars.

The second reason why strategy and strategic thinking is important to you is because it's a critical life skill that will serve you well in every endeavor to which you aspire. Seriously. I mean, let's face it—you've been planning and executing strategy ever since you figured out how to get more attention from a parent or caregiver by putting on a cute smile or how to get more cookies from the cookie jar or how to get that special someone's attention or get a teacher to agree to a grade change. You already *are* a strategist, so let's put some refinement and precision to your strategic thinking and give you some tools and processes that will benefit you even more, whether you're huddled in a planning cell devising the air campaign against our next enemy or setting up the department picnic or leading the club fundraising project. So, please trust me. This is important to you.

What exactly is strategy? The concept is very simple. At its core, strategy is *figuring out how to use what I've got to get what I want*. This is sometimes phrased as reconciling ends, ways, and means:

Ends = *What I want*
Ways = *Figuring out how*
Means = *What I have*

Thinking strategically is really nothing more than a problem-solving methodology. There are certainly plenty of nuances and a great deal of complexity involved, not least of which is the fact that in military strategy you're dealing with a very challenging operating environment where—oh, by the way—the enemy doesn't want to cooperate and, in fact, likely wants you dead. Tricky. We'll address some of this complexity shortly, but let's introduce some general concepts at the start.

LEVELS OF WARFARE AND INSTRUMENTS OF NATIONAL POWER

There are different levels of warfare. Strategic thinking (reconciling ends, ways, and means) can, and is, executed at all levels.

Grand Strategic Level

This is at the nation-state strata and involves more than just military power. At its simplest, grand strategy is what our political leaders do in order to make our world look the way we'd like. Think big-picture politics here: a free and democratic nation secure from threats, with a healthy and growing global economy and a portfolio of dynamic allies. You get the idea.

Political leaders generally have four tools, or instruments, at their disposal with which to achieve grand strategic objectives. These instruments are abbreviated as DIME:

Diplomacy: Politics. Negotiating. Facilitating. Collaborating. Agreeing.
Information: Marketing. Spreading our message. Obtaining buy-in and support.
Military: Force and/or the threat of force. Kinetic and nonkinetic "effects."
Economic: Monetary or resource incentives and disincentives.

Obviously, the military service branches primarily support and pursue our political leaders' grand strategic objectives through the application of the military instrument of power. But it's absolutely essential for you to understand that this does not occur in a vacuum. These four instruments of national power are more like colors on a painter's palette, integrated (sometimes better than others) in efforts to get the world to be the way *our nation* wants it. Simple in concept, but clearly very complex in reality.

Strategic Level

This could also be called the *military* strategic level. This is the *M* in DIME. It's how we use our joint military capabilities to help achieve grand strategic objectives. The strategic level of warfare is primarily at the national military–to–national military level of interaction and impact.

Operational Level

Think "campaign." Think "regional." The operational level of war is where we orchestrate and direct and manage the many, many tactical pieces toward the larger military strategic objectives for the operation. Our joint warfighting capabilities are organized into components, closely aligned to warfare domains: air, land, maritime, space, and cyber. Airpower is typically planned and orchestrated within and from an air operations center (AOC). The integration of space and cyber power is critical to the execution of airpower, and these could be directed from within the AOC or through stand-alone space or cyber operations centers.

Tactical Level

This is force-on-force with individual maneuvering units or entities. Think combat and weapons employment. Warfighters typically begin their career training to become an expert at the tactical level of warfare.

An example to tie this all together: You are a combat systems operator (CSO) on an RC-135V/W Rivet Joint signals intelligence aircraft supporting EA-18Gs conducting a suppression of enemy air defense (SEAD) mission. You detect an active enemy surface-to-air missile target-tracking radar and relay the location to the SEAD package commander, who repositions her assets and engages weapons against the radar, destroying it and opening up a corridor in the enemy's integrated air-defense system. F-15Es successfully penetrate the enemy missile engagement zone unharmed and strike their target, a garrison of enemy armor preparing to mobilize against our forwardmost Marine forces. These would all be activities at the *tactical level.*

At the *operational level*, using airpower to conduct interdiction strikes against the armor garrison has significantly impeded the enemy's ability to counter our land forces. Within hours, Marine units have capitalized on this gain and rapidly advanced to secure two major production and staging areas, both of which are critical to the enemy's ability to supply and sustain its military forces in the region.

This alters the thinking of the enemy leadership at the *strategic level.* Senior military leaders now realize that their ability to counter a US-led military coalition will not succeed. These military resources were critical to their plans, and without them they lack both the capability and the will to fight a war against a clearly superior force. They advise their political leaders that negotiations may be the best alternative.

In the following days, our enemy's political leaders sue for peace and tacitly acquiesce, ultimately agreeing to all coalition demands, hence meeting our *grand strategic* objectives.

Good job, warfighter! Your tactical savvy had tie-ins at all levels and directly helped us win the war and get the world we want!

PLANNING AND EXECUTING MILITARY STRATEGY

The role of military leaders, then, is to direct forces in changing the military situation between ourselves and an adversary in order to help achieve grand strategic (national) objectives. Easy, right?

At the risk of embarrassingly oversimplifying this, here's how it's done.

Step 1, Ends: *Define the Desired Military End State*

Start by knowing what your political leaders seek and very clearly understanding the national-level objectives we are trying to obtain. What does our world look like now, and how should our world look when this is all done? Then—and this is not easy—determine what the military instrument of power can and should do to support this. What will victory look like? And does this precisely and unequivocally map to achieving our political objectives?

This typically involves using our joint forces to change either the way an enemy thinks (its *will*) or what it can do (its *capability*). Often it's a combination of both.

On one hand, we could seek to destroy every single military resource an adversary possesses until it is physically unable to resist us. History is full of examples where states have embarked on this type of strategy. No surprise, this can be long and costly.

Conversely, perhaps we never destroy a single enemy resource and instead, through deliberate strategic messaging and threats, simply "help" our enemy change its mind.

Honestly, it's going to be a blend of both. As an adversary loses its ability to resist, its thinking is likely going to change. Our desired military end state (DMES) is going to be defined in terms of what the adversary thinks (will) and what it can do (capability) at the end of the conflict. DMES might be "unconditional surrender" (e.g., Germany and Japan in World War II) or maybe "withdrawal from seized territory and inability to threaten neighboring states" (e.g., Iraq in Operation Desert Storm). In these cases, we used force to *compel* our adversary to do or change something.

DMES might also be having our adversary *not* do something—*deterring* it. "Declining to pursue the development, acquisition, or employment of nuclear weapons" (e.g., Iran at present). The challenge is to determine what effects we can and should make on the enemy systems in order to achieve our DMES—at its most basic, "What targets do we need to hit?" The key to success is soundly connecting the means (forces, assets, capabilities) with the ways (operations and tactics) in order to get the effects we want.

Effects can be *kinetic* or *nonkinetic*. Basically, it's what we want to "happen" to the enemy that ultimately achieves our DMES. Effects include terms such as:

- degrade
- deny
- disrupt
- ensure
- prevent
- subvert

Effects are what changes in the enemy system in order to accomplish our DMES. Perhaps a nonkinetic effect of jamming an enemy communication capability (deny, degrade) allows us to strike a command headquarters (disrupt) prior to the enemy scrambling air interceptors, which, in turn, leads to us achieving the operational objective of air superiority, the strategic objective of capturing the enemy's territory, and the grand strategic objective of defeating the enemy and removing it as a threat to regional stability.

The kinetic and nonkinetic effects we levy on our enemy can have impact at any or all levels of warfare. So, next, figure out what you need and how to use it to get the effects you want on the enemy.

Step 2, Means: *Determine Your Resources*

This is not nearly as straightforward as it may seem. Think economics: cost and benefit, competing demands for scarce resources, operating budgets, manpower, force structure, weapon-procurement programs, competing regional threats, installation, and fuel and logistics requirements. Despite being the greatest military power in the history of the world, the United States will always have to make hard decisions about configuring limited amounts of forces to match military needs.

We use a joint force structure to organize our capabilities into components. The goal is to efficiently integrate and harmonize a diverse array of military capabilities in order to put precise and formidable pressure on an adversary. In my humble opinion, we're very good at this. The United States possesses, maintains, and continues to develop and acquire a very agile portfolio of systems capable of providing military leaders some very robust asset options.

Hint: Select forces (means) based on how appropriate they are to achieving the effect you want on the enemy. Example: If we want to degrade the enemy's ability to counter us in the air, perhaps, at the outset, a squadron of F-22s on 24/7 defensive counterair (DCA) combat air patrol, although very effective, might not be as efficient as using submarine-launched Tomahawk cruise missiles to destroy enemy aircraft in shelters or B-2–launched precision munitions to destroy key taxi-runway intersections that prevent them from becoming airborne. It's all about the effect, not so much about the specific platform.

Step 3, Ways: *Develop Your Plan of Action*

How do we specifically match appropriate weapon systems against targets in order to achieve the kinetic and nonkinetic effects that we know (think, hope) will bend our enemy's capability or will to our preference? One method to accomplish this is through *operational design*, a planning process that ties ends, ways, and means together into an execution plan. It's basically a to-do chart, a graphical representation of the military tasks we need to accomplish sequentially or simultaneously in order to achieve effects that compel and/or deter our adversary.

This will be where you encounter the complexities of constraints and restraints as well as the dynamic tension between doctrine and innovation.

It should not surprise you that culture, ethics, politics, and morality will largely frame the options available to us in the conduct of warfare. Yes, in the 1960s and 1970s, the United States was certainly capable of destroying North Vietnamese military capability through large-scale invasion—or even through the employment of nuclear weapons. Yikes. But that likely would've invited a reaction from China and/or the Soviet Union (and from our allies) that we did not desire, so we opted not to. "Restraints" are limits *we impose on our own actions*, likely in efforts to support an overarching political requirement or simply to comply with the laws of armed conflict. "Constraints" are external factors *imposed upon us* that limit our options. An example of the latter was in 2003's Operation Enduring Freedom, when conducting air missions from bases on the Arabian Peninsula into Afghanistan, but most definitely without overflight authorization from Iran, resulted in a very complex air-refueling bridge to and through Pakistan and an emphasis on carrier-based and long-range bomber strikes from bases in the Indian Ocean.

And, finally, let's briefly discuss doctrine and innovation. Doctrine is the codification of previous lessons learned. It's what we've determined from previous successes and failures is the best way to do things. We typically think of doctrine as residing at the operational level of war, but there is certainly strategic-level and tactical-level doctrine as well. Doctrine is simply an effort to induce efficiency into our planning processes—an effort to not be forced to "reinvent the wheel" every time we go into a conflict. It works. At its best, it's an off-the-shelf guide for how to conduct operations. But, more realistically, it's often a baseline from which to start planning. Most operations involve a doctrinal foundation that is quickly amended and adjusted as the operation unfolds. Enter innovation.

At the other end of the spectrum from doctrine is innovation (and her siblings, resourcefulness and creativity). The American military enterprise has a long history of being exceptionally innovative. This, coupled with our fundamental doctrine of centralized command, decentralized execution, has proven time and again that we are an immensely adaptive and surprisingly agile military force. But, as I was told as a lieutenant, "in order to think outside of the box, you first need to understand what the box looks like." That's why, early in this book, we explore the basic whos and hows of US military doctrine. We need to understand the tools in our tool box and how they are designed to be used so that we can then critically explore options and alternatives for innovatively applying them to future wicked military problems.

MILITARY STRATEGY: SOME PERSPECTIVES AND LEARNING POINTS

I'd like to wrap this up with some thoughts for you to keep in mind as you learn and explore military strategy. Please take these points, largely based on personal perspective with some scholarly grounding, and critically consider them as you engage with this text and develop your strategic thinking:

1. There is no one right, predefined strategy. There are macrolevel documents titled "strategy" that provide a framework for grand strategic and military strategic objectives. There is operational doctrine. There are tactics, techniques, and procedures (TTPs), which are just tactical-level doctrine renamed. There are off-the-shelf operations plans. But when the war starts, there is no set playbook. You will have to rely on your education, your training, and your experience to take what you know and apply it to problems that are new, very complex, and hard to define.
2. Always, always, always start with the question "What's the desired end state?" It's surprising to me how many times, and from what a wide array of rank and experience, the first questions tend to be "What do we have and what can we do with it?" Wrong. Always start by clearly defining what you want it to be like when you're done. Always.
3. The enemy always has a DES too. Think about that. Use your regional/cultural and intelligence experts to define what that looks like for your adversary. Understanding your enemy's DES will help you identify effects to compel and/or deter it.
4. Like us, our adversaries are also secretive, illusive, adaptive, skilled, smart, and lethal. The enemy always gets a vote—at every play, and between plays if it can get away with it. It wants to win. It likely wants you dead. It likely has different values than you do. And it will not adhere to our restraints. Influencing, changing, or defeating adversaries like this requires strategic thinkers who are bold, aggressive, and precise.
5. Your strategy will and must change as the operation unfolds. Political guidance, enemy and coalition actions, fog (unknowns), and friction (inherent inefficiencies)

will require you to adjust. Plan for it and think forward to, and through, as many contingencies as you can realistically forecast.

6. There is no such thing as a stand-alone military operation. Any conflict we enter will involve agents and stakeholders from the other instruments of power—other government agencies (OGAs), such as the Department of State, the Federal Bureau of Investigation, and the Central Intelligence Agency, as well as nongovernmental organizations (NGOs), such as the International Red Cross/Crescent and the World Health Organization. And coalition military partners and allies of varying degrees of capability, commitment, and, candidly, trustworthiness. And host-nation civilians and political leaders. And the press, the world stage, and the social media universe. And the American voter. The sooner you embrace the complexity and diverse landscape of military strategic operations, the less frustrating it will be when you enter it for real.
7. Jointness works. For those that will have the opportunity to work in a streamlined, well-functioning joint planning environment with military professionals who are experts at matching capabilities and effects to targets in order to bend the enemy—it is a thing of true beauty.
8. Read more. History provides the relevant context of our current environment. Through an understanding of the context, we know what has and has not worked in the past. This knowledge helps us develop new ways of thinking and new theories to guide the eventual application of military power in the future. Therefore, it's imperative to continue reading and to learn through this interdisciplinary *context-theory-application* paradigm to truly understand and appreciate how and why we use military force today and into the future.
9. Tactics, operations, and strategy are not in opposition to one another. Young military operators are expected to be expert tacticians. Later they grow into planners, managers, leaders, and decision-makers at the operational and strategic levels of war. Learn now how these levels blend and interface.
10. Never forget: Compelling an adversary to change is a complex endeavor and the military instrument of power is a dynamic capability in our national tool kit. There is no one right way to design strategy and apply military force. What works now will almost certainly be less effective—or wrong—later. The enemy adjusts, our resources and capabilities change, and our political and military goals evolve.

SUMMARY

Strategy is simply tying together ends, ways, and means. Military strategy (*M*) complements the other instruments of national power. Always start by defining the DMES. Determine which kinetic and nonkinetic effects should be sought in order to change the system into what we want. Match weapons and platforms/assets to targets to get these effects. Tie it all together in an operational timeline of tasks. Execute and adjust. Simple, right? Please have fun. Learn lots. And thanks for reading!

—Col. Thomas T. Swaim, USAF
Permanent Professor and Head
Department of Military and Strategic Studies
United States Air Force Academy

ACKNOWLEDGMENTS

We are grateful to Don Jacobs and the staff at Georgetown University Press for their assistance throughout the book development process. We are grateful to the chapter authors for the contributions. We would like to thank the following for their insightful comments and constructive feedback on draft chapters: LTC Aaron Cross, LTC James “Cutch” Cutchin, LCDR Corey Fogle, Lt. Col. Keith German, and Lt. Col. Donnie Hodges. Thank you for your willingness to contribute to the development of our future leaders. Each chapter endured multiple iterations of peer review from subject-matter experts representing a diverse background in academic and professional perspectives.

This work reflects the views of the authors and does not necessarily represent the view of the US government, the Department of Defense, the military services, or their academic institutions.

We dedicate this second edition to the past, present, and future cadets of military and strategic studies at the US Air Force Academy. As we evolved the curriculum in recent years, the book has vastly benefited from cadet discussions and feedback with faculty and authors. This second edition codifies the evolution of our teaching style and philosophy in the pursuit of knowledge in the contemporary context, theory, and application of military strategy. Go forth and continue to spread airpower and jointness.

Introduction

Ryan Burke

Since its inception in 1999, the Department of Military and Strategic Studies (MSS) at the United States Air Force Academy (USAFA) has assumed the charge of educating academy cadets in the study of military strategy, theory, art, and science. Today MSS is arguably the only academic discipline that differentiates USAFA's core academic curriculum from that of any other elite college or university. Most colleges and universities offer a range of courses in a variety of disciplinary fields—but few require their students to study war. Moreover, while we certainly need officers educated in disciplines spanning science, technology, engineering, math, the humanities, and the social sciences, educating future officers in the *context*, *theory*, and *application* of military strategy and operational art is unique to the mission of the military service academies and the Reserve Officer Training Corps (ROTC). With four thousand USAFA cadets and twelve thousand ROTC cadets, all of whom volunteer to serve their nation as military officers upon graduation, the relevance, applicability, and significance, therefore, of the discipline to the educational development of military officers in training is unquestioned. This book purposefully focuses cadet education within this frame.

War, and the study of the same, is inherently interdisciplinary, and so is this book. Throughout the pages of this second edition, we integrate material from security studies, public policy, political science, history, international relations, and many other fields. We apply a context-theory-application paradigm to the study of military strategy in the contemporary environment with an emphasis on the operational level of war, or the nexus between grand strategic thinking and tactical engagement. At the strategic level, we focus on the combination of military *means* and *ways* to achieve desired *ends*.[1] On the other end of the spectrum, the tactical level of war emphasizes decisions about the mechanics of employing those means and ways at the point of decision to achieve desired ends. The operational level of war bridges this gap, residing at "the level that embraces battles in their dynamic totality, in which generic methods of war are developed, debated, and applied."[2] We focus our analysis at the operational level where strategy and theory meet doctrine and art.

A theory *describes* a phenomenon or occurrence, *explains* why it happens, and *predicts*—based on the occurrence of similar observations—what will happen in the future. Military *theory*, specifically, enjoys a rich depth of scholarly contributions informing the application of military power today. Deterrence, coercion, command of the commons, attrition, and others permeate the military theory literature espousing descriptions, explanations, predictions, and even prescriptions for how, when, and why states use military force. Theorists develop their analytical frames through a deep understanding of the relevant *context*, or the lessons of history carried forward to contemporary analysis. With a contextual understanding of past events leading to the development of military theory, strategists use these frames to inform the general *application* of military power in the contemporary environment. Military doctrine codifies the prescriptions for how militaries apply theory to employ force. Among other things, it defines the essence of operational art and planning—that which links strategic decision to tactical action. It is a national imperative for future military officers to have a working knowledge of the relevant context informing the development of military theory and how those theories influence the decision to apply the military instrument of power to achieve our desired national ends. This progressive thread encapsulates the context-theory-application paradigm informing the book.

This book is intended for future leaders in the military profession, whose "primary function is the application of violence," as Samuel Huntington bluntly put it.[3] This book provides cadets the foundation from which to develop and hone their working knowledge of *how* and *why* the United States uses military power and to what end.

The United States has deployed military forces overseas every decade of its existence.[4] Absent a radical and acute shift in US foreign policy, every graduating cadet will find himself or herself serving a military committed to overseas operations in some form or capacity, be it cooperation, conflict, or everything in between. Many cadets—regardless of their chosen specialty code—will engage in the business of warfighting upon graduation and must comprehend how they will contribute as an individual and as part of an organization to advancing US national interests and achieving objectives.

Because of this, an instruction from the chairman of the Joint Chiefs of Staff (CJCS) mandates that all precommissioning professional military education programs—including those of the service academies, ROTC, and Officer Training School (OTS), are responsible for "instilling Joint education early in officer development."[5] More specifically, this instruction specifies that students must have knowledge of the nature of American military power and joint warfare, with complementary learning areas emphasizing military capabilities, organizations, foundations of warfare, and the profession of arms. The instruction further stipulates that the various military services are responsible for applying its requirements to inform their respective service-specific, precommissioning education curriculums.

Building on this, US Air Force Instruction 36-2014 establishes commissioning education requirements in the form of institutional competency learning outcomes (ICLOs) linked to the CJCS instruction. This specific Air Force instruction ensures that the precommissioning student (USAFA, ROTC, or OTS) "understands and applies operational and strategic art in conventional and irregular warfare, peacekeeping, and homeland defense operations."[6] It requires commissioning sources to educate students in the employment of military capabilities in the joint environment.

With that, it is prudent to discuss the purpose of the text and how to read it. This book serves as the primary course text for MSS 251: Airpower and Joint Operations Strategy. The content of the book, therefore, closely relates to the course material. Chapters provide foundational lesson readings throughout the course and present abridged overviews of several important topics for consideration in today's contemporary military environment. While the book's intended purpose is to serve as the foundational reading for this specific USAFA course, the content does not confine it to the walls of Fairchild Hall. As its focus includes joint operations and airpower across all levels of war, the book's applicability reaches beyond

USAFA. Air Force ROTC programs nationwide can and will find relevant and useful material in this text to supplement their current curriculum. In addition, Air Force OTS and similar programs will find relevance and utility in the content.

While the text emphasizes airpower as a core theme, the material is widely scoped to include joint operations and can therefore find value in Army and Navy ROTC curriculums as well. Regardless of the end user, the book's organization allows the student to read in or out of sequence, consuming material as desired rather than through prescriptive and progressive means. Whether reading in order or by content interest, readers will note that each chapter offers a similar progression through the context-theory-application paradigm noted. This is the MSS lens, the framework of our collective disciplinary vision, and how we approach our educational mission. We invite and encourage our readers to engage with this material critically and thoroughly, as often some of our material is wholly consistent with the current state of the field, whereas other material deliberately departs from the foundational concepts permeating the literature today. We do this to generate discussion and to challenge—and advance—those concepts most influential to today's discourse informing the application of military power in the contemporary environment.

To this point and as a final thought, we must remind our readers that there is not a single correct answer to the military problems of today. This is not a how-to manual for developing military strategy and achieving military effects but rather a series of chapters discussing some of the considerations in today's contemporary military environment. This book follows our first edition and remains to the extent of our knowledge the first—and to date only—military strategy textbook intended for an undergraduate audience specifically focused on contemporary strategy with particular emphasis on airpower in the joint environment. Because of this, the book targets undergraduate cadets enrolled at USAFA and those participating in the many Air Force ROTC programs nationwide. With this text, our readers will develop a familiarization with the military instrument of national power and the many ways in which we apply military means to advance national interests and to achieve, or contribute to achieving, national objectives.

In developing a second edition, we made numerous changes. This iteration more deliberately targets those topics of importance in the evolving military strategy discourse. We reproduced some of the original chapters from the first version, though they have been repurposed and modernized to reflect the many changes since the first edition's publication. Recognizing change in the contemporary environment also necessitated alterations to the book's content. This second edition includes mostly new chapters integrating discussions on such things as strategic foundations and national security interests, the instruments of national power, and the spectrum of conflict. We also offer new chapters on the joint force: the Army, Navy, Air Force, Space Force, and Marine Corps. There is a newly written special operations chapter and rewritten chapters on cyber power, intelligence, surveillance, reconnaissance, and even weapons of mass destruction. We repurposed our military theory and operations chapters from the first edition with evolved discussion for the second edition more directly situated in the context-theory-application paradigm. Finally, our emphasis on operational art, planning, and design now enjoys its own part, complete with multiple chapters outlining the layered operational design processes. Rather than a single chapter detailing a rough overview of the cornerstone-planning construct, we devote an entire part of the book and specific chapters to each element of the operational design model. Nearly a complete rewrite from our first edition, this book also incorporates a number of new authors, most of whom are current MSS faculty members at USAFA.

In advancing cadets and other future leaders toward this goal, this second edition contains five parts. We designed this iteration to be similar to how one might learn to play chess. To understand the game, a player must first understand the board, or the context of their environment. In this way, we begin with an overview of the national security and defense environment, emphasizing the factors shaping US national security interests and how the military instrument of power advances toward these goals. Additionally, we discuss the military's role as a national instrument of power relative to diplomatic, informational, and economic means and the advantages and disadvantages of each to achieve national ends. To conclude the opening part, we outline the military's role across the modern spectrum of conflict and differentiate between military missions ranging from peacekeeping to conventional war. With an understanding of the game board—in this case, the national security environment and the military's utility within—we move to discussing the pieces.

In part II, we provide an overview of the joint force structure and how each military service uniquely contributes to national security interests, or what each piece does on the metaphorical board. We discuss the roles and missions of the Army, Navy, Coast Guard, Air Force, Marine Corps, and Space Force in the contemporary environment, differentiating between each service's role and contribution to the joint force.

In part III, we discuss the functional roles and contributions of special operations forces, cyber power, intelligence, surveillance, and reconnaissance as well as weapons of mass destruction. Employed jointly, these functional area contributions provide the US military additional options and capabilities to employ hard power and contribute to national security objectives. After players understand both the board and its pieces, they can begin to formulate strategies for employment.

Part IV begins to merge the previous part's content and describes the strategic foundations for military employment. Here our readers gain exposure to classic military theories and their origins with an emphasis on airpower theory. The discussion transitions from classic to contemporary as readers learn how modern forces apply evolving theories to achieve strategic effect. Readers engage with the differences between deterrence, compellence, and cooperation before learning how each influences US approaches to both irregular and conventional warfare.

Part V concludes this second edition with a series of chapters devoted to operational art, planning, and design in the contemporary military environment. We emphasize the purpose and utility of operational design in the joint force, its process, and the procedural method planners use in both analyzing and designing operational plans. Chapters detail elements of the operational design construct, including end states and objectives and methods for evaluating the operational environment, understanding and applying center of gravity analysis, and building lines of effort. Cadets engage with a layered discussion of operational design intended to expose them to the intricacies of the model and aid in their own design and development of the same, both in their undergraduate military classes and beyond as they become military officers.

While current and former military personnel and combat veterans—many of whom are accomplished academics—wrote the content of the book, we take some liberties with our interpretations and welcome future discourse. We seek to advance the academic discussion in the military and strategic studies discipline not through a summary of and strict adherence to existing military doctrine and established paradigms but rather an emphasis on our own paradigm focused on the relevant context, theory, and application of military power in the contemporary profession of arms. With this text, we intend to push the boundaries of thought and advance the discussion into new frontiers of contemporary military strategy. In the world of evolving and complex global threats to national and international security, we need proactive ideas and adaptive execution to outthink our adversaries and galvanize relations with allies. We must resist adopting the convenient or safe approaches simply because they worked before and continue to expand the discussion to promote thinking in unconventional and nonlinear vice conventional and linear ways. How can we reconcile means and ways to produce combined effects that ultimately lead to accomplishing desired ends? These are the questions and the paradigms we continue to emphasize in the latest edition of the book—the concepts we encourage you, as future officers, to consider. We wrote this book for you, the future military leaders of America who will one day represent and defend our nation and its ideals on the global stage. Thank you for answering the call and covering our six. You have the watch.

NOTES

1. Lawrence Freedman, *Strategy: A History* (Oxford: Oxford University Press, 2013), xii; Arthur F. Lykke Jr., *Toward an Understanding of Military Strategy* (Carlisle, PA: US Army War College, 1989), 3–5.

2. Edward N. Luttwak, *Strategy: The Logic of War and Peace* (Cambridge, MA: Belknap Press of Harvard University Press, 2003), 112.

3. Samuel P. Huntington, *The Soldier and the State: The Theory and Politics of Civil-Military Relations* (Cambridge, MA: Belknap Press of Harvard University Press, 1957), 11. As explained in chapter 3, militaries also perform nonviolent functions. But violence continues to be the raison d'être of military forces.

4. Richard Grimmett, *Instances of Use of United States Armed Forces Abroad, 1798–2010* (Washington, DC: Congressional Research Service, 2011), A-A-1.

5. "Officer Professional Military Education Policy," Chairman of the Joint Chiefs of Staff Instruction 1800.01F, May 15, 2020, Department of Defense, Washington, DC.

6. Secretary of the Air Force, "Pre-Commissioning Programs," Air Force Instruction 36–2104, July 15, 2019, Department of Defense, Washington, DC, 13.

PART I

NATIONAL SECURITY AND DEFENSE

CHAPTER 1

Strategic Foundations and National Security Interests

John T. Farquhar

Comprehending strategy requires understanding factors that shape national security interests. A host of influences, including human nature, politics, society, economics, geography, and technology, shape strategic considerations.[1] Decision-making does not occur in a vacuum, and shrewd strategic thinkers draw wisdom from past masters. Although many strategic thinkers span the ages, the "big three" classical strategists provide breadth, depth, and nuance for the foundations of strategy. Thucydides, Carl von Clausewitz, and Sun Tzu provide insights that enhance understanding of the nature of war by examining those elements that are common to all wars and are fundamental to comprehending war's complexity and timelessness. Although separated in time, culture, and context, the thoughts of Thucydides, Clausewitz, and Sun Tzu enrich a modern understanding of strategy and war's purpose.

In the *History of the Peloponnesian War*, Thucydides, an Athenian Greek citizen soldier and statesman (c. 460–400 BCE), presents the first Western book to analyze warfare and strategy. Thucydides examined three themes: (1) war consists of both rational and irrational elements, (2) in vital matters, the irrational usually wins out over the rational, and (3) the first casualty of war is the moral and ethical standards of a society. Thucydides captures the reasons nations go to war: the moral, political, economic, and emotional elements involved in a society's most momentous decision. He presents concepts that define Western strategic culture, including freedom, honor, democracy, bravery, and civic obligation. Thucydides argues that both rational and irrational elements influence war. Any rational policy considerations that ignore the emotions and passions of the people are doomed to fail.

In the history's section "The Debate at Sparta," Thucydides presents speeches from those about to go to war, including appeals to both emotion and reason. The Corinthians appeal to liberty and fairness: "When one is deprived of one's liberty one is right in blaming not so much the man who puts fetters on as the one who had the power to prevent him, but did not use it."[2] The rival Athenians present a rational statement: "We did not gain this empire by force. . . . It was the actual course of events which first compelled us to increase our power to its present extent: fear of Persia was our chief motive, though afterwards we thought, too, of our own honor and our own interest. . . . And when tremendous dangers are involved no one can be blamed for looking to his own interest."[3] The Athenians evoke power politics:

> So it is with us. We have done nothing extraordinary, nothing contrary to human nature in accepting an empire that was offered to us and then in refusing to give it up. Three very powerful motives prevent us from doing so—security, honor, and self-interest. And we were not the first to act in this way. Far from it. It has always been a rule that the weak should be subject to the strong; and besides, we consider that we are worthy of our power. Up till the present moment you, too, used to think we were; but now, after calculating your own interest, you are beginning to talk in terms of right and wrong. Considerations of this kind have never yet turned people aside from the opportunities of aggrandizement offered by superior strength.[4]

Contrasting the nature of power with moral imperatives of right and wrong, the Athenians caution regarding the consequences and uncertainties of war:

> Think, too, of the great part that is played by the unpredictable in war; think of it now, before you are actually committed to war. The longer a war lasts, the more things tend to depend on accidents. Neither you nor we can see into them: we have to abide their outcome in the dark. And when people are entering upon a war they do things the wrong way round. Action comes first, and it is only then they have already suffered that they begin to think.[5]

Joining Thucydides on the rational and irrational dimensions of war, Carl von Clausewitz's book, *On War*, provides a foundation for comprehending military theory and strategy. A timeless masterpiece, it discusses issues that span the nature of war, military theory, politics, strategy, and tactics. Clausewitz provides a conceptual framework for the study of war and its relationship to the state. Because his book represents a kind of intellectual wrestling match, Clausewitz requires careful reading and deep thinking.[6]

Although he never commanded in combat, Clausewitz fought in actions ranging from small-unit engagements to the epic battles of Borodino and Waterloo. His combat experience, high-level staff duties, and intense military education supported his quest to create a military theory.[7]

Clausewitz presents five ideas that help define the nature of war:

- the dual nature of war—tension between war's theoretical unchecked violence and limits imposed by politics and "fog and friction"
- war as an instrument of politics
- the paradoxical trinity—war as a balance of passion, chance, and reason
- "fog and friction"—danger, exertion, chance, uncertainty that define "real war"
- military genius as a counter to fog and friction

Clausewitz's "dual nature of war" represents an attempt to explore war's essential nature. Clausewitz presents a thesis that the ideal, or "absolute," form of war is total war: "War is thus an act of force to compel our enemy to do our will. . . . If one side uses force without compunction . . . [it] will force the other side to follow suit; each side will drive the other to extremes."[8] In its absolute form, "there is no logical limit to the application of . . . force."[9] Clausewitz counters with an antithesis: in reality, political objectives and "fog and friction" (danger, exertion, uncertainty, chance—the factors that separate war on paper from war in reality) impose limits on war's violence. Understanding Clausewitz's dialectical approach provides a key to unlocking his insights.[10] Clausewitz envisions a dual nature of war, a battle between absolute versus limited war—war in theory versus real war.

Inherent in his concept of the dual nature of war, Clausewitz argues that war is an instrument of politics: "War Is Merely the Continuation of Policy by Other Means."[11] Nations go to war to achieve a political purpose and politics provides the reason for war. Clausewitz's original word, "*Politik*," means either "politics" or "policy" in English, where "politics" refers to the conduct of political affairs (the battle of ideas that make governments work) and "policy" means a plan of action—"those political acts that lead to war, determine its purpose, influence its conduct, and bring about its termination."[12] Both concepts apply: war is a continuation of policy by other means, referring to diplomacy, international affairs, and political objectives as described above, and war is a continuation of politics, both domestic and international. The competition of political leaders, parties, factions, and ideas does not cease during a war. Hence, war is a political instrument of the policymaker. He attacks the notion that military necessity overrides political objectives: "Subordinating the political point of view to the military would be absurd, for it is policy that has created war. Policy is the guiding instrument and war only the instrument, not vice versa. No other possibility exists, then, than to subordinate the military point of view to the political."[13]

Further developing both the nature of war and war's political dimension, Clausewitz introduces a theoretical construct known as the "paradoxical trinity":

> War is more than a true chameleon that slightly adapts its characteristics to the given case. As a total phenomenon its dominant tendencies always make war a paradoxical trinity—composed of primordial violence, hatred, and enmity, which are to be regarded as a blind natural force; of the play of chance and probability within which the creative spirit is free to roam; and of its element of subordination, as an instrument of policy, which makes it subject to reason alone.
>
> The first of these three aspects mainly concerns the people; the second the commander and army; the third the government. The passions that are to be kindled in war must already be inherent in the people; the scope which the play of courage and talent will enjoy in the realm of probability and chance depends on the particular character of the commander and the army; and the political aims are the business of the government alone.[14]

A genuine theory of war must address all three aspects and their relationships to each other. The trinity is an object that "maintains a balance between the three entities, like an object suspended between three magnets."[15] While some simplify the trinity as a triangle depicting people, commander and army, and government, others emphasize violence or passion, chance and probability, and reason.[16] Although the people, commander/army, and government triangle appeals for its simplicity, the passion, chance, and reason triangle better captures Clausewitz's key insights that wars are inherently psychological and war's nature transcends time and culture.

If Clausewitz's paradoxical trinity provides an overall conceptual framework for how to think about war, his emphasis on "friction" reflected his twenty years of combat experience. In other words, "everything in war is very simple, but the simplest thing is difficult. The difficulties accumulate and end by producing a kind of friction that is inconceivable unless one has experienced war."[17] Friction distinguishes real war from war on paper. Military organizations are composed of individuals, each of whom retains a potential for friction (Murphy's law). Friction is always in contact with uncertainty, chance, and probability, elements he describes as the "fog" of war. The combination of fog and friction causes effects that cannot be measured or entirely anticipated.[18] Clausewitz cautions: "Action in war is like a movement in a resistant element. Just as the simplest and most natural of movements, walking, cannot be easily performed in war, so in war it is difficult for normal efforts to achieve even moderate results."[19]

Clausewitz's answer to fog and friction is the concept of "military genius." He defines genius as "a very highly developed mental aptitude for a particular occupation" and says that we must "survey all those gifts of mind and temperament that in combination bear on military activity. . . . Genius consists *in a harmonious combination of elements*, in which one or the other ability may predominate, but none may be in conflict with the rest"[20] (emphasis in original).

What did Clausewitz mean by "military genius"? Since wars embody danger, courage is the first requirement. "Courage is of two kinds: courage in the face of personal danger and courage to accept responsibility." Since war features physical exertion and suffering, a leader must possess "a certain strength of body and soul." Clausewitz continues: "War is the realm of uncertainty; three quarters of the factors on which action in war is based are wrapped in a fog of greater or lesser uncertainty. A sensitive and discriminating judgment is called for; a skilled intelligence to scent out the truth." Since war is "the realm of chance," Clausewitz called for a "quick recognition of a truth the mind would ordinarily miss or would perceive only after long study and reflection." He further explains the concept with a French term, *coup d'oeil*, "*an intellect, that even in the darkest hour, retains some glimmerings of the inner light which leads to truth*" (emphasis in original). Linked to this instinctive ability, Clausewitz stresses determination, "the courage to follow this faint light wherever it may lead." While Clausewitz acknowledges the importance of intelligence, his concept of military genius emphasizes physical and moral courage, physical and moral strength, truth, and determination.[21]

A brilliant mind could be a detriment to a military leader: "Intelligence alone is not courage; we often see that the most intelligent people are irresolute. . . . In short, we believe that determination proceeds from a special type of mind, from a strong rather than a brilliant one."[22] Since the clock rules every military plan, intelligence must be matched with resolve and the ability to make decisions.[23] Military genius combines strength of mind with strength of character. Strength of mind focuses on the mental and physical energy required to meet the unexpected. It calls for staunchness, the will's resistance to a heavy blow; endurance, the will's capability for prolonged resistance; and self-control, "the gift of keeping calm under the greatest stress." Strength of character is the ability to stick to convictions.[24] Clausewitz's "military genius" blends intelligence, temperament, and action: "Truth in itself is rarely sufficient to make men act. Hence the step is always from cognition to volition, from knowledge to ability. The most powerful springs of action in men lie in his emotions. He derives his most vigorous support . . . from that blend of brains and temperament which we have learned to recognize in the qualities of determination, firmness, staunchness, and strength of character."[25]

War is not waged against an inanimate object: "War, however, is not the action of a living force upon a lifeless mass . . . but always the collision of two living forces."[26] Too often military theorists reduce war to objective, quantifiable factors.[27] Clausewitz rejects this tendency and stresses the uncertain and variable. In war, the enemy is a living being who thinks and reacts, quite often in unexpected ways. Therefore, theory cannot lead to complete understanding, but it can strengthen and refine judgment. Military theory can show how one thing is related to another, and it can separate the important from the unimportant.[28] Clausewitz provides ideas to stimulate thinking and an intellectual process to educate our minds. Those looking for formulas to solve problems or concrete principles for success will be disappointed.

Joining Clausewitz as a pillar of strategic thought, Chinese military philosopher Sun Tzu assumes a special place in military theory. Like Clausewitz and Thucydides, Sun Tzu provides pithy, quotable statements that contain genuine pearls of wisdom.[29] Scholars disagree over whether Sun Tzu ("Master Sun") actually constitutes a historical figure (who lived between 500 and 200 BCE) or simply a body of knowledge (i.e., Sun Tzu represents observations of a series of scholars over time), but, for simplicity, this text will treat Sun Tzu as an individual.[30] Translations vary, but readers like Sun Tzu's brevity, simplicity, and wisdom.[31] Of the classic theorists, Sun Tzu best articulates the relationship of war, strategy, and economics.[32]

"War is a matter of vital importance to the state; a matter of life and death, the road either to survival or to ruin. Hence, it is imperative that it be studied thoroughly."[33] Where Clausewitz uses dialectical reasoning to create a rational argument, Sun Tzu presents a series of succinct conclusions. While Clausewitz focuses on narrow, in-depth examination of war and combat, Sun Tzu articulates a broad perspective encompassing both military and nonmilitary (i.e., diplomatic, economic, and psychological) factors.[34]

Sun Tzu provides foundational ideas for the strategist. He argues that, before entering a war, the wise must calculate and assess the probability of success:

> Therefore, appraise [war] in terms of the five fundamental factors and make comparisons of the various conditions of the antagonistic sides in order to ascertain the results of a war. The first of these factors is politics; the second, weather; the third, terrain; the fourth, the commander; and the fifth, doctrine. Politics means the thing which causes the people to be in harmony with their ruler so that they will follow him in disregard of their lives and without fear of any danger.[35]

The sovereign or military adviser must answer seven questions:

1. Which ruler is wise and more able?
2. Which commander is more talented?
3. Which army obtains the advantages of nature and the terrain?
4. In which army are regulations and instructions better carried out?
5. Which troops are stronger?
6. Which army has the better-trained officers and men?
7. Which army administers rewards and punishments in a more enlightened and correct way?[36]

Contrasting Clausewitz's emphasis on battle, Sun Tzu stresses deception as the key to victory: "All warfare is based on deception. Therefore, when capable of attacking, feign incapacity; when active in moving troops, feign inactivity. When near the enemy, make it seem that you are far away; when far away, make it seem that you are near. Hold out baits to lure the enemy. Strike the enemy when he is in disorder. . . . Avoid the enemy for the time being when he is stronger."[37] Many authorities consider this passage as Sun Tzu's essential contribution to comprehending warfare.

In his chapter "Waging War," Sun Tzu presents another key precept: avoid prolonged war:

> A speedy victory is the main object in war. If this is long in coming, weapons are blunted and morale depressed. If troops are attacking cities, their strength will be exhausted. When the army engages in protracted campaigns, the resources of the state will fall short. . . . Thus, while we have heard of stupid haste in war, we have not yet seen a clever operation that was prolonged. For there has never been a protracted war which benefited a country. . . . Hence, what is valued in war is victory, not prolonged operations.[38]

In "Offensive Strategy," Sun Tzu outlines his ideal: victory without fighting. "Generally, in war the best policy is to take a state intact; to ruin it is inferior to this. To capture the enemy's entire army is better than to destroy it. . . . For to win one hundred victories in one hundred battles is not the acme of skill. To subdue the enemy without fighting is the supreme excellence." He then proposes what some call "the four attacks" that prioritize strategic operations:

> Thus, what is of supreme importance in war is to attack the enemy's strategy. Next best is to disrupt his alliances by diplomacy. The next best is to attack his army. And the worst policy is to attack cities. Attack cities only when there is no alternative.
>
> Thus, those skilled in war subdue the enemy's army without battle. They capture the enemy's cities without assaulting them and overthrow his state without protracted operations. Their aim is to take all under heaven intact by strategic considerations.[39]

In other words, the enemy's center of gravity (to use Clausewitz's concept) is the enemy's strategy and alliances. Victory will go to those who understand the enemy's vision of ends, ways, and means. For Sun Tzu, diplomatic moves are as important as military maneuvers.

How does a commander or political leader actually accomplish Sun Tzu's ideas? Tough thinking occurs not in reading Sun Tzu but in figuring out how to bring his ideas to fruition. "Offensive Strategy" concludes with perhaps Sun Tzu's most famous line: "Therefore, I say: Know the enemy and know yourself; in a hundred battles, you will never be defeated." Unfortunately, many readers ignore the remainder of the passage: "When you are ignorant of the enemy but know yourself, your chances of winning or losing are equal. If ignorant both of your enemy and of yourself, you are sure to be defeated in every battle."[40]

Sun Tzu demonstrates considerable powers of observation and attention to detail. He continues his themes of deception, surprise, and using terrain and maneuver for advantage. Although his "Maneuvering" chapter examines tactical maneuvers and how to gain a position of advantage, Sun Tzu again stresses deception and wise alliances:

> One who is not acquainted with the designs of his neighbors should not enter into alliances with them. Those who do not know the conditions of the mountains and forests, hazardous defiles, marshes and swamps, cannot conduct the march of an army. Those who do not use local guides are unable to obtain the advantages of ground. Now, war is based on deception. Move when it is advantageous and create changes in the situation by dispersal and concentration of forces.[41]

In other words, what are the political objectives of your allies? What do they seek from the alliance? To what extent do their objectives match your own? Sun Tzu concludes his operational chapters with a summary:

> If I know that my troops are capable of striking the enemy, but do not know that he is invulnerable to attack, my chance of victory is but half. If I know that the enemy is vulnerable to attack, but do not know that my troops are incapable of striking him, my chance of victory is but half. . . . And, therefore, I say: Know the enemy, know yourself: your victory will never be endangered. Know the ground, know the weather; your victory will then be complete.[42]

Along the same lines, Sun Tzu provides a stunning philosophical observation:

> If not in the interests of the state, do not act. If you cannot succeed, do not use troops. If you are not in danger, do not fight a war. A sovereign cannot launch a war because he is enraged, nor can a general fight a war because he is resentful. For while an angered man may again be happy, and a resentful man again be pleased, a state that has perished cannot be restored, nor can the dead be brought back to life.[43]

The passage reinforces emphasis on rational calculation before entering a war and to reject emotional policy responses. Like Clausewitz's observations on fog and friction and military genius, the irrational and emotional realms of war are ever present and often triumph over cold rationality.

Sun Tzu concludes with his chapter "Use of Spies" that links the military, political, economic, and psychological aspects of war:

> Now, the reason a brilliant sovereign and a wise general conquer the enemy whenever they move and their achievements surpass those of ordinary men is their foreknowledge of the enemy situation. This "foreknowledge" cannot be elicited from spirits, nor from gods, nor by analogy with past events, nor by astrologic calculations. It must be obtained from men who know the enemy situation. . . . There is no place where espionage is not possible. . . . And, therefore, only the enlightened sovereign and the wise general who are able to use the most intelligent people as spies can achieve great results. Spy operations are essential in war: upon them the army relies to make its every move.[44]

The "big three" classic strategists provide the foundation of strategy, the reconciling of ends, ways, and means. Thucydides, Clausewitz, and Sun Tzu describe factors that shape national security interests and define the nature of war. Strategy involves both rational and irrational elements, including fear, honor, and self-interest, as the reasons nations go to war. For Thucydides, war is unpredictable: "The longer a war lasts, the more things tend to depend on accidents."

Clausewitz's *On War* provides tools for thought, not a checklist for action. He stresses that war is not performed against an inanimate object but is always the collision of two living forces—that is, your enemy gets a vote in the outcome of a war. The following strategic ideas stand out:

- War has a dual nature marked by ever increasing violence (absolute or theoretical war) and limits imposed by politics and "fog and friction" (real war).
- War is an instrument of politics; political objectives trump military necessity.
- Success in war is a balance of passion, chance, and reason—the paradoxical trinity—represented by the people, military, and government.

- Fog and friction limits both absolute violence and normal efficiency.
- Military genius (courage, intelligence, determination, character) counters fog and friction.

Sun Tzu presents a host of political, economic, and social observations that describe the character and nature of war. Among the most famous and influential:

- All warfare is based on deception.
- A speedy (or swift) victory is the main object of war.
- Prolonged war never benefits a country.
- "To subdue the enemy without fighting is the supreme excellence."
- Attack the enemy's strategy, alliances, army, and, last, his cities.
- Know yourself and know your enemy.
- One must know the designs (intentions, aspirations, perspective) of current and potential allies.
- Speed is the essence of war.
- If you cannot succeed, do not use troops. If you are not in danger, do not fight.
- There is no place where espionage is not possible (for your enemy or for yourself).

Classic military thinkers stimulate our thinking on war, politics, power, strategy, and other topics. Changes in time, technology, and other circumstances limit the "classics" as practical tools for policymakers but unlock the mind, raise timeless questions, and spur serious thinking on the nature of war, war aims, political uncertainties, moral dilemmas, and other vital concerns. The challenge for the modern strategist is how to apply the wisdom of the past.

LEARNING REVIEW

- Describe the factors that shape national security interests.
- Explain the concepts of fog and friction and their relevance to Clausewitz's "real war."
- Describe how military training creates experiences to facilitate the emergence of military geniuses.
- Recall the challenges associated with applying military theories to a strategic problem.

NOTES

1. Colin S. Gray, *Modern Strategy* (Oxford: Oxford University Press, 1999), 16–47. In the chapter "The Dimensions of Strategy," Gray categorizes influences into People and Politics (people, society, culture, politics, ethics), Preparation for War (economics and logistics, organization, military administration, information and intelligence, strategic theory and doctrine, technology), and War Proper (military operations, geography, friction, chance and uncertainty, time).
2. Thucydides, *History of the Peloponnesian War*, trans. Rex Warner (New York: Penguin Classics, 1954), 74.
3. Thucydides, 79–80.
4. Thucydides, 80. Some translations use "fear" instead of "security."
5. Thucydides, 81–82.
6. This chapter synthesizes Carl von Clausewitz, *On War*, ed. and trans. Michael Howard and Peter Paret (Princeton, NJ: Princeton University Press, 1976); Peter Paret, "Clausewitz," in *Makers of Modern Strategy from Machiavelli to the Nuclear Age*, ed. Peter Paret (Princeton, NJ: Princeton University Press, 1986); Michael I. Handel, *Masters of War: Classical Strategic Thought*, 3rd ed. (London:

Frank Cass, 2001); Gray, *Modern Strategy*; and Michael Howard, *Clausewitz* (Oxford: Oxford University Press, 1983). Three essays in the Howard and Paret translation of *On War* were valuable: Peter Paret, "The Genesis of *On War*"; Michael Howard, "The Influence of Clausewitz"; and Bernard Brodie, "The Continuing Relevance of *On War*."

7. Paret, "Clausewitz," 195.

8. Clausewitz, *On War*, 75–76.

9. Clausewitz, 77.

10. Some scholars refer to "limited war" instead of "real war." I will use "absolute war" and "ideal war" as equivalent terms and consider "real war" and "limited war" to be synonyms. Paret, "Genesis of *On War*," 22; Paret, "Clausewitz," 199–200.

11. Clausewitz, *On War*, 87.

12. *The American Heritage Dictionary*, 2nd college ed. (Boston: Houghton Mifflin, 1985), 959–60; Paret, "Clausewitz," 210.

13. Clausewitz, *On War*, 607.

14. Michael Howard and Peter Paret also call the "paradoxical" trinity the "remarkable" trinity. In the 1976 version, they used "remarkable" but changed it to "paradoxical" in the 1984 paperback. Clausewitz, 89.

15. Clausewitz, 89.

16. Clayton K. S. Chun, *War, Military Theory, and Strategy: An Introduction* (Boston: Houghton Mifflin, 2002), 26; Paret, "Clausewitz," 201; Michael Handel, "The Trinitarian Analysis," in *Masters*, 102–7.

17. Clausewitz, *On War*, 119.

18. Clausewitz, 119.

19. Clausewitz, 120.

20. Clausewitz, 100.

21. Clausewitz, 100–103.

22. Clausewitz, 102–3.

23. Gray, *Modern Strategy*, 42.

24. Clausewitz, *On War*, 105–7.

25. Clausewitz, 112.

26. Clausewitz, 77, 149.

27. Williamson Murray and Mark Grimsley, "Introduction: On Strategy," in *The Making of Strategy: Rulers, States, and War*, ed. Williamson Murray, MacGregor Knox, and A. Bernstein (Cambridge: Cambridge University Press, 1994), 1.

28. Paret, "Clausewitz," 193.

29. Although most Western scholars adopted "Sun Zi" as the most appropriate transliteration in accordance with the *pinyin* system, the traditional and most common translation, "Sun Tzu," is used by Yuan Shibing, the translator of Gen. Tao Hanzhang's *Sun Tzu's Art of War: The Modern Chinese Translation*. To avoid confusion, "Sun Tzu" is used.

30. In 2009, the National Defense University sponsored a "Teaching Sun Zi" conference where the consensus was that *The Art of War* represented the thoughts of a number of scholars that evolved over time. This contrasts the Chinese interpretation that stresses Sun Zi as a historical person. Some in China view such Western debates as an attempt to rob China of a national hero and its historical greatness.

31. I recommend the following translations as the most readable: Roger T. Ames, ed. and trans., *Sun Tzu: The Art of Warfare* (New York: Ballantine Books, 1993); Ralph D. Sawyer, ed. and trans., *Sun Tzu: The Art of War* (New York: Barnes & Noble, 1994); and Samuel B. Griffith, ed. and trans., *Sun Tzu: The Art of War* (London: Oxford University Press, 1963). See also a cartoon version, *Sunzi Speaks: The Art of War*, adapted and illus. Tsai Chih Chung, trans. Brian Bruya (New York: Anchor Books, 1994).

32. Michael I. Handel, *Masters of War: Classical Strategic Thought*, 3rd ed. (London: Frank Cass, 2001), 3.

33. Hanzhang, *Sun Tzu's Art of War*, 22.

34. Handel, *Masters of War*, 22–23.

35. This passage is a departure from other translations. Whereas the Hanzhang translation states, "The first of these is *politics*. . . . *Politics* means the thing which causes the people to be in harmony

with their ruler," Samuel Griffith translates, "The first of these is *moral influence*. . . . By *moral influence* I mean that which causes the people to be in harmony with their leaders." Ralph Sawyer uses *Tao* (which means "the Way"): "The *Tao* causes the people to be fully in accord with their ruler." Brian Bruya and Tsai Chih Chung use *Dao*: "Establishing a moral cause means that there must be a common conviction shared by the both the people and the government." (Emphasis added in each case.) There is a difference between the word "politics" and the term "*Tao*" (or *Dao*), or "moral influence." *Tao* implies a moral, philosophical, or spiritual dimension missing from "politics" that better captures Sun Tzu's association of harmony between the people and ruler. Hanzhang, *Sun Tzu's Art of War*, 22; Sun Tzu, *The Art of War*, trans. Samuel B. Griffith (London: Oxford University Press, 1977), 63–64; Sun Tzu, *The Art of War*, trans. Ralph D. Sawyer (Boulder, CO: Westview, 1994), 167; *Sunzi Speaks*, 24–25.

36. Hanzhang, *Sun Tzu's Art of War*, 23–24.
37. Hanzhang, 24–25.
38. Hanzhang, 29–30.
39. Hanzhang, 33–34.
40. Hanzhang, 36.
41. Hanzhang, 56–57.
42. Hanzhang, 56–57.
43. Hanzhang, 89–90.
44. Hanzhang, 96.

CHAPTER 2

Integrating the Instruments of Power

Paul Bezerra, Marybeth Ulrich, and Mark Grotelueschen

Thucydides states that humans are motivated to fight by fear, honor, self-interest, or a combination of all three.[1] Sun Tzu advises leaders to know one's enemies and know oneself before making war.[2] Clausewitz expounds upon war's unchanging nature; its chameleon-like character; the interplay of reason, hatred, and chance; and the inextricable link between warfare and politics.[3] But how is a modern state supposed to arrange and employ its resources to ensure its national interests?

This chapter offers an answer in three sections. First, we identify the US actors responsible for planning, coordinating, and implementing the instruments of power (IOPs) toward national security objectives. Second, we discuss the individual IOPs. Finally, we provide a way to describe how the United States decides to use its IOPs in international affairs.

PRESIDENT AND CONGRESS AS COEQUAL BRANCHES

The US Constitution sets forth a system based on equally shared but separate powers across the government's executive, legislative, and judicial branches. Since the executive and legislative branches both control when, where, how, and why the IOPs are used, coordination across these branches is necessary to ensure national security. For example, the president sets strategic goals or ends. At the same time, Congress provides or withholds funding to pursue those goals—illustrating Congress's power to check the president's prerogatives or impulses through its "power of the purse." Likewise, the Constitution identifies the president as the "Chief Administrator" of the government and provides the president the authority to appoint officials to carry out the administration's policies. But again, the Senate's ability to confirm the president's appointees checks the president's influence on how the government operates.

The separation of powers ensures that no branch of government dominates another.[4] Yet while Congress has significant national security responsibilities, the presidency is a unitary actor capable of acting with speed and decisiveness. Unlike Congress, the president is an actor that can quickly set the US national security agenda and respond to national security challenges and opportunities.

The President's Agenda-Setting Role

The president sets national security policy direction and navigates a complicated national security enterprise including

- more than two hundred and fifty diplomatic missions worldwide, staffed by more than thirteen thousand Foreign Service officers,[5]
- eighteen distinct intelligence organizations,[6]
- five functional and six geographic combatant commands,[7]
- 1.3 million active-duty military and 845,000 military reserve and National Guard personnel,[8] and
- approximately $19.2 billion in development and humanitarian assistance.[9]

In addition to the Department of State (DOS), the US intelligence community, and the Department of Defense (DOD), the president leads the "collective executive" featuring other executive departments and agencies such as the National Security Council (NSC), the Department of Homeland Security (DHS), and the Office of Management and Budget.[10] The efforts of these departments and agencies toward the president's objectives are largely coordinated through the NSC's interagency process while being mindful of other influential actors, including Congress, the courts, the media, think tanks, and interest groups.[11]

Congress's Oversight Role

As the US defense establishment grew, Congress established committees to exercise oversight over the executive's actions and pass legislation relevant to the structure and regulation of the national security enterprise. The House Armed Services Committee and Senate Armed Services Committee authorize funding across the DOD and influence policy through legislation setting the terms of DOD activities and programs—that is, what the DOD can and cannot do.[12] The House and Senate appropriations committees determine the actual funding of bills—that is, what the DOD and others may spend. The Senate Committee on Foreign Relations approves treaties and ambassadorial nominations per the "advice and consent" authority given to it in the Constitution. The House Foreign Affairs Committee leverages its aforementioned "power of the purse" in coordination with the House Budget Committee.[13] Both the Senate Committee on Foreign Relations and the House Foreign Affairs Committee also have jurisdiction over humanitarian assistance, human rights, and the activities of multilateral institutions in various regions of the world as well as arms exports and security assistance, the use and deployment of US armed forces, and any other national security developments affecting foreign policy.[14]

Overall, Congress influences national security decision-making through the budget process, oversight, committee reports, and the Senate's confirmation power as well as media statements and writing letters to executive branch officials.[15] Congress can also explicitly legislate outcomes. For example, Congress limited the Barack Obama administration's ability to transfer detainees from the prison at Guantanamo Bay to facilities in the United States.[16] Congress also reorganized the DOD to strengthen civilian control, improve the provision of military advice to political leadership, give combatant commanders clear command responsibility, and improve the military's "jointness" with the Goldwater-Nichols Act (1986)—despite active resistance of the military services to the changes.[17]

CRAFTING STRATEGY THROUGH THE INTERAGENCY PROCESS

The interagency process is how the executive branch develops national security options for the president. The National Security Act of 1947 established the NSC "to advise the President with respect to the integration of domestic, foreign, and military policies relating to the national security so as to enable the military services and the other departments and agencies of the Government to cooperate more effectively in matters involving the national security."[18] The membership of the NSC varies from president to president. In the Joe Biden administration, the NSC includes the president, the vice president, and the secretaries of state, treasury, defense, energy, and homeland security. Other regular attendees in the Biden White House include the attorney general, the US ambassador to the United Nations, the administrator of the US Agency for International Development (USAID), the White House chief of staff, the director of the Office of Science and Technology Policy (OSTP), and the national security adviser (NSA). The chairman of the Joint Chiefs of Staff and the director of National Intelligence provide military and intelligence advice to the NSC. Other administration members may attend NSC meetings when national security issues under consideration affect their agencies or departments.[19]

While the NSC system was initially created to coordinate the efforts of the DOS and DOD, other agencies and departments increasingly participate. For example, USAID officials offer essential insights on international development issues. The Department of Energy, which has jurisdiction over nuclear policy, offers crucial expertise on arms control treaties. The Department of the Treasury is needed when dealing with foreign financial crises and implementing economic sanctions. The Biden administration's inclusion of the director of the OSTP signals the importance it places on the role of scientific expertise in policymaking.

The NSC and the NSA

The NSC provides the president national security policy recommendations, a venue for crisis management, and the interagency process's coordinating mechanism. The NSC staff directorates are divided into regional and functional areas, and staff members typically come from executive departments, academia, and think tanks, although the exact structure varies.[20] The NSC staff fulfills four primary roles:

- advising the president on national security affairs
- managing policy coordination across agencies and departments
- coordinating and monitoring the implementation of policy
- "staffing" the president, including preparing the president for engagements with foreign leaders, summits, trips, and events.[21]

The Scowcroft Model

In 1947, President Dwight Eisenhower created the position of assistant to the president for national security affairs to coordinate the interagency process and act as a personal adviser to the president.[22] Nearly thirty individuals have held this role since then, including prominent figures such as Henry Kissinger, Colin Powell, and Condoleezza Rice. But scholars and practitioners alike have held up Brent Scowcroft, the NSA to President Gerald Ford (1975–77) and President George H. W. Bush (1989–93), as the exemplar for approaching the role as an archetypical "honest broker." This means Scowcroft focused on coordinating interagency actors' inputs to develop policy options for the president's decision rather than acting as a policy advocate pushing specific ideas. To develop policy options and efficiently utilize senior officials' limited availability, Scowcroft instituted a four-level deliberation process in the NSC:

- The NSC: A statutory forum from which the president may request and receive national security advice; the president chairs NSC meetings.
- The Principals Committee (PC): a meeting of the NSC members without the president, chaired by the NSA.
- The Deputies Committee (DC): a meeting chaired by the deputy NSA that includes the deputy secretaries of the NSC members, whose job is finding consensus on interagency policy formulation, monitoring policy implementation, and engaging in crisis management.
- The interagency policy committees (IPCs): IPCs function at various levels below the DC, are chaired by NSC senior directors, and meet regularly to coordinate interagency assessment of and participation in national security issues. IPCs propose policy options for possible adoption at the DC and PC levels.[23]

Scowcroft intended the four-level system to produce consensus policy options and implementation, at the lowest level possible, with only the most sensitive and intractable issues rising to senior officials' attention at higher levels.[24] Of course, some presidents have preferred to rely on informal advisory groups instead of a more formal NSC system, but the NSC still performs the same function.[25]

INSTRUMENTS OF POWER

Whether US national security decision-making flows from Congress, the president, the NSC, informal advisory bodies, or a combination of these actors, the United States relies on a limited number of "tools," or IOPs, to realize its objectives. The acronym DIME (for diplomacy, information, military, and economic) captures the tools that national security decision-makers utilize independently or in combination as part of a strategy to achieve objectives.[26]

Diplomacy

Diplomacy is both an action and a skill set enabling the other IOPs, making it unique among them. As an action, diplomacy is the process of communicating with counterparts in world affairs—that is, formulating and sending messages, including written, verbal, and nonverbal interactions, as well as receiving and interpreting the same from peers.[27] As a skill set, diplomacy is one's ability to realize objectives through negotiations—the ability to exploit or leverage the information, military, and economic IOPs to realize preferred outcomes. Diplomats well skilled in negotiation can realize preferred outcomes with only minimal information, military, and economic power.[28] US diplomats have the luxury of negotiating with lots of power and potential leverage over counterparts, but this luxury alone does not guarantee optimal uses of the diplomacy IOP.[29]

Information

The information IOP takes active and inactive forms and might be the most diverse IOP in terms of who wields it and how one does so, given the ease of accessing and using the Internet. In its active form, states, nonstate actors, nongovernmental organizations, and even individuals may pursue goals using the information IOP. Despite their diversity, all actors actively using it do so to gain strategic advantages by[30]

- influencing the distribution of information to clarify or otherwise inform target audiences' perceptions in favorable ways or
- manipulating information to corrupt others' perceptions and response capabilities or deny adversaries from doing the same.[31]

In its inactive form, the information IOP is not directly wielded by any actor. Instead, it simply manifests or exists as a matter of institutional or ideological appeal. National security decision-makers might attempt to indirectly increase institutional or ideological appeal through mechanisms such as increased budget funding or favorable policy statements. Nonetheless, the end result is still dependent upon a third party's perception. For example, the US could increase science- and technology-related research funding to higher education institutions, but whether foreign students are attracted to such opportunities depends on their individual interest in science and technology research. In the US context, inactive information power flows from others' attraction to

- US-based universities,
- US-based media, entertainment, and advertising industries,
- US-based content held on the Internet or by libraries, museums, endowments, foundations, or nongovernmental organizations, and
- the prevalence of American English around the world.[32]

Military

The military IOP achieves objectives by applying force, threatening the use of force, and enabling others to use force. Two points are critical. First, armed forces are responsible for wielding this IOP but may also wield and support other IOPs. For example, combatant commanders exercise diplomacy when engaging with foreign counterparts. Overseas military bases are a point of economic leverage—opening or expanding a base increases local prosperity, and closing or downsizing a base has the opposite effect. Likewise, the Navy uses its ships as diplomacy and information power by showing the American flag to shape both friends' and would-be adversaries' perceptions in near and distant locales. Second, agencies or departments outside the armed forces—notably, the Central Intelligence Agency (CIA)—may use the military IOP, too, but on a much smaller scale.

Economic

Governments exercise economic power by either enhancing or restricting a targeted actor's fiscal prosperity or wealth.[33] Doing so is accomplished via development assistance (aid), trade flows, or finance opportunities and provides leverage because countries can withdraw these opportunities or even impose sanctions. However, national security decision-makers must carefully weigh the use of the economic IOP because it may negatively impact domestic audiences in ways no other IOP can—just as the Jimmy Carter and Donald Trump administrations' trade policies toward the Soviet Union and China, respectively, harmed American farmers.[34]

US ACTIONS IN INTERNATIONAL POLITICS

The president attempts to realize US objectives worldwide by selecting policy options often developed through the NSC that rely on combinations of IOPs, if not all IOPs. However, every president is a unique individual subject to unique decision-making biases, risk tolerances, and political constraints, among other decision-making factors. Likewise, the exact process within the NSC for preparing policy options for the president is also somewhat variable and dependent on the specific preferences of the NSA. As a result, no one perfect way exists for understanding when, why, toward whom, and how the United States acts in international politics. One can still broadly understand the process for determining US actions when national security challenges and opportunities arise, by focusing on three questions characterizing it:

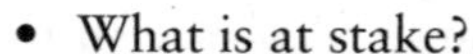

- What is at stake?
- How could the US proceed?
- How should the US proceed?

What Is at Stake?

The first question can be answered by identifying US national interests. US national interests are now commonly articulated in a document called the National Security Strategy (NSS). In short, national interests may be considered the ideas or outcomes the US is willing to spend resources pursuing—including financial, human, physical, and social capital. Each presidential administration prepares unique NSS documents per requirements set by Congress. Still, four enduring national interests have been somewhat consistent across administrations:

1. defense of the US and its constitutional system
2. enhancement of US economic well-being and promotion of US products abroad
3. creation of a favorable world order (international security environment)
4. promotion abroad of US democratic values and the free-market system[35]

Admittedly, in practice, not every US action abroad will appear to be connected clearly to a specific national interest. However, in theory, US national interests provide reliable rules of thumb for understanding why or when the United States will respond to national security challenges or opportunities.

How Could the US Proceed?

The second question can be answered by thinking about power—the ability of one actor to get what it wants from another actor—using IOPs across a spectrum ranging from soft to hard.[36] Hard and soft power both try to realize cooperation as an end but differ in terms of the way this end is realized. Generally speaking, actors use hard power to coerce or otherwise induce another into taking actions, halting ongoing actions, or avoiding unfavorable actions.[37] When the US uses hard power, it tries to bring about compliance toward its objectives by creating fear of negative consequences among other actors for resisting or by bribing other actors to cooperate. In effect, when the US uses hard power, it is leveraging "carrots" or "sticks" or a combination of both.

Soft power tries to co-opt others to achieve compliance toward objectives rather than coerce them.[38] Actors use soft power to influence others toward deciding on their own to take actions, halt ongoing actions, or avoid unfavorable actions as a result of the perceived legitimacy or morality or inherent appeal of doing so. In effect, when the US relies on soft power, it is leveraging others' faith or confidence or trust in its preferences or respect for its views. As with hard power, the US can use soft power directly through such means as diplomatic statements or calls to action; unlike with hard power, the US can benefit from soft power indirectly through such means as others' regard for its institutions, values, culture, or policies. When soft power is effective, others want what the US wants because what the US wants is seen to be more attractive or desirable than any alternatives. Fear or bribes are not required.[39]

Consider the cases of the pope and Osama bin Laden, who both exercise or exercised soft power. Catholics around the world observe the pope's teachings on capital punishment because Catholics consider the pope a relevant moral authority on the topic. This is soft power. Catholics do not follow the pope's teachings because the pope threatens Catholics with excommunication from the Catholic Church for doing otherwise. This would be hard power. Likewise, some radical Islamists around the world supported bin Laden's actions because they believed in his goals—again, soft power. If bin Laden had bribed them to do so or threatened them for not doing so, he would have been leveraging hard power.[40]

Two common misconceptions characterize the use of power in international affairs. The first misconception is that specific IOPs are always hard or soft power. For example, the military IOP is considered hard power. Still, it need not be the only IOP associated with hard power since the US may use its economic IOP to coerce others into agreement or submission via sanctions too. The military IOP can also be a potent mechanism of US soft power demonstrating compassion and concern for others by performing humanitarian assistance and disaster relief operations, as it did in the wake of the 2004 Indian Ocean earthquake and tsunami. Likewise, the diplomacy IOP is often associated with soft power since it relies on communication and negotiation rather than force, but diplomats sometimes deliver fear-inspiring ultimatums as a mechanism supporting other IOPs—as in the case of Secretary of State John Foster Dulles's many statements on Eisenhower's strategy of "massive retaliation." Any IOP can be hard or soft power.

The second misconception concerns whom hard and soft power target—namely, that hard power is useful only against adversaries and soft power only with partners. One can typically assume the US and its partners share national security objectives. Still, significant disagreements between partners are possible, making the use of hard power as plausible as soft power. For example, the US applied hard power via economic sanctions against its NATO ally Turkey in 2020 because Turkey purchased Russian-made air-defense systems over US appeals to the value or importance of unity within the NATO alliance. The US and its adversaries can typically be assumed to prefer different, even opposite, national security objectives that would make soft power seem implausible. But when mutual interests or values align, soft power may lead to cooperation among adversaries—such as the US helping further Russian

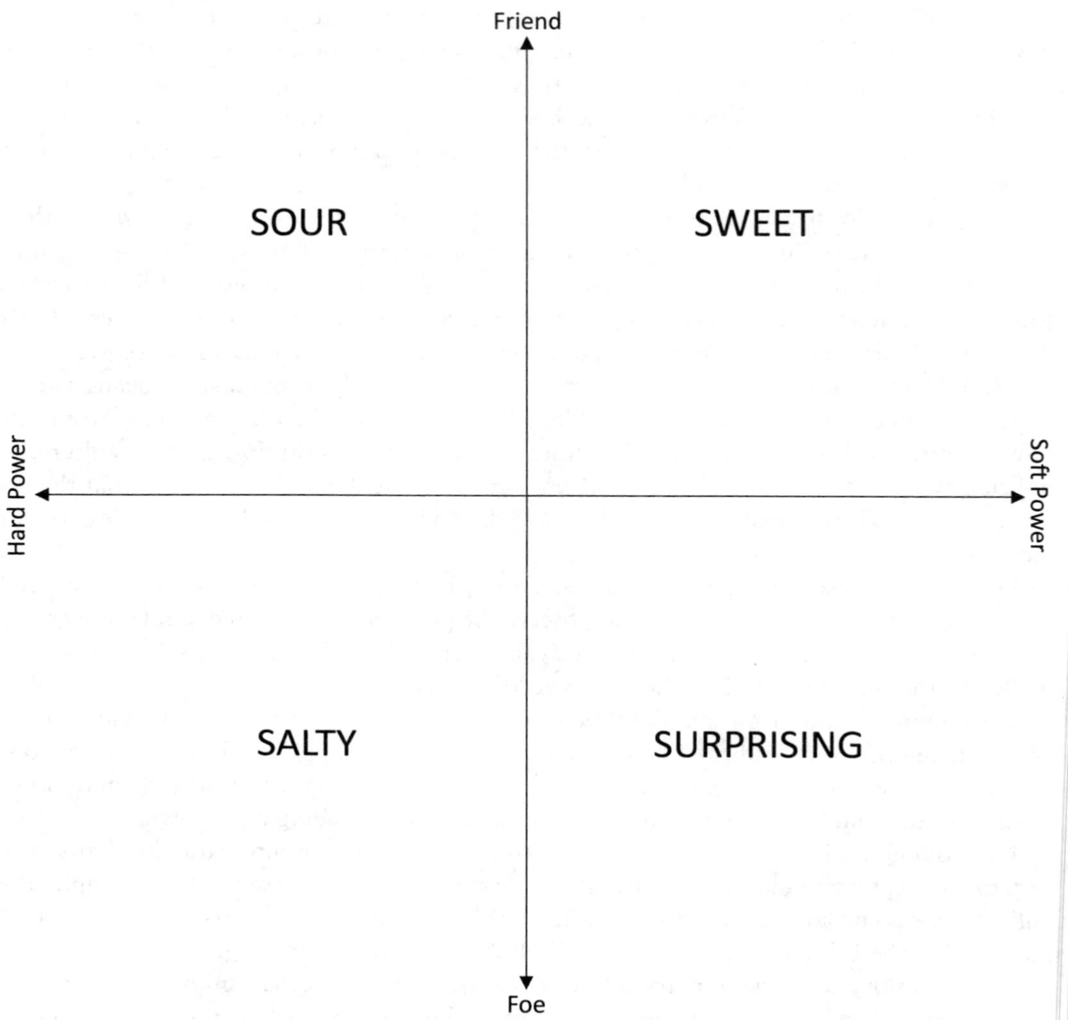

Figure 2.1. Elements of US Responses to National Security Challenges

economic integration into Europe following the collapse of the Soviet Union. Any actor can use any form of power toward another.

Describing how the US responds to national security challenges and opportunities can be challenging, given these common misconceptions surrounding power and IOPs. A potentially helpful way for describing US actions is to identify (1) the nature of the relationship between the US and its target, ranging from "friend" to "foe," and (2) the form of power the US is applying against its target, ranging from hard to soft. Figure 2.1 visualizes these elements and provides a basis for describing policy options. Very simply, one might describe options as sweet, sour, salty, or surprising:

- sweet: using soft power to attract friends
- sour: using hard power to coerce friends

- salty: using hard power to coerce foes
- surprising: using soft power to attract foes

How Should the US Proceed?

The third question can be answered by considering (1) the importance of realizing a favorable outcome in specific national security opportunities or challenges and (2) doing so proportionately to the issue's importance and probability of success. When determining the importance of realizing a favorable outcome, national security decision-makers may assess factors related to potential costs, risks, and values,[41] in addition to considering any potential impacts for failing to do so.[42] Each president is likely to weigh these factors differently.

When determining proportionality to importance and likelihood of success, national security decision-makers and their subordinates may assess the advantages and disadvantages, or limitations, of different strategic options. Admittedly, national security decision-makers and their subordinates do not follow one approach to make such an assessment. But one method for doing so common among military planners that can characterize NSC planning is to analyze the ways and means proposed to achieve objectives based upon metrics of each option's feasibility, acceptability, suitability, and risk—also known as FAS-R tests.[43] FAS-R tests scrutinize each component of the proposed strategy for the following:[44]

- Feasibility: Are the means available to execute the option's proposed ways or courses of action?
- Acceptability: Does the proposed way have the necessary support from domestic and international stakeholders? Is it legal, ethical, or otherwise worth the potential costs?
- Suitability: Will the ways and means assessed realize the objective?
- Risk: Is there a gap between the objective to be achieved and the ways and means available to achieve it?[45] Do any circumstances threaten the course of action's success? Will the course of action produce undesirable secondary or tertiary effects?

National security decision-makers can then compare strategic options while updating FAS-R tests as circumstances and context evolve and suggest changes in strategy to the president as needed.[46]

CONCLUSION

The United States possesses impressive diplomatic, information, military, and economic power. While individual government departments have the lead regarding certain IOPs, such as the DOS controlling diplomacy and the DOD managing the military, many agencies coerce, persuade, or attract.

The proper coordination of all the IOPs is among the most significant challenges for a large, complex, powerful state like the US as it seeks to achieve national security objectives efficiently and effectively. Successful strategies bring high rewards; failed strategies bear high costs. It is crucial that national security policymakers know how to use each IOP, the differences between hard and soft power, and how to evaluate different strategic options. The challenge for US national security professionals is understanding the IOPs and using the right IOPs toward the right targets at the right moment. The difficulty of this challenge cannot be overstated.[47]

LEARNING REVIEW

- Identify key interagency partners involved in the national security decision-making process.
- Recall the difference between the legislative and executive roles in US national security decision-making.
- Explain how the DIME IOPs are used across the national security structure to achieve national security objectives.
- Describe the difference between hard power and soft power.
- Based on the relative advantages and limitations, select and justify an appropriate IOP, or IOPs, to achieve strategic objectives.

NOTES

1. Thucydides, *History of the Peloponnesian War*, trans. Rex Warner (New York: Penguin, 1972), 80.

2. Tao Hanshang, *Sun Tzu's Art of War: The Modern Chinese Interpretation*, trans. Yuan Shibing (New York: Sterling Innovation, 2007), 36.

3. Carl von Clausewitz, *On War*, trans. Michael Howard and Peter Paret (Princeton, NJ: Princeton University Press, 1976), 87, 100–112, 119.

4. Richard E. Neustadt, *Presidential Power* (New York: New American Library, 1960), 42. See also Michael J. Meese, Suzanne C. Nielsen, and Rachel Sondheimer, *American National Security*, 7th ed. (Baltimore: Johns Hopkins University Press, 2009), 97.

5. Julia Nutter, "Where We Stand," *Foreign Service Journal* 97, no. 1 (2021): 60.

6. "Members of the IC," Office of the Director of National Intelligence, accessed April 5, 2021, https://www.dni.gov/index.php/what-we-do/members-of-the-ic.

7. Kathleen J. McInnis, *Defense Primer: Commanding U.S. Military Operations* (Washington, DC: Congressional Research Service, 2020).

8. "Demographics of the U.S. Military," Council on Foreign Relations, July 13, 2020, https://www.cfr.org/backgrounder/demographics-us-military; "The Biggest Armies in the World Ranked by Active Military Personnel in 2020," Statista, December 1, 2020, https://www.statista.com/statistics/264443/the-worlds-largest-armies-based-on-active-force-level/.

9. "Fiscal Year (FY) 2020 Development and Humanitarian Assistance Budget Request," United States Agency for International Development online, February 10, 2020, https://www.usaid.gov/sites/default/files/documents/1868/FinalFY20FactSheet.pdf.

10. Meese, Nielsen, and Sondheimer, *American National Security*, 100.

11. Roger Z. George and Harvey Rishikof, *The National Security Enterprise* (Washington, DC: Georgetown University Press, 2011), 3.

12. George and Rishikof, 129.

13. George and Rishikof, 130.

14. "Jurisdiction," US House of Representatives Committee on Foreign Affairs, accessed April 5, 2021, https://foreignaffairs.house.gov/about.

15. Gerald Felix Warburg, "Congress: Checking Presidential Power, in George and Rishikof, *National Security Enterprise*, 228.

16. Toni Johnson, "Congress and U.S. Foreign Policy," Council on Foreign Relations, January 24, 2013, https://www.cfr.org/backgrounder/congress-and-us-foreign-policy.

17. Barry Goldwater Department of Defense Reorganization Act Pub. L. No. 99-433 (1986), *U.S. Statutes at Large* 100 (1986): 992–1075b.

18. National Security Act, US Code 50 (1947), §402.

19. "National Security Council," White House, accessed April 5, 2021, https://www.whitehouse.gov/nsc.

20. David Auerswald, "The Evolution of the NSC Process," in George and Rishikof, *National Security Enterprise*, 32.

21. Richard D. Hooker, *The NSC Staff: New Choices for a New Administration* (Washington, DC: Institute of National Strategic Studies, 2016), 1.

22. Meese, Nielsen, and Sondheimer, *American National Security*, 102.

23. Gabriel Marcella, "National Security and the Interagency Process: Forward into the 21st Century," in *Organizing for National Security*, ed. Douglas T. Stuart (Carlisle Barracks, PA: Strategic Studies Institute), 168. The IPCs can also be referred to as policy coordination committees.

24. Charles P. Ries, *Improving Decision Making in a Turbulent World* (Santa Monica, CA: RAND Corp., 2016), 13.

25. Meese, Nielsen, and Sondheimer, *American National Security*, 102; John J. Rosenwasser and Michael Warner, "History of the Interagency Process for Foreign Relations in the United States: Murphy's Law?," in George and Rishikof, *National Security Enterprise*, 18.

26. While DIME is the most common acronym, some use DIMEFIL, MIDLIFE, and MIDFIELD to highlight the importance of finance, intelligence, law enforcement, or development.

27. Christer Jönsson, "Diplomacy, Communication and Signaling," in *The SAGE Handbook of Diplomacy*, ed. Costas M. Constantinou, Pauline Kerr, and Paul Sharp (London: SAGE, 2016), 80–82.

28. For greater discussion on the relationship between US ambassadors, the traditional US diplomatic representatives, and combatant commanders (a US military official increasingly performing diplomatic functions in the post-9/11 era), see Shoon Murray and Anthony Quainton, "Combatant Commanders, Ambassadorial Authority, and the Conduct of Diplomacy," in *Mission Creep: The Militarization of U.S. Foreign Policy?*, ed. Gordon Adams and Shoon Murray (Washington, DC: Georgetown University Press, 2014). In short, DOD activities after 9/11 have increased available resources characterizing diplomatic activities as opposed to usurping ambassadorial roles and responsibilities.

29. An example is when the US was unable to secure Turkey's blessing to position sixty-two thousand troops at Incirlik Air Base in advance of the 2003 Iraq invasion despite substantial negotiation and incentives.

30. Inconsistent use of terms in US government publications has conflated information with intelligence. Intelligence informs decision-making but is not an IOP. See Adrian Wolfberg and Brian A. Young, "Is Intelligence an Instrument of National Power?," *American Intelligence Journal* 33, no. 1 (2016): 26–30.

31. Steven Heffington, Adam Oler, and David Tretler, eds., *A National Security Strategy Primer* (Washington, DC: National Defense University Press, 2019), 26–27.

32. Donald M. Bishop, "DIME, Not DiME: Time to Align the Instruments of U.S. Informational Power," The Strategy Bridge, June 20, 2018, https://thestrategybridge.org/the-bridge/2018/6/20/dime-not-dime-time-to-align-the-instruments-of-us-informational-power.

33. Heffington, Oler, and Tretler, *National Security Strategy Primer*, 31–32.

34. Frank Morris, "Farmers Say Current Trade War Mirrors 1980 Russian Grain Embargo," Harvest Public Media, August 20, 2018, https://www.harvestpublicmedia.org/post/farmers-say-current-trade-war-mirrors-1980-russian-grain-embargo#:~:text=Farmers%20Say%20Current%20Trade%20War%20Mirrors%201980%20Russian%20Grain%20Embargo,-By%20Frank%20Morris&text=Harvest%20season%20isn't%20far,one%20day%20to%20the%20next.

35. Donald E. Nuechterlein, *America Recommitted: A Superpower Assesses Its Role in a Turbulent World* (Lexington: University Press of Kentucky, 2015), 16.

36. Joseph S. Nye Jr., "Get Smart: Combining Hard and Soft Power," *Foreign Affairs* 88, no. 4 (2009): 160; Joseph S. Nye Jr., *The Paradox of American Power: Why the World's Only Superpower Can't Go It Alone* (New York: Oxford University Press, 2002), 4.

37. Robert J. Art and Kelly M. Greenhill, "Coercion: An Analytical Overview," in *Coercion: The Power to Hurt in International Politics*, ed. Kelly M. Greenhill and Peter Krause (New York: Oxford University Press, 2018), 4–5; Nye, "Get Smart," 160.

38. Nye, "Paradox," 8–12; Nye, "Get Smart," 160.

39. For a definitive treatment of hard and soft power, see Joseph S. Nye Jr., *Soft Power: The Means to Success in World Politics* (New York: PublicAffairs, 2009), 1–18.

40. These examples are sourced from Nye, *Soft Power*, 2.

41. Nuechterlein, *America Recommitted*, 26–27.

42. Robert E. Hamilton, ed., *National Security Policy and Strategy Course Directive* (Carlisle, PA: US Army War College, 2018), 88.

43. Hamilton, 84–87; H. Richard Yarger, "Toward a Theory of Strategy: Art Lykke and the Army War College Strategy Model," in *Army War College Guide to National Security Issues, Vol. I: Theory of War and Strategy*, ed. J. Boone Bartholomees (Carlisle Barracks, PA: Strategic Studies Institute, 2012), 48–49.

44. Each of these elements is elaborated further in US Joint Chiefs of Staff, *Joint Planning* (Washington, DC: Department of Defense, 2020).

45. Yarger, "Toward a Theory of Strategy," 49.

46. Special attention must be given to the decision to pursue objectives via war rather than other strategies. To be viewed as legitimate or "just," war is broadly scrutinized by five so-called *jus ad bellum* elements: whether the perpetrator is acting with the right intention, whether the perpetrator possesses the proper authority to do so, whether the perpetrator's use of military force is proportionate to the desired objective, whether the perpetrator is using military force as a last resort, and whether the perpetrator's use of military force is likely to succeed. Full discussion of each element is beyond the scope of our chapter, but it should suffice to suggest might does not equal right on its own. See Brown, Seyom, "The Just War Tradition (*Jus ad Bellum*)," in *The Use of Force: Military Power and International Politics*, ed. Robert J. Art and Kelly Greenhill (Lanham, MD: Rowan & Littlefield, 2015), 75–79.

47. For information on this challenge, see Daniel W. Drezner, ed., *Avoiding Trivia: The Role of Strategic Planning in American Foreign Policy* (Washington, DC: Brookings Institution Press, 2009); and Amy B. Zegart, *Flawed by Design: The Evolution of the CIA, JCS, and NSC* (Stanford, CA: Stanford University Press, 1999).

CHAPTER 3

The Spectrum of Conflict and Range of Military Operations

Danielle Gilbert and Kyleanne Hunter

"War is merely a continuation of policy by other means."[1] This quote from Carl von Clausewitz lays a foundation for the *spectrum of conflict*—the continuum of national security and foreign policy challenges that range from peace to war. The military is an instrument of politics. While the military is uniquely suited to engage in combat in all its forms, it has many other capabilities that are crucial for pursuing and protecting national interests. As one of the authors of the 2017 National Security Strategy stated, "By failing to understand that the space between war and peace is not an empty one—but a landscape churning with political, economic, and security competitions that require constant attention—American foreign policy risks being reduced to a reactive and tactical emphasis on the military instrument by default."[2]

This chapter emphasizes that it is crucial for the United States to employ the full range of its instruments of power—not just military but also diplomatic, information, and economic—to achieve national security and foreign policy objectives in peace and in war. At the same time, there are a wide range of missions that the military *can* undertake, ranging from conventional and unconventional war to military operations that include peacekeeping, security cooperation, humanitarian response, and national defense. Historically known as military operations other than war (MOOTW),[3] these operations exercise the power and skill set of the armed forces without resorting to deadly force. This chapter outlines military missions in the *range of military operations* (ROMO), providing a framework for thinking about the scope of military engagement.[4]

THE MILITARY AND THE RANGE OF MILITARY OPERATIONS

How does the military exercise power? This question often brings to mind ground combat or an aerial bombing campaign—but the military does so much more. From preparing for the potential of large-scale nuclear war to providing humanitarian relief in the wake of natural disasters, militaries engage daily in a wide range of operations across the spectrum of conflict. The ROMO includes major-theater conventional war, unconventional war, and operations to aid and bolster allies. To illustrate how the military operates along this spectrum, this chapter spotlights a single month of US activity—May 2011—to show the variety of operations in which the military can be engaged. A single month was chosen to highlight the concurrent engagement in multiple types of operations. A decade after the terrorist attacks of September 11, the US was still on the hunt for the perpetrators of the attacks on the World Trade Center and Pentagon and embroiled in years-long conflicts in Iraq and Afghanistan while also responding to humanitarian crises, engaging in training activities, and responding to new threats. Illustrating military operations in this way both shows that the military is engaged in activities across the spectrum of conflict at any given time and that activities themselves change across the spectrum of conflict.

Operation Tomodachi (Japan, March–May 2011)

In March 2011, a magnitude 9.0 earthquake struck Japan, causing a devastating tsunami and major accident at the Fukushima Daiichi nuclear power plant. With victims dead or missing estimated at 19,300, the powerful earthquake and subsequent tsunami constituted one of the deadliest natural disasters in Japanese history.[5] The next day, the US military initiated support efforts under Operation Tomodachi (literally "Operation Friend[s]")—a six-week mission to support Japanese recovery efforts. The United States mobilized 24,500 troops from the Army, Navy, Air Force, and Marines to aid in the $90 million effort, which was lauded as a success for the depth of its cooperation, demonstrating US commitment to its Japanese ally.

The effort drew on personnel from twelve US military bases in Japan; it involved 189 aircraft and twenty-four naval ships, including a carrier strike group and elements from a Marine Expeditionary Unit. For instance, USS *Cowpens*, USS *Preble*, USS *Shiloh*, and USS *Curtis D. Wilbur* searched for human remains off the coast of Honshu, while helicopters from USS *Ronald Reagan* and one P-3 Orion aircraft provided aerial reconnaissance.[6] A remotely piloted aircraft (RPA, aka a drone), the RQ-4 Global Hawk, was deployed from Anderson Air Force Base in Guam and used radar and optical surveillance to assess the extent of infrastructure damage.[7] By the end of the mission, the US Seventh Fleet had delivered more than 260 tons of relief supplies to a grateful Japanese public. Japanese defense minister Toshimi Kitazawa delivered a message from Prime Minister Naoto Kan stating that "the entire Japanese people are deeply moved and encouraged by the scenes of US military members working hard to support the relief efforts. Both Japan and the United States are true 'TOMODACHI' (friends)."[8] The operation strengthened the US-Japan alliance and demonstrated American soft power on the world stage.

Exercise Atlas Drop and Training by US Advisers (Uganda, 2011)

For decades, the government of Uganda battled the brutal tactics of the Lord's Resistance Army (LRA), a heterodox Christian extremist rebel group, and its leader, Joseph Kony. Throughout the conflict, more than two million Ugandans were displaced from their homes, more than sixty-six thousand children were forcibly recruited to the LRA as child soldiers, and countless Ugandans were raped, tortured, kidnapped, and killed by the rebels.[9] While the US military had provided limited support to the Ugandan government for years, it meaningfully increased support in 2011.

In May 2010, the US Congress passed the Lord's Resistance Army Disarmament and Northern Uganda Recovery Act, which committed the US to "providing political, economic, military, and intelligence support for viable multilateral efforts to protect civilians from the Lord's Resistance Army, to apprehend or remove Joseph Kony and his top commanders from the battlefield in the continued absence of a negotiated solution, and to disarm and demobilize the remaining Lord's Resistance Army fighters." The legislation also committed to providing humanitarian assistance to neighboring Democratic Republic of Congo, Sudan, and the Central African Republic, while requiring the president of the United States to outline updated policy toward Uganda in the subsequent 180 days.[10]

In February 2011, the US military began its sixteenth Exercise Atlas Drop, an annual joint training exercise by US and foreign forces. Atlas Drop 11 took place in Uganda and featured troops from the Georgia National Guard and the Utah National Guard training soldiers from the Ugandan Peoples Defense Forces in aerial resupply and cargo drops.[11] In the aftermath of congressional action and building on the existing cooperation forged during the annual joint exercises, President Barack Obama committed a more dedicated presence to supporting and training Ugandan troops, sending approximately one hundred "combat-equipped"[12] troops "to Central Africa to provide assistance to regional forces that are working toward the removal of Joseph Kony from the battlefields."[13] This deployment included "associated headquarters, communications, and logistics personnel." While combat-equipped, these service members were deployed with a noncombat mandate: "they will only be providing information, advice, and assistance to partner nation forces, and they will not themselves engage LRA forces unless necessary for self-defense."[14] In early 2017, US Africa Command announced the end of the successful "counter-LRA" mission: the rebels had been reduced from thousands of fighters to fewer than one hundred.[15]

Expansion of the Global War on Terror (Yemen, May 2011)

The global war on terrorism (GWOT) has not been confined to operations in Iraq and Afghanistan. As part of the hunt for al-Qaeda in the Arabian Peninsula (AQAP) operatives, the US military, led by Joint Special Operations Command, deployed to Yemen in late 2010. Prior to May 2011, the US military presence had been primarily preventive in nature—with both US boots on the ground and naval warships in the Red Sea acting as a deterrent against Yemeni support for AQAP. This early presence was also essential for gathering information about AQAP locations, as Yemen's rough terrain provided cover and concealment.

In May 2011, US forces escalated their operations and launched their first personality-targeted drone strike against AQAP.[16] Drone strikes were a way to pinpoint single individuals and avoid large-scale combat operations. There is evidence that this attack was intended to assassinate Anwar al-Awlaki, an American-Yemini cleric who was a primary AQAP funder and organizer.[17] Al-Awlaki was not killed in this attack, though three individuals were. The strike in May marked an escalation into more lethal operations from previous deterrence missions and began a series of targeted drone strikes that lasted until 2020, including the one that ultimately killed al-Awlaki in September 2011.

Operation Neptune Spear (Pakistan, May 2011)

Perhaps the most famous US military mission of May 2011 was Operation Neptune Spear—the killing of Osama bin Laden in Abbottabad, Pakistan. Over the previous four years, US intelligence officials began linking the name and details of one of bin Laden's couriers to a large, secure compound outside of Islamabad. By April 2011, intelligence sources were confident that the compound served as bin Laden's hideout, and President Obama authorized Navy SEAL Team Six, a special operations unit, to conduct a raid.

Just after midnight (Pakistan time) on May 2, President Obama formally authorized the mission, and MH-60 Black Hawk and MH-47 Chinook helicopters carrying twenty-five SEALs took off from Afghanistan. Over a "nearly flawless" forty minutes, SEAL Team Six found and killed the world's most wanted terrorist and four other individuals in the compound.[18] The SEALs collected intelligence information from the compound, destroyed a helicopter that had crashed during the mission, and departed without loss of life among them—arriving safely back in Afghanistan only four hours after they left.

Operation New Dawn (Iraq, September 2010–December 2011)

While military operations in one GWOT theater were intensifying, operations in another were cooling. In September 2010, Operation Iraqi Freedom transitioned to Operation New Dawn. This marked a transition in US force posture from a combat and occupation mission to one of security force assistance. The initial timeline for Operation New Dawn had US combat troops fully withdrawn from Iraq by the end of 2011. However, in May 2011, President Obama and Iraqi prime minister Nouri al-Maliki recognized the need for a more robust status-of-forces agreement to expand the training role of US forces in Iraq due to changing security situations.[19]

Operation New Dawn represented a transition in both force strength and mission. The status-of-forces agreement reduced the number of US troops from almost half a million to fifty thousand.[20] In May 2011, the British military withdrew the last of its forces as well, shifting the burden of operations from a coalition to a US-only activity. The mission also changed significantly. The kinetic aspects of operations in Iraq were transitioned to Iraqi forces, and US forces took on an expanded training and support role. Operation New Dawn shows how the role of the US military can also transition down the spectrum, moving from combat to support operations without fully disengaging from the conflict.

Operation Odyssey Dawn and Unified Protector (Libya, March–October 2011)

In early 2011, a wave of protests against autocrats swept the Middle East and North Africa in the "Arab Spring." While some leaders were quickly ousted, others—including Libya's longtime ruler, Muammar Qaddafi—responded by violently repressing the demonstrations. In escalating violence against civilians, Libyan security forces attacked demonstrators with lethal force from the ground and air. As Qaddafi's position hardened, some Libyan political and military figures defected from the regime, siding with the demonstrators in armed rebellion. At the same time, the United Nations Security Council began pressuring Qaddafi to step down, employing sanctions, travel restrictions, and an arms embargo.[21]

In the face of these diplomatic and economic measures, Qaddafi ramped up his attacks. With support from the United States, France, and the Arab League, and citing the 2005 Responsibility to Protect commitment in the case of the Libyan people, the United Nations Security Council adopted Resolutions 1970 and 1973, which called for a no-fly zone over Libya.[22] From March 19 to 31, the US used Operation Odyssey Dawn to enforce the no-fly zone, destroy several surface-to-air missile sites, and attack Qaddafi's ground forces.[23] On March 31, the US transferred control to the North Atlantic Treaty Organization under the banner of Operation Unified Protector.

These operations were launched to protect the people of Libya from Qaddafi's attacks, but in enforcing a no-fly zone they supported the rebel efforts to remove Qaddafi from power. By October 2011, the rebels had taken the capital city of Tripoli and Qaddafi was dead.

CONCEPTS: THE SPECTRUM OF CONFLICT

Each of the above cases can be conceptualized along the spectrum of conflict in four dimensions: *type of power projection*, *relationship between militaries*, *lethality of military action*, and *immediacy of physical threat*. They include both the way that the military operates (the type of power projection and the lethality of military action) and the external environment in which the military must operate (the relationship between militaries and the immediacy of physical threat).

Figure 3.1 illustrates the range of these military operations along the spectrum of conflict. First, what type of power does the government want the military to project? Power is defined as the ability to get others to do what they otherwise might not do. But not all power involves physical force and coercion; it can also include persuasion and co-option. As discussed in chapter 2, this can be distinguished between two broad categories of power: soft power, which occurs "when one country gets other countries to *want* what it wants," versus hard power, understood as "*ordering* others to do what it wants" (emphasis in original).[24] The military can engage in operations that span the spectrum from soft to hard power. Soft power activities might include personnel exchanges, overseas basing, and humanitarian assistance, while hard power activities include actions such as dropping bombs.

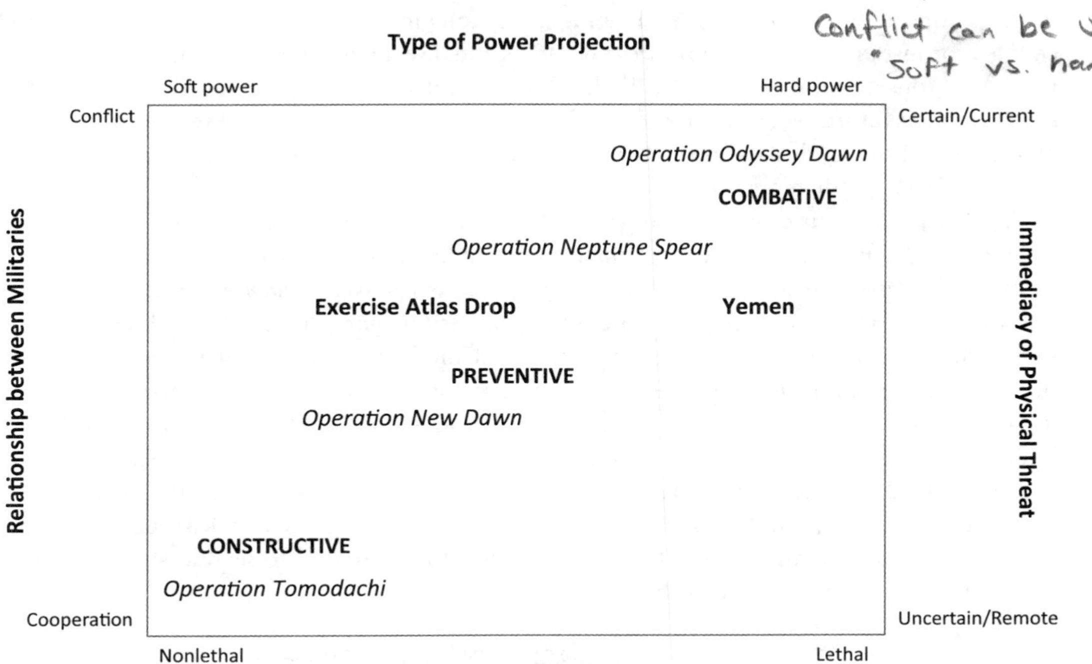

Figure 3.1. Range of Military Operations along the Spectrum of Conflict

Second, how does the military relate to the country in which it is operating? The relationship between the military and that of other countries ranges from cooperative to combative. Cooperative relationships can be formally codified alliances or not, such as a country's request for humanitarian assistance.[25] Combative relationships most often involve the use of force and similarly may be formally codified (as in a declaration of war) or not (as in a spontaneous attack).

Third, how lethal is the military action? The military is a warfighting institution and, as such, is often tasked with using deadly force to achieve political outcomes. Yet not all military action is lethal, and in fact the government often tasks the military with saving lives. The US military is responsible for providing humanitarian assistance, disseminating and evaluating information related to American security, and developing infrastructure and building security force capacity in partner states. Additionally, new technologies are allowing for targeted ends to be achieved in a less lethal manner. For example, in 2019, the US reportedly conducted a cyberattack that crippled Iran's ability to engage in kinetic attacks against US vessels.[26] Military action can be highly lethal (as in nuclear weapons) or kill a few targeted individuals (as in precision drone strikes), or it can save many lives (as in providing medical care after a natural disaster).

Last, how immediate or proximate is the underlying threat? This last dimension captures the time horizon for dealing with risks and challenges. On one end of the spectrum, there are threats that are certain and immediate—a launched missile, an earthquake, an outbreak of a deadly disease. These threats must be countered immediately, decisively, and forcefully to preserve safety and security. On the other end of the spectrum, however, some risks are distant, uncertain, and may take years to unfold. These risks tend to come not from rival states or even nonstate actors but from changing conditions in the international system. Climate change, for instance, poses a vital threat to US national security interests—but its risks manifest in the long term. Nevertheless, the US military considers it important to deal with this risk to ensure future security. Moreover, these uncertain and remote threats can exacerbate and catalyze existing threats, as the world has seen with increasing political instability during the COVID-19 pandemic.[27]

Together, these four dimensions describe the spectrum of conflict as it relates to the range of military operations. Bringing the dimensions together, military operations along this spectrum can be grouped into three desired effects: *constructive*, *preventive*, and *combative*. Constructive operations focus on building capacity with partner nations and shaping the international environment to the advantage of the United States. Preventive operations focus on reducing the opportunity or likelihood of future conflict and combat. Combat operations use military force against an adversary. These categories exist on a continuum, and many military operations blur the lines between them. Counterinsurgency activities, for example, often slide between prevention (e.g., village-stability operations) to combat (e.g., killing insurgents) to construction (e.g., building schools). The military often engages in constructive, preventive, and combat operations simultaneously and must be prepared to seamlessly move from one part of the spectrum to the other.

APPLICATION: CLASSIFYING OPERATIONS

Each of the cases of military activity of May 2011 falls on the four dimensions of the spectrum of conflict and range of military operations. These operations often move along the spectrum and can move between being constructive, preventive, and combative. Exploring real examples shows how the different dimensions can explain military action while illustrating the way that operations can change over time and move along the spectrum of conflict.

At one end of the spectrum, Operation Tomodachi epitomizes a *constructive* military mission: by *cooperating* with the Japanese military to provide *nonlethal* (and even life-saving) support to the Japanese people, the US military used *soft power* to strengthen a relationship with an important ally. On the fourth dimension—the immediacy of the threat—responding to a natural and humanitarian disaster is undoubtedly time sensitive. But in doing so, the United States not only responded to the ongoing crisis in Japan but also strengthened an alliance important to the future. Japanese policymakers viewed the large-scale US cooperation in relief efforts as bolstering Japan's ability to respond to its regional rivals.[28]

Exercise Atlas Drop features elements of *constructive*, *preventive*, and destructive *combat* operations. The mission included elements of both hard and soft power and of cooperation and conflict. While the US advisers were prepared for combat, it was not the purpose of their mission. Rather, they aimed to use nonlethal tactics to support the Ugandans in deterring and defeating the ongoing, immediate threat of the LRA.

The activities under the umbrella of the GWOT in Yemen highlight how external factors influence the way that the military acts. Concerning the relationship between actors, tensions were rising as it became evident that Yemeni officials were not cooperating with requests to give up locations of AQAP fighters.[29] As US troops discovered these locations, the threat became more immediate. The escalation of tensions coupled with immediacy of threat resulted in the decision to increase the lethality of actions—moving from training and intelligence-gathering operations to engaging in RPA strikes. The use of RPAs often falls between the *preventive* and *combat* categories. Proponents of their use assert that they are necessary, especially in counterinsurgency and counterterrorism operations, to achieve targeted decapitations without having to engage in full-scale combat operations.[30] However, they fall high on both the lethality, hard power, and conflict scales, making others view them as combat operations.[31]

Operation Neptune Spear had two distinct desired effects. First, the mission had clear elements of *combat*, including the use of hard power and lethal, kinetic operations against a proximate adversary. The mission punished Osama bin Laden for perpetrating the deadliest terrorist attack on American soil. At the same time, the mission included *preventive* elements as well: it worked to stave off future attacks by crippling the organization by removing its leader and sending a warning to other armed groups considering an attack on the United States.

Operation New Dawn demonstrates how operations move along the spectrum of conflict in response to changes in both internal priorities and environmental factors. During the 2003 invasion, the relationship between the US and Iraq was one of hostility. But with the removal of Saddam Hussein and the subsequent establishment of a democratic government, the relationship moved from fighting against a state military toward cooperation in defeating an insurgency, changing the way in which the militaries interacted. Operation New Dawn represented a step in formalizing the de-escalation from hostilities to advising and training.

Finally, Operation Odyssey Dawn / Unified Protector is a clear case of combative operations. Though the stated purpose of the operation was to protect civilians (per the UN resolutions), the actions taken to do so employed lethal, hard power. Further, the threat to civilians on the ground in Libya was imminent, requiring the use of kinetic operations.

THE MILITARY BEYOND WAR

There are several reasons why the US military is called on to conduct operations in contexts other than war. First, it is exceptionally capable of dealing with massive logistic challenges all over the world. The US military has an extensive budget and equipment supply, and its members receive substantial training in logistics, engineering, strategy, and combat. The military is also continually forward deployed, capable of rapid global mobility through airlift, and service members are based around the world. This allows for quick reaction to crises as they emerge. Additionally, the military planning process enables quickly disseminating orders through the chain of command.

In addition to a desire to help those in need, the government derives benefits from the military's involvement in noncombat missions.[32] Participation in noncombat operations is preparation for future threats. For example, when Hurricane Florence hit the Carolinas in 2018, the response from the US Marines not only helped disaster recovery; it also served as a real-world exercise in the logistic integration needed for deploying to combat.[33] From a strategic level, US involvement in many noncombat missions also bolsters the public perception of America as a force for good in the world.[34]

However, the ability of the military to conduct such a wide range of operations comes with risks: the government might employ the military to solve foreign policy problems when other instruments of power would be more appropriate.[35] As Abraham Maslow wrote in 1966, "When all you have is a hammer, everything looks like a nail."[36] Rosa Brooks applied this directly to the US military, stating, "If your only functioning government institution is the military, everything looks like a war."[37] This expresses the concern that the US government has become overreliant on the military to solve all problems—both foreign and domestic.

Increased participation in operations other than war creates potential for "mission creep." Since the attacks of September 11, 2001, the military has taken on more domestic roles. President George W. Bush ordered the creation of the Department of Homeland Security (DHS) and US Northern Command (USNORTHCOM).[38] Domestically, the Department of Defense legally serves in a support role to DHS during domestic missions, referred to as defense support of civil authorities (DSCA). Its logistic capability, mission-planning processes, and scalability of operations provides civilian authorities critical capabilities to prevent suffering, save lives, and mitigate damage at home.[39] Though the military is legally subordinate to civilian authorities, the capabilities that it brings often result in the military serving in a more prominent position, leading to questions about the expanding roles that it is playing at home.[40]

Military engagement around the world can also hurt public perception of the United States. While some foreign audiences might see US global engagement as a sign of goodwill, others might interpret American action as meddling or coercion. Especially in the Middle East and Latin America—regions long accustomed to US interference over the last century—governments and populations may prefer for the US military to stay far away.[41] To that end, the US has pledged to use the military as a tool of last resort, prioritizing "diplomacy, development, and economic statecraft" to achieve the goals of US foreign policy.[42]

Balancing the logistic, operational, and planning benefits of military engagement with the risks of mission creep and public perception is difficult. An understanding of the inputs into the spectrum of conflict help to make sense of how the military is used.

CONCLUSION

While many may think of the military as an organization focused solely on combat, it is involved in a wide range of operations that span the spectrum of conflict from peace to war. As shown by the above examples, which illustrate only a fraction of the military's activity at one point in time, the spectrum of conflict represents a continuum of operations and activities; operations move up and down, depending on internal and external factors. Though not an absolute, it is an important ordering principle for us to understand how the military interacts with other instruments of national security.

Using the four dimensions of the spectrum of conflict puts in perspective that the military weighs a range of internal and external factors—including the threat environment and desired effects—in designing appropriate and effective military operations. Last, the spectrum of conflict conceptualizes how to classify, prepare for, and confront future threats. Constructive and preventive operations allow the military to pursue desired effects today so that the country is prepared for what tomorrow brings.

LEARNING REVIEW

- Differentiate between military missions across the spectrum of conflict and the range of military operations.
- Describe the desired effects of soft power military missions.
- Evaluate the pros and cons of using the military for missions other than major theater war.

NOTES

1. Carl von Clausewitz, *On War*, ed. and trans. Michael Howard and Peter Paret (Princeton, NJ: Princeton University Press, 1976), 87, 605.
2. Nadia Schadlow, "Peace and War: The Space Between," War on the Rocks, August 18, 2014, https://warontherocks.com/2014/08/peace-and-war-the-space-between/.
3. Joint Chiefs of Staff, *Joint Publication 3-07: Joint Doctrine for Military Operations other than War* (Washington, DC: June 16, 1995), i.
4. "Airpower and the Range of Military Operations," Curtis E. LeMay Center for Doctrine Development and Education, Annex 3-0 Operations and Planning, November 4, 2016.
5. Kenneth Pletcher, "Japan Earthquake and Tsunami of 2011," Britannica, https://www.britannica.com/event/Japan-earthquake-and-tsunami-of-2011.
6. "Timeline of Operation Tomodachi," National Bureau of Asian Research, https://www.nbr.org/publication/timeline-of-operation-tomodachi/.
7. Andrew Feickert and Emma Chanlett-Avery, *Japan 2011 Earthquake: U.S. Department of Defense (DOD) Response*, Congressional Research Service, June 2, 2011, https://fas.org/sgp/crs/row/R41690.pdf.
8. "Timeline of Operation Tomodachi."
9. Pub. L. No. 111-172, May 24, 2010, 111th Cong., https://www.congress.gov/111/plaws/publ172/PLAW-111publ172.pdf.
10. Pub. L. No. 111-172.
11. "Atlas Drop," GlobalSecurity, https://www.globalsecurity.org/military/ops/atlas-drop.htm. Accessed December 28, 2021.
12. Jack Goldsmith, "The Uganda Intervention and the WPR 60-Day Clock," Lawfare, December 14, 2011, https://www.lawfareblog.com/uganda-intervention-and-wpr-60-day-clock.

13. "Letter from the President to the Speaker of the House of Representatives and the President Pro Tempore of the Senate Regarding the Lord's Resistance Army," White House Office of the Press Secretary, October 14, 2011, https://obamawhitehouse.archives.gov/the-press-office/2011/10/14/letter-president-speaker-house-representatives-and-president-pro-tempore.

14. "Letter from the President to the Speaker of the House."

15. Robert Chesney, "Close Enough: The Quiet Conclusion of the Combat-Equipped Deployment to Uganda," Lawfare, April 18, 2017, https://www.lawfareblog.com/close-enough-quiet-conclusion-combat-equipped-deployment-uganda.

16. Jeb Boon and Greg Miller, "US Drone Strike in Yemen Is First since 2002," *Washington Post*, May 5, 2011, https://www.washingtonpost.com/world/middle-east/yemeni-official-us-drone-strike-kills-2-al-qaeda-operatives/2011/05/05/AF7HrzxF_story.html.

17. Mark Maxetti, "Drone Strike in Yemen Was Aimed at Awlaki," *New York Times*, May 7, 2011, https://www.nytimes.com/2011/05/07/world/middleeast/07yemen.html.

18. Julie Marks, "How SEAL Team Six Took Out Osama bin Laden," History, August 2, 2019, https://www.history.com/news/osama-bin-laden-death-seal-team-six.

19. Ryan N. Mannina, "How the 2011 US Troop Withdrawal from Iraq Led to the Rise of ISIS," Small Wars Journal, December 23, 2019, https://smallwarsjournal.com/jrnl/art/how-2011-us-troop-withdrawal-iraq-led-rise-isis.

20. "Operation New Dawn," US Army, August 31, 2010, https://www.army.mil/article/44526/operation_new_dawn#:~:text=The%20transition%20to%20Operation%20New%20Dawn,%20Sept.%201,,advising,%20assisting%20and%20training%20Iraqi%20Security%20Forces%20(ISF).

21. Editors of Encyclopaedia Britannica, "Libya Revolt of 2011," Britannica, https://www.britannica.com/event/Libya-Revolt-of-2011.

22. "Security Council Approves 'No-Fly Zone' over Libya Authorizing 'All Necessary Measures' to Protect Civilians," UN press release, March 17, 2011, https://www.un.org/press/en/2011/sc10200.doc.htm.

23. "Rebel Forces Hold Key City, Advance West," CNN, March 26, 2011, http://edition.cnn.com/2011/WORLD/africa/03/26/libya.war/index.html.

24. Joseph S. Nye Jr., "Soft Power," *Foreign Policy*, no. 80 (Autumn 1990): 153–71.

25. Schadlow, "Peace and War."

26. Julian Barnes, "US Cyber Attack Hurts Iran's Ability to Target Oil Tankers, Officials Say," *New York Times*, August 28, 2019, https://www.nytimes.com/2019/08/28/us/politics/us-iran-cyber-attack.html.

27. Jonathan D. Moyer and Oliver Kaplan. "Will the Coronavirus Fuel Conflict?," *Foreign Policy*, July 6, 2020.

28. Richard J. Samuels, *3.11: Disaster and Change in Japan* (Ithaca, NY: Cornell University Press, 2013), 103–7; Jennifer D. P. Moroney et al., "Lessons from Department of Defense Disaster Relief Efforts in the Asia-Pacific Region," RAND Corporation, (2013), 100; Erik Lin-Greenberg, "Non-Traditional Security Dilemmas: Can Military Operations other than War Intensify Security Competition in Asia?," *Asian Security* 14, no. 3 (2018).

29. Kali Robinson, "Backgrounder: Yemen's Tragedy," Council on Foreign Relations, February 5, 2021, https://www.cfr.org/backgrounder/yemen-crisis.

30. James Andrew Lewis, "Drone Strikes, Complicated by Necessary," Center for Strategic and International Studies, July 5, 2016, https://www.csis.org/analysis/drone-strikes-complicated-necessary.

31. James I. Walsh and Marcus Schulzke, *The Ethics of Drone Strikes: Does Reducing the Cost of Conflict Encourage War?* (Carlisle Barracks, PA: Strategic Studies Institute, 2015).

32. Ryan Burke, *Toward a Unified Military Response: Hurricane Sandy and the Dual Status Commander* (Carlisle Barracks, PA: US Army War College Press, 2015).

33. Kevin Reilley, Graham Flagan, and Daniel Brown, "How US Marines Respond to Hurricanes," Insider, August 27, 2020, https://www.businessinsider.com/how-us-marines-respond-to-natural-disasters-hurricane-2019-8.

34. Richard Wike, "Does Humanitarian Aid Improve America's Image?," Pew Research Center, March 6, 2012, https://www.pewresearch.org/global/2012/03/06/does-humanitarian-aid-improve-americas-image/.

35. Robert M. Gates, "The Overmilitarization of American Foreign Policy," *Foreign Affairs*, July/August 2020, https://www.foreignaffairs.com/articles/united-states/2020-06-02/robert-gates-over militarization-american-foreign-policy.

36. Abraham H. Maslow, *The Psychology of Science: A Reconnaissance* (NY: HarperCollins: 1966).

37. Rosa Brooks, *How Everything Became War and the Military Became Everything: Tales from the Pentagon* (New York: Simon & Schuster, 2016).

38. USNORTHCOM is a geographic combatant command with homeland defense (HD) and defense support of civil authorities (DSCA) as its primary mission sets.

39. William J. Lynn, "Defense Support of Civil Authorities (DSCA)," Department of Defense Directive 3025.18, December 29, 2010, https://www.dco.uscg.mil/Portals/9/CG-5R/nsarc/DoDD %203025.18%20Defense%20Support%20of%20Civil%20Authorities.pdf.

40. Thomas Goss, Barry Cardwell, and Jimmie Perryman, *Who's in Charge? New Challenges in Homeland Defense and Homeland Security* (Peterson Air Force Base, CO: US Northern Command, 2006).

41. Christopher Marquis, "After the War: Opinion; World's View of the U.S. Sours after Iraq War, Poll Finds," *New York Times*, June 4, 2003, https://www.nytimes.com/2003/06/04/world/after-the-war -opinion-world-s-view-of-us-sours-after-iraq-war-poll-finds.html.

42. Joseph R. Biden Jr. "Interim National Security Strategic Guidance," White House, March 3, 2021, https://www.whitehouse.gov/wp-content/uploads/2021/03/NSC-1v2.pdf.

PART II

MILITARY FORCES AND THE JOINT FIGHT

CHAPTER 4

The US Joint Force Structure

Buddhika Jayamaha

The United States, of all the great powers, continues to maintain a global security architecture. This global presence allows its military to respond to both security challenges and humanitarian disasters at a moment's notice. This global security architecture, built around the joint force structure, was successfully used during the 1990s and today makes it possible for the US to maintain its global presence. Why and how did this joint force structure emerge? How does it function, and is this the most appropriate security architecture as the US enters an era of great-power competition?

In answering those questions, this chapter is separated into three sections. The first provides a brief explanation from the end of World War II to the emergence of the joint force. The second section describes the joint force structure. The third section briefly focuses on empirical examples in an attempt to highlight how the joint force functions in reality. The chapter concludes by briefly exposing the reader to contemporary strategic challenges the joint force faces.

COMBINED ARMS TO JOINT FORCE

Land was the defining domain until World War I, with sea power playing an auxiliary role.[1] Consequently, combined-arms approaches that focused on the land domain—the synchronized utilization of combat arms to create complementary effects in battle that would create greater total effect than if they were employed independently or sequentially—dominated military strategic thinking. World War II was a total war along national lines that was a clash of industrial organizations and is an anomaly in the annals of war rather than the norm. It was defining because in addition to land, sea and air became equally critical domains. As a consequence, military strategy in World War II required thinking at the national level. Creating effects now required the deployment of combat power in all three domains to create complementary effects across domains. It gave rise to the joint force concept.

Though winning World War II required thinking along the lines of the joint force concept, at the tactical and operational level each branch largely fought its own battles. The military organizational innovations and institutional structures that emerged during World War II were formalized in the National Security Act of 1947. It created the Air Force; made the National Security Council (NSC) the statutory forum where the president discussed national security issues; merged the War Department and the Navy Department into a National Military Establishment (NME), with civilian secretaries for the Department of the Army, the Department of the Navy, and the Department of the Air Force; and created the secretary of defense as a civilian cabinet position. The act was amended in 1949 and renamed the NME the Department of Defense (DOD).[2] Despite this reorganization, each branch retained its own service chief, and the chairman of the Joint Chiefs of Staff (CJCS) remained part of the operational chain of command. The idea of "joint" remained only at the strategic level, but in reality each branch concentrated on its own domain, fought its own war, and there was little to no integration across domains at the operational and tactical levels.

At the height of the Cold War, the US faced a strategic challenge at the national level. The Soviet Union advanced its nuclear deterrence and expanded and modernized its conventional forces to the point that Warsaw Pact forces in Europe outnumbered North Atlantic Treaty Organization (NATO) forces by a ratio of three to one.[3] The Soviet strategic challenge coupled with challenges the US faced in Korea and Vietnam revealed the shortcomings of the existing institutional architecture. Later, failures in Iran and near failures in Grenada further exposed that the separation between branches created incongruities at strategic, operational, and tactical levels of warfighting reducing military effectiveness, at times resulting in disastrous consequences.[4] Faced with this dual challenge—military ineffectiveness and Soviet strategic advantage in nuclear and conventional forces—the US was forced to come up with *institutional*, *matériel*, *doctrinal*, and *personnel* solutions. The joint force is the cumulative result of those solutions.

CREATING THE JOINT FORCE

At the *institutional* level, the Goldwater-Nichols Department of Defense Reorganization Act of 1986 operationalized the joint force concept by instituting sweeping changes across branches. The CJCS became the highest-ranking military officer and principal military adviser to the president, the NSC, and the secretary of defense. The act transferred legal authority for combat operations from services to combatant commands (COCOMs), with a four-star general or admiral at the helm.[5] It created a dual chain of command, each with a unique role. Services retained the authority to organize, train, and equip forces and make them combat-ready for use by the COCOMs. The COCOMs were given the authority to conduct operations across the spectrum of conflict once directed by the president or the secretary of defense.[6] While the CJCS advises the president, the CJCS is technically not in the warfighter's chain of command. Instead, combat authority is delegated from the president to the secretary of defense to the appropriate combatant commander (see figure 4.1).[7]

The Unified Command Plan, modified every few years, delineates the areas and domains of responsibility for each of the geographic and functional COCOMs. Functional COCOMs operate worldwide across geographic boundaries and provide unique capabilities to geographic COCOMs. Each combatant commander is assigned component commanders for land, air, maritime, and special operations. Making these component commanders report to the unified commander rather than to service chiefs facilitated unity of command and minimized interservice rivalry. With the addition of US Space Command in 2019 (previously established in 1985 and deactivated in 2002), the DOD exercises its combat authorities through eleven COCOMs, six with authorities based on geographic location and five with global authorities based on specific functions or domains (see table 4.1). Operations in the land and maritime domains are critical to controlling resources and the movement of

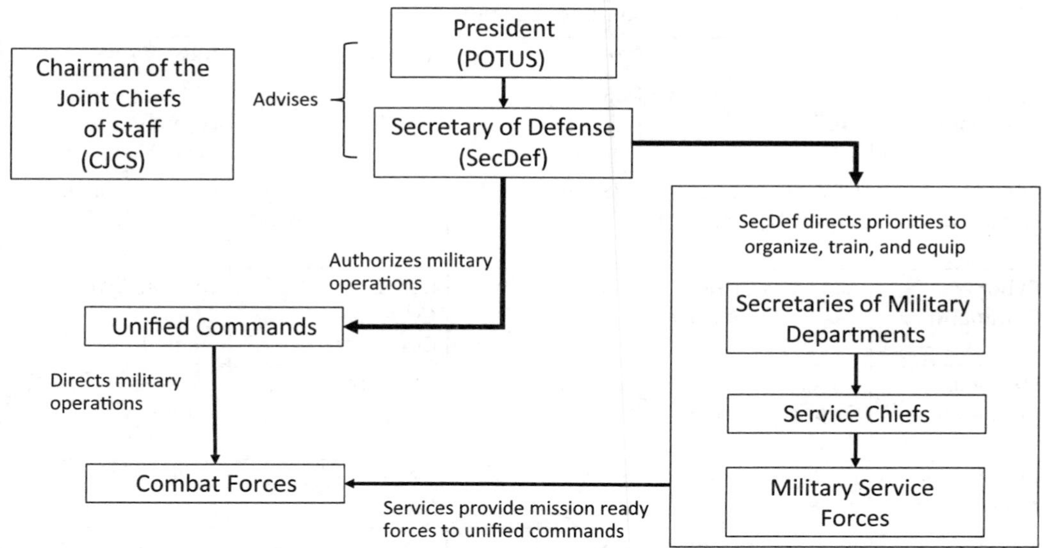

Figure 4.1. US Joint Force Organizational Structure

supplies. Forces in these domains are relatively slow and constrained by terrain compared to forces in the air domain. US Cyber Command and US Space Command are responsible for the cyber and space domains, respectively. Cyber and space forces operate at much higher speeds but require long lead times to set up their forces for execution.

US Special Operations Command conducts counterterrorism missions across the globe. US Transportation Command provides sustainment and moves forces between the geographic commands. Each COCOM (except for US Space Command) has supporting service component commanders. These component commands are often the combatant commander's first option to lead the creation of a new joint task force (JTF) headquarters or to staff a joint force component command.

When a new JTF is established, it will also be assigned joint force component commands to suit the mission. Figure 4.2 depicts four types: joint force air component commander (JFACC), joint force land component commander (JFLCC), joint force maritime component commander (JFMCC), and joint special operations component commander (JFSOCC).[8] The JTF headquarters, in coordination with its subordinate joint force component commands, is where joint operations are synchronized and integrated.

This institutional level solution was complimented with *matériel* solutions. Given NATO's inability to quantitatively match the numbers of Warsaw Pact military forces, the US looked to technology to serve as a force multiplier, to qualitatively exceed the Warsaw Pact. For example, if the US could not balance military power soldier for soldier or tank for tank, it could leverage technology to multiply the value of its tanks, soldiers, aircraft, etc. relative to its Warsaw Pact counterpart. Labeled the Offset Strategy, it is now typically referred to as the Second Offset Strategy, with the first offset being nuclear weapons.[9]

Doctrinal solutions came in the form of developing new joint doctrine and joint tactics, techniques, and procedures (TTPs). Doctrinal innovations were implemented with multiple joint exercises from the strategic level to the operational and tactical. For example, the Air Force's C-17 Globemaster and C-5 Galaxy are mobility assets maintained by the Air Force's

Table 4.1. Combatant Commands' Component Commands

	Air Force	Army	Marine Corps	Navy
Africa Command	US Air Forces Africa	US Army Africa	USMC Forces Africa	US Naval Forces Europe-Africa (Sixth Fleet)
Central Command	US Air Forces Central (Ninth Air Force)	US Army Central	USMC Forces Central Command	US Naval Forces Central Command (Fifth Fleet)
Cyber Command	Air Forces Cyber (Sixteenth Air Force)	US Army Cyber	USMC Forces Cyberspace Command	US Fleet Cyber Command (Tenth Fleet)
European Command	US Air Forces in Europe	US Army Europe	USMC Forces Europe	US Naval Forces Europe-Africa (Sixth Fleet)
Indo-Pacific Command	Pacific Air Forces	US Army Pacific	USMC Forces Pacific	US Pacific Fleet
Northern Command	Air Forces Northern (First Air Force)	US Army North	n/a	US Naval Forces Northern Command
Southern Command	Air Forces Southern (Twelfth Air Force)	US Army South	USMC Forces South	US Naval Forces Southern Command (Fourth Fleet)
Space Command	n/a	n/a	n/a	n/a
Special Operations Command	Air Force Special Operations Command	US Army Special Operations Command	US Marine Forces Special Operations Command	US Naval Special Warfare Command
Strategic Command	Air Force Global Strike Command	US Army Space and Missile Defense Command	n/a	n/a
Transportation Command	Air Mobility Command	Military Surface Deployment and Distribution Command	n/a	Military Sealift Command

Air Mobility Command. Though mobility assets, there are airborne operations–qualified C-17 and C-5 pilots who train with Army paratroopers conducting joint forcible-entry exercises, in which paratroopers are dropped from an altitude of eight hundred feet above ground level.[10] On the one hand, joint training missions have the direct impact of making it possible for soldiers, airmen, marines, and sailors to improve their joint tactical and operational skills. On the other hand, since each service and unit retains its unique cultural attributes, joint exercises provide leaders with opportunities to better understand and better navigate service cultures.

Personnel solutions included mandatory joint training along with the requirement of completing a joint assignment mandatory for promotion to flag rank. For example, officers can reach the rank of lieutenant colonel (or equivalent) holding command positions in a specific service. But before being promoted to colonel and definitely before taking command at the strategic level, they are required to complete a joint tour, where they get the opportunity to

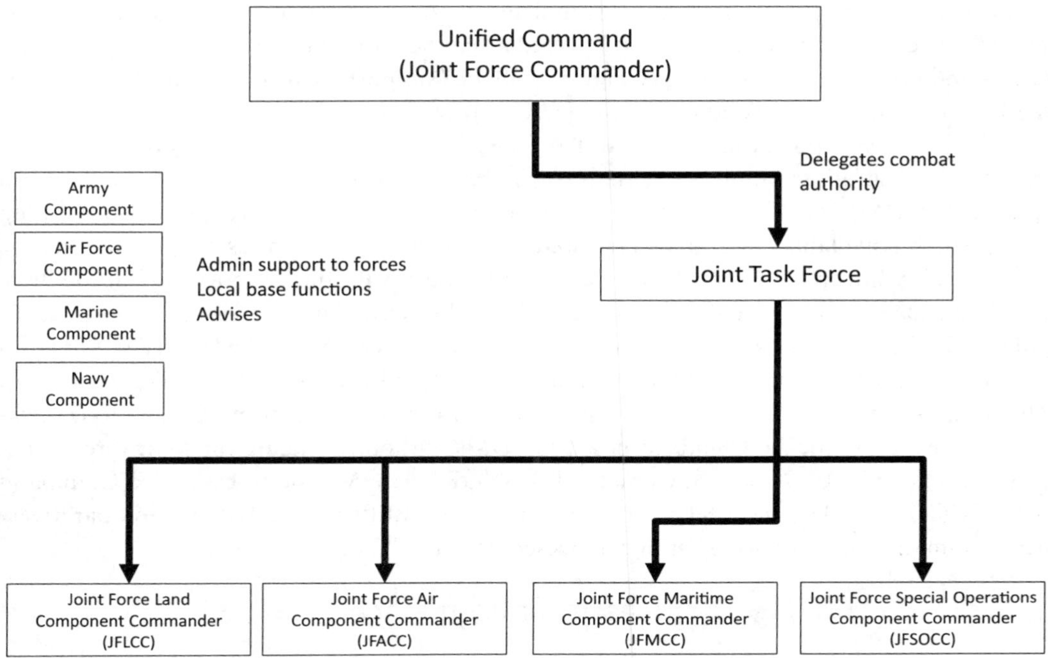

Figure 4.2. Joint Force Components

work with and learn from other services. Personnel solutions also included the creation of joint professional military education institutions for both officers and senior noncommissioned officers, managed by the joint education branch in the office of the Joint Chiefs of Staff. The combination of the above solutions work to align the tactical, operational, and strategic levels under the joint force concept and have vastly improved military effectiveness.

JOINT FORCE AT WORK

The joint force concept was soon put to the test during Operation Just Cause (Panama, 1989) and Operation Desert Storm (1991). During the US invasion of Panama, the joint forces commander, an Army general, had full operational control of all naval, air, Marine Corps, Army, and special operations assets, proving the viability of the joint concept. It was the first time that a commander from a different service had operational control of units from other services.[11] During Operation Desert Storm, the joint force concept was augmented with coalition forces, turning it into a combined joint task force. And, again, the outcome matched the aspirations.

During Operation Desert Storm, the combatant commander of US Central Command (USCENTCOM) had complete operational control, with a codified division of labor among component commanders. The JFMCC, with the use of naval and air assets, dominated the Arabian Gulf and implemented a blockade.[12] The JFACC conducted the air campaign while the JFMCC enabled Marine amphibious exercises to deceive Iraqis as other Marine air-ground task force (MAGTF) units conducted operations in shaping the battlespace. Though the MAGTF was subordinated to the JFMCC, those marines on the ground were subordinated to the JFLCC, which had complete operational control of all land components. Though special operations forces (SOF) played a significant role in taking out early-warning radars and providing reconnaissance and surveillance support, instead of being placed under the JFSOCC they were passed out to the JFACC, JFLCC, and JFMCC to be utilized as they saw fit.[13] US Transportation Command (USTRANSCOM), a functional command that transcends geographic boundaries, enabled the buildup of forces. US Strategic Command (USSTRATCOM), working with US Space Command (USSPACECOM), provided warning of ballistic missile launches and also ensured the functioning of various supporting satellite networks. US European Command (USEUCOM) and US Pacific Command (USPACOM), which is today US Indo-Pacific Command (INDOPACOM), provided forces and logistics hubs to USCENTCOM as well as aircraft that were under USCENTCOM/JFACC operational control based out of USEUCOM (i.e., Turkey) and USPACOM (i.e., Diego Garcia). The joint concept again proved itself during Operation Iraqi Freedom. As the global strategic context evolved, the US added new COCOMs without changing the joint force structure. For example, US Northern Command (USNORTHCOM, 2002), US Africa Command (USAFRICOM, 2007), and US Cyber Command (USCYBERCOM, 2010) are comparatively new commands that did not exist during Desert Storm.

FUTURE OF THE JOINT FORCE

The joint force concept served the US well during the 1990s. However, the nation is entering a changed global strategic context with peer and near-peer adversaries, while it remains wedded to the joint concept.

This joint design is running on the fumes of the Second Offset. Instead of matching US strengths, peer competitors developed capabilities that focused on unconventional forces. Advanced antiaccess/area-denial (A2AD) capabilities (e.g., advanced air defenses, ballistic missiles, antisatellite weapons, offensive cyber capabilities, and disruptive information campaigns) have the potential to disrupt US/NATO Cold War–era command and control (C2). Despite increasing interdomain dependency in modern military operations, existing DOD and NATO planning and operational processes are insufficiently integrated and synchronized. Too many processes are stovepiped and linear, limiting their utility in rapidly changing, dynamic situations. Anticipated disruptions in traditional C2 will require increasingly delegated decision-making. To an extent, this delegated decision-making will require an increase in data/information integration/fusion.[14]

As the "new kids on the block," the cyber and space domains are the primary challenges for integration and synchronization into the other domains. The challenges of this integration, combined with increasing threat of peer competition, particularly in the space and cyber domains, led to the development of concepts such as joint all-domain operations (JADO) and multidomain operations (MDO).

Good military planners are asset and domain agnostic. That is, they must evaluate the relative advantages and disadvantages of operating in each domain to select the optimum asset (means) to conduct tasks (ways) that provide a capability to achieve desired effects and end states (ends). Every capability is the result of a combination of an asset with a task. Capabilities can be provided by a variety of different assets using different ways. For example, antisubmarine warfare can be performed by ships, fixed-wing aircraft, helicopters, mines, and submarines. Each of these assets has a unique task that it performs to contribute an antisubmarine capability. In many cases, the integration of these assets will result in a sum that is greater than the parts. Working together provides a better overall capability than a large number of a single type of asset. This will be critical as the world shifts toward a multipolar world strategically and the military is expected to ready for a joint all-domain fight. The joint force will have to work to either reassess the COCOM structure or learn to reconcile how to better integrate geographic and functional focus of COCOMs across domains so as to maintain American combat primacy in a joint all-domain operational environment.

LEARNING REVIEW

- Differentiate between the roles of the services and those of the COCOMs.
- Identify the key responsibilities of each geographic and functional COCOM.
- Recall the role of the secretary of defense and the CJCS.
- Describe the advantages and disadvantages of joint command structure.
- Describe the concept of multidomain operations and all-domain operations.
- Based on the military capabilities required to address a strategic issue, justify the likely necessary components for a JTF.
- Given the advantages and disadvantages of operating in each domain, justify the optimum domain to achieve a given objective.

NOTES

1. For more on domains, see Jeffrey Reilly, "Over the Horizon: The Multi-Domain Operational Strategist (MDOS)," Over the Horizon, November 8, 2018, https://othjournal.com/2018/11/08/oth-mdos-reilly/.

2. Ryan Burke, "The Uncommon Defense Policy: History, Evolution, and Future Directions," *Journal of Policy History* 33, no. 2 (2021): 210.

3. Hugh W. A. Jones, "Multi-Domain Operations: Expanding the Battlefield and Re-establishing America's Military Offset," Strategy Research Project, Army War College Fellows, March 2021, 61.

4. William C Flynt III, *Broken Stiletto: Command and Control of the Joint Task Force during Operation Eagle Claw at Desert One* (Plano, TX: Tannenberg, 2015).

5. Cynthia Watson, *Combatant Commands: Origins, Structure and Engagements* (Westport, CT: Praeger, 2010).

6. Watson.

7. Tommy Franks, *American Soldier* (New York: HarperCollins, 2004). General Franks's memoir provides a clear overview of the chain of command and how it worked in real life during his experience commanding Operation Iraqi Freedom in 2003. Gen. Norman Schwarzkopf's memoir, *It Doesn't Take a Hero: Autobiography of General Norman Schwarzkopf* (New York: Bantam, 1992) also provides a clear overview of the chain of command as well as the nature of the discord that rose between the CJCS and the JFCs.

8. Over time, as the Space Force and Cyber Command get better institutionalized, it is likely that space and cyber component commanders will be an integral part of the COCOM staff organizational structure.

9. Jones, "Multi-Domain Operations," 62.

10. Operation Northern Delay, the airborne operation conducted by the 173rd Airborne Brigade during Operation Iraqi Freedom, consisted of twenty-two C-17 aircraft and one thousand paratroopers.

11. Ronald H. Cole, *Operation Just Cause: The Planning and Execution of Joint Operations in Panama February 1988–January 1990* (Washington, DC: Joint History Office, Office of the Chairman of the Joint Chiefs of Staff, 1995).

12. Schwarzkopf, *It Doesn't Take a Hero.*

13. Schwarzkopf.

14. Sandeep S. Mulgund and Mark D. Kelly, "Command and Control of Operations in the Information Environment," *Air and Space Power Journal* (Winter 2020).

CHAPTER 5

The US Army and the Land Domain

Brian Drohan

In 1958, as the US government sought to reorganize its defense establishment, President Dwight D. Eisenhower argued that "separate ground, sea and air warfare is gone forever. If ever again we should be involved in war, we will fight in all elements, with all services, as one single concentrated effort."[1] Eisenhower based this assessment on his experiences as the supreme Allied commander in Europe during World War II, but his insight has had a tremendous influence on the way that the armed services fight. Today the armed services operate as a joint force, yet each service provides important capabilities, some of which are unique to that service alone. This chapter analyzes the capabilities of the US Army within the context of the land domain.

CONTEXT

The land domain is defined by both human and physical geography. There are two key characteristics of the land domain that fundamentally shape military operations: (1) the large-scale permanent presence of human populations and (2) the variety and complexity of terrain. Land operations ultimately involve controlling terrain and people—effects that can require different mixtures of assets, capabilities, and tasks based on highly localized conditions that can vary dramatically from one place to the next.

First, the land is the only domain in which humans live on a permanent basis. Constant interaction with large human populations is therefore a normal feature of land operations.[2] The fact that humans live on land, societies are organized on land, and governments are based on land means that warfare in any domain must ultimately impact the land domain.[3] This characteristic does not diminish the importance of the other domains. In fact, the ability of warfare in the air, at sea, in space, and in cyberspace to influence the land domain highlights the interconnectedness of all the domains and the importance of joint operations.

Second, terrain also shapes the dynamics of land operations. Terrain, in a sense, exists in all domains—air pressure, temperature, and wind patterns affect air operations, for instance—but it is the sheer variety of terrain that distinguishes the land domain. Differences of climate, vegetation, elevation, and human improvements such as roads and settlements create a multitude of different environments in which to conduct military operations. The land domain, therefore, consists of a vast range of subdomains. Furthermore, variations in terrain do not necessarily affect each combatant in the same way. For a defender, mountains and cities provide many natural obstacles that can slow down an attacker, whereas an attacker may find that open terrain provides an advantage in mobile warfare. Such local variations can have a tremendous impact on the conduct of operations and the capabilities necessary to achieve desired effects.[4]

Army Roles and Missions

The US Army fulfills four strategic roles: to shape the operational environment, to prevent conflict by deterring adversaries, to prevail in ground combat, and to consolidate gains achieved during prior operations.[5] It organizes, trains, equips, and maintains the readiness of its forces and provides them to joint force commanders, who employ them in joint operations.

The Army shapes the operational environment by providing forces to joint force commanders for operations such as training partner forces or developing logistic infrastructure. The development of logistic infrastructure helps to "set the theater," which is how the Army contributes to the joint force's ability to seize the initiative in the early stages of a conflict. Setting the theater includes intelligence and communication support, opening ports and airports for follow-on forces, air defense, and logistics. These activities are often conducted as part of reception, staging, onward movement, and integration (RSOI) operations. RSOI is the process in which follow-on forces arrive in theater and are prepared for combat.[6] The Army plays a key role in joint RSOI due to its significant sustainment capabilities.

Efforts to shape the operational environment can also help prevent conflict by deterring potential adversaries. One example of conventional deterrence is the long-term forward stationing of ground forces, which can deter adversary aggression while also reassuring friendly countries of American commitment. This was the rationale for the deployment of US forces in Western Europe during the Cold War, for example.

The Army's main strategic role, however, is to prevail in ground combat by conducting sustained land operations, which require the endurance to continue operations for months or years. The Army therefore mans, trains, and equips ground forces with an emphasis on close combat and sustainment.[7] Close combat—warfare waged primarily with direct-fire assets—is a key feature of land operations due to the influence of terrain and human populations. Enemies that operate in complex terrain, such as mountainous or urban areas, can often use the terrain to their advantage to conceal their activities. The presence of large human populations requires target discrimination—that is, soldiers must be able to engage enemy combatants while minimizing civilian casualties.[8] In addition to close combat, the Army maintains strong sustainment capabilities that enable expeditionary deployments while also maintaining a robust force during long-term combat operations. Army sustainment capabilities include the ability to rotate fresh forces into the fight, refit and rearm combat units, and supply deployed forces.

The fourth strategic role, consolidating gains, involves translating military success into enduring strategic results. Military victories are only temporary unless other operations help to establish the conditions for a sustainable and stable postconflict environment. Actions conducted to consolidate gains can include eliminating enemy forces that had initially been bypassed, securing key routes and critical infrastructure, restoring stability and essential government services within population centers, and providing humanitarian relief.[9]

The Army accomplishes its strategic roles through four kinds of operations: offense, defense, stability, and defense support to civil authorities (DSCA). Offense and defense involve attacking or defending against enemy forces; stability operations include establishing civil security, restoring essential services and governance, and conducting security cooperation missions with allies and partners. DSCA missions occur within the United States and include humanitarian assistance, disaster response, and support to law enforcement during domestic emergencies.[10] The Army Reserve and the National Guard play key roles in these operations.

The Army conducts operations by synchronizing the use of six warfighting functions through combined arms. Combined arms involves the simultaneous, synchronized employment of multiple capabilities in complementary ways "to achieve an effect greater than if each element was used separately."[11] Each of these individual elements is called a warfighting function. The six warfighting functions are command and control, movement and maneuver, intelligence, fires, sustainment, and protection. Commanders integrate their capabilities through command and control. Movement and maneuver positions forces at a point of relative advantage over the enemy. Intelligence helps commanders understand the enemy and the environment. Fires enable additional operations through artillery fire, electronic warfare, cyber operations, and attack aviation. Sustainment is the provision of logistic support and human services (such as personnel management and medical care) to ensure freedom of action and the ability to continue long-term operations. The protection function involves securing routes and bases as well as conducting air and missile defense and chemical, biological, radiological, nuclear, and explosive (CBRNE) operations.[12] By integrating the six warfighting functions, commanders can create more problems for the enemy because if the enemy counteracts one capability, it becomes vulnerable to another. For example, if the mission is to seize a hill occupied by an enemy force, commanders can use intelligence to identify enemy troop concentrations, then suppress the enemy with fires, which would prevent the enemy from moving to another location while friendly ground forces maneuver into position to seize the hill.

ARMY SUPPORT TO THE JOINT FORCE

Army forces primarily support joint force commanders by providing air-defense forces to the area air-defense commander (AADC) and ground forces to the joint force land component commander (JFLCC). Because the bulk of air-defense assets in a theater are often provided by the Army, the senior Army air-defense commander is usually designated as the deputy area air-defense commander (DAADC) and supports the AADC, who is usually an Air Force officer also serving as the joint force air component commander (JFACC). Within a joint task force (JTF), the AADC oversees defensive counterair operations.[13] The AADC's main priority is to protect critical assets in the JOA. The AADC allocates air-defense capabilities to protect as many critical assets as possible based on their priority. The resulting list is called the defended asset list (DAL).[14]

The JFLCC is responsible for the employment of available land forces as well as planning and coordinating land operations. The JFLCC reports to either a combatant commander (CCDR) or a JTF commander. Typically, the JFLCC is a division or corps commander. A division headquarters is commanded by a major general and can function as a JTF or JFLCC headquarters during limited contingency operations and short-duration missions.[15] A division can command and control two to five brigade combat teams (BCTs) in addition to enabler brigades. Above divisions, corps serve as joint headquarters during major combat operations and large-scale, long-term contingencies as the Army's preferred element for a JTF HQ. A corps is commanded by a lieutenant general who oversees two to five divisions along with additional enabler forces.[16] As of 2020, the Army has ten active division headquarters and eight National Guard division headquarters as well as four active corps headquarters.[17]

While divisions and corps serve as headquarters elements for Army forces, the units provided to joint force commanders are primarily organized as brigades. Army combat forces are primarily organized as BCTs of approximately four thousand to forty-five hundred soldiers. The number of BCTs has varied over the past two decades. The active Army had thirty-two BCTs in 2001. This number grew to forty-five during Operation Enduring Freedom and Operation Iraqi Freedom. In 2015, the active force was reduced to thirty BCTs before being increased again in 2018, to thirty-one BCTs. There are an additional twenty-seven BCTs in the National Guard.[18] These units are self-contained organizations with all the core capabilities needed for close combat and maneuver, with the exception that there are no organic aviation elements in a BCT, which are instead externally sourced to support it. Direct-fire weapons can range from several hundred meters (rifles and machine guns) to three to five kilometers (main battle tanks and antitank guided missiles). "Enabler" brigades include aviation (helicopters), field artillery, intelligence, air defense, sustainment, and maneuver enhancement (engineers and military police). Many of these enabler units provide supplies and security for BCTs. Field artillery, air defense, and attack aviation, however, can degrade enemy forces before they draw close enough to fight infantry or armor units.[19]

Brigade Combat Teams

BCTs come in three configurations. First, armored BCTs (ABCTs)—with tanks, armored reconnaissance, engineers, mechanized infantry, and self-propelled artillery—provide a powerful offensive, forced-entry capability as well as the ability to defend against strong enemy conventional forces (see figure 5.1). With over eighty M1A2 Abrams tanks and over 150 M2/M3 Bradley fighting vehicles, ABCTs combine firepower and maneuver to defeat adversaries, but they lack strategic mobility.[20] It takes time to transport an ABCT from a home station to a crisis zone because the ABCT's heavy vehicles must be loaded onto cargo ships for weeks-long voyages to a theater of operations. In some theaters where a rapid response is essential, such as the Persian Gulf and South Korea, the Army has established prepositioned stocks of ABCT equipment so that ABCTs can deploy faster by flying soldiers from home station without having to wait for their equipment to arrive by ship.[21]

Second, the medium-weight Stryker BCT (SBCT), equipped with over two hundred wheeled rather than tracked fighting vehicles, retains some of the tactical mobility of an ABCT but lacks the same degree of firepower (see figure 5.2). Even so, the SBCT's lighter equipment allows for greater strategic mobility. Rather than fighting from their vehicles as ABCTs do, SBCTs rely on their lighter, faster vehicles to carry infantry into the vicinity of combat, where the infantry dismounts to fight on foot. This capability provides improved tactical mobility for the infantry.[22]

Third, infantry BCTs (IBCTs) are the most rapidly deployable (see figure 5.3). They are built around dismounted infantry and a small ratio of lightly armored utility and transport vehicles. This reliance on dismounted infantry provides an advantage in dense urban areas and rugged mountainous terrain in which vehicle-bound forces struggle to maneuver. IBCTs are therefore best suited for providing a rapid-response force as well as clearing and securing complex terrain. Their greatest disadvantages, however, are that they lack the firepower of ABCTs and the tactical mobility of SBCTs.

Furthermore, IBCTs can provide two specialized capabilities. Air-assault IBCTs use helicopters to "leap" from one landing zone to another, maneuvering across the battlefield at distances as far as a hundred miles at a time, but are less strategically mobile because of the

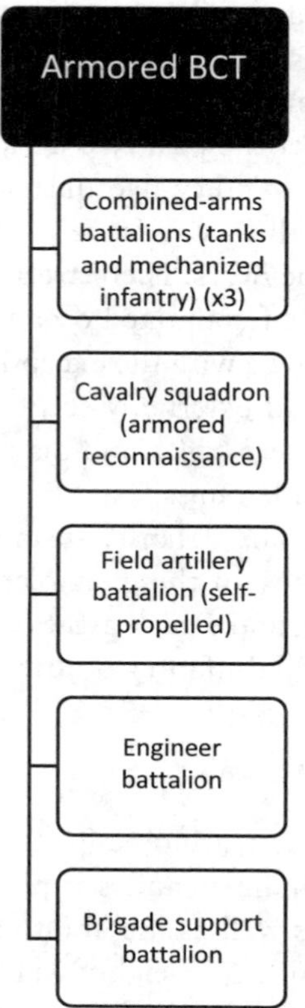

Figure 5.1. Armored Brigade Combat Team

Note: 4,182 soldiers, 120 Bradley fighting vehicles, and 87 Abrams tanks in total:

- six tank companies
- four infantry companies
- three cavalry troops
- three battalion scout platoons
- three self-propelled 155mm artillery batteries (eighteen guns)

Data Source: US Army Maneuver Center of Excellence, *Supplemental Manual 3-90: Force Structure Reference Data: Brigade Combat Teams* (Washington, DC: Department of the Army, October 2015).

need to transport a large number of helicopters into the theater.[23] In contrast, airborne IBCTs are capable of seizing an assigned objective in any theater of operations by parachuting onto or near it. Airborne forces therefore offer strategic mobility and a forced-entry capability. The challenge with air-assault and airborne operations, however, is that both require protection from enemy air defenses and aircraft.[24]

Security Force Assistance Brigades

In February 2018, the Army activated the first of six planned security force assistance brigades (SFABs), which are designed to advise foreign forces. These brigades are not BCTs, but each SFAB is designed to mirror the structure of either an IBCT or an ABCT. Security force assistance is considered a subset of stability operations, but SFABs are designed to advise partner forces during peace or war. Each SFAB consists of eight hundred personnel who are

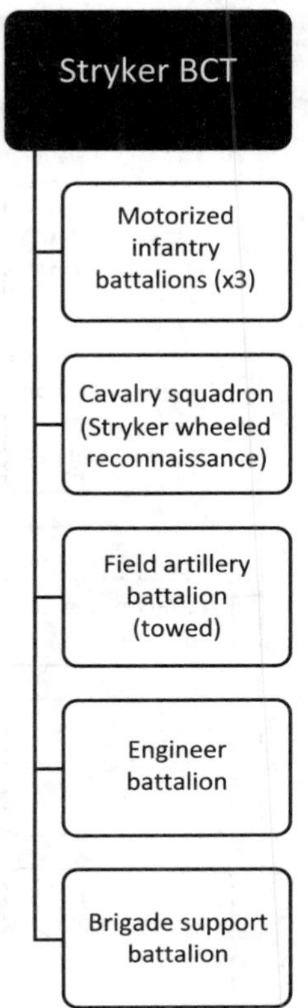

Figure 5.2. Stryker Brigade Combat Team

Note: 4,388 soldiers and over two hundred Stryker vehicles of multiple variants in total:

- nine infantry companies
- one weapons company (mounted on light utility vehicles and armed with heavy machine guns, grenade launchers, and antitank guided missiles)
- three cavalry troops
- three battalion scout platoons
- three towed 155mm artillery batteries (eighteen guns)

Data Source: US Army Maneuver Center of Excellence, *Supplemental Manual 3-90: Force Structure Reference Data: Brigade Combat Teams* (Washington, DC: Department of the Army, October 2015).

primarily senior noncommissioned officers (NCOs) and experienced officers, in addition to a security force element to protect the advisers. Each SFAB consists of a brigade headquarters element, two maneuver battalions, a reconnaissance squadron, a field artillery battalion, an engineer battalion, a support battalion, and enablers such as intelligence and communications companies. In times of crisis, SFABs can form the foundation for "growing" additional BCTs. Because they are largely staffed by experienced officers and NCOs, these units could be rounded out with newly recruited soldiers.[25]

Field Artillery

Field artillery supports the fires warfighting function by delivering lethal or nonlethal effects on a designated target at a specific time and place. Artillery weapons include cannons, rockets,

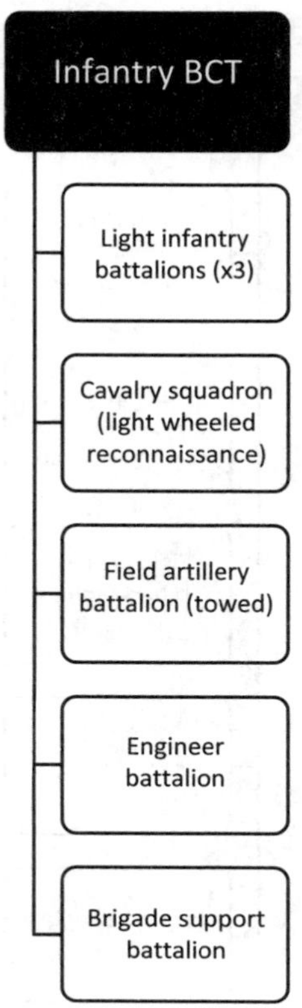

Figure 5.3. Infantry Brigade Combat Team

Note: 4,216 soldiers total:

- nine infantry companies
- one weapons company (mounted on light utility vehicles and armed with heavy machine guns, grenade launchers, and antitank guided missiles)
- three cavalry troops
- three battalion scout platoons
- two towed 105mm artillery batteries (twelve guns)
- one towed 155mm artillery battery (six guns)

Data Source: US Army Maneuver Center of Excellence, *Supplemental Manual 3-90: Force Structure Reference Data: Brigade Combat Teams* (Washington, DC: Department of the Army, October 2015).

and surface-to-surface missiles. Artillery assets are organized as internal elements of BCTs and divisions as well as separate brigades. Each BCT's artillery battalion is typically equipped with eighteen cannons.[26] Cannon artillery can cover 360 degrees, is available regardless of weather, and can respond within minutes to any fire mission. ABCTs are equipped with tracked, self-propelled cannons, whereas IBCTs and SBCTs are equipped with towed cannons that must be transported by truck and unlimbered before being fired. The main disadvantage with current US Army cannon artillery is its relatively short range: twenty-four kilometers for regular shells and thirty kilometers for rocket-assisted shells.[27] In addition to cannons, maneuver battalions have mortars for local fire support at ranges up to nine kilometers. Cannons and mortars fire unguided projectiles, but cannons can also fire precision-guided munitions. At the division level, the division artillery (DIVARTY) headquarters is responsible for coordinating fires from the field artillery battalions in each BCT.[28]

Separately organized field artillery brigades (FABs) provide the ability to synchronize fires in support of operations above the division level. FABs are task-organized for the mission at hand. Although often attached to divisions, FABs can also support corps or JFLCC requirements with medium- and long-range fires. Rocket and missile artillery units are typically assigned to FABs. The tracked, self-propelled multiple-launch rocket system (MLRS) and a lighter, wheeled variant, the high-mobility artillery rocket system (HIMARS), provide high-volume, rapid-fire support. These assets are usually used to attack high-payoff targets, strike targets deeper into enemy lines, or mass effects against a specific area to facilitate an armored breakthrough. Like cannon artillery, rockets and missiles operate regardless of weather, cover 360 degrees, and respond rapidly. However, rockets and missiles have a longer range than cannons. Basic unguided rockets can reach twenty-six kilometers; extended-range rockets can travel forty-five kilometers. The Guided Multiple Launch Rocket System (GMLRS) provides precision rocket fires up to seventy kilometers. Missile artillery, in the form of the Army Tactical Missile System (ATACMS), provides precision engagement up to three hundred kilometers.[29] Rocket battalions differ in organization, but they typically consist of sixteen to eighteen firing systems.[30]

Air-Defense Artillery

Army air and missile defense commands (AAMDCs) and air-defense artillery (ADA) brigades integrate a variety of air-defense assets into a coherent area air-defense plan. These assets provide the capability to conduct early warning, coordinate airspace control and to conduct counterair and countermissile operations to protect friendly forces. AAMDCs operate at the theater level. ADA brigades support the AAMDC by defending designated assets—such as specific forces, bases, and population centers—based on the commander's priorities.[31] The Army currently has three active-duty AAMDCs and seven active-duty ADA brigades.

The organization of ADA brigades differs based on the mission, but each brigade normally commands two to four subordinate battalions. Most units are organized as either a short-range air-defense (SHORAD) battalion, capable of engaging low-altitude air threats up to four kilometers away, or as a longer-range Patriot missile battalion capable of engaging aircraft and missile threats at ranges up to seventy kilometers and at a maximum altitude of twenty-four kilometers.[32] Both SHORAD and Patriot battalions can be deployed to specific conflict zones around the globe. In addition to these units, some brigades are also assigned separate terminal high-altitude area-defense (THAAD) batteries. THAAD units exist to destroy ballistic missiles in their terminal (incoming) phase and can engage targets at ranges up to two hundred kilometers and at altitudes of up to one hundred and fifty kilometers.[33] One ADA brigade—the 100th Missile Defense Brigade—differs from all others in that it is a mixed active-duty and National Guard organization responsible for strategic missile defense of the US homeland.

Aviation

Rotary-wing aircraft capabilities support the fires, intelligence, and movement and maneuver warfighting functions. All CABs include a mix of attack, reconnaissance, air-assault, and general-support aviation battalions. Attack aviation assets destroy enemy forces using direct fire. Reconnaissance assets ("air cavalry") identify enemy formations and collect information on their activities to inform the intelligence picture of the battlefield. Air-assault assets transport soldiers and equipment rapidly over vast distances, which enables large flanking movements or deep strikes behind enemy lines. Attack battalions and reconnaissance squadrons each consist of twenty-four AH-64 Apache helicopters. Air-assault battalions have thirty UH-60 Blackhawk helicopters, whereas the heavier general-support aviation battalions include a mix of UH-60s, specialized medical evacuation helicopters, and at least twelve CH-47 Chinook helicopters—the largest helicopter in the Army inventory.[34] UH-60s have a maximum range of over five hundred kilometers, AH-64s can range nineteen hundred kilometers, and CH-47s six hundred kilometers.[35] There are currently twelve CABs in the active-duty Army: one per division and per two separate brigades. CABs are particularly valuable because they provide long-range reconnaissance and attack capabilities as well as enhanced mobility.

LAND POWER THEORY

The conceptual basis for conducting the Army's missions, employing its capabilities, and synchronizing the warfighting functions is the notion of land power. Officially, the Army defines land power as "the ability—by threat, force, or occupation—to gain, sustain, and exploit control over land, resources, and people."[36] Land power's importance stems from the notion that the land domain matters most—it is the only domain that humans permanently inhabit, which means that control over it bears significant political consequences. Even air travel, maritime commerce, and reliance on space-based satellites for communication and navigation make sense only in the context of human life on land.[37] It follows that control over human populations or resources available to them is a vital aspect of warfare. Human civilization is inseparable from the land domain.

The primary use of land power that distinguishes it from other forms of military power is its ability to exercise control over land, resources, and people.[38] With land power, seizing and holding a territory or population translates into political control, which creates the conditions for achieving the ultimate policy goals for which military force was used in the first place. Control does not always imply aggressive behavior, however. Control can be used to protect land, resources, or people by preventing them from being controlled by an adversary.

Ground forces exert control by engaging with other human beings at the local level on an enduring basis—whether friends, enemies, or simply bystanders caught up in the conflict. Operating in and among human populations provides ground forces with the ability to conduct sustained local social and cultural engagement that may be vital to success in a conflict. The localized nature of land power also makes it the most discriminatory in terms of differentiating between civilian, friendly, and enemy personnel. For example, ground forces generally see their adversaries at closer ranges than air or maritime forces, allowing them to exercise discretion and restraint by deciding not to engage a target if civilians are present. This ability to influence a conflict at the local level and on an enduring basis is a key characteristic of land power.[39]

Land power, however, cannot function alone. The presence of the Atlantic and Pacific Oceans insulates the United States from ground invasion but also makes it difficult to project land power from the homeland. Army deployments from the US therefore require the use of sealift and/or airlift to transport ground forces to the theater of operations. This imperative helps explain the value of overseas bases for the employment of US land power. Forward-deployed ground forces provide readily available land power assets that would otherwise take weeks or months to arrive from the continental US.[40]

Although exercising control is a powerful military tool, it is not absolute. Even when control is achieved, it can be challenged. Enemy decisions, the presence of civilians on the battlefield, the challenges of traversing difficult terrain, miscommunication, and other events create friction—unforeseen confusion on the battlefield—that can disrupt friendly plans, cause higher casualties, or lead to delays that allow the enemy to regroup. Control of the land can also be contested with relatively few resources. It takes far fewer industrial or financial resources to organize a terrorist campaign or insurgency than it does to produce aircraft, missiles, or warships necessary for combat in the maritime or air domains. The result is a paradox: land power provides an exceptionally powerful tool for controlling land, resources, and people but is also the easiest form of military power for an adversary to challenge.[41]

Consequently, employing land power is inherently risky. For instance, it is expensive to deploy and maintain large ground forces. In 2016, the cost of operating one ABCT was estimated at $500 million per year. When including the support infrastructure and services needed to sustain that ABCT, the estimate increased to $2.6 billion annually.[42] These estimates do not include the costs of deploying the ABCT overseas. Beyond financial costs, there is the potential for casualties and the political danger in failing to achieve one's objectives. Such risks make land power, in the words of one strategist, "often the most politically contentious of all instruments of national power."[43]

These risks, however, are not confined to a single action, because land power's ability to achieve control arises from the combination of smaller actions that build on each other. This notion of "accumulative success" means that one defeat or miscalculation will not necessarily lead to catastrophe; likewise, victory in a single battle is rarely sufficient to ensure long-term success. The Army wages campaigns that link several smaller engagements to a broader purpose that leads to a strategic-level outcome.[44] The idea is that the combination of tactical actions and engagements will result in the achievement of a strategic goal. Individual battles must be tied to a larger objective to achieve success.[45]

CONCLUSION

Land power provides an enduring presence in and among human communities, giving commanders the ability to protect, influence, or control people on a very personal level—face-to-face contact that the maritime or air domains cannot provide. This capability is especially useful in stability operations and irregular warfare, where fighting tends to occur in heavily populated areas with the goal of controlling civilian populations. Historian and former US Army officer T. R. Fehrenbach described this essential feature of land power in the aftermath of the 1950–53 Korean War: "You may fly over a land forever; you may bomb it, atomize it, pulverize it and wipe it clean of life—but if you desire to defend it, protect it, and keep it for civilization, you must do this on the ground."[46]

Ground forces can physically separate warring communities, stabilize postconflict zones, and control territory in perpetuity through close combat in terrain as varied as densely populated cities, empty deserts, and rugged mountain ranges. The Army's capabilities are designed to provide policymakers and joint force commanders with a range of useful options for the employment of military force in the land domain. Above all else, capabilities across all domains must serve strategy—such capabilities exist to help the United States achieve its objectives. Fundamentally, military capabilities are tools of statecraft that serve political ends.

LEARNING REVIEW

- Recall the primary role of the US Army.
- Recall how the Army presents forces to the joint force commander in the form of brigade combat teams.
- Recall how Army forces deploy to support the joint force.
- Describe the conditions under which land forces would be the preferred focus for a military option.
- Given a land-power scenario, identify the optimum asset to provide a specific capability.

NOTES

1. Dwight D. Eisenhower, "Special Message to the Congress on Reorganization of the Defense Establishment," April 3, 1958, University of California, Santa Barbara, American Presidency Project, http://www.presidency.ucsb.edu/ws/?pid=11340.

2. Lukas Milevski, "Fortissimus Inter Pares: The Utility of Landpower in Grand Strategy," *Parameters* 42, no. 2 (Summer 2012): 8–10.

3. Colin S. Gray, *Always Strategic: Jointly Essential Landpower* (Carlisle Barracks, PA: US Army War College Press, 2015), 8–9.

4. John M. Collins, *Military Geography for Professionals and the Public* (Washington, DC: National Defense University Press, 1998); Harold A. Winters, *Battling the Elements: Weather and Terrain in the Conduct of War* (Baltimore: Johns Hopkins University Press, 1998).

5. *ADP 1: The Army* (Washington, DC: Department of the Army, 2019), 1-1, 2-4.

6. *ADP 1*, 2-8.

7. *ADP 1*, 1-1.

8. *ADP 3: Operations* (Washington, DC: Department of the Army, 2019), 1-10–1-11.

9. *ADP 3*, 3-5–3-7.

10. *ADP 1*, 1-3, 3-7.

11. *ADP 3*, 5-2.

12. Prior to July 2019, the command and control function was called "mission command."

13. *US Air Force Doctrine Publication 3-01: Counterair Operations* (Montgomery, AL: Air University Press, 2019), 11.

14. Joint Chiefs of Staff, *Joint Publication 3-01: Countering Air and Missile Threats* (Washington, DC: Department of Defense, 2018), II-4, III-15–III-16.

15. Joint Chiefs of Staff, *Joint Publication 3-0: Joint Operations, Incorporating Change 1* (Washington, DC: Department of Defense, 2018), GL-11, V-5.

16. *FM 3-94: Theater Army, Corps, and Division Operations* (Washington, DC: Department of the Army, 2014), 4-8, 6-2.

17. "Army Announces Activation of Additional Corps Headquarters," US Army, February 11, 2020, https://www.army.mil/article/232649/army_announces_activation_of_additional_corps_headquarters.

18. Todd South, "The Army Is Converting Two BCTs as It Beefs Up Its Fighting Force for the Next Big War," *Army Times*, September 20, 2018, https://www.armytimes.com/news/your-army/2018/09/20/the-army-is-converting-two-bcts-as-it-beefs-up-its-fighting-force-for-the-next-big-war/.

19. John A. Bonin and Telford E. Crisco Jr., "The Modular Army," *Military Review* 84, no. 2 (2004): 21–27.

20. *FM 3-96: Brigade Combat Team* (Washington, DC: Department of the Army, 2015), 1-10–1-12.

21. John A. Bonin, ed., *Army Organization and Employment Data* (Carlisle, PA: Center for Strategic Leadership, 2015), 41–42.

22. *FM 3-96*, 1-6–1-9.

23. John D. Broderick, *Air Assault Logistics during Desert Storm: A Personal Experience Monograph* (Carlisle, PA: US Army War College, 1993).

24. *FM 3-96*, 1-1–1-6.

25. Nathan A. Jennings, "Security Force Assistance Brigades: The U.S. Army Embraces Antifragility," *Small Wars Journal*, August 11, 2017; Morgan Smiley, "Security Force Assistance Brigades: It's About Time," *Small Wars Journal*, September 16, 2017; *ATP 3-96.1: Security Force Assistance Brigade* (Washington, DC: Department of the Army, 2018).

26. *FM 3-09: Field Artillery Operations and Fire Support* (Washington, DC: Department of the Army, 2014), 1-1, 1-37–1-39.

27. "M777 155mm Ultralightweight Field Howitzer," Army Technology, accessed April 9, 2020, https://www.army-technology.com/projects/ufh/; "Paladin M109A6 155mm Artillery System," Army Technology, accessed April 9, 2020, https://www.army-technology.com/projects/paladin/.

28. *FM 3-09*, 1-35–1-40.

29. *ADP 3-19: Fires* (Washington, DC: Department of the Army, 2019), 2-1.

30. *FM 3-09*, 1-36–1-37.

31. *ATP 3-01.7: Air Defense Artillery Brigade Techniques* (Washington, DC: Department of the Army, 2016, 1-2–1-3.

32. "Stinger Man-Portable Air Defence System (MANPADS), Army Technology, accessed April 10, 2020, https://www.army-technology.com/projects/stinger-man-portable-air-defence-system-manpads/; "Patriot Missile Long-Range Air Defence System," Army Technology, accessed April 10, 2020, https://www.army-technology.com/projects/patriot/.

33. "THAAD Missile System," Army Technology, accessed April 10, 2020, https://www.army-technology.com/projects/thaad/.

34. *FM 3-04: Army Aviation* (Washington, DC: Department of the Army, 2020), 1-2, 2-7–2-10.

35. "UH-60M Blackhawk Multi-Mission Helicopter," Army Technology, accessed April 10, 2020, https://www.army-technology.com/projects/uh-60m-black-hawk-multi-mission-helicopter/; "Apache Attack Helicopter," Army Technology, accessed April 10, 2020, https://www.army-technology.com/projects/apache/; "CH-47D/F and MH-47E Chinook Helicopter," Army Technology, accessed April 10, 2020, https://www.army-technology.com/projects/chinook/.

36. *ADP 1*, v.

37. Gray, *Always Strategic*, 23.

38. Milevski, "Fortissimus Inter Pares," 9.

39. Gray, *Always Strategic*, 12–14, 39.

40. Gray, 3; Milevski, "Fortissimus Inter Pares," 10.

41. Milevski, "Fortissimus Inter Pares," 11–13.

42. Adam Talaber, *The U.S. Military's Force Structure: A Primer* (Washington, DC: Congressional Budget Office, 2016), 10.

43. Lukas Milevski, "Variable Heroism: Landpower in US Grand Strategy since 9/11," in *Landpower in the Long War: Projecting Force after 9/11*, ed. Jason W. Warren (Lexington: University Press of Kentucky, 2019), 19.

44. Antulio J. Echevarria II, "American Operational Art, 1917–2008," in *The Evolution of Operational Art: From Napoleon to the Present*, ed. John Andreas Olsen and Martin van Creveld (Oxford: Oxford University Press, 2011), 137.

45. Michael R. Matheny, *Carrying the War to the Enemy: American Operational Art to 1945* (Norman: University of Oklahoma Press, 2011), xix.

46. T. R. Fehrenbach, *This Kind of War: The Classic Korean War History* (Washington, DC: Potomac Books, 2001), 290.

CHAPTER 6

The US Navy and the Maritime Domain

James Holmes

The US Navy conducts "combat incident to operations at sea . . . from deep water to the littorals."[1] The Navy is a multidomain service that operates on, above, and beneath the sea's surface as well as in cyberspace. It prosecutes a mix of defensive and offensive functions in company with the US Marine Corps, the US Coast Guard (USCG), and land-based joint forces, shielding the homeland, allies, and partners from aggression while projecting influence into distant theaters. Together, the Navy, Marine Corps, and the USCG constitute the US Naval Service.

THE CONTEST FOR ACCESS

Strategy is the use of power to achieve national security objectives. Maritime strategy uses sea power to achieve objectives relating to the nautical realm.[2] For Capt. Alfred Thayer Mahan (1840–1914), the second president of the Naval War College and history's most influential historian of saltwater affairs, the goal of maritime strategy is access to important regions "to secure commerce, by political measures conducive to military, or naval, strength. This order is that of *actual relative importance* to the nation of the three elements—*commercial*, *political*, *military*"[3] (emphasis added).

Commerce is king. Governments seek diplomatic access to promote commercial access. Military access supports diplomacy by force of arms should commercial access come under duress from foreign competitors. Maritime strategy is not about battle for its own sake. A navy furnishes a backstop for diplomatic efforts to open, nourish, and safeguard commercial access and the economic prosperity it brings. Indeed, war "has ceased to be the natural, or even normal, condition of nations."[4] Military might is "accessory and subordinate to the other greater interests, economical and commercial."[5] In turn a navy is a beneficiary of prosperity, since economic vitality generates the revenue needed to fund it.

Mahan's contemporary, English historian Sir Julian Corbett (1854–1922), agrees on the importance of seaborne commerce but widens his gaze to encompass other worthy naval endeavors. According to Corbett, "The function of the fleet, the object for which it was always employed, has been threefold: firstly, to support or obstruct diplomatic effort; secondly, to protect or destroy commerce; and thirdly, to further or hinder military operations ashore."[6] A navy exists to help joint forces shape events on land. After all, that is where humanity lives. Wars are settled on dry earth "either by what your army can do against your enemy's territory and national life or else by the fear of what the fleet makes it possible for your army to do."[7]

Sea power is the control of mercantile and naval supply chains, known as sea lines of communication (SLOCs). SLOCs are made up of three links—namely, production, distribution, and consumption. Manufacturers distribute goods through transportation networks such as roads, railways, airports, and seaports. The naval supply includes production of warships, maritime thoroughfares, and bases such as Yokosuka and Sasebo in Japan.

Ships of war demand ample supplies of fuel and stores as well as occasional repairs and refits. Hence the need for access to foreign harbors. The commercial supply chain generates wealth, some of which can go to fund a navy to protect commerce. Maritime statecraft aims at keeping the virtuous cycle among commerce, diplomacy, and the navy churning. SLOCs are those primary sea lanes that ships use to transport from port to port. Securing SLOCs ensures uninterrupted merchant shipping as well as sealift for the army and logistics sustainment required by all deployed forces. To ensure this security, maritime forces will occasionally conduct freedom-of-navigation operations (FONOPS) to ensure that coastal states do not infringe on freedom of the sea as codified in the United Nations Convention on the Law of the Sea.

FLEET FUNCTIONS AND SHIP TYPES

Ship types fall into three categories: the battle fleet, made up of heavy warships able to fight peers for control of SLOCs; "cruisers," an assortment of smaller, more lightly armed, and cheaper fighting ships that are affordable in large numbers; and the "flotilla," composed of still smaller, even more lightly armed craft that discharge the mundane duties all navies must discharge—generally close to shore owing to limited fuel capacity.[8] The battle fleet seeks to defeat an enemy battle fleet or blockade it in port so that lighter vessels can fan out to police the sea lanes in relative safety. If successful, Corbett's scheme denies the enemy the ability to use the sea while assuring friendly shipping can pass safely.

These convenient categories were upended by technology, initially by the advent of steam propulsion, armor plating, and big guns during the late nineteenth century. Naval weapons technology made it possible for torpedo boats and submarines—quintessential flotilla craft—to carry armaments able to strike heavy blows against heavy warships. No longer were big guns the sole determinant of victory at sea. Torpedoes and sea mines upended naval warfare, compelling fleet commanders to worry about defending high-end ships of war.

This challenge was compounded by the introduction of military aviation and guided missiles. Constant improvements in range and precision empowered small craft at the same time they enabled ground-based aircraft and missiles to lash out at fleets hundreds of miles out to sea.

Mahan defines capital ships as "the vessels which, by due proportion of defensive and offensive powers, are capable of taking and giving hard knocks."[9] For the US Navy, the nuclear-powered aircraft carrier (CVN) is an obvious candidate for the status of premier fighting ship. Carriers have constituted the core of American naval power since World War II. A modern carrier is large and ruggedly built, helping it withstand punishment. It carries scores of aircraft capable of helping defend the fleet against air and missile attack while striking at rival fleets or shore targets hundreds of miles distant. US law currently requires the Navy to maintain a fleet of eleven flattops.

Yet carriers' survivability has come into question. Shore-based armaments such as China's DF-21D and DF-26B antiship ballistic missiles now outrange the carrier air wing, meaning that carrier strike groups (CSGs) must venture deep into harm's way to strike targets at sea or on distant shores.[10] They appear vulnerable to "saturation" missile attacks that could, if not sink them, put them out of action for long enough for a foe to fulfill its goals. Saturation barrages overload shipboard defenses, flinging more projectiles at them than they can shoot down.[11] Whether the aircraft carrier still meets the Mahanian standard for defensive resilience in this operational environment is hotly debated among naval specialists.

Much the same can be said for multimission surface combatants such as guided-missile cruisers (CGs) and destroyers (DDGs). These are lightly armored to keep costs down. Destroyers tend to be smaller and cheaper than cruisers. However, even the design of cruisers is cost-conscious. For example, the guided-missile cruisers, the *Ticonderoga* class, were built on destroyer hulls to hold down costs.[12] CGs and DDGs are meant to stop threats before they strike home, not to take a punch and fight on. The revolution in naval technology allowed shipwrights to fit them with the latest in offensive weaponry. The result is a cruiser-type asset sporting capital-ship armament. Like the carrier, cruisers and destroyers pack a formidable punch via scores of vertical launch system (VLS) silos embedded in their decks. Depending on the mission, a vessel carries a mix of surface-to-air missiles (SAMs) to guard against air and missile attack, antiship missiles for battling hostile surface fleets, and antisubmarine munitions and helicopters to assail enemy subs.

The result of this muddying of distinctions is a genre of ships that perform a variety of functions. They are overdesigned for some missions. It does not take a frontline *Arleigh Burke*–class destroyer to conduct counterpiracy or counterproliferation missions. The Navy has been casting about for something more suitable for errands like those Corbett assigned to the flotilla. The Navy's littoral combat ships (LCS)—small, single-mission combatants designed to be repurposed at short notice for inshore surface combat, mine warfare, or antisubmarine warfare—constitute a partial gap filler for flotilla and cruiser missions. They are not fully satisfactory for the Navy's purposes.[13]

More recently Navy leaders have inaugurated a project intended to put to sea a guided-missile frigate (FFG), the *Constellation* class.[14] These multimission vessels may restore some order to the makeup of the fleet, taking on lower-end missions while freeing cruisers and destroyers to take on higher-end missions.

What about submarines? Undersea warfare remained mostly a thing of the future until World War I. It never would have occurred to Mahan, who perished before the United States joined the war, or Corbett, who died soon after peace came at Versailles, to think diesel-electric subs might become capital ships in their own right. They were lethal—if they could get within range of shipping to fire torpedoes. They were also slow and had to surface frequently to charge their batteries.

Diesel submarines advanced by World War II, devastating Japan's fleet of oilers, freighters, and transports. Undersea technology underwent a leap during the 1950s with USS *Nautilus*, the world's first nuclear-powered attack submarine (SSN). SSNs, known as "attack boats," boast impressive complements of torpedoes and, these days, antiship and land-attack cruise missiles. Indeed, the latest "flight" of US Navy *Virginia*-class subs has a hull insert, or "payload module," that boosts each boat's missile inventory, valuable for fighting enemy fleets.

In defensive power, subs have hulls built to withstand deepwater pressure; they are not thickly armored to survive torpedo blasts. These craft substitute stealth for defense. Naval nuclear propulsion lets them stay underwater for indefinite stretches of time, limited only by supplies of food and stores. Elaborate machinery-quieting measures help them elude acoustic detection, the principal method for sub hunting. Whether they fit into the fleet as capital ships or something else is worth pondering.

Several other ship types fill out the US Navy inventory and assuredly do not qualify as capital ships. Nuclear-powered ballistic-missile submarines (SSBNs) are the undersea component of the US strategic deterrent force and are not meant to fight enemy navies. While crucial to national defense, they are an outlier in the Corbettian scheme. They exist to vanish into the deep sea to provide an invulnerable second-strike option in the event of a nuclear war. US naval leaders deem replacing the Cold War–era fleet of *Ohio*-class SSBNs with a dozen new-construction *Columbia*-class SSBNs their top shipbuilding priority. Even so, they stand apart from the Navy's fleet as traditionally understood.

Amphibious ships of various kinds ferry US Marines to foreign beaches. Some are equipped with "well decks," which, with ballasting, allow waterborne small craft to float in and out to speed up sea-to-shore movement. Some amphibious assault ships resemble light aircraft carriers and indeed have dimensions similar to those of World War II–era fleet carriers. These helicopter landing docks (LHDs) and landing helicopter assault ships (LHAs) were constructed primarily to operate helicopters but can also support short-takeoff, vertical-landing jets such as the F-35C joint strike fighter. However, the amphibious, or "gator," fleet does not fight for control of the sea; it takes advantage of control of the sea once secured by the battle fleet.

Lastly, the US Navy depends on a combat-logistics fleet operated by the US Merchant Marine to refuel its warships at sea. Oilers, refrigerated-stores ships, and ammunition ships rendezvous with combat formations at sea to carry out "underway replenishment," a technique whereby the delivery and receiving ships cruise on parallel courses at intimate range—less than two hundred feet—pass wires and hoses between them, and transfer matériel via this temporary rigging. Also commonplace is "vertical replenishment" employing cargo helicopters to deliver lighter shipments.[15] This logistic capability provides what is called a "blue-water" navy, making the US Navy less reliant than others on foreign ports. Auxiliary ships do not fight the enemy directly—but victory at sea would be impossible without the stores they bear. Even a nuclear-powered carrier, which can steam indefinitely, needs regular resupply lest the air wing empty the ship's tanks of jet fuel.

This is an idle-seeming debate—battle fleet, cruisers, or flotilla?—that matters. Julian Corbett observes three basic strategic options for commanders. They can fight for outright maritime supremacy. If not strong enough yet, they can strive to deny an enemy maritime supremacy until the fleet is strong enough for toe-to-toe battle. They can exploit maritime supremacy once the battle has been won or the hostile battle fleet is otherwise out of action.[16] Now suppose that antiaccess weaponry so imperils high-end combatants such as carriers, cruisers, and destroyers that commanders have to turn to other units—submarines, perhaps, along with small surface craft of various sorts—to bear the initial brunt of the fighting.

If that were the case, the battle fleet would start to look suspiciously like the cruiser or flotilla contingent, forced to shelter out of range of hostile missile and air forces and await the results of battle before getting to work in relatively safe seas and skies. Why is that a problem? Because domestic politics could well turn against building major combatants that then sat out the Navy's foremost function: major combat at sea. The American people and their elected representatives might balk at spending $13 billion on a *Ford*-class aircraft carrier that no longer appeared to be a frontline asset.[17] Corbett presents us an analytic tool that remains handy for appraising the design of fleets a century after his passing.

Naval power is in flux just as it was during the age of Corbett and Mahan. The coming years could see traditional ship types such as those profiled here give way to very different implements of sea combat. The reasons are strategic and technological in nature. US naval strategy increasingly views a fleet of more numerous, smaller, less pricey vessels as the right weapon to accomplish the nation's aims at sea. If equipped to concentrate firepower at the scene of action while spreading out on the map, it could fulfill strategic aims more effectively than a fleet composed exclusively of traditional ship types. Such a dispersed fleet could afford to lose individual ships in battle and still fight on, whereas today's fleet loses a substantial percentage of its combat power if a single carrier, cruiser, or destroyer is put out of action.[18] Resilience lies in numbers.

Technology offers considerable promise as fleet designers try to put the vision of a "distributed" force into practice. Like their counterparts in armies and air forces around the globe, US naval engineers are experimenting with unmanned or "optionally manned" vehicles of all types. For example, an unmanned tanker aircraft, the MQ-25 Stingray, is on its way to the fleet to help extend the combat reach of carrier warplanes.[19] If these experiments bear fruit, the sea services could afford to construct low-cost platforms in bulk to supplement the fleet's fighting power. The degree to which unmanned technology will transform naval warfare remains to be determined. Navies tend to harness newfangled technology as an auxiliary to what they already do well until it proves its worth in real-world operations. A century ago, for instance, commanders regarded aircraft carriers as an adjunct to the battleship fleet, useful chiefly for scouting and gunfire spotting. Only after fleet experimentation, and only until aircraft and weapons design lent carrier planes heavy-hitting firepower, did the flattop take the battleship's place at the center of oceangoing navies. It is possible that today's high technology will have the same revolutionary impact.

TYPES OF NAVY AND MARINE FORMATIONS

The chief of naval operations, the United States' top uniformed naval officer, is entrusted with training, manning, and equipping forces to be supplied to regional combatant commanders as directed by the Pentagon. Formations dispatched for overseas duty typically fall into three categories. First, the carrier strike group is an organizational construct of fairly recent vintage, replacing the larger Cold War–era carrier battle group, or CVBG.[20] Carrier strike groups need not be identical in makeup, but in general a group consists of a nuclear-powered aircraft carrier with an embarked air wing centered primarily on different variants of the F-18 Super Hornet fighter/attack jet; a guided-missile cruiser; several other surface combatants, mainly guided-missile destroyers; a nuclear-powered attack submarine; and a combat-logistics ship.

The CSG had its origins during the post–Cold War years, after the Soviet Navy had been disbanded and before new "peer" challengers arose. Hence the "strike" label, as opposed to "battle." Terminology matters. During the Cold War, Navy leaders assumed they would have to do battle for sea control against an adversary on par with the US Navy in combat power. Designating a formation as a strike group assumes the US Navy will not need to fight for maritime command; it will control the sea from the outset. The sea will be a more or less safe sanctuary, meaning Navy formations can dispense with part of the self-defense capability they needed to vanquish Soviet opposition. They can concentrate more or less exclusively on strike missions.

A CSG is designed to be self-sufficient and defend itself against surface, subsurface, and air attack in low- to medium-threat environments. Typical missions include "forward presence," meaning mounting a peacetime show of force to impress allies, friends, and adversaries with American power and resolve; protecting or attacking seaborne trade; protecting amphibious forces en route to distant beaches; and projecting power onto foreign shores using air or missile strikes or naval gunfire. It remains to be seen whether the naval leadership will restore the carrier battle group, a formation more lavishly furnished with surface-ship escorts, to cope with China's and Russia's resurgent maritime forces.

Second, an amphibious ready group (ARG) typically transports a Marine expeditionary unit (MEU; see chapter 7). Carrying the embarked Marines will be an amphibious assault ship, either a landing helicopter dock (LHD) or a landing helicopter assault ship (LHA); an amphibious transport dock ship (LPD); and an amphibious dock landing ship (LSD). Surface combatants and combat-logistics ships commonly steam in company with an amphibious ready group, depending on the threat environment and the mission.

In peacetime, an ARG might conduct theater-security cooperation efforts to bolster regional security. Because an MEU is modest in numbers and capability, naval commanders would probably combine expeditionary groups into larger formations in wartime—much as they would probably combine carrier strike groups into larger formations or even operate entire fleets at sea at the same time. They will tailor the force to the contingency.

And third, Navy commanders can assemble surface action groups (SAGs) as circumstances warrant. After the Cold War, when the threat remained negligible, it was commonplace to dispatch individual surface combatants on individual missions. With the return of great-power competition, the Navy has taken to operating multiple combatants together in a variety of contexts. There is no set layout for a SAG. For instance, a recent group consisting of two destroyers conducted routine patrols, maritime security operations, and theater-security cooperation.[21] SAGs can also be assigned as escorts for an ARG to create an expeditionary strike group (ESG).

Just as naval technology is in transition, so are naval organizations. As noted, the naval leadership wants to rebalance the fleet toward more, smaller, cheaper hulls to boost its ability to withstand a punch and battle on. As the rebalancing process progresses, it is a reasonable guess that new formations will come into being to fit the new mode of naval warfare. For instance, the Marine Corps is already instituting "littoral regiments" for island-hopping in Pacific combat.[22] Dispersed regiments will require dispersed Navy units to transport and retrieve them—implying a substantial revision to the ARG as an organizational construct, if not something altogether new. Nevertheless, knowing the makeup and uses of carrier, amphibious, and surface groups as they stand today provides a yardstick to measure the evolution of sea strategy and operations.

The Coast Guard is the third component of the Naval Service. The USCG is distinct in that it is part of the Homeland Security Department in peacetime, is primarily a law-enforcement and lifesaving service, and yet can be incorporated into the Navy in wartime. Like the Navy and Marine Corps, the USCG is charged with protecting the homeland while furthering US interests overseas. It is the main defender of US sovereignty in the territorial sea, contiguous zone, and exclusive economic zone (EEZ), belts of water adjoining US shores where the United States enjoys special legal rights and prerogatives under the law of the sea.[23] It trains foreign partners and can also supply detachments on Navy ships to conduct boarding operations in counterpiracy, counterdrug, and counterproliferation operations. USCG cutters routinely deploy to such expanses as the Persian Gulf and the South China Sea to perform constabulary missions of this type. For instance, the USCG maintains a standing contingent of six patrol craft in Bahrain to bolster maritime security, protect maritime infrastructure, and undertake theater security cooperation with partners in the region.[24]

The USCG fleet is lean in the extreme, considering the breadth of the missions assigned to it. The service operates fourteen high-endurance cutters (WHECs), similar to frigates (which are smaller than destroyers), and is planning to procure a flotilla of twenty-five smaller offshore patrol cutters (OPCs) to replace aging midsized vessels.[25] This fleet must police the world's second-largest EEZ, with sea areas in two oceans, the Caribbean Sea, and the Gulf of Mexico. USCG cutters sometimes cruise with naval formations.[26] In light of the distinct nature of the USCG's police duties, competing demands on its fleet, and its modest numbers, it is doubtful that the service would attach more than one cutter to a CSG, ARG, or SAG. The last time USCG vessels took part in traditional combat operations was during the Vietnam War.[27] During Desert Storm, the USCG deployed personnel, but no ships, to enhance port security at ports throughout the region, which were key to the debarkation of land forces (and some Air Force equipment) and supplies for their sustainment.

COMMAND AND CONTROL: A CASE STUDY IN DEFENDING TAIWAN

To project power, the US and the North Atlantic Treaty Organization rely heavily on SLOCs. Due to this reliance, every joint task force is assigned a joint force maritime component commander (JFMCC). In some scenarios, the JFMCC will be the lead component. Consider the case of Taiwan, a likely Pacific battleground in this age of great-power strategic competition. China's People's Liberation Army (PLA) is a peer competitor for the US armed forces in the Pacific, including the Japan-based US Seventh Fleet and US Air Force, Army, and Marine forces scattered about allied countries in East Asia. Taiwan lies in the shadow of mainland China, meaning that any fight would take place within reach of not just the PLA Navy surface and subsurface fleets but also shore-based aircraft and missiles. China watchers debate the likelihood of a Chinese offensive against the island, but Beijing's ultimate goal is to occupy it. It might try indirect measures such as a naval blockade or air and missile strikes on critical infrastructure to soften up the defenders. To seize ground, however, the PLA would eventually be forced to mount an amphibious offensive across the Taiwan Strait. The American goal would be to help Taiwan's armed forces stymie such an offensive.

A cross-strait war would represent a high-end contingency. To blunt a Chinese offensive in China's own backyard would demand a combined effort from the Seventh Fleet, the larger US Pacific Fleet stationed in Hawaii and along the US West Coast, and joint air and ground forces along with Taiwanese forces (and potentially forces supplied by other allies as well, although no capital is committed by treaty to intervene on the island's behalf). Some of the Navy's air component would be needed for fleet defense and would be retained under the JFMCC. Those not needed for fleet defense might be assigned to the JFACC to conduct strikes that might slow down the enemy's attacks.

The threat would emanate from multiple domains, coming at the US expeditionary force from above, on, and under the sea as well as cyberspace and the electromagnetic spectrum. The PLA's operational aim would be to stop US forces from reaching the scene of battle or to slow them down enough to permit Chinese forces to win the battle before rescuers could reach the scene. PLA commanders would present their foes as a fait accompli—daring them to reverse what had been done. Beijing would have calculated that friends of Taiwan would decline to try to overturn the verdict of arms, judging the costs and risks prohibitive.

To survive the onslaught and prevail, US commanders would feel compelled to deploy enough combat power to ward off PLA antiaccess weaponry coming from multiple dimensions and axes of attack. Conceptually, the land-, sea-, and air-based missile defenses would be consolidated under the JFACC's area air-defense commander. Only thus would they stand much chance of enabling Taiwan's military to frustrate the cross-strait amphibious invasion. That would mean committing multiple CSGs to the fight and potentially multiple ARGs as well. In all likelihood, US commanders would decline to send heavy forces into the strait itself, where they would be exposed to threats at close range and their freedom of maneuver would be constrained by the waterway's cramped topography. Carrier and amphibious groups would operate to the island's east, still within reach of their firepower but with freedom to maneuver and evade counterattacks. Taiwan's armed forces would bear the brunt of operations in the strait, then, with heavy US backup. While afloat on the ARG, the MEUs are subordinate to the JFMCC. Presumably, Taiwan would be in need of additional ground forces. Once the Marines touch land, they would become subordinate to the JFLCC. If there were a need for direct action or other specialty missions, Navy special operations forces might be assigned to the JFSOCC.

Lesser Pacific contingencies are certainly thinkable. China covets the Senkaku Islands to Taiwan's north and has manufactured and fortified islets in the South China Sea. A conflict around one or more of these potential hot spots would pit China against US treaty allies such as Japan or the Philippines or partners such as Vietnam. The composition of US naval forces for such a contingency would depend on the nature of US aims and the prospects that the encounter might escalate into a larger war. The larger the war, the more closely the intervening force would resemble the one sent for an all-out battle off Taiwan.

Like fellow armed services, the Naval Service constantly conducts war games to help foresee future scenarios and what they would demand of the US Navy, Marine Corps, and Coast Guard. Projecting alternative futures can help students of military affairs understand the naval contribution to joint operations and strategy and measure the adequacy of US maritime forces for the tasks they are likely to shoulder.

LEARNING REVIEW

- Recall the primary role of the US Navy.
- Recall how the Navy presents forces to the joint commander in the form of CSGs, SAGs, ESGs, and ARGs.
- Recall the primary roles of the USCG when working with the Department of Defense.
- Recall how Navy forces deploy to support the joint force (i.e., the logistics of forward presence).
- Describe the conditions under which maritime forces would be the preferred focus for a military option.
- Given a maritime-focused scenario, identify the optimum assets to provide specific capabilities.

NOTES

1. "Mission," US Navy, accessed December 24, 2020, https://www.navy.mil/About/Mission/.
2. See James R. Holmes, *A Brief Guide to Maritime Strategy* (Annapolis, MD: Naval Institute Press, 2019).
3. Alfred Thayer Mahan, *Retrospect and Prospect: Studies in International Relations, Naval and Political* (Boston: Little, Brown, 1902), 246.
4. Mahan, 246.
5. Mahan, 246.

6. Julian S. Corbett, *England in the Seven Years' War: A Study in Combined Strategy*, vol. 1 (London: Longmans, Green, 1907), 6.

7. Julian S. Corbett, *Some Principles of Maritime Strategy* (1911; repr., Annapolis, MD: Naval Institute Press, 1988), 16.

8. Corbett, 107–27.

9. Alfred Thayer Mahan, *The Interest of America in Sea Power, Present and Future* (Boston: Little, Brown, 1897), 198.

10. See "Missiles of China," Center for Strategic and International Studies, accessed December 29, 2020, https://missilethreat.csis.org/country/china/.

11. See "Chinese Anti-Shipping Missiles," GlobalSecurity.org, accessed December 29, 2020, https://www.globalsecurity.org/military/world/china/missile-ashm.htm.

12. Conversely, the Navy's stealthy new *Zumwalt*-class destroyers have cruiser dimensions, outweighing the *Ticonderoga* by 50 percent. Spiraling costs truncated the *Zumwalt* class to three hulls. See Ron O'Rourke, *Navy DDG-51 and DDG-1000 Destroyer Programs: Background and Issues for Congress* (Washington, DC: Congressional Research Service, December 17, 2019).

13. Ron O'Rourke, *Navy Littoral Combat Ship (LCS) Program: Background and Issues for Congress* (Washington, DC: Congressional Research Service, October 22, 2018).

14. Ron O'Rourke, *Navy Frigate (FFG[X]) Program: Background and Issues for Congress* (Washington, DC: Congressional Research Service, July 21, 2020).

15. "Underway Replenishment (UNREP)," Federation of American Scientists, accessed January 3, 2021, https://fas.org/man/dod-101/sys/ship/unrep.htm.

16. Corbett, *Some Principles of Maritime Strategy*, 161–67.

17. This figure accounts for the hull alone, not counting the cost of aircraft or stores. Ron O'Rourke, *Navy Ford (CVN-78) Class Aircraft Carrier Program: Background and Issues for Congress* (Washington, DC: Congressional Research Service, December 22, 2020).

18. Thomas Rowden, Peter Gumataotao, and Peter Fanta, "Distributed Lethality," *Proceedings* 141, no. 1 (January 2015).

19. "MQ-25A Stingray," Naval Air Systems Command, accessed January 3, 2021, https://www.navair.navy.mil/product/MQ-25A-Stingray.

20. "Carrier Strike Group," GlobalSecurity.org, accessed January 3, 2021, https://www.globalsecurity.org/military/agency/navy/csg-intro.htm.

21. Trevor Walsh, "Surface Action Group: A Key to Maintaining Maritime Superiority," *Surface Warfare* 54 (Spring 2017).

22. Philip Athey, "Corps to Launch 3-Year Marine Littoral Regiment Experiment Using Hawaii Marines," *Marine Corps Times*, September 22, 2020.

23. United Nations Convention on the Law of the Sea, United Nations, accessed January 4, 2021, https://www.un.org/Depts/los/convention_agreements/texts/unclos/unclos_e.pdf.

24. "5th Fleet Bolstered by Arrival of Two Coast Guard Fast Response Cutters," *Seapower*, May 26, 2021, https://seapowermagazine.org/5th-fleet-bolstered-by-arrival-of-two-coast-guard-fast-response-cutters/.

25. US Coast Guard, "The Cutters, Boats, and Aircraft of the US Coast Guard," accessed January 4, 2021, https://www.uscg.mil/Portals/0/documents/CG_Cutters-Boats-Aircraft_2015-2016_edition.pdf?ver=2018-06-14-092150-230.

26. "Coast Guard Cutter Munro Joins RIMPAC Following 37-Day Alaska Patrol," US Indo-Pacific Command, August 24, 2020, https://www.pacom.mil/Media/News/News-Article-View/Article/2322847/coast-guard-cutter-munro-joins-rimpac-following-37-day-alaska-patrol/.

27. US Coast Guard Historian's Office, "Vietnam Commemoration: 50 Year Anniversary," US Coast Guard, accessed January 4, 2021, https://www.history.uscg.mil/Our-Collections/Commemorations/Vietnam/.

CHAPTER 7

The US Marine Corps and Expeditionary Power Projection

Ryan Burke and Kyleanne Hunter

The United States has an Army to fight on the land, a Navy to fight in the sea, an Air Force to fight in the air, and now even a Space Force to (potentially) fight in space. In the simplest manner of speaking, all domains are covered. So, why does the United States have a Marine Corps that fights in the air, on land, and at sea? The redundancy of the Marine Corps seems undeniable, at least on the surface. Those who do not understand the Marine Corps relative to the other services may think of it as a "jack of all trades," whereas the others are "masters of one." In truth, former Marine Corps general Victor H. Krulak put it best in 1957: "The United States does not *need* a Marine Corps. However, for good reasons which completely transcend cold logic, the United States *wants* a Marine Corps."[1] So why does the United States want something it does not need?

CORPS CONTEXT: MISSIONS AND ORGANIZATION

The US Marine Corps's value proposition—its utility while receiving only 7 percent of the annual US defense budget (compared with 26 percent for the Army, 24 percent for the Air Force, and 23 percent for the Navy)—extends beyond its iconic uniforms and mythological status. On any given day, the Marine Corps is forward deployed, present, engaged, and prepared to rapidly respond to crisis and contingencies. In short, marines train and maintain readiness to conduct expeditionary operations in "every clime and place."[2] The Marine Corps is America's expeditionary force in readiness—its military multipurpose tool that can be both lethal and lifesaving. While America may not *need* a Marine Corps, the tradition, history, mystique, and lore of the Marine Corps ensures that Americans continue to *want* a Marine Corps to the point that the mission, purpose, and even the size of the Marine Corps, unlike that of other services, remains codified in law.

Legal Structure of the Marine Corps

Following World War II, the United States questioned the necessity of maintaining a Marine Corps as a distinct service from the Army, noting obvious parity and similarity in the two services' roles during the war, albeit in different theaters. The result of this debate manifested in the language of the National Security Act of 1947, codifying a distinct role for the Marine Corps.

The National Security Act mandates that marines be versatile and adaptable. The first two decades of the twenty-first century necessitated that marines engage in land-based combat operations in Iraq, Afghanistan, Syria, and Mali. And while the Marine Corps was celebrated for its role in them, they again raised questions about its differentiation from the Army. To some, the Marine Corps's role in the global war on terrorism (GWOT) was redundant, thus compelling deliberate discussion about the Corps's intended function in the contemporary strategic toolbox. A closer look at the past twenty years shows that even though both services conducted land-based operations, there is a significant contribution that marines make to the joint force. The US Army owns the ground. Its primary function is to conduct and sustain combat operations on land. The Marine Corps can—and does—project land power but organizationally lacks the long-term capability to sustain ground-combat operations for extended periods. And whereas the Army *can* conduct amphibious operations, it is not its primary role or function, just as where the Marine Corps *can* conduct sustained ground combat operations, that is not its primary role or function. While there is overlap in the ability to conduct many operations, the Marines are *optimized* for amphibious operations. The Marine Corps emphasizes forcible entry from the sea as a core tenet of its amphibious mission. However, the Corps conducts forcible entry over land as well, serving as the shock force for entry into contested regions prior to the introduction of the Army for sustained land operations. For example, the Marine Corps was forward deployed to take Baghdad, Fallujah, Ramadi, and Nasiriyah in Iraq before the Army. The Corps is a lightweight force in readiness, with versatile and hard-hitting shock troops capable of rapid deployment and power projection across the range of military operations, both from the sea and over land.

Despite twenty years of land-based operations and being the nation's expeditionary force in readiness, the Marine Corps is foremost a naval force. According to the United States Code, which establishes the function and purpose of the Marine Corps, it "shall be organized, trained, and equipped to provide Fleet Marine Forces of combined arms, together with supporting aviation forces, for service with the fleet in the seizure and defense of advanced naval bases and for the conduct of such land operations as may be essential to the prosecution of a naval campaign."[3] Amphibious by nature and expeditionary by necessity, the Marine Corps also performs "other such duties as the President may direct," including providing security at US embassies, consulates, and even the White House. Among other requirements and consistent with its ties to the Navy, marines serve on Navy ships, protect Navy stations and bases, and conduct expeditionary operations in "the littorals and other challenging environments."[4] To execute these responsibilities, the Marine Corps is legally mandated to maintain "not less than three combat divisions, three aircraft wings, and other organic land combat forces, aviation, and other services."[5] The nature of the roles and missions of the Marine Corps makes it uniquely suited to respond to crises and contingencies and to rapidly project lethal combat power to "assure access" to and within contested environments. A unique feature of this ability is the deliberate design to work within the enemy's weapons engagement zone (WEZ). While technology has enabled greater standoff capability for engaging the enemy, there are times when direct engagement is essential. Operating within the WEZ gives joint force commanders critical capabilities, including "attriting adversary forces, enabling joint force access requirements, complicating targeting and consuming adversary ISR [intelligence, surveillance, and reconnaissance] resources, and preventing fait accompli scenarios."[6] With

90 percent of the world's population residing in the littoral regions, these are areas of the world most likely to see conflict. Thus, it is imperative for the United States to be able to project military power in the littorals and for the joint force to have a way to create maneuver and decision space in such regions. The Marine Corps serves this purpose.

A force charged with an amphibious mission requires the versatility and ability to execute multidomain operations from the air, on land, and at sea. This amphibious and expeditionary multidomain focus necessitates a self-sustaining combined-arms approach in both organization and execution.

The Marine Corps is a military service residing within the Department of the Navy. As such, the Navy and Marine Corps operate in a team construct, combining combat capabilities of both services toward the same ends. Forward-deployed amphibious units are the backbone of the Navy–Marine Corps team. Navy amphibious assault ships—including landing helicopter assault (LHA), landing helicopter dock (LHD), landing platform dock (LPD), and dock landing ship (LSD)—make up the amphibious readiness group (ARG) that carries marines and their equipment aboard. The ARG ferries marines to the littoral regions and allows them to project power ashore in ship-to-shore operations. Doing so requires a full complement of aviation, logistic, and ground-combat capabilities. This concept is known as the Marine air-ground task force (MAGTF).

Organization of the Marine Corps

MAGTFs are scalable and "balanced, air-ground, combined-arms formations under a single commander."[7] MAGTFs come in the same shape, though different sizes. Regardless of size, all MAGTFs have the same four elements: command element (CE), ground combat element (GCE), aviation combat element (ACE), and logistics combat element (LCE) (see figure 7.1).

The CE, GCE, ACE, and LCE

The command element functions as the MAGTF headquarters, planning and directing combat power-projection activities. The ground combat element provides the MAGTF with a ground force capable of executing missions, including forced entry, terrain seizure, and even short-term occupation. The GCE consists of infantry marines whose primary mission is to locate, close with, and destroy the enemy through fire and maneuver or to repel the enemy assault by fire and close combat. Marine Corps infantry units are supported by Marine artillery units as well as reconnaissance units as required on the ground. Until 2020, the Marine Corps had armor units (tanks). However, in its latest reorganization effort to reflect the needs of a modern and lightweight, mobile shock force, the Marine Corps recommended disbanding all

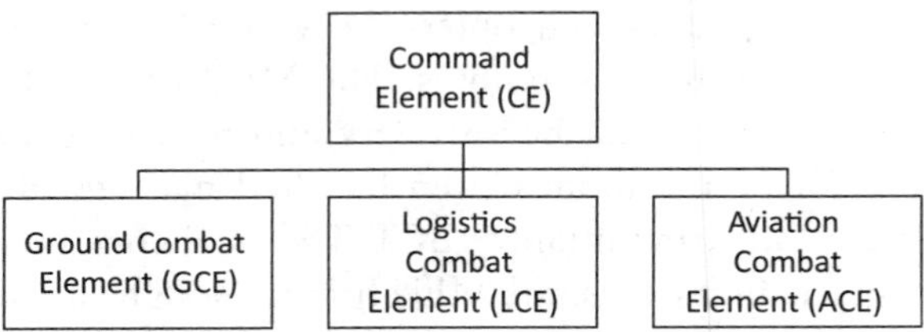

Figure 7.1. Elements of a MAGTF

armor units within its ranks and structure. Tanks are now the sole capability of the Army's armored brigade combat teams (ABCTs). In the air, the ACE augments the GCE and provides both fixed-wing and rotary assets for close air support, aerial reconnaissance, and assault support, among other combat-support functions. Unlike forward-deployed Air Force and Army aviation assets, Marine aviation assets function principally to support Marine ground units first and only support joint forces (other than marines) when there are untasked resources otherwise unnecessary for MAGTF support at the time. Because of this, Marine aviation will rarely be assigned to the joint force air component commander (JFACC).

In addition to supporting the GCE, the ACE augments the logistics combat element for ship-to-shore combat support or through aerial lift to resupply forward forces. To this point and similarly unique to the Marines, when operating within a JTF, marines aboard ship ("boots wet," in the colloquial phrasing) are under the command and control of the joint force maritime component commander (JFMCC). When marines execute ship-to-shore movements and arrive on land (or go "boots dry"), they become come under the joint force land component commander (JFLCC). The LCE is often the enabler of this unique force transition and functions to sustain the MAGTF's forward power projection, providing vital sustainment to forward-deployed forces. The LCE can deliver supplies in myriad ways from the air, including via external sling loading from helicopters or via air delivery, from the land via logistics convoys, or from the sea via ship-to-shore transport and coordinated beach operations. The LCE is capable of resupplying Marine Corps ground units in austere and contested areas to enable continued forward presence and power projection.[8] To put it more simply, the MAGTF elements operate together; the LCE goes where the GCE goes, and the ACE supports both.

The four MAGTF elements work in concert to form the organic, self-sustaining basis of the Marine Corps's unique power-projection model. Organic and self-sustaining functions enable the Marine Corps to rapidly deploy and operate with an expeditionary mind-set, limiting its force structure and enhancing its maneuverability. The elegant simplicity of the MAGTF promotes a modular and scalable construct that can be tailored to a specific mission or purpose.[9] This gives the joint force a powerful tool for rapid force projection, rapid response, and shaping the battlefield. Though tailorable to meet specific requirements, the Marine Corps maintains three standard MAGTF structures that it deploys worldwide.

Types of MAGTFs

The typical forward-deployed MAGTF is a Marine expeditionary unit (MEU). The MEU's versatility enables it to conduct a range of military operations. MEUs are capable of forcible entry and direct combat action, operating in contingency or security cooperation efforts, and executing rapid-response missions, including emergency disaster relief or noncombatant evacuation operations. The MEU's aviation combat element maintains a reinforced tilt-rotor squadron containing attack helicopters, heavy-lift helicopters, and vertical/short-takeoff-and-landing fixed-wing fighter-bombers. The MEU's ground combat element is a reinforced infantry battalion with attached artillery and reconnaissance elements called a battalion landing team. There are about eleven hundred marines in the MEU's GCE, or about one-third the size of an Army infantry BCT. The LCE consists of a combat logistics battalion. Due to ship space limitations, the MEU brings enough supplies for fifteen days of self-sustainment before it requires supplemental support for continued operations. Between the CE, GCE, LCE, and ACE, the MEU comprises approximately twenty-two hundred marines deployed aboard Navy ships. At any given time, there are two to three MEUs afloat around the world, ready and able to respond to crises and contingencies at a moment's notice. While afloat marines are not just waiting for crises—they are continually training with our allies and partners and engaged in security cooperation missions. Prior to deployment, MEUs train to conduct a range of operations from humanitarian assistance and security missions to major combat. MEUs are the Marine Corps's versatile, forward-deployed crisis-response forces.

While MEUs are capable of a range of operations, some missions require a specific focus. For more specific missions requiring a particular capability, the marines form a special-purpose MAGTF (SPMAGTF). A SPMAGTF is usually smaller than a MEU and prepares for a defined mission such as humanitarian assistance or security cooperation.[10] Recent SPMAGTFs include the response to Hurricane Katrina in New Orleans, Louisiana; an SPMAGTF providing immediate crisis-response capabilities for the US Central Command combatant commander; and an SPMAGTF providing immediate crisis response for the US Africa Command combatant commander. Marines assigned to these SPMAGTFs train for the most likely crisis-response situations in their designated area of responsibility, including noncombatant evacuation, high-value target identification and direct action, and humanitarian response. SPMAGTFs focus on regional expertise. As the Marine Corps shifts its focus to US Indo-Pacific Command, maintaining crisis-response capabilities in other regions remains a core capability.[11] While SPMAGTFs are agile and specially tailored, they lack the firepower and logistic capability of a full MEU.[12]

The midsized MAGTF is the Marine expeditionary brigade (MEB). While the MEB is similarly structured to a MEU, it is capable of generating greater combat power for longer periods. MEBs can conduct self-sustaining operations for up to thirty days before requiring resupply. MEB elements are roughly three times larger than their MEU counterparts. The CE can oversee larger combat forces and other supporting functions, including communications, intelligence, and engineering. The MEB's ACE generally contains three to five helicopter squadrons and three to five aircraft squadrons. The GCE's main component is an infantry regiment with three battalions and additional artillery and reconnaissance units. The LCE consists of a combat logistics regiment that typically houses various units, including landing support and transport companies. In summary, a MEB is task organized to meet the specific needs of a combatant commander.[13]

The biggest MAGTF is a Marine expeditionary force (MEF). The Marines maintain three active-duty and one reserve MEF headquarters in order to meet its congressionally mandated size. A MEF can conduct major combat operations for upward of sixty days before requiring resupply. A MEF is not a combination of MEBs. Rather, it is—like other MAGTFs—a tailorable force able to conduct major combat operations that is approximately three to five times larger than its equivalent MEB element. The MEF CE can function as a joint task force headquarters, something its MEB and MEU counterparts cannot do. Though the MEF can serve as a JTF, the Army corps is typically the preferred structure due to the Army's capacity for conducting sustained operations relative to the Marine Corps's design as an expeditionary mobile force. The MEF's combat elements consist of a Marine division, a Marine aircraft wing, and a Marine logistics group, each of which can be structured for a particular mission. The MEF is the Marine Corps's most capable MAGTF in terms of its size and command capacity. MEFs can command multiple Marine divisions if needed, as was the case in the 2003 US invasion of Iraq when the I MEF headquarters commanded several Marine Corps units as well as a British armored division.[14]

Corps Theory: Applying the MAGTF through Maneuver Warfare

The MAGTF organization allows marines to practice maneuver warfare. Maneuver warfare is both a spatial and psychological concept, based on "rapid, flexible, and opportunistic" employment of forces.[15] The self-sustaining MAGTF package allows marines to both physically and temporally outmaneuver the enemy. The integrated logistics keeps marines better supplied and capable of a faster operating tempo than the enemy. The speed at which Marine units are able to operate due to their integrated air and logistics elements gives them a psychological advantage that can be exploited to shape the battlefield. The rapid deployment of the MAGTF's self-sustaining units is designed to disrupt the enemy's ability to make a meaningful decision—known as the observe-orient-decide-act (OODA) loop—and contribute to their systemic disruption and ultimate destruction. Focusing simultaneously on logistically supported air and ground assets toward creating effects on the same targets or objectives enables the Marine Corps to get inside the enemy's OODA loop and degrade its decision-making capacity. The goal of maneuver warfare is not necessarily the overwhelming annihilation of enemy forces but the rapid destruction of the enemy's most critical components.

Maneuver warfare provides the joint force a critical advantage in shaping the battlefield and creating the decision space necessary for sustained operations. Historic examples of maneuver warfare are celebrated throughout not just Marine Corps history but also American history. From the raid on British forces in Nassau during the Revolutionary War to the island-hopping campaigns in World War II memorialized with the flag raising on Iwo Jima, the Marines' ability to engage in forward-projected maneuver warfare has contributed to military success since the country's founding.

In the months following the 2001 terrorist attacks, marines from the 15th MEU conducted forward operations throughout Kandahar, Afghanistan, seizing critical airstrips and setting conditions for the Army and Air Force to conduct sustained operations as part of Operation Rhino. The 2003 invasion of Iraq similarly employed maneuver-warfare tactics in a landlocked environment, ultimately resulting in marines seizing and securing Ayn Al Asad Air Base, the centerpiece of US operations in Iraq throughout the war. Maneuver warfare is most often described as a combat concept; however, it is also the backbone of the range of operations in which marines engage. The speed at which marines operate has not only led to combat success but also contributed to their success in operations ranging from humanitarian assistance to the evacuation of noncombatants. Their self-sustained organizational structure coupled with the principles of maneuver warfare makes marines adept at operations that blur the lines between combat and noncombat operations. For example, in 1915, after the assassination of the Haitian president, marines were sent to help ensure order. In this instance, they had to both forcibly enter and hold a contested maritime port and provide humanitarian assistance to a population that was being cut off from its normal supply routes. Marines were once again used in Haiti in 2010 during Operation Unified Response using their unique ship-to-shore logistics capabilities to provide humanitarian earthquake relief to areas that were impassible by road.[16]

Beyond humanitarian response, the MAGTF's employment of maneuver warfare is a critical tool for conducting operations across the range of military operations (ROMO). The ability to outmaneuver enemy forces has been essential for noncombatant evacuation missions. The integration of air, ground, and logistics allows marines to simultaneously engage the enemy while removing civilians safely from conflict zones. Marines have been responsible for saving the lives of noncombatants across the globe, ranging from Vietnam and Cambodia to Lebanon and Somalia. The rapid-response and self-sustainment capabilities of the MAGTF give joint force commanders yet another powerful tool to meet their strategic goals. And while there are specialty Army units capable of such operations, the Marine Corps's focus on operating inside the WEZ gives them the skills necessary for evacuating civilians during hostile conditions.

CONCLUSION

The Marine Corps does not dominate a single domain and instead serves as an expeditionary power-projection force in readiness.[17] To conduct critical missions abroad on short notice, the Marine Corps is often described as a "middleweight" force: light enough "to quickly get to the scene of action, yet heavy enough to either accomplish the mission or provide a stopgap pending the arrival of additional forces."[18] But they are far more than just a smaller Army. Their scalability, maneuverability, rapid-response capability, and forward presence provide the joint force with a multifunction tool to shape the battlefield. Though America will always *want* a Marine Corps, in an ever-changing environment the joint force will continue to need a service capable of maneuvering inside the enemy's WEZ to shape the environment.

LEARNING REVIEW

- Recall the primary role of the US Marines.
- Identify the trade-offs between deploying the Marines versus the Army.
- Recall how the US Marine Corps presents forces to the joint commander in the form of a MAGTF.
- Recall how Marine forces deploy to support the joint force.
- Describe the conditions under which marines would be the preferred focus for a military option.
- Describe the logistic pros and cons of expeditionary warfare, forward presence, prepositioned assets, and the trade-offs of using airlift versus sealift.
- Given a complex scenario, identify the optimum Marine Corps assets to provide specific capabilities.

NOTES

1. Victor H. Krulak, *First to Fight: An Inside View of the US Marine Corps* (Annapolis, MD: Naval Institute Press, 2013), xv (italics in original).
2. "Marines' Hymn," Marine Corps University, https://www.usmcu.edu/Research/Marine-Corps-History-Division/Frequently-Requested-Topics/Marines-Hymn/.
3. US Code Title 10. Armed Forces, section 5063.
4. 10 USC 5063.
5. 10 USC 5063.
6. US Marine Corps (USMC), *Force Design 2030* (Quantico, VA: Headquarters Marine Corps, March 26, 2020).
7. USMC, *MCDP 1-0, Warfighting* (Washington, DC: Department of the Navy, 2016), 2-6.
8. On logistics, see also USMC, *MCWP 3-40: Logistics Operations* (Washington, DC: Department of the Navy, 2016).
9. USMC, *MCDP 1-0*, 2-6–2-8.

10. USMC, 2-13–2-14.

11. Gordon Emmanuel and Justin Gray, "The Marine Corps' Evolving Character and Enduring Mission," War on the Rocks, May 6, 2019, https://warontherocks.com/2019/05/the-marine-corps-evolving-character-and-enduring-purpose/#:~:text=The%20Marine%20Corps%20must%20continue,blunt%2C%20surge%2C%20and%20homeland.

12. Mark Cancian, *U.S. Military Forces in FY 2021: The Last Year of Growth?*, Center for Strategic and International Studies International Security Program (Lanham, MD: Rowman & Littlefield, 2021).

13. USMC, *MCDP 1-0*, 2-11.

14. Michael R. Gordon and Bernard E. Trainor, *Cobra II: The Inside Story of the Invasion and Occupation of Iraq* (New York: Pantheon Books, 2006), 222. For order-of-battle information, see Nicholas E. Reynolds, *U.S. Marines in Iraq, 2003: Basrah, Baghdad and Beyond* (Charleston, SC: CreateSpace, 2007), 165–72.

15. USMC, *MCDP-1*.

16. This was also the first humanitarian mission to use MV-22 Ospreys for disaster relief.

17. Office of the Secretary of Defense, "DOD Directive 5100.01," 31.

18. USMC, *MCDP 1-0*, 1-1–1-2. See also USMC, *Expeditionary Force 21: Forward and Ready; Now and in the Future* (Washington, DC: Department of the Navy, 2014); and USMC, *Marine Corps Vision and Strategy 2025* (Washington, DC: Department of the Navy, 2013).

CHAPTER 8

The US Air Force and the Air Domain

Heather Venable

The US Air Force (USAF) provides global awareness, mobility, and long-range strike capabilities. The USAF develops and employs a wide array of nonkinetic and kinetic, lethal and nonlethal capabilities to the joint force commander for a spectrum of missions, from humanitarian operations to counterinsurgency to near-peer conflict to nuclear deterrence.

During the global war on terrorism, close air support (CAS), or the orchestrated delivery of munitions in support of those on the ground, provided one example of how the USAF contributes to joint warfare. During recent counterinsurgencies, ground forces came to expect CAS and on-demand intelligence, surveillance, and reconnaissance (ISR). This relationship between air and ground forces requires communication and coordination in a dynamic battlespace.[1] In future wars, CAS may be a lower priority, at least initially. Airpower also provides the ability to bypass the enemy's army and directly strike targets deep into its heartland. (Chapters 14 and 15 will discuss strategic bombing theory in more detail.) A wide range of platforms and capabilities enables American airpower primacy in every region of the world, from the tactical level to the strategic.

This chapter provides an overview of airpower and the ways in which it is coordinated within the joint force structure. It details capabilities and mission sets for the USAF, including its five core missions of air and space superiority, ISR, rapid global mobility, global strike, and command and control (C2). Finally, the chapter explores what the future holds.

AIRPOWER'S UNIQUE CAPABILITIES

What is airpower, what are the characteristics of the air domain, and what does airpower add to the joint fight?

Airpower is "the ability to project military power or influence through the control and exploitation of air, space, and cyberspace to achieve strategic, operational, or tactical objectives."[2] The air domain provides "complete freedom of action and direction," unlike the sea or land domains.[3] Airpower can attack from any direction at any time, making defense inefficient. The three characteristics of airpower—"speed, reach, and height"—enable "ubiquity, agility, and concentration."[4] Ubiquity is the ability to be anywhere one chooses to be. When considering how airpower should be used in the joint context, Colin Gray's explanation in table 8.1 is germane:

Table 8.1. Airpower Strengths and Weaknesses

What can airpower do uniquely?	What can airpower do well?
• directly assault physical centers of gravity regardless of distance • attack opponent from inside to outside • project force around the world quickly • transport people and supplies in limited quantities rapidly • insert and supply small numbers of troops	• protect its land and sea forces from an opponent's airpower • deter in conventional conflicts • engage in strategic attack in conventional conflicts • be a force multiplier for land and sea forces • interdict or impede enemy access or resupply • prevent enemy from seizing or holding objective • like spacepower, observe "over the hill"
What does airpower often do poorly?	**What is airpower unable to do?**
• occupy territory from the air alone • send clear diplomatic messages • close with and grip an opponent continuously • wage strategic attack in primarily irregular conflicts • discriminate reliably between friend and foe	• bulk transport (at least not in a cost-effective manner) • seize and hold territory • accept enemy surrender

Source: Adapted from Colin S. Gray, *Airpower for Strategic Effect* (Maxwell Air Force Base, AL: Air University Press, 2012), 281.

Whether employed tactically or strategically, airpower has some important capabilities. But what falls under the air domain? The USAF considers it to be "the atmosphere, beginning at the Earth's surface, extending to the altitude where its effects upon operations become negligible."[5] However, most typically rely on the Kármán line (about one hundred kilometers above the surface of Earth) as differentiating the air and space domains.

Perhaps more so than other domains, airpower benefits from how it is organized due to its long reach and speed. In one popular analogy, it makes more sense to use airpower like a fire hose than "sprinklers" in which it is parceled out in small numbers to Army commanders. Such centralization has increased over time, particularly in Operation Desert Storm in 1991 where the services better planned and coordinated airpower under a single commander for the first time.[6]

However, airpower capabilities require tremendous structures and logistics to sustain them.[7] Air bases provide the ability to "translate military potential into military force."[8] The need for foreign basing rights and overflight permissions can hinder military operations. For instance, Turkey prevented the United States from using Incirlik Air Base for offensive operations against Iraq in 2003. As air bases can be a liability, the USAF has "devoted most of its attention to improving airborne performance," which now increasingly affects an air commander's ability to operate without well-dispersed and protected bases to facilitate employment.[9]

ORGANIZING AIRPOWER FOR THE JOINT FIGHT

In peacetime, the USAF is organized into major commands (MAJCOMs), of which there are nine currently, such as Air Mobility Command (AMC), Air Combat Command (ACC), and Pacific Air Forces (PACAF). MAJCOMs divide up the training and equipping of units based on different missions, typically separated functionally or geographically. Below them, numbered air forces (NAFs) provide operational leadership and supervision to wings, groups, and squadrons.[10] Within this overarching structure, the USAF presents forces to the joint commander in the form of a tailorable air expeditionary task force (AETF). The advantages of this organizational construct stem from the fact that the AETF offers a "scalable, tailorable organization with three elements: a single, clearly designated commander, appropriate C2 mechanisms, and tailored and fully supported forces."[11]

As introduced in chapter 4, the joint force air component commander (JFACC)—or the combined force air component commander (CFACC)—will advise the joint task force commander how to apportion airpower. For example, the JFACC might suggest allotting 75 percent of aircraft to counterair missions on the first day of an operation, 10 percent to strategic attack, and the remaining 15 percent to counterland targets. Additional responsibilities include but are not limited to developing a joint air operations plan while managing airspace and area air defense.[12]

The JFACC provides unity of command and unity of effort by being responsible for planning and tasking the majority of air assets regardless of whether they come from the USAF or from other services.[13] This has been an area of historical contention, with individual services resisting this notion, a problem mostly resolved by Operation Iraqi Freedom in 2003, in part because the CFACC established strong relationships with other branches capable of providing airpower.[14] The JFACC need not be from the USAF, but he or she typically is because the USAF usually provides most of the forces for the JFACC.[15]

The JFACC relies on the air operations center (AOC) to provide the C2 for airpower.[16] When engaged in coalition warfare, the AOC generally is referred to as the combined air operations center (CAOC). The AOC provides the basics of air strategy and planning that integrate air, space, and cyberspace.[17] It is divided by five core functions:

1. The strategy division focuses on long-range planning.
2. The combat plans division (CPD) produces the master air-attack plan (MAAP) and the daily air tasking order (ATO).
3. The combat operations division (COD) monitors and executes operations.
4. The ISR division allocates, collects, and disseminates ISR resources and products.
5. The air-mobility division oversees diplomatic clearances and movement of cargo and high-ranking officials.

Airpower planning is a cycle:

> The cycle begins with joint force commander [JFC] and component commander guidance. The CAOC strategy division then determines the task to be accomplished in the next cycle. This, in turn, is developed into targets that are vetted through a joint and coalition selection and approval process. This prioritized list then goes to the master air attack plan (MAAP) team that assigns air assets to the targets. The ATO production team then builds the ATO and sends it out to the various units for execution. After execution, the results flow back into the CAOC, where the assessment team determines the outcome and the combat effects achieved. This feedback then flows back to the JFC, the component commanders, and the strategy division, where the cycle starts all over again.[18]

The cycle lasts about seventy-two hours but can be compressed, notably, for time-critical targets. Some criticize the process as inefficient and clumsy, while others worry that speeding up the process might result in a perspective that is too tactical.[19] The cycle is a comprehensive method to plan the application of airpower in a cohesive and coherent manner involving what can be thousands of aircraft per day from multiple service and allied aircraft.

EMPLOYING AIRPOWER IN THE JOINT FIGHT

Airpower contributes to the joint fight in six areas:

1. Counterair includes integrated air and missile defense to "ensure freedom to maneuver, freedom to attack, and freedom from attack."[20] Defensive counterair (DCA) and offensive counterair (OCA) sweep missions attack enemy fighters and missiles. OCA missions might strike aircraft on the ground or the air base's supporting infrastructure. Suppression of enemy air defenses (SEAD) and destruction of enemy air defenses (DEAD) attack enemy radars and surface-to-air missiles (SAMs). The counterair mission is increasingly challenged by antiaccess/area-denial (A2/AD) technologies, making it easier to detect stealth aircraft that have small radar cross sections (RCS). As a result, airmen increasingly talk not of achieving air superiority over the entire country but rather seeking out periods of localized air superiority.[21]
2. Strategic attack seeks to directly achieve objectives typically by targeting C2, communications, infrastructure, and war-supporting industry and/or other centers of gravity. The intent is to produce the greatest effect for the least cost in lives, resources, and time.[22] For example, strategic attack in Operation Desert Storm had a debilitating effect on the functioning of Iraq's forces.[23]
3. Counterland includes air interdiction and CAS. Interdiction targets could include an army's C2 nodes, a transportation hub, forces moving into position and/or supply trucks. Interdiction requires less complicated coordination with ground troops. CAS, by contrast, attacks enemy forces that are close to friendly forces (e.g., troops in contact [TIC]).[24]
4. Countersea operations employs airpower to achieve maritime superiority. USAF assets might provide ISR, interdict surface forces, and conduct aerial minelaying, antisubmarine warfare, aerial refueling, or airborne C2.[25] The Air Force is pursuing an expanded inventory of countersea weapons.[26]
5. Air mobility quickly transports people and matériel, including aerial refueling and aeromedical evacuation.[27] Tankers provide in-flight fueling, which provides the endurance and range for global power projection.
6. Information operations (IO) ensures "synchronized messaging" and seeks to affect an opponent's "behavior and decision making." The USAF uses behavioral influence analysis in seeking to understand an opponent's thinking in order to select and strike information-related targets.[28]

THINKING ABOUT AIRPOWER

The USAF seeks an effects-based approach to operations (EBAO) in which "operations are driven by desired ends (objectives and end states), and should be expressed in terms of desired effects, not defined by what available forces or capabilities can do."[29] One example of an application of this idea is how the USAF does not consider a bomber to be inherently "strategic" or a fighter inherently "tactical."[30] Rather, it is the effect that the bomber or the fighter has when employed that provides the conceptual framework for thinking about airpower employment. As Colin Gray explains, everything a military does is "tactical in the doing."[31] That means that even the act of dropping a nuclear weapon is tactical, although it might have strategic effects.

The USAF believes it brings a different perspective to the joint fight—sometimes called "airmindedness." The USAF conceives of itself as more strategically minded because of the speed of its operations and ubiquity, and it is not as bound to the terrain or what it can see in front of it. Hence, the USAF has a "functional" approach that is "unconstrained by operating areas."[32] It is a "global, strategic mind-set through which the battlespace is not constrained by geography, distance, location, or time."[33]

Although airmen use airmindedness to suggest how airpower should be employed properly, it is ultimately up to elected leaders to decide when and how to use it. Politicians often prefer airpower for a number of reasons, such as avoiding US ground troop casualties and limiting collateral damage. As such, it has come to be seen as a "coercive option that is precise, scalable, rapid, and relatively risk-free." And, in such situations, it can be employed relatively quickly.[34]

THE USAF BY THE NUMBERS

In 2019, the USAF had about 4,147 aircraft (see table 8.2).[35] The table is slightly misleading, as the far greatest number of aircraft in the ISR/BM (battle management)/C2 category is the MQ-9 Predator, which has an important attack role against mobile and high-value targets, even if it carries far less ordnance than manned platforms. Of course, the mix is constantly changing as the USAF develops future aircraft such as the KC-46 air refueler and the B-21 stealth bomber.

While the United States counts more tanker aircraft in its inventory than any other nation, ever-increasing requests for airborne fuel combined with aging fleets and lagging recapitalization programs continue to strain the force. Table 8.3 (see below) explains that six F-15Cs

Table 8.2. US Air Force Mix of Aircraft

Aircraft type	Percentage of total
Fighter/attack	48.6
Transport	15.9
ISR/BM/C2	12.5
Tankers	11.4
Helicopters	4.5
Bombers	3.8
Special ops	3.3

Source: "Major Commands and Air National Guard," *Air Force Magazine*, June 2020, 64, https://www.airforcemag.com/app/uploads/2020/06/June2020_Fullissue5.pdf.
Note: BM = battle management; C2 = command and control; ISR = intelligence, surveillance, and reconnaissance.

Table 8.3. KC-46 Tanker Aircraft Requirements

Aircraft number and type	1,000 nm	3,000 nm	6,000 nm
6 F-15C	—	3	9
6 F-16	—	2	7
6 F-22	1	5	8
1 C-17	—	—	2

Source: Air Force Pamphlet 10-1403: Air Mobility Planning Factors (Washington, DC: Secretary of the Air Force, October 24, 2018), 21.

require the use of three KC-46 tankers to travel three thousand nautical miles without landing. However, mission planning variations for both tankers and receivers such as airspace (flyover approval, contested, congested), cruise altitudes, low-level flying, cargo and munitions load, airfield density altitude, possible weather divert, and maintenance options affect the number of required tankers, often increasing rather than decreasing them.

Interestingly, while tanker assets are often used to fuel organic receivers, many nations share capacity, therein increasing capability. The US has receiver compatibility with at least twenty-five international tankers.[36] Thus, aerial refueling is not only a key joint capability but a coalition advantage.

Battle management, by contrast, has become an increasingly important capability since Operation Desert Storm. Two important aircraft for this role are the E-3 Airborne Warning and Control System (AWACS) and the E-8 Joint Surveillance and Target Attack Radar System (JSTARS). The former, used for air defense, can track aircraft, including low-flying ones. The latter are used to track ground movement. These aircraft are becoming increasingly vulnerable in the A2/AD environment, necessitating innovative solutions to maintain these capabilities in the future.

Electronic warfare (EW) aircraft are those with the ability to both seek to deny an opponent the ability to use the electromagnetic spectrum, including infrared energy and radio waves, and ensure that its own forces can. For example, electronic warfare helps to protect aircraft when attacking enemy air defenses. The USAF no longer has specific EW aircraft, having retired the EF-111A in 1998, and instead relies upon Navy EA-18Gs. The USAF believes the F-35 has some promising abilities in this arena, which can be supplemented by the EC-130H Compass Call's provision of long-range EW, while the EC-130J Commando Solo provides support for information operations.[37]

Transport aircraft can be divided into two types: intratheater and intertheater. Intratheater transport aircraft operate in a theater of operations, while intertheater transport operate between theaters. Intratheater transport can be conducted with aircraft such as the C-130, which can land on short dirt strips. Intertheater transport, on the other hand, connects the theater over a longer distance, such as to the continental United States. Key intertheater aircraft include the C-17, which is capable of landing on rough, semiprepared runways, and the enormous C-5, which can hold two M1 Abrams tanks. Air transport moves equipment and personnel quickly but in small quantities compared to land and sea transport. For example, a single armored brigade combat team has ninety tanks, but there are under forty C-5s in the inventory, with an even smaller number mission-capable. For a more practical option, a six-hundred-person airborne battalion requires twelve C-17s (half for troops, half

LEARNING BOX 8.1. APPLICATION SCENARIO

Identify the optimum joint air assets to employ in reference to the following scenario:

Russian irregular forces have captured Vilnius, the capital city of Lithuania. They have overthrown the government and installed a puppet government while launching cyber-attacks, cutting power to homes and businesses. The Russian outpost of Kaliningrad, equipped with short-range ballistic missiles that can deliver tactical nuclear weapons and a strong air-defense system of S-400 and S-300V4 missiles, is only about one hundred miles away. Lithuania, as a member of the North Atlantic Treaty Organization (NATO), has invoked Article 5, leading to all NATO member states mobilizing forces to defend Lithuania.

NATO is preparing a ground operation that will require airpower support to retake the city. A US carrier strike group is being sent, including a Marine expeditionary unit (MEU). Both will be positioned two hundred miles away in the Baltic Sea. Air bases across Europe are standing by to provide kinetic and nonkinetic capabilities, and air force bases in the US are preparing to deploy whatever assets might be needed to retake Lithuania.

How do you suggest the JFACC advise the JFC as to what airpower capabilities can and should do? What limitations should the JFACC discuss with the JFC? What information do you need to know before planning? How much air superiority is required before you can fly interdiction, strategic attack, and CAS missions? How will you deconflict and command and control these joint air operations? How do you integrate NATO allies into your planning?

Use this chapter's appendix to facilitate your planning and decisions and the assets needed.

for equipment).[38] More specifically, the purpose of strategic brigade airdrop is to deliver a brigade—consisting of more than three thousand airborne soldiers and three thousand tons of equipment—from the US into combat thousands of miles away to set up an area from which to launch further operations, all within twenty-four hours and possibly using austere airfields.[39]

ISR provides key information from a range of air assets. USAF ISR is inherently joint. While the other services use most of their ISR assets for their own organic needs, most USAF ISR is tasked to support joint or national requirements.[40] For more on ISR, see chapter 12.

PREPARING FOR THE FUTURE JOINT FIGHT

As the USAF continually assesses how it will contribute to the joint fight, it is engaged in numerous debates about the future of airpower. Envisioning this future force means not thinking about how many bombers or fighters or tankers are needed but what capabilities it might require, such as range, persistence, and survivability.

With many nations having increased their A2/AD capabilities to deter US airpower, it is important to note the pendulum swing from airpower's offensive advantage at its inception to today. Arguably, A2/AD capabilities have shifted to provide defensive depth with a significant advantage.

Ongoing debates continue to occur in the realm of platforms. For example, the future of the A-10 fighter-bomber, designed to attack ground targets, has been particularly contentious. While CAS can be provided by any aircraft with precision weapons, ground forces prefer the support of the A-10. Unfortunately, the A-10 lacks survivability in today's A2/AD environments. These kinds of debates have been ongoing since the USAF first used jets for CAS in the Korean War, when the troops on the ground preferred slower, propeller-driven aircraft for their long loitering time, while the USAF argued for more survivable and faster jets.[41] As a result, for example, the Army developed and employed attack helicopters in the Vietnam War to provide its own close air support.

Similar debates that have continued since the Cold War have concerned the right balance of capabilities among the platforms as well as how much should be invested in what T. X. Hammes has called the "exquisite few" versus large numbers of platforms.[42] The USAF has tended to invest in top-of-the-line aircraft. One notable exception was the largely simultaneous development of the F-15 and the F-16, with the F-15 being the more expensive aircraft designed specifically for air superiority and the F-16 being the more numerous multirole platform due to its cost. An analogous relationship in regard to roles can be seen in the F-22, envisioned as primarily an air-superiority fighter, as compared to the F-35, envisioned as a multirole, affordable fighter.[43] A number of reasons have contributed to the F-35 being far less affordable than originally intended.[44] The recent purchase of the F-15X is a way of having partial fifth-generation capabilities sans stealth.

Increasingly, the US seeks to combine the "exquisite few" with the "cheap many" by using F-35s as "quarterbacks" or motherships, networked to a large number of attributable, inexpensive drones to provide the required mass. Australia is designing an unmanned wingman to accompany the F-35.[45]

Some ethical concerns have centered on the use of artificial intelligence (AI) in unmanned weapons and platforms. The Department of Defense (DOD) insists that it will keep humans "in" or "on the loop" in regard to decision-making, although others take a more cynical view of this claim because decisions will need to be made more quickly than humans can react.[46] Indeed, the USAF's 2019 AI Strategy mentions ethics a handful of times but provides little indication of how it will implement AI ethically beyond a vague assurance to "staying engaged, informed, and accountable" and "leading dialogue."[47]

Of equal concern is the actual employment of AI. From the chips themselves to the networked hardware to the actual code, reliability and security may be highly suspect and vulnerable to rogue entry and jamming. Hence, the security and reliability of supply chains will be a major vulnerability to all US military weapon systems and future warfighting.

Organizationally, the USAF has gotten away from the idea of the AOC being a physical place near combat operations by moving the AOC that supports US Central Command from Al Udeid Air Base, Qatar, to Shaw USAF Base, South Carolina.[48] A distributed AOC provides redundancies and backups that could be connected through a combat cloud. ACC defines the cloud as an "overarching meshed network for data distribution and information sharing with a battlespace, where each authorized user, platform, or node transparently contributes and receives essential information."[49] Some caution that joint commanders must be colocated in order to provide the best mutual support, in part because strong relationships and seamless communication are foundational to joint effectiveness.[50]

The Air Force Warfighting Integration Capability (AFWIC) is the USAF's think tank for the long-term future. It proposed three possible visions. First, an "evolutionary" one focuses on how to draw on its current capabilities more "effectively" in regard to tactics and technology.

Second, a more "revolutionary" future stresses a more "stand-off" approach to future warfare. Finally, a "disruptive" approach considers "doing away with crewed aircraft altogether in favor of big bets on drones, hypersonic missiles, or laser weapons."[51]

CONCLUSION

The AOC plans and synchronizes USAF forces, deployed in the form of an AETF, with the air arms of the other services and countries to achieve security objectives for the joint force commander. However, not all aircraft will be under the command of the AOC as the other services will retain some of their air assets to support their operations on the land or sea. Airpower alone might be a preferred national security option for those situations requiring power projection while minimizing risk and vulnerability. Airpower provides leadership with strategic alternatives not available any other way.

LEARNING REVIEW

- Recall the primary role of the USAF.
- Recall how the USAF presents forces to the joint commander in the form of a tailorable AETF and AOC.
- Recall how air forces deploy to support the joint force (i.e., logistics).
- Describe the conditions under which air would be the preferred focus for a military option.
- Given a complex scenario, identify the optimum joint air assets to provide a specific set of capabilities.

APPENDIX: USAF CAPABILITIES

Table 8.4 lists sample USAF assets aligned by Air Force core function:

Table 8.4. Air Force Assets Aligned by Air Force Core Function

Capability	Mission/Task	Primary platform(s)
	Air superiority	
Protect the joint force from attack	DCA	F-22, F-15C
Protect the joint force's ability to attack	OCA sweep	F-22, F-15C
Protect air strike packages from surface threats (SAMs, AAA, EW/GCI)	SEAD/DEAD	F-16
Deny the adversary the ability to conduct air missions	OCA strike	F-35, F-15E, F-16, B-1, B-2, B-52
	Global integrated ISR	
Periodic reconnaissance of potential targets	IMINT	U-2, RQ-4 Global Hawk
Periodic monitoring of high-value targets	FMV	MQ-9
Analyze communications and radar signals	SIGINT	RC-135 Rivet Joint
Track ground targets across a wide area	GMTI	JSTARS
Process, analyze, and disseminate intelligence from airborne ISR	Manage airborne IMINT and FMV missions	DCGS
	Global precision attack	
Destroy enemy centers of gravity	Strategic attack	F-35, F-15E, F-16, B-1, B-52, B-2
Deny enemy ability to resupply or reinforce	Air interdiction	F-35, F-15E, F-16, B-1, B-52, B-2
Support friendly troops in close contact	CAS	A-10, AC-130, or any precision attack
	PR	
Recover downed airmen	CSAR	HH-60, CV-22
	C2	
Provide TACON of aircraft assigned to execute the day's air tasking order	C2	AWACS, ground-based ACSs, AOCs

Note: AAA = antiaircraft artillery; ACS = air-control squadron; AOC = air operations center; AWACS = Airborne Warning and Control System; CAS = close air support; CSAR = combat search and rescue; C2 = command and control; DCA = defensive counterair; DCGS = distributed common-ground system; DEAD = destruction of enemy air defenses; EW = electronic warfare; FMV = full-motion video; GCI = ground-control intercept; GMTI = ground moving-target indicator; IMINT = imagery intelligence; ISR = intelligence, surveillance, and reconnaissance; JSTARS = Joint Surveillance and Target Attack Radar System; OCA = offensive counterair; SAM = surface-to-air missile; SEAD = suppression of enemy air defenses; SIGINT = signals intelligence; TACON = tactical control.

Table 8.5 lists operational planning factor estimates, which can vary depending on the tactical context—adversary, weather, route selection, and mission type:

Table 8.5. Operational Planning Factor Estimates

Aircraft	Combat radius[1]	Cruise speed[2]	Optimum on-station time	Typical firepower[3]
F-22	500 nm	1.0 Mach	One-hour CAP	Six AIM-120 and two AIM-9X air-to-air missiles. For air-to-ground missions, two AIM-120, two AIM-9X, and two 1,000 lb. bombs. When stealth is not required, additional weapons can be mounted externally.
F-35	500 nm	0.8 Mach	Fifteen minutes for CAS	Four 2,000 lb. bombs
F-15C	500 nm	0.8 Mach	Fifteen minutes for CAS	Six AIM-120, two AIM-9X
F-15E	500 nm	0.8 Mach	Fifteen minutes for CAS	Four 2,000 lb. bombs
F-16CM	500 nm	0.8 Mach	Fifteen minutes for CAS	Two HARMs or two 2,000 lb. bombs
A-10	250 nm	0.5 Mach	One hour for CAS	Two AIM-9X but no AMRAAMs; 30mm cannon plus variety of bombs and Maverick missiles optimizes it against armored vehicles and tanks
HH-60	200 nm	0.2 Mach	n/a	Can refuel at forward operating base
U-2	3,000 nm	0.6 Mach	n/a	High-altitude flight path keeps it out of most air defenses
RQ-4	10,000 nm	0.5 Mach	n/a	High-altitude flight path
MQ-9	1,000 nm	0.3 Mach	Twelve hours	Two 500 lb. bombs and four hellfire missiles
RC-135, JSTARS, AWACS	HVAA orbit	0.7 Mach	Twelve hours	Advanced sensors and robust communications

Note: AMRAAM = advanced medium-range air-to-air missile; AWACS = Airborne Warning and Control System; CAP = combat air patrol; CAS = close air support; HARM = high-speed antiradiation missile; HVAA = high-value airborne asset; JSTARS = Joint Surveillance and Target Attack Radar System.

[1] Assumes a round-trip flight with a full weapons load and external fuel tanks when available. If air refueling, this would be the potential distance from the tanker(s) to target(s). Combat radius (and/or on-station time) can be increased by reducing the weapons load. Alternatively, planners may want to shorten the distance in order to improve the on-station time.

[2] For planning purposes, this is a fuel-efficient transit speed that maintains aircraft maneuverability.

[3] There are a multitude of variations. This lists a typical loadout for this mission type. Note that air-to-ground fighters typically carry two AIM-120 and two AIM-9X air-to-air missiles for self-protection. Although armed with a 20mm cannon, fighters typically do not strafe due to the risk of ground fire. The A-10 is the exception to both of these: it does not carry AIM-120s, but due to its slow speed and high survivability against ground fire when not in A2/AD conditions, its 30mm cannon is especially effective in supporting ground forces.

NOTES

1. Phil Haun and Colin Jackson, "Breaker of Armies: Air Power in the Easter Offensive and the Myth of Linebacker I and II in the Vietnam War," *International Security* 40, no. 3 (2016): 139–78.

2. "Air Force Updates Doctrine Documents," US Air Force, November 16, 2011, https://www.af.mil/News/Article-Display/Article/112104/air-force-updates-doctrine-documents/#:~:text=That%20definition%20defines%20airpower%20as,%2C%20operational%20or%20tactical%20objectives.%22. The Air Force may modify this definition, given the newly established Space Force.

3. Giulio Douhet, *The Command of the Air* (1921; repr., Maxwell Air Force Base [AFB], AL: Air University Press, 2019), 8.

4. Colin S. Gray, *Airpower for Strategic Effect* (Maxwell AFB, AL: Air University Press, 2012), 280.

5. "Introduction to Counterair Operations," *Annex 3-01: Counterair Operations* (Maxwell AFB, AL: Curtis E. LeMay Center, September 6, 2019).

6. Viktoriya Fedorchak, *Understanding Contemporary Air Power* (New York: Routledge, 2020), 77.

7. Jarrod Pendlebury, Foreword, in Peter Layton, *Surfing the Digital Wave: Engineers, Logisticians and the Future Automated Airbase* (Canberra, Australia: Air Power Development Centre, 2020), iii.

8. Layton, *Surfing the Digital Wave*, 1.

9. Price T. Bingham, "The Air Base: The Air Force's Achilles Heel? Understanding the Key Role Air Bases Play," Mitchell Institute for Aerospace Studies, May 2020, https://mitchellaerospacepower.org/wp-content/uploads/2021/02/a2dd91_5e66fb274bb74aa2afcfd7ca2550b7a1.pdf.

10. "Major Commands and Reserve Components," 2013 USAF Almanac, *Air Force Magazine*, https://www.airforcemag.com/PDF/MagazineArchive/Magazine%20Documents%2F2013%2FMay%202013%2F0513MC_RC.pdf.

11. US Air Force, *Air Force Doctrine Publication 3-30 Command and Control* (Maxwell AFB, AL: Curtis E. LeMay Center, 7 January 2020), 28.

12. *Air Force Doctrine Volume 3: Command*, "The Joint Force Air Component Commander" (Maxwell AFB, AL: Curtis E. LeMay Center, November 12, 2019).

13. Joint Chiefs of Staff, *Joint Publication 3-30: Joint Air Operations* (Washington, DC: Department of Defense, July 25, 2019).

14. Benjamin Lambeth, *Unseen War: Allied Air Power and the Takedown of Saddam Hussein* (Annapolis, MD: Naval Institute Press, 2013), 124–25.

15. C. Q. Brown Jr. and Rick Fournier, "No Longer the Outlier: Updating the Air Component Structure," *Air and Space Power Journal* 30, no. 1 (Spring 2016): 4–15.

16. *Air Force Doctrine, Annex 3-30: Command and Control* (Maxwell AFB, AL: Curtis E. LeMay Center, January 7, 2020), "Appendix B: The Air Operations Center," https://www.doctrine.af.mil/Doctrine-Publications/AFDP-3-30-Command-and-Control/.

17. *Air Force Doctrine, Annex 3-30*, 57.

18. Quoted in Lambeth, *Unseen War*, 207–8.

19. Lambeth, 214.

20. *Annex 3-01*, 2.

21. *Annex 3-01*, 1; Phillip S. Meilinger, "Supremacy in the Skies," *Air Force Magazine*, February 2016, 46–50.

22. "Introduction to Strategic Attack," in *Air Force Doctrine Annex 3-70: Strategic Attack* (Maxwell AFB, AL: Curtis E. LeMay Center; last updated July 12, 2019), 2.

23. David A. Deptula, "Desert Storm at 30: Aerospace Power and the U.S. Military," War on the Rocks, March 1, 2021, https://warontherocks.com/2021/03/desert-storm-at-30-aerospace-power-and-the-u-s-military/; *Gulf War Air Power Survey*, vol. 2, *Operations, Effects and Effectiveness* (Washington, DC: Government Printing Office, 1993), 343.

24. Mike Pietrucha, "The Myth of High-Threat Close Air Support," War on the Rocks, June 30, 2016, https://warontherocks.com/2016/06/the-myth-of-high-threat-close-air-support/.

25. *Annex 3-04 Countersea Operations*, "Air Force Operations" (Maxwell AFB, AL: Curtis E. LeMay Center, November 12, 2019).

26. Joseph Trevithick, "The Air Force Is Developing Smart Bombs with 'Torpedo-Like' Ship Killing Capability," The War Zone, September 2, 2021, https://www.thedrive.com/the-war-zone/42234/the-air-force-is-developing-smart-bombs-with-torpedo-like-ship-killing-capability.

27. *Air Force Doctrine Annex 3-17: Air Mobility Operations*, "Introduction to Air Mobility Operations" (Maxwell AFB, AL: Curtis E. LeMay Center, June 28, 2019).

28. *Air Force Doctrine Annex 3-13*, "Airman's Perspective on Information Operations" (Maxwell AFB, AL: Curtis E. LeMay Center, April 28, 2016).

29. "The Effects-Based Approach to Operations (EBAO)," US Air Force, November 22, 2016, 1.

30. *Air Force Doctrine,* vol. 1, *Basic Doctrine*, "Uses of Doctrine," February 27, 2015, 1.

31. Gray, *Airpower for Strategic Effect*, 288.

32. US Air Force, "USAF Doctrine Update on Airmindedness" (Maxwell AFB, AL: Curtis E. LeMay Center, January 4, 2013), https://www.doctrine.af.mil/Portals/61/documents/doctrine_updates/du_13_01.pdf. See also Jason Trew, "Rescuing Icarus: The Problems and Possibilities of 'Air-Mindedness,'" *Air and Space Power Journal* 33, no. 2 (Summer 2019): 48–60.

33. US Air Force, Volume I, "Airmindedness" (Maxwell AFB, AL: Curtis E. LeMay Center, January 4, 2013). See also Gray, *Airpower for Strategic Effect*, 290.

34. Daniel L. Byman, Matthew C. Waxman, and Jeremy Shapiro, "The Future of US Coercive Airpower," in *Strategic Appraisal: United States Air and Space Power in the 21st Century*, ed. Zalmay Khalilzad and Jeremy Shapiro (Santa Monica, CA: RAND Corp., 2001), 51.

35. "Aircraft Total Active Inventory (TAI)," *Air Force Magazine*, 2019 USAF Almanac, June 2019, 56–60, https://www.airforcemag.com/article/usaf-almanac-2019/.

36. United States ATP 3.3.4.2 (D) Standards Related Document, September 10, 2021, 38–39, https://www.japcc.org/?file=5154.

37. Loren Thompson, "The F-35 Isn't Just 'Stealthy': Here's How Its Electronic Warfare System Gives It an Edge," *Forbes*, May 13, 2019.

38. Stanley McChrystal, *Team of Teams: New Rules of Engagement for a Complex World* (New York: Penguin, 2015), 33.

39. Danita L. Hunter, "C-17s Deliver a Brigade in 30 Minutes or Less," *Air Force News*, February 22, 2000.

40. Author's correspondence with Tyler Morton, May 22, 2020.

41. Conrad Crane, *American Airpower Strategy in Korea* (Lawrence: University Press of Kansas, 2000), 26, 172.

42. T. X. Hammes, "The Future of Warfare: Small, Many, Smart vs. Few and Exquisite," War on the Rocks, July 16, 2014, https://warontherocks.com/2014/07/the-future-of-warfare-small-many-smart-vs-few-exquisite/.

43. Jeremiah Gertler, *F-35 Joint Strike Fighter (JSF) Program* (Washington, DC: Congressional Research Service, 2020).

44. See, e.g., Sydney J. Freedberg Jr., "Lockheed's Not Cutting F-35 Costs Enough, but We Know How: Assad Bogdan," Breaking Defense, March 22, 2017, https://breakingdefense.com/2017/03/lockheeds-not-cutting-f-35-costs-enough-but-we-know-how-assad-bogdan/.

45. Robbin Laird, "The Future Is Now: The RAAF and Boeing Australia Build F-35's Unmanned Wingman" Breaking Defense, February 27, 2019, https://breakingdefense.com/2019/02/the-future-is-now-the-raaf-and-boeing-australia-build-an-f-35-unmanned-wingman/.

46. Sydney J. Freedberg Jr., "Why a 'Human in the Loop' Can't Control AI: Richard Danzig," Breaking Defense, June 1, 2018, https://breakingdefense.com/2018/06/why-a-human-in-the-loop-cant-control-ai-richard-danzig/; Jackson Barnett, "AI Needs Humans 'on the Loop' Not 'in the Loop' for Nuke Detection, General Says," Fedscoop, February 14, 2020, https://www.fedscoop.com/ai-should-have-human-on-the-loop-not-in-the-loop-when-it-comes-to-nuke-detection-general-says/.

47. US Air Force, "Artificial Intelligence Annex to the Department of Defense Artificial Intelligence Strategy," 2019, https://www.af.mil/Portals/1/documents/5/USAF-AI-Annex-to-DoD-AI-Strategy.pdf, 6.

48. Joseph Trevithick, "Air Force Just Tested Its Big Backup Plan if Its Air Ops Center in Qatar Gets Attacked," The Drive, September 30, 2019, https://www.thedrive.com/the-war-zone/30099/air-force-just-tested-its-big-backup-plan-if-its-air-ops-center-in-qatar-gets-attacked.

49. Quoted in Jacob Hess, Aaron Kiser, El Mostafa Bouhafa, and Shawn Williams, *The Combat Cloud: Enabling Multidomain Command and Control across the Range of Military Operations*, Wright Flyer Paper No. 65 (Maxwell AFB, AL: Air University Press, 2019), 1.

50. Author's correspondence on May 22, 2020, with Matthew Powell, author of *The Development of British Tactical Air Power, 1940–1943* (New York: Palgrave, 2016).

51. Sydney J. Freedberg Jr., "Beyond 386 Squadrons: AFWIC's Four Futures for the Air Force," Breaking Defense, December 19, 2018, https://breakingdefense.com/2018/12/beyond-386-squadrons-afwics-four-futures-for-the-air-force/.

CHAPTER 9

The US Space Force and the Space Domain

Michael Martindale

The National Defense Authorization Act for Fiscal Year 2020 established the United States Space Force (USSF) to "(1) protect the interests of the United States in space; (2) deter aggression in, from, and to space; and (3) conduct space operations."[1] The USSF organizes, trains, and equips forces to support the joint force by maintaining space dominance in the face of great-power competition from China and Russia. This chapter introduces spacepower, the space domain, the organization of the USSF, spacepower theory, and the application of spacepower through the lens of assets and capabilities to complete space tasks and create effects in multiple domains.

SPACEPOWER

Spacepower is "the sum of a nation's capabilities to leverage space for diplomatic, information, military, and economic activities in peace or war in order to attain national objectives."[2] *National spacepower* is "the totality of a nation's ability to exploit the space domain in pursuit of prosperity and security."[3] *Military spacepower* is "the ability to accomplish strategic and military objectives through the control and exploitation of the space domain."[4] "Space-faring" nations have assets on orbit providing a service to terrestrial users. Spacepower nations have an indigenous ability to produce satellites and space-lift vehicles and put those satellites into orbit. Space is relatively new as a medium for conflict. Strategists should comprehend the space domain, its capabilities, space superiority, the environment, and the utility of spacepower.[5]

CHARACTERISTICS OF THE SPACE DOMAIN

Early on, the US Air Force (USAF) attempted to secure primary responsibility for space for military purposes by using the term "aerospace" to represent a continuous domain from the surface of Earth to the far reaches of space.[6] However, the air and space domains are significantly different.

There is no accepted definition for the barrier between the two domains. The National Aeronautics and Space Administration (NASA) considers seventy-six nautical miles to be the reentry altitude for spacecraft. The USAF awards astronaut wings for pilots who have flown above fifty nautical miles. The Kármán line, at sixty-two nautical miles (one hundred kilometers) is the altitude at which the physics of orbital forces dominate the physics of aerodynamics.[7] At eighty-one miles, objects can maintain an orbit.

Space is a unique domain. Maneuver is the primary restricted factor. In space, maneuver is limited to slow, deliberate changes due to the weight cost of fuel, a finite resource. Maneuvers are considered only when necessary or a part of the mission plan.[8]

The Space Environment

Space is congested, contested, and competitive.

Congested: Of the over twenty-two thousand cataloged objects in space, about eleven hundred are functional satellites. The rest—95 percent—are debris.[9] The probability of a collision is presently small. As the number of objects increases, however, the probability of a catastrophic collision increases. Many objects will remain in orbit over one hundred years unless removed. Time scales are very long in space; actions taken today can produce effects in the space environment suffered by all space-faring states for more than a century.

On February 10, 2009, the US Iridium 33 satellite and the Russian Cosmos 2251 intersected, creating the first instance of an accidental collision causing catastrophic damage. The result was a debris ring centered on the original orbits, and eventually "shells" of debris spread at the same orbital altitudes. The impact produced at least 200,000 objects, of which 1,602 from Cosmos 2251 and 597 from Iridium 33 were at least ten centimeters in diameter.[10] Objects of this size are tracked and can cause catastrophic damage to a satellite. While nearly half of the debris safely reentered Earth's atmosphere, half remains in orbit and a potential threat to other satellites.[11]

On February 21, 2008, the Aegis cruiser USS *Lake Erie* launched a Standard Missile–3 (SM-3) to intercept and deorbit the defunct USA-193 satellite. The trajectory of the intercept ensured that most of the debris would safely enter the atmosphere within twenty-four to forty-eight hours and the remaining debris within forty days.[12] The United States chose to deorbit USA-193 because its thousand-pound tank of frozen hydrazine propellant posed a toxic risk to humans should it survive reentry. The choice to use the SM-3 to initiate the deorbit allowed for some control as to where the reentering portions might fall and some assurance that the hydrazine tank would be destroyed prior to reentry. Some speculated that the real mission was to destroy classified components or to respond to China's antisatellite (ASAT) test the previous year.[13] Regardless, the mission demonstrated both the US capability to kinetically destroy satellites and the desire to act responsibly by limiting debris.

Contested: The Soviet Union and United States both pursued space weapons but ultimately abandoned their programs.[14] With more space-faring states, states are contesting the US advantage in space. This is prescient since nearly every military asset benefits from space-based services, in particular precision navigation and timing (PNT) provided by the Global Positioning System (GPS). While all military forces can operate without GPS, the accuracy and ease of navigation significantly simplifies operations.

Space-faring states are developing ASAT weapons and nonkinetic means to disrupt communication to space assets. China's direct-ascent ASAT test destroyed its weather satellite, added three thousand pieces of debris, ended a norm against space weapons, and sent a signal that space will be contested in future conflicts. China continues to test space weapons,[15] and it is doing so in parallel with efforts to create international bans to the same class of weapons.[16] The two-pronged strategy of space weapons development coupled with diplomatic efforts to make such weapons illegal creates uncertainty as to China's intent.

Competitive: The economics of space is more competitive as more seek to capture market share.[17] Regardless of the financial gains, capturing market share is important to national security to maintain expertise in space science and engineering technologies. In 1998, the United States conducted thirty-five of a worldwide total of eighty-two space launches. From 1998 to 2015, the US market share of space launches dropped from 43 percent to 23 percent.[18] This change indicates greater competition in space lift. The US runs the risk of losing expertise in space lift and associated jobs to Russia, China, the European Space Agency, Japan, and Israel.

ORGANIZATION OF THE SPACE FORCE

The USSF mission is essentially the same as the other services but with the focus on providing space capabilities to the joint force. The USSF's headquarters and the Office of the Chief of Space Operations are subordinate to the secretary of the Air Force, similar to the arrangement for the US Marine Corps under the secretary of the Navy.

The initial force structure of the USSF was limited to the former Air Force Space Command (AFSPC).[19] All military capabilities that produce effects or operate in, from, and through the space domain have the potential to be transferred to the USSF from the other services.[20] On September 21, 2021, the CSO announced that eleven satellite communications units from the US Army and four from the US Navy were identified for transfer to the USSF in October 2021.[21] The transferred units will provide additional space capabilities required to provide defense of US interests in the space domain.

The USSF includes three major commands: Space Operations Command (SpOC), Space Systems Command (SSC), and Space Training and Readiness Command (STARCOM). The SpOC provides capabilities to the joint force. The SSC does development, acquisition, testing, maintenance, and space lift.[22] STARCOM trains space professionals. Subordinate to each command are "deltas," which are roughly equivalent to the USAF wing. The deltas have subordinate squadrons, but the USSF did not adopt the USAF group command level that is between the wing and the squadron.[23]

The primary combatant command assigned USSF forces is US Space Command (USSPACECOM). It "conducts operations in, from, and to space to deter conflict, and if necessary, defeat aggression, deliver space combat power for the Joint/Combined force, and defend U.S. vital interests with allies and partners."[24] USSPACECOM has two subordinate commands, the Combined Force Space Component Command (CFSCC) and the Joint Task Force–Space Defense (JTF-SD). The CFSCC is focused on delivering combat-relevant space capabilities to support the joint fight. The JTF-SD focuses on "space superiority operations to deter aggression, defend U.S. and Allied interests, and defeat adversaries throughout the continuum of conflict."[25]

The SpOC commands nine space deltas and two garrisons:[26]

- Space Delta 1: Provides initial, specialized, and advanced space training.
- Space Delta 2: Space Domain Awareness (SDA). "Integrates ISR [intelligence, surveillance, and reconnaissance], space observation and environmental monitoring to enable space battle management and support ground operations."
- Space Delta 3: Space Electronic Warfare. "Operates electronic attack, protection, and support capabilities to protect and defend the space domain."
- Space Delta 4: Missile Warning. "Provides strategic and theater missile warning to the United States and our International Partners."

- Space Delta 5: Command and Control (C2). "Maintains global awareness of operational environments and space forces to enable data-driven decisions."
- Space Delta 6: Cyberspace Operations. "Executes cyber operations to protect space operations, networks, and communications, and operates the Air Force Satellite Control Network."
- Space Delta 7: Intelligence, Surveillance, and Reconnaissance. "Provides intelligence data to allow for the detection and characterization of adversary space capabilities."
- Space Delta 8: Satellite Communications, Navigation Warfare. "Provides position, navigation, timing and satellite communications to U.S. military, coalition partners, interagency partners, and commercial/civilian users."
- Space Delta 9: Orbital Warfare. "Conducts protect and defend operational from space and provides response options to deter and defeat adversary threats in space."
- Peterson-Schriever Garrison: Includes Peterson Space Force Base (SFB), Schriever SPB, Thule Air Base, Cheyenne Mountain Space Force Station (SFS), Kaena Point SFS, New Boston SFS, and sixteen USSF mission locations worldwide.
- Buckley Garrison: Includes Buckley SFB, Cape Cod SFS, Clear SFS, and ten USSF mission locations worldwide.

The Peterson-Schriever Garrison at Peterson SFB and the Buckley Garrison at Buckley SFB, both in Colorado, provide installation support for the USSF around the globe.[27]

SPACEPOWER THEORY

There is no one theory of spacepower.[28] One approach focuses on space exploration and commerce.[29] The USSF's foundational perspective defines five core competencies of military spacepower as space security, combat power projection, space mobility and logistics (SML), information mobility, and SDA.

Space security protects civil, commercial, intelligence, allied, and military interests in space. The USSF leverages multinational partners, provides SDA, ensures access to space, and conducts offensive and defensive space control to ensure space security.[30]

Combat power projection provides freedom of action in space. Military space forces deter adversaries and conduct offensive and defensive operations. Defensive operations, both active and passive, protect space assets and reduce the effectiveness of threats.[31]

Space mobility and logistics includes movement of military equipment and personnel to, from, or through space. SML includes space lift to sustain and replenish constellations. Possible future capabilities include refueling, repairing, and maintaining satellites in orbit and transporting personnel and equipment through space for time-sensitive operations in terrestrial domains.[32]

Information mobility requires planning for information collection and transportation for a variety of purposes and via multiple communication paths and linkages. Information mobility is provided through satellite communications, but the effort must be supported with terrestrial assets to send and receive, store, protect, and share data and information for all levels of war.[33]

Space domain awareness is an enabler for all space operations. SDA is composed of three dimensions: physical, network, and cognitive. The physical includes the natural space environment, spacecraft, and orbital debris. The network includes the links and nodes, communications and sensor frequencies, locations, and awareness of the electromagnetic spectrum to enable orbital flight and the movement of information in, from, and through space. The cognitive focuses on the human element and includes the space systems they rely on, decision-making processes, biases, cultural values, and psychological tendencies. Collectively, the three dimensions provide a framework for understanding the space domain and human activities within it in order to make more effective decisions regarding the pursuit of space superiority.[34] Spacepower provides strategic, operational, and tactical advantages for the United States and its allies. Applications of space technologies in six mission areas make spacepower a critical enabler in all other domains.

APPLICATION OF SPACEPOWER

The USSF has eight interrelated missions that enable, or are enabled by, space superiority.[35]

Space superiority "is a relative degree of control in space of one force over another that would permit the conduct of its operations without prohibitive interference from the adversary while simultaneously denying their opponent freedom of action in the domain at a given time."[36] Space superiority requires effective SDA, space control, C2 of space forces, space operations, and space service support. Space superiority enables space forces to provide space support to operations; support to nuclear C2, communications, and nuclear detonation detection; missile warning; and space support to missile defense.

SDA "encompasses the effective identification, characterization and understanding of any factor associated with the space domain that could affect space operations and thereby impact the security, safety, economy, or environment of our Nation."[37] SDA enables space superiority through an understanding of the space environment and an understanding of activity in space to inform threat assessments and responses, which can range from diplomacy to satellite maneuver to offensive or defensive space control options.

Offensive and defensive space control combine to "ensure freedom of action in space and, when directed, defeat efforts to interfere with or attack US or allied space systems. Space control uses a broad range of response options to provide continued, sustainable use of space."[38] Offensive space control (OCS) does activities to deceive, disrupt, deny, degrade, or destroy adversary space assets and activities. Defensive space control (DSC) does active and passive measures to prevent adversary OCS.[39] OCS and DCS determine the degree of control in space.

Command and control of space forces / satellite operations is "the exercise of authority and direction by a properly designated commander in the accomplishment of a mission."[40] The C2 of space forces is similar to C2 of forces in the other domains. C2 is the means for communicating a commander's intent, organizing and unifying effort, delegating decision-making authority, and providing frameworks or boundaries for decision-making. The nature and character of space make the C2 of space forces unique. First, orbital flight and the application of space capabilities to all levels of war create a situation that can lead to strategic compression, "blurring the distinctions between the tactical, operational, and strategic levels of war."[41] The remoteness of space adds complexity to gathering information, and decision-making is complicated by time compression and the necessity to coordinate with multiple organizations with equities in the outcomes of the decision. C2 of space forces requires SDA that is timely, anticipatory, and is shared vertically and horizontally across space units at all echelons.[42] Satellite operations are the tactical actions space units take to ensure mission success within the C2 structure. C2 of space forces and satellite operations directly influence the capability to gain and maintain space superiority. The C2 of space forces and the dominant tactical execution of satellite operations by the space operations crews will determine the level of space superiority achieved by space forces.

Space support to operations provides "capabilities to aid, protect, enhance and complement the activities of other military forces, as well as intelligence, civil, and commercial users."[43] These functions include ISR; detection, tracking, and warning of threat missile launches; environmental monitoring; SATCOM; and PNT provided by GPS.[44] Failure in the space superiority mission will challenge the ability to provide space support to forces in the air, land, and maritime domains.

Space service support provides "access to, transport through, operations in, and, as appropriate, return from space through reliable, flexible, resilient, responsive, and safe launch and satellite operations."[45] The primary functions are space lift, space range, and satellite operations. Space lift provides the ability to place objects in orbit. Space range operations are analogous to airfield operations with focus on infrastructure, volume of airspace, and the transition to Earth orbit for space lift. Satellite operations include all activities to maintain the satellite and its payload and maneuver, configure, and sustain in-orbit assets.[46] Space service support operations maintain the capacity and health of satellite constellations. In contested environments, space service support operations contribute to satellite constellation resilience through satellite status maintenance, satellite maneuver, and replenishment and reconstitution of degraded or destroyed satellites and constellations.

Space support to nuclear command, control, communications (NC3) and nuclear detonation detection encompasses the mission of potentially highest consequence for space forces. Space forces provide warning of missile launches, including nuclear missiles, using overhead persistent infrared (OPIR) sensors and ground-based radars. Detecting, tracking, and characterizing missile attacks, combined with nuclear detonation detection, provide information for the president, the secretary of defense, and commanders to make decisions on the use of nuclear forces.[47]

Missile warning and space support to missile defense: Some of the same OPIR and ground-based radars that support the NC3 mission produce information to support missile defense by detecting, tracking, characterizing, and reporting on missile launches from rogue states.[48] Space support to NC3, nuclear detonation detection, missile warning, and space support to missile defense missions rely on space superiority. Without space superiority, these other critical high-consequence missions can be threatened.

CONDITIONS UNDER WHICH SPACEPOWER WOULD BE THE PREFERRED OPTION

Spacepower options are presently limited to supporting forces in the terrestrial domains. Space combat is unprecedented and will remain so if the deterrence mission succeeds. Assessing the conditions under which spacepower would be the preferred option is speculative with regard to active conflict. However, the history of space activities offers insight for the short term as to when spacepower provides preferred options.

Space capabilities enable coordination, synchronization, and communication across geographically dispersed forces. Space-based capabilities first proved their value in the execution of Operation Desert Storm in 1991. While only a part of the strategy for victory, satellite communications, GPS, and space-based ISR enabled the coalition forces arrayed against the Iraqi military to conduct a combined air and ground campaign across the entirety of Iraq and Kuwait, which achieved its strategic goals in just forty-three days of combat. Space forces provide the ability to effectively communicate on the scale required to support maneuver forces dispersed across broad geographic areas.

Similarly, geographically isolated forces without access to terrestrial communications often rely on space-based capabilities, especially satellite communications and PNT, to maintain contact with command and support elements. The success of Task Force Dagger in the opening months of Operation Enduring Freedom in 2001 offers an example of small tactical forces producing significant strategic effects partly through the aid of space-based capabilities.

Space-based ISR provides access to geographically denied areas. Geographically denied territory that limits the knowledge of the adversary military force presents problems for understanding adversary actions and intent. International law and practice ensure the freedom of overflight by any nation's satellites over any other nation's territory. The United States and the Soviet Union both used this aspect of law to their mutual advantage to monitor each other's military activities, prevent surprises, and maintain a stable relationship in the context of the Cold War. Space capabilities provide a unique advantage by providing access to remote territory to monitor activities, whether those are the tactical activities of a terrorist group in a remote mountain region or the strategic activities of a great power in its protected interior.

GREAT-POWER COMPETITION AND THE SPACE DOMAIN

Considering the space domain within the context of great-power competition requires the strategist to think of a broader national grand strategy. A narrow focus on military spacepower risks the larger great-power competition within the space domain. Assessments of the advantages of providing and maintaining space capabilities, particularly military space capabilities, look inward to human activities on Earth. The inward look is important; however, it is limited and stunts the growth of ideas of how to expand and extend space activities beyond Earth-facing, Earth-orbiting satellites and the services they provide. A new vision for the US space enterprise and the USSF is growing that extends its sights to the moon, asteroids, Mars, and beyond—not as fanciful science fiction but as hard realist imperatives for maintaining US economic and military strategic advantages over its competitors.

Within US military circles, the intellectual lead and champion is retired USAF lieutenant general Steven L. Kwast, who argues for the pursuit of space economic development to provide enough electrical energy to power the globe and ease climate stress through solar-power-collecting satellites and for extracting materials from celestial bodies to further enable a space economy.[49] At the core of Kwast's vision is the idea that if the United States does not win the race to develop such a space economy, it will become and remain inferior to the nation that wins the race.

Spacepower theorists have matured Kwast's vision. Brent Ziarnick has developed a theoretical model for understanding the grammar and logic of spacepower in terms of access to space, the resources in it, and the ability to conduct activities there.[50] Joshua Carlson has compared Chinese spacepower theory and strategy to those of the United States to inform his Space Development Theory, which he proposes as a US strategy for winning the competition with China for space economic dominance.[51] Namrata Goswami and Peter Garretson have championed the idea that the competition for space domain dominance, and the vast energy and material resources in the space domain, will be the central competition between great powers in the twenty-first century.[52]

Whether or not the individual space strategist agrees with the policy prescriptions offered by the adherents to Kwast's vision, the fact remain that the stakes in great-power competition in the space domain extend both to outcomes on Earth and potential futures beyond Earth's orbit. It is possible that competition in the space domain will be the central feature of great-power competition in the twenty-first century. It is also possible that competition in the space domain will be only one of several central elements of great-power competition in the foreseeable future. Given the increasing importance of the space domain to economies and militaries over the past thirty years, it is less likely that the space domain competition will be of little importance in the future.

CONCLUSION

The space domain is a complicated environment that requires technical knowledge of the dynamics of operations to, in, from, and through space as well as the implications of space activities for governments, militaries, and societies. The cognitive requirements to develop a space strategy that integrates with joint all-domain operations for warfighting is the same as those levied on strategists for any domain: the strategist must comprehend more than just the single domain and systems employed. Rather, the strategist must be an expert in the specific domain and the implications for operations in all other domains for any strategy developed. The space strategist must comprehend the current and potential future for the USSF as a part of a broader national space strategy to win in the competition with great powers.

It is hoped that this chapter has set a foundation for comprehending the role of the USSF and the space domain and, in concert with the other chapters in this volume, for developing an understanding of joint all-domain operations and joint warfighting. The student of space strategy must build on such a foundation through deep study of orbital mechanics, specific space systems, systems in other domains using space-based services, and C2. Only with a comprehension of the technology, procedures, and national and international implications of how best to gain advantage in using space assets will the space strategist be able to effectively connect tactical-level actions through operational processes to achieve strategic objectives for the defense of the nation.

The space strategist must consider the proper balance between achieving immediate objectives of supporting joint warfighting and the potential strategic advantages of building a space force capable of supporting national objectives, which extend beyond immediate terrestrial concerns to empower commerce and exploration far beyond Earth's gravity well.

LEARNING REVIEW

- Recall the primary role of the US Space Force.
- Recall how the Space Force presents forces to the joint commander.
- Recall how air forces "deploy" to support the joint force (i.e., logistics).
- Describe the conditions under which space forces would be the primary focus for a military option.
- Given a scenario, identify the optimum assets to provide specific capabilities.

NOTES

1. National Defense Authorization Act for Fiscal Year 2020, December 20, 2020.
2. Defense Space Strategy Summary, June 2020, 1, https://media.defense.gov/2020/Jun/17/2002317391/-1/-1/1/2020_DEFENSE_SPACE_STRATEGY_SUMMARY.PDF.

3. US Space Force (USSF), *Spacepower: Doctrine for Space Forces*, Space Capstone Publication (Arlington, VA: Headquarters USSF, 2020), 13.

4. USSF, 21.

5. A knowledge of physics, chemistry, and engineering and of the challenges in deploying and operating in space will equip the strategist to leverage space assets for conflict in any domain.

6. Delbert R. Terrill Jr., *The Air Force Role in Developing International Outer Space Law* (Maxwell Air Force Base [AFB], AL: Air University Press, 1999), 38; Sean N. Kalic, *US Presidents and the Militarization of Space, 1946–1967* (College Station: Texas A&M University Press, 2012), 40–42.

7. Eric Betz, "The Karman Line: Where Does Space Begin?," *Astronomy*, March 5, 2021, https://astronomy.com/news/2021/03/the_krmm-line-where-does-space-begin.

8. Wiley Larson and James R. Werts, eds., *Space Mission Analysis and Design*, 3rd ed. (Torrance, CA: Microcosm, 1999).

9. "About Space Debris," European Space Agency, accessed April 27, 2017, http://www.esa.int/Our_Activities/Operations/Space_Debris/About_space_debris.

10. R. L. Wang, W. Liu, R. D. Yan, and J. C. Gong, "Thinking Problems of the Present Collision Warning Work by Analyzing the Intersection between Cosmos 2251 and Iridium 33," Proceedings of the Sixth European Conference on Space Debris, Darmstadt, Germany, April 22–25, 2013, https://conference.sdo.esoc.esa.int/proceedings/sdc6/paper/45/SDC6-paper45/pdf.

11. National Aeronautics and Space Administration, "Consequences of the Collision of Iridium 33 and Cosmos 2251," Presentation to the Fifty-Second Session of the Committee on the Peaceful Uses of Outer Space, United Nations, June 3–12, 2009, https://www.unoosa.org/pdf/pres/copuos2009/tech-27.pdf.

12. Jamie McIntyre, Suzanne Malveaux, and Miles O'Brien, "Navy Missile Hits Dying Space Satellite, Says Pentagon," CNN, February 21, 2008, http://www.cnn.com/2008/TECH/space/02/20/satellite.shootdown/index.html.

13. Yousaf Butt, "Technical Comments on the US Satellite Shootdown," *Bulletin of the Atomic Scientists*, August 21, 2008, http://thebulletin.org/technical-comments-us-satellite-shootdown; T. S. Kelso, 2007, "Analysis of the 2007 Chinese ASAT Test and the Impact of Its Debris on the Space Environment," 2007 AMOS Conference Technical Paper, Center for Space Standards and Innovation, 1, https://celstrak.com/publications/AMOS/2007/AMOC-2007.pdf.

14. Article V of the Interim Agreement between the United States of America and the Union of Soviet Socialist Republics on Certain Measures with Respect to the Limitation of Strategic Offensive Arms (SALT I), July 1, 1968; Article XII of the Treaty between the United States of America and the Union of Soviet Socialist Republics on the Limitation of Anti-Ballistic Missile Systems, October 3, 1972; Article XV of the Treaty between the United States of America and the Union of Soviet Socialist Republics on the Limitation of Strategic Offensive Arms (SALT II), June 18, 1979; and Article IX of the Treaty between the United States of America and the Union of Soviet Socialist Republics on the Reduction and Limitation of Strategic Offensive Arms and Associated Documents, July 31, 1991. However, the Treaty between the United States of America and the Russian Federation on the Further Reduction and Limitation of Strategic Offensive Arms, January 3, 1993, does not specify noninterference with NTM but does discuss the use of NTM for verification. Accessible at Arms Control Association, https://www.armscontrol.org/treaties.

15. Zachary Keck, "China's Next Super Weapon Revealed: Satellite Destroyers," *National Interest*, April 15, 2015, http://nationalinterest.org/blog/the-buzz/chinas-next-superweapon-revealed-satellite-destroyers-12640.

16. Louis de Gouyon Matignon, "Treaty on the Prevention of the Placement of Weapons in Outer Space," *Space Legal Issues* (May 8, 2019), https://www.spacelegalissues.com/treaty-on-the-prevention-of-the-placement-of-weapons-in-outer-space-the-threat-or-use-of-force-against-outer-space-objects/. The Treaty on Prevention of the Placement of Weapons in Outer Space and of the Threat or Use of Force against Outer Space Objects (PPWT) was introduced on June 10, 2014, to United Nations Conference on Disarmament by the Russian Federation representative as an update to a previous version submitted by the People's Republic of China, May 8, 2019.

17. The global space market in 2014 totaled $330 billion, including commercial and government infrastructure, products, and services and US and non-US government space budgets. *The Space Report: The Authoritative Guide to Global Space Activity* (Colorado Springs, CO: Space Foundation, 2015), 1.

18. Ed Kyle, Space Launch Report, accessed May 5, 2017, www.spacelaunchreport.com/log2015.html.

19. National Defense Authorization Act for Fiscal Year 2020.

20. Barbara Barrett, *Comprehensive Plan for the Organizational of the U.S. Space Force* (Washington, DC: Department of the Air Force, 2020).

21. Sandra Erwin, "Space Force Reveals Which Army and Navy Units Are Moving to the Space Branch," *SpaceNews*, September 21, 2021.

22. Barret, *Comprehensive Plan.*

23. Sandra Erwin, "Space Force to Stand Up Three Major Commands, Lower Echelons to Be Called 'Deltas,'" *SpaceNews*, June 30, 2020.

24. Organizational Fact Sheet, USSPACECOM, June 18, 2020, https://www.spacecom.mil/Portals/32/USSPACECOM%20Fact%20Sheet%2018Jun20.pdf?ver=2020-06-18-155219-363.

25. Organizational Fact Sheet.

26. "Space Operations Command: Space Missions Deltas and Garrisons" Space Force Public Affairs, March 25, 2021, https://www.spoc.spaceforce.mil/About-Us/Fact-Sheets/Display/Article/2550627/space-operations-command.

27. "Space Force Begins Transition into Field Organizational Structure," Space Force Public Affairs, July 24, 2020, https://www.spaceforce.mil/News/Article/2287005/space-force-begins-transition-into-field-organizational-structure/.

28. Everett C. Dolman, *Astropolitik: Classical Geopolitics in the Space Age* (New York: Frank Cass, 2006); John J. Klein, *Space Warfare: Strategy, Principles, and Policy* (New York: Routledge, 2006); Charles D. Lutes and Peter L. Hays, eds., *Toward a Theory of Spacepower: Selected Essays* (Washington, DC: National Defense University, 2011); James E. Oberg, *Space Power Theory* (Colorado Springs, CO: US Air Force Academy, 1999).

29. Brent Ziarnick, *Developing National Power in Space: A Theoretical Model* (Jefferson, NC: McFarland, 2015).

30. USSF, *Spacepower*, 35.

31. USSF, 36.

32. USAF, 37; "USTRANSCOM Announces the Next Frontier for Logistics: Space," US Transportation Command Public Affairs, October 7, 2020, https://www.ustranscom.mil/cmd/panewsreader.cfm?ID=29ADE173-D927-8E46-7C6CBC100BAD9F71&yr=2020.

33. USSF, *Spacepower*, 38.

34. USSF, 38–39.

35. USSF, 6.

36. USSF, 30.

37. USSF, 34.

38. Joint Chiefs of Staff (JCS), *Joint Publication 3-14: Space Operations; Incorporating Change 1* (Washington, DC: Department of Defense, October 26, 2020), https://www.jcs.mil/Portals/36/Documents/Doctrine/pubs/jp3_14ch1.pdf?ver=qmkgYPyKBvsIZyrnswSMCg%3D%3D, II-2.

39. JCS, II-2–II-3.

40. USSF, *Spacepower*, 40.

41. USSF, 41.

42. USSF, 40–43.

43. *US Air Force Basic Doctrine*, volume 1, publication 3-14, *Counterspace Operations* (Maxwell AFB, AL: Curtis E. LeMay Center for Doctrine Development and Education, August 27, 2018), https://www.doctrine.af.mil/Portals/61/documents/AFDP_3-14/AFDP-3-14-Counterspace-Ops.pdf. Interestingly, the secretary of the Air Force codified "space support to operations" as a function of the USSF, yet USSF doctrine does not directly define the term.

44. *US Air Force Basic Doctrine.*

45. *US Air Force Basic Doctrine.*

46. *US Air Force Basic Doctrine.*

47. *Space Operations*, II-7.

48. Missile Defense Agency, https://www.mda.mil.

49. Steven L. Kwast, "The Urgent Need for a U.S. Space Force," presentation to Hillsdale College, December 5, 2019, YouTube, https://www.youtube.com/watch?v=KsPLmb6gAdw.

50. Ziarnick, *Developing National Power.*

51. Joshua Carlson, *Spacepower Ascendant: Space Development Theory and a New Space Strategy* (self-pub., 2020).

52. Namrata Goswami and Peter A. Garretson, *Scramble for the Skies: The Great Power Competition to Control the Resources of Outer Space* (Lanham, MD: Lexington Books, 2020).

PART III

SYNCHRONIZING OPERATIONS

CHAPTER 10

Special Operations

Jon McPhilamy

Special operations has a unique and specialized role in achieving national security objectives. This chapter details how US Special Operations (USSOCOM) operates and integrates with other combatant commands to bring special operations forces (SOF) to the joint fight. SOF employ a unique command and control (C2) structure. While they are highly capable, SOF are not a "one size fits all" approach to solving military problems. They are optimized for specific problem sets, such as the Russian-sponsored civil war in Ukraine.

ORGANIZATION: THE UNIFORMED SERVICES

The concept of "specially trained and equipped units" dates to World War II.[1] Due to intraservice competition, much of SOF's history consisted of fighting a two-front bureaucratic war for relevance and resources among national security decision-makers and service chiefs.[2] After the Goldwater-Nichols Department of Defense Reorganization Act of 1986 reorganized the military structure (see chapter 4), in 1987 Congress passed the Nunn-Cohen amendment, which established USSOCOM as a "combatant command."[3] From the hard-earned successes in Vietnam to the tragedy of Operation Eagle Claw in 1980, the failed rescue of American hostages in Iran, SOF have always had to fight for legitimacy.[4]

USSOCOM has been at the forefront of the fight against terrorism for the past twenty years.[5] As a result of the terrorist attacks on September 11, 2001, "the nature and urgency of the threat led the Secretary of Defense to designate USSOCOM a 'supported' command with umbrella authority for the military campaign against Al-Qaeda worldwide."[6] Overnight, a small command that had fought for relevance was ordered to not only lead but be supported by the conventional services. The fringe capabilities that were once rejected by the conventional services as unnecessary budgetary drains made USSOCOM "the only military service capable of directly attacking the primary American targets in the war."[7]

Popular culture incorrectly characterizes SOF, often oversimplifying and dramatizing the roles and scope. USSOCOM is a "unified Combatant Command (COCOM) responsible for organizing, training, and equipping all U.S. SOF units."[8] SOF draw forces from all four service branches. USSOCOM is different "in that it performs Service-like functions and has Military Department–like responsibilities and authorities."[9] USSOCOM defense budget appropriations draw from a different funding authority than the conventional services.[10] This different

Table 10.1. SOF Assets

Command	Assets
US Army Special Operations Command (USASOC)	• Special Forces (Green Berets) • Rangers • Special operations airlift • Civil affairs • Psychological operations / MISO
Naval Special Warfare Command (NAVSPECWARCOM)	• Sea, Air, Land (SEALs)
Air Force Special Operations Command (AFSOC)	• Combat controller team • Personnel recovery (CV-22) • SOF ISR (e.g., U-28, MC-12) • SOF airlift (MC-130, C-145, C-146) • SOF strike (e.g., AC-130) • MISO (e.g., Commando Solo)
Marine Forces Special Operations Command (MARSOC)	• Raiders

Note: ISR = intelligence, surveillance, and reconnaissance; MISO = military information support operations; SOF = special operations forces.

"pot of money" enables a unique autonomy and keeps USSOCOM out of the conventional budget battles that can slow down the traditional services.[11] In short, USSOCOM provides specialized activities in the air, land, and sea domains while being responsible for the organization, training, and equipping of the SOF elements across the services.

USSOCOM is a joint command supported by service components, including US Army Special Operations Command (USASOC), Naval Special Warfare Command (NAVSPECWARCOM), US Air Force Special Operations Command (AFSOC), and US Marine Corps Forces Special Operations Command (MARSOC). Table 10.1 summarizes the units that make up the US SOF community.[12]

Joint Special Operations Command (JSOC) is a "sub-unified command charged to study special operations requirements and techniques, ensure interoperability and equipment standardization, plan and conduct special operations exercises and training, and develop joint special operations tactics."[13]

There exists a historical tension between what is known as "white" SOF and "black" SOF that dates back to the inception of the service. Black SOF units are "units (often referred to as special mission units or SMUs) whose existence is not acknowledged and whose operations are not only always classified/clandestine, but often covert, meaning that the operation is not readily observable and can be plausibly denied by the US government."[14] More simply, "black" refers to the unobserved and often unacknowledged existence of these highly specialized units. These units reside under JSOC, and while this command is under USSOCOM, JSOC was founded to "oversee the SMUs and command black SOF activities."[15]

White SOF have historically "focused on unconventional warfare and foreign internal defense [FID]."[16] White SOF consist of "units whose existence is openly acknowledged by the US government even if their operations are almost always classified and clandestine (clandestine meaning that the effect is observable even if it cannot be attributed)."[17] It is important to note that while there is differentiation, the previous decades of sustained combat operations have blurred the mission-specific lines that once separated these two communities. In fact, "SOCOM increasingly emphasizes direct action and counter-terrorism, the 'door-kicking' activities such as commando raids, special reconnaissance, hostage rescue, and terrorist hunting."[18] These activities produce fast and tangible results to battlefield commanders. While black SOF have enjoyed (ironically) more publicity over the past decade, the role white SOF play is no less important. For instance, in "2008, the Department of Defense directive [stated] that irregular warfare is as strategically important as conventional warfare."[19] Even today, there is a growing competition for relevance, funding, and priority within the command.

COMMAND AND CONTROL

USSOCOM integrates into the geographic combat commands (GCCs).[20] This integration is depicted in figure 10.1 below, which illustrates how the "operational requirements and missions may be served most efficiently by multiple SOF organizations."[21]

The joint force special operations component commander (JFSOCC) is "the commander within a unified command, subordinate unified command, or JTF responsible to the establishing commander for making recommendation on the proper employment of assigned, attached, and/or made available for accomplishing such operational missions as may be assigned."[22] The JFSOCC is the equivalent of the JFLCC or JFACC.

USSOCOM can also integrate into the GCCs through theater special operations commands (TSOCs), which "operate with the conventional forces of the Joint Force."[23] The GCCs have operational control of their TSOC.[24] While a TSOC provides a SOF capability to the GCC, there are situations within a theater that require a specialized C2 structure.

A special operations forces joint task force (SOJTF) is a "modular, tailorable, and scalable SOF organization that allows USSOCOM to more efficiently provide integrated, fully capable, and enabled joint SOF to GCCs and subordinate JFCs based on the strategic, operational,

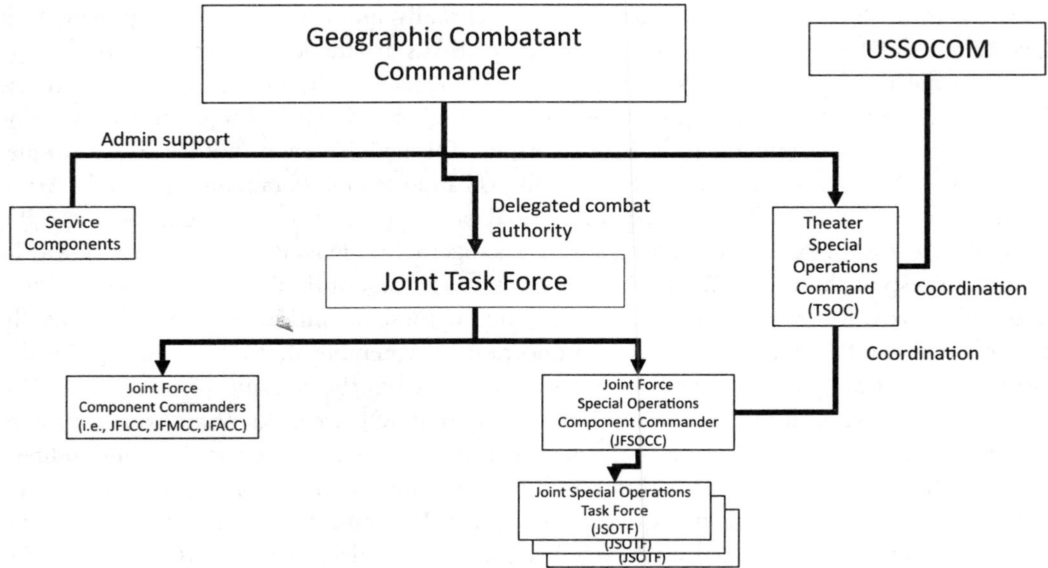

Figure 10.1. Notional SOF Theater Command Structure

Source: Joint Chiefs of Staff, *Joint Publication 3-05: Special Operations* (Washington, DC: Department of Defense, 2014), III-8.

and tactical context."[25] A SOJTF can also act as a JTF headquarters of a JFSOCC.[26] SOJTFs are formed in response to "military engagements, security cooperation, and deterrence operations."[27] Afghanistan provides an example of how a SOJTF would fit into the larger C2 picture. US Central Command (USCENTCOM) has operational control over Afghanistan. The TSOC, Special Operations Command Central Command (SOCCENT), provides the special operation forces to the AOR. SOJTF-Afghanistan provides a "more robust SOF presence and engagement" within the country.[28] The same way the JFACC in Afghanistan would have operational control over all the air assets in country, the JFSOCC (controlling the SJOTF) would have operational control over all the SOF assets in country.

An additional example of the modular nature of the SOJTF is the joint special operations task force (JSOTF). A JSOTF can "be established and deployed from outside the theater into the AOR in coordination with that GCC."[29] JSOTFs typically are "composed of units of two or more SOF Service components formed to unilaterally carry out special operations or activities."[30] A recent example is the JSOTF–Philippines, which was tasked to counterterrorism and to provide stability in the region.[31] TSOCs have flexible and adaptable C2 configurations that can respond with proper size and capability within the assigned geographic region. Unlike the conventional JFACC or JFLCC, USSOCOM has a unique C2 structure that can be customized to provide the GCC the capabilities needed. Modularity is its strength.

CAPABILITIES

When examining capabilities, "SOF are organized into small, flexible, and agile self-contained teams that can operate without support in ambiguous, austere, and dynamic environments for short periods."[32] SOF are unique in that specific activities are designed to facilitate these joint capabilities tailored to a specific end. When thinking about SOF, it is tempting to fall into two traps. First, there is a tendency to conceptually link a particular component to a specific activity. For example, some assume Navy SEALs are the ideal asset to capture a terrorist. As the activity table shows below, no specific unit has exclusive rights over an activity. The second trap is these activities are geographically located. More simply stated, no geographic combatant command privileges a certain SOF activity over another. For example, USCENTCOM does not get only SEALs while US Indo-Pacific Command gets only Army Special Forces (SF). USSOCOM provides global power projection, and there is a specific planning process that goes into putting SOF units together to deliver a specific activity within an area of responsibility (AOR). Table 10.2 gives a brief description of each specific activity. In order to provide a required level of understanding, these definitions are stated specifically as defined in Joint Publication 3-05. It is important to remember that the "asset type" is the most likely (but not exclusive) unit to be tasked to carry out the activity.

While the activities listed in table 10.2 may imply that SOF are jacks-of-all-trades, masters of none, it is more helpful to think of the activities in terms of direct action (DA) and indirect action. It has been argued that within the SOF community there is DA (search and rescue [SR], countering weapons of mass destruction [CWMD], and counterterrorism [CT]) and indirect action (unconventional warfare [UW], FID, civil affairs operations [CAO], and military information support operations [MISO]), with SOF also conducting security force assistance (SFA), hostage rescue and recovery, counterinsurgency (COIN), foreign humanitarian assistance (FHA), and CAO.[33] The direct and indirect action debate stems from the historical competition mentioned previously between black and white SOF. While there is some merit

Table 10.2. SOF Activities

Special operations core activities	Asset type	Description
DA	• SF • Rangers • SEALs • Raiders	• Short strikes. • Small-scale offensive actions. • High-value targets. • Precise or discriminate use of force.
SR	• SF • Rangers • SEALs • Raiders • SOF ISR	• Recon conducted in a clandestine or covert manner to collect or verify information of strategic or operational significance.
CWMD	• SF • Rangers • SEALs • Raiders	• Curtail the development, materials, technologies, and means of delivery of WMDs by state and nonstate actors.
CT	• SF • Rangers • SEALs • Raiders • SOF strike	• Neutralize terrorists and their networks. • Shape and stabilize operational environment to erode capabilities of terrorist organizations.
UW	• SF • Rangers • SEALs • Raiders	• Enable a resistance movement or insurgency to coerce, disrupt, or overthrow a government or occupying power. • Operated through or with an underground, auxiliary, or guerrilla force in a denied area.
FID*	• SF	• Support internal defense (DIME-wide). • Protect against subversion, insurgency, and terrorism.
SFA*	• SF • Raiders	• Support reforming, training, and equipping armed forces. • Can include police, border patrol, coast guard, and customs.
Hostage rescue and recovery	• SEALs • Raiders	• Sensitive crisis-response missions in response to terrorist threats and incidents.
COIN*	• SF • Rangers • SEALs • Raiders • SOF strike	• Comprehensive civilian-military effort to defeat and contain insurgency and address its root causes. • Often includes supporting activities such as DA, SR, CT, FID, SFA, MISO, and CAO.
FHA*	• SF • Rangers • SEALs • Raiders • SOF airlift	• Deliver supplies (e.g., tents, food, water, clothing, sanitation, medical supplies). • Medical care. • Demining operations. • Security to enable supply storage and delivery. • Restore basic infrastructure (communications, transportation, port).
MISO*	• Psyops • MISO	• Convey information to influence emotions, motives, objective reasons, and behaviors.
CAO	• Civil affairs	• Enhance the operational environment. • Identify and mitigate underlying causes of instability within civil society.

*This mission can also be assigned to conventional forces. SOF will typically be assigned when the mission requires a very small footprint, a clandestine operation, or is time-sensitive.

Note: CAO = civil affairs operations; COIN = counterinsurgency; CT = counterterrorism; CWMD = countering weapons of mass destruction; DA = direct action; DIME = diplomatic, informational, military, and economic; FHA = foreign humanitarian assistance; FID = foreign internal defense; ISR = intelligence, surveillance, and reconnaissance; MISO = military information support operations; SF = Special Forces; SFA = security force assistance; SR = special reconnaissance; UW = unconventional warfare; WMD = weapon of mass destruction.

to thinking of these capabilities in terms of direct or indirect, a key question remains: under what circumstances SOF should be used?

EMPLOYMENT

SOF rarely operate in a vacuum. SOF have been a victim of their own success. Operations done with a heightened level of secrecy are most often associated with SOF, and "some policy-makers will always be drawn to the 'quick-fix,' only to discover that it seldom stays fixed for long."[34] SOF provide relief to "budget pressures and exhaustion with large-scale wars [that] now place a premium on small-footprint operations and partnering with allies to provide cost-effective defense."[35] SOF are not designed to replace armies, navies, or air forces on the battlefield.[36] SOF are not a one-size-fits-all approach to achieving military objectives. Arranging these concepts in the correct order produces a flowchart of SOF employment:

Environment → Characteristic of operation → Activity → SOF unit

Given that the previous section has outlined activity and unit, it becomes necessary to identify the specific conditions that lend themselves to favoring SOF over the conventional forces. It is important to take two conditions into consideration: the characteristics of the environment and the characteristics of the operation.

SOF missions take place in "hostile, denied, or politically and/or diplomatically sensitive environments."[37] Where SOF diverge from conventional forces centers on the characteristics of the environment in which they are employed. However, it is difficult to understand the environment without knowing the characteristics of the types of operations SOF conduct. SOF operations typically are characterized by "time-sensitivity, clandestine or covert nature, low visibility, [whether they are conducted] with or through indigenous forces, and a high degree of risk."[38] Even when describing when to use SOF and when to use conventional forces, it is cumbersome to differentiate the *when*, *where*, and *how* aspects of force employment. Afghanistan provides a useful scenario where it would be difficult to imagine an Army Stryker brigade combat team sent in to capture a single terrorist. When thinking about when to use SOF, the footprint, time sensitivity, and requirement for secrecy are critical to take into account.[39] These defining characteristics, taken with the environment SOF operate in, shed light on the type of operations SOF are called to conduct.

In the past, things were difficult for situations that fell outside of the Unified Command Plan (UCP). Previously, the UCP generically stated that "USSOCOM [was] responsible only for synchronizing planning for global operations to combat terrorist networks."[40] TSOCs provided a pathway for the GCCs to synchronize efforts within their AORs. Historically, there was a tendency to rely on SOF to counter any problem with quick and specific results, yet SOF are a fixing agent, not traditionally a deterrent. In 2014, the main limit to USSOCOM was its inability to conduct activities "designed to deter emerging threats."[41] With emerging great-power threats and a move toward countering conventional potential rivals, SOF have been forced to adapt.

APPLICATION: THE UKRAINE CASE

Can SOF be effectively used to counter a great power? Russia has been waging a hybrid war in Eastern Europe, and Ukraine's engagements with Russia represent a challenging battlespace for USSOCOM. SOF have been at the forefront of US military counterterrorism operations over the past decade,[42] yet Russian activities, both overt and covert, signal a troubling narrative using Ukraine as a test bed in attempts to destabilize not only the Ukrainian government but also other North Atlantic Treaty Organization (NATO) allies, specifically the Baltic states. Fighting a war in the shadows permits the Russian government a degree of deniability while achieving political goals.

The implications of the "annexation of Crimea and the subsequent large-scale deployment of Russian troops near the Russo-Ukrainian boarder"[43] rippled throughout the world and created a dangerous international situation. The military engagement known as Operation Russian Spring started on August 11, 2014, with a large-scale invasion by conventional Russian troops into eastern Ukraine.[44] It was described that the "Russian military operation against Ukraine is instructive, having been waged in accordance with the Gerasimov Doctrine of Ambiguous Warfare."[45] The belief that Russia appeared to develop a new approach to warfare is misguided, and "despite the attention the topic has received among Western audiences, Russia's 'newly' launched information war is no different from the disinformation instruments that were widely used by the Soviets against the West in the second half of the 20th century."[46] This type of warfare is known in Russia as "reflexive control."[47]

The Baltic states viewed Russian activities in Ukraine as a shift in strategy, and from the Russian standpoint "Ukraine is supposed to be a close ally or, at best, neutral, [and Russia] considers the involvement of the United States and the European Union to be a direct confrontation to its regional interests."[48] The way Russia prosecuted the campaign in Ukraine raises the question of which forces the US would use. The example of reflexive control occurred when Eastern Europe witnessed Russia use "denial and deception operations to conceal or obfuscate the presence of Russian forces in Ukraine, including sending in 'little green men' in uniforms without insignia."[49] Russia appears to be using a SOF-specific approach (UW) to advance political and territorial agendas in Ukraine.

STARTING POINT

What is USSOCOM's role against state actors? The environment along the Ukrainian eastern front is one of a competition short of conflict, and there is a sense of urgency to develop a new SOF activity. Do SOF provide enough impact to make a difference? Are the critical conditions of time sensitivity, footprint, and environment present? At the very least, Russia knows SOF are training the Ukrainians and would certainly factor this into the calculation about starting a conflict that could involve American troops. It is not a far assessment to conclude that US SOF on the ground, training near the Russian boarder, would be comparable in the Kremlin's eyes to US aircraft flying over the same area.

Some see this conflict not as a black-and-white conventional conflict, as illustrated by a 2015 USSOCOM white paper detailing the concept of the "gray zone," defining it as "competitive interactions among and within state and non-state actors that fall between traditional war and peace duality."[50] While the term is sometimes used to describe the conventional competition that takes place short of war, USSOCOM realizes that when looking over the horizon at future threats, "challenges [continue] to rise above normal, everyday peacetime geo-political competition and are aggressive, perspective-dependent, and ambiguous."[51] Due to political sensitivities, it is likely that SOF will not be called on to conduct direct-action missions inside the "potentially contested" border of a great power, but what can SOF provide to the joint force against a near-peer adversary? While SOF have enjoyed the front-page headlines over the past decade, in the past hundred years of American military involvement, there have been fifty-seven instances of the US military conducting foreign operations.[52] Many of these engagements do not rise to the level of contested interaction with a state actor.

In competitions short of conflict, where SOF would likely be called to operate, adversaries conducting operations such as reflexive control and defined in the West as "combined conventional, irregular, and asymmetric means, including the persistent manipulation of political and ideological conflict"[53] have the potential to create problems. What makes this type of competition so difficult for SOF stems from the nature of required or desired mission sets. SOF and reflexive control are arguably both offensive measures, so one has to ask whether they are compatible to compete against each other or, more simply, how SOF fit in dealing with a great power.

The recent rise of Russian activity in Ukraine highlights the aggressive nature of reflexive control and raises the question of a US response. The reality of this new type of aggression being administered by Russian authorities requires a commitment from not only the uniformed services but also the political will of the United States. Is the US ready and willing to fight a proxy war in Ukraine to thwart subversive Russian goals? Was it right to send SOF into Ukraine? If the answer to both of the questions is yes, the question then becomes whether SOF offer the right capability to defend US interests in the region. After examining the activities of Russian involvement and reflexive control strategy, USSOCOM offers three specific activities to achieve the required objectives in Ukraine: FID, SFA, and MISO.

ACTIVITY 1: FOREIGN INTERNAL DEFENSE

UW operates against the host government, while FID protects the host government. UW is support to "an insurgency or resistance movement [from within] against a nation state."[54] The United States is supporting Ukraine, and therefore the operations fall under FID, which is "support[ing] a nation state against an insurgency, resistance, or terrorists [from the outside]."[55]

FID includes indirect support, direct support (not involving combat operations), and combat operations "to protect against subversion, lawlessness, insurgency, terrorism, and other threats to their internal security and stability."[56] Given the hesitation to directly engage Russia, USSOCOM should focus its efforts on indirect support. This type of support involves training, advising, and assisting the Ukrainian special operations forces to strengthen them. The main effort would involve training their forces to combat the "asymmetrical actions . . . [including] special-operations forces [which seek] to create a permanently operating front through the entire territory of the state."[57] The approach would provide activities to provide defense against Russian aggression and influence.

ACTIVITY 2: SECURITY FORCE ASSISTANCE

The arguably more difficult, but necessary, activity for USSOCOM to facilitate is SFA to help a partner country "defend against internal and transnational terrorist threats to stability [and] to defend against external threats and to perform as part of a multinational force (MNF)."[58] The value of SFA is that it directly targets the third phase of Russia's "new-generation warfare." The third phase calls for "intimidation, deceiving, and bribing government and military officers with the objective of making them abandon their service duties."[59]

To simplify, the Russians have "placed the idea of influence at the very center of their operational planning and used all possible levers to achieve this."[60] SFA is an activity to counter this idea.

Russia will attempt to influence every level of possible resistance in Ukraine, and SFA will strengthen the mechanisms of providing "safety, security, and justice with civilian government oversight."[61] SFA and FID, while separate core activities, should be joined in unison to enable Ukraine to successfully counter Russian influence in the region.[62]

Activity 3: Military Information Support Operations

The final area where USSOCOM should focus its efforts is MISO, which is "planned to convey selected information and indicators to foreign audiences to influence their emotions, motives, objective reasoning, and ultimately the behavior of foreign governments, organizations, groups, and individuals in a manner favorable to the originator's objectives."[63] MISO fights to control the information in and around the battlespace.

MISO is highly needed due to specific tactics used by Russian forces. The National Defense Academy of Latvia's Center for Security and Strategic Research stated that when the Russians invaded Crimea, "their second operational phase consisted of psychological warfare, intimidation, bribery, and internet/media propaganda to undermine resistance, thus [successfully] avoiding the use of firepower."[64] Russia understands the impact of psychological warfare, and SOF must provide a useful activity to Ukraine in an attempt to counter a powerful narrative going on in the country.

Russian military strategists base their theory of new-generation warfare on the concept that the "main battlespace is in the mind and new-generation wars are to be dominated by information and psychological warfare."[65] The need for MISO lies in the concept that once psychological operations commence, it is difficult to regain the advantage without sustaining significant setbacks. USSOCOM understands the importance of MISO and states that "SOF should plan MISO to support all phases of operations and campaigns."[66] Policymakers and military strategists must realize that Russia's involvement in Ukraine is not an Iraq-like insurgency and resist the urge to pull COIN off the shelf and insert into Eastern Europe.

Moving Forward

Whether they label it reflective control, new-generation warfare, or irregular warfare, the Russians seek to gain influence in Ukraine through an "invisible military occupation."[67] Russian aggression in Ukraine represents an interesting shift in strategy that sees nations move toward using small unconventional forces as a means of promoting national objectives. It is fair to argue that most SOF capabilities are inherently offensive, which makes the task of employing them as a preventive capability in Ukraine all the more challenging. The above example also demonstrates how SOF's white mission capabilities are critical in advancing national-level security objectives.

Given that USSOCOM operates in a resource-constrained environment, it is important not to stretch the force too thin by asking this small, specialized force to try to conduct all twelve of its core activities. Rather, a focused approach of providing FID, SFA, and MISO activities to Ukraine can provide enough of a deterrent toward a full-scale Russian invasion. USSOCOM conducting FID, SFA, and MISO would clearly signal to Russia that even asymmetrical warfare will be challenged in Eastern Europe.

CONCLUSION

USSOCOM is a highly specialized functional combatant command made up of elements of all four of the armed services. This chapter has described the makeup of SOF and how such units are employed to the GCCs through TSOCs. TSOCs then are able to employ SOF personnel to utilize their core activities in support of military objectives. The use of SOF is not a one-size-fits-all solution; rather, they should be used to fight in high-risk, time-sensitive, and politically sensitive environments. The case study of SOF in Ukraine illustrates the potential opportunities of using SOF activities to help achieve military objectives as the country pivots toward great-power competition. The true contribution of SOF to the joint force is not with daring missions and attention-grabbing headlines but when they are used in the correct environment to achieve the specifically identified national security–level objectives.

LEARNING REVIEW

- Recall the key capabilities that SOF bring to the joint fight.
- Recall the advantages and disadvantages of using SOF relative to alternative military options.
- Describe the conditions under which SOF would be the preferred focus for a military mission.
- Given a scenario, identify the optimum SOF asset type (and C2 structure) to provide a specific capability.

NOTES

1. Christopher Marsh, James Kiras, and Patricia Blocksome, "Special Operations Research: Out of the Shadows," *Special Operations Journal* 1, no. 1 (2015): 1–6.
2. Susan L. Marquis, *Unconventional Warfare: Rebuilding U.S. Special Operations Forces* (Washington, DC: Brookings Institution, 1997).
3. David Tucker and Christopher Lamb, *United States Special Operations Forces* (New York: Columbia University Press, 2019). Chapter 3 provides a detailed history on the formation of USSOCOM. Chapter 2 provides a detailed history on the formation of USSOCOM.
4. Daniel Byman and Ian A. Merritt, "The New American Way of War: Special Operations Forces in the War on Terrorism," *Washington Quarterly* 41, no. 2 (2018): 79–93.
5. Byman and Merritt.
6. Colin Jackson and Austin Long, "The Fifth Service: The Rise of Special Operations Command," in *U.S. Military Innovation since the Cold War: Creation without Destruction*, ed. Harvey M. Sapolsky, Benjamin H. Friedman, and Brendan Rittenhouse Green (London: Routledge, 2009), 150.
7. Richard K. Betts, *Soldiers, Statesmen, and Cold War Crises* (Cambridge, MA: Harvard University Press, 1977); Jackson and Long, "Fifth Service," 150.
8. Andrew Feickert and Barbara Salazar Torreon, *Defense Primer: Special Operations Forces* (Washington, DC: Congressional Research Service, 2020).
9. Joint Chiefs of Staff (JCS), *Joint Publication 3-05: Special Operations* (hereafter *JP 3-05*) (Washington, DC: Department of Defense, 2014), ix.
10. Jackson and Long, "Fifth Service."
11. Jackson and Long.
12. USSOCOM Office of Communication, *Fact Book: 2021* (MacDill Air Force Base, FL: USSOCOM), https://www.socom.mil/latest-factbook.
13. USSOCOM Office of Communication, I-4.
14. Jackson and Long, "Fifth Service," 139.
15. Jackson and Long, 142.

16. Jackson and Long, 141.
17. Jackson and Long, 139.
18. Harvey M. Sapolsky, Eugene Gholz, and Caitlin Talmadge, *US Defense Politics: The Origins of Security Policy*, 4th ed. (New York: Routledge, 2021), 136; see chap. 6, "Service Politics."
19. Christopher Marsh, James D. Kiras, and Patricia J. Blocksome, eds. *Special Operations: Out of the Shadows* (Boulder, CO: Lynne Rienner, 2020), 68; see chap. 6, "Terrorism and Unconventional Warfare," by Dan Cox.
20. JCS, *JP 3-05*, III-8.
21. JCS, III-7.
22. JCS, III-7.
23. Feickert and Torreon, *Defense Primer*.
24. Andrew Feickert, *U.S. Special Operations Forces (SOF): Background and Issues for Congress* (Washington, DC: Congressional Research Service, 2021).
25. JCS, *JP 3-05*, III-4.
26. JCS, III-5.
27. JCS, III-4.
28. JCS, III-5.
29. JCS, III-8.
30. JCS, III-7.
31. Richard Oakley, "Operation Enduring Freedom Philippines FID Success and the Way Forward," *Special Warfare* 27, no. 1 (January–March 2014): 46–51.
32. JCS, *JP 3-05*, I-5.
33. Eitan Shamir and Eyal Ben-Ari, "The Rise of Special Operations Forces: Generalized Specialization, Boundary Spanning and Military Autonomy," *Journal of Strategic Studies* 41, no. 3 (August 2016): 335–71, 339. Shamir and Ben-Ari provide a useful discussion about direct and indirect missions. Direct missions typically provide immediate strategic, operational, or tactical results. Indirect missions are more postured toward building a specific capability or nonkinetic outcome.
34. David Isenberg, *The Pitfalls of US Covert Operations*, Cato Institute Policy Analysis No. 118 (Washington, DC: Cato Institute, 1989), 11.
35. Linda Robinson, *The Future of US Special Operations Forces* (New York: Council on Foreign Relations, 2013), 3.
36. JCS, *JP 3-05*, I-6.
37. JCS, I-1.
38. JCS, I-1.
39. David Ellis, Charles Black, and Mary Nobles, "Thinking Dangerously: Imagining United States Special Operations Command in the Post-CT World," *Prism: A Journal of the Center for Complex Operations* 6, no. 3 (December 2016): 110–29. Ellis, Black, and Nobles provide a useful discussion about when to use SOF.
40. Feickert, *U.S. Special Operations Forces*.
41. Feickert.
42. Feickert.
43. Igor Sutyagin, *Russian Forces in Ukraine*, RUSI Briefing Paper 9 (London: Royal United Services Institute, 2015), 1.
44. Sutyagin, 1.
45. Sutyagin, 1.
46. Maria Snegovaya, *Putin's Information Warfare in Ukraine: Soviet Origins of Russia's Hybrid Warfare*, Russia Report 1 (Washington, DC: Institute for the Study of War, 2015), 12.
47. Snegovaya, 7.
48. Jānis Bērziņš, *Russia's New Generation Warfare in Ukraine: Implications for Latvian Defense Policy*, Policy Paper no. 2 (Riga: National Defence Academy of Latvia, 2014), 1.
49. Snegovaya, *Putin's Information Warfare*, 7.
50. USSOCOM, "The Gray Zone," https://army.com/sites/army.com/files/Gray%20Zones%20-%20USSOCOM%20White%20Paper%209%20Sep%202015.pdf, 2015, 1.
51. USSOCOM, 1.
52. USSOCOM, 3.

53. US Army Special Operations Command (USASOC), *Counter-Unconventional Warfare*, September 1, 2014, https://info.publicintelligence.net/USASOC-CounterUnconventionalWarfare.pdf, 3. The American definition of hybrid warfare is parallel to the Russian doctrine of reflexive control.

54. JCS, *JP 3-05*, II-2.

55. JCS, II-2.

56. JCS, II-10.

57. USASOC, *Counter-Unconventional Warfare*, 4.

58. JCS, *JP 3-05*, II-11.

59. Bērziņš, *Russia's New Generation Warfare*, 6.

60. Bērziņš, 6.

61. JCS, *JP 3-05*, II-11.

62. While SFA can be conducted by non-SOF units, the environment, politically sensitive nature, and small footprint are sufficient conditions to warrant SOF in this scenario.

63. JCS, *JP 3-05*, II-14.

64. Bērziņš, *Russia's New Generation Warfare*, 4.

65. Bērziņš, 5.

66. JCS, *JP 3-05*, II-14.

67. Bērziņš, *Russia's New Generation Warfare*, 7.

CHAPTER 11

Cyber Power

Judson C. Dressler

The digital age has changed the way the world functions. Cyberspace has become a pervasive element of daily life, with interconnected computers held in the palm of our hand, facilitating everything from ordering a pizza to controlling the world's energy, transportation, financial, and military systems. The open and interconnected nature of the Internet, for the most part unhindered by international law, has invigorated *adversaries* to use the cyber domain to "steal technology, disrupt our government and commerce, challenge our democratic process, and threaten our critical infrastructure."[1] Russia's recent bellicose actions against its neighbors (e.g., Estonia, Georgia, Ukraine) and interference in the 2016 US presidential election demonstrates that the cyber domain is now a significant component of geopolitical competition, which is relevant across all four pillars of national power (i.e., diplomatic, informational, military, and economic).

According to the Department of Defense (DOD) Cyber Strategy, "computers and network technologies underpin US military warfighting superiority by enabling the Joint Force to gain the information advantage, strike at long distance, and exercise global command and control [C2]."[2] This operational dependency places the nation at risk because any disruption would significantly impact the ability of the US to properly function and defend itself.[3] As a result, the DOD has recognized cyberspace as an operational domain on par with land, sea, air, and space. Such a domain-specific focus has enabled the capability to project power in and through cyberspace in support of its forces and to defend US global interests.[4]

The primary objective of this chapter is to familiarize readers with the fundamentals of cyberspace operations, the key capabilities that the cyber domain brings to the joint fight, its advantages and disadvantages relative to alternative military operations, and the conditions under which the cyber domain would be the preferred focus for a military operation.

OPPORTUNITIES AND CHALLENGES TO THE JOINT FORCE'S USE OF CYBERSPACE

Cyberspace is a *man-made domain*. It was created by, and for, people. Started for a community of a few dozen researchers, it was designed to be fast, open, and frictionless—a medium to share thoughts and ideas around the world.[5] Now accessible by over five billion people, it is ever-growing and changing, a dynamic combination of hardware and software, security policies, procedures, and configurations.[6] It is malleable and complex, and at times its structures seem fragile and ephemeral. This makes it different from traditional warfighting domains, as "mountains and oceans are hard to move, but portions of cyberspace can be turned on and off by throwing a switch."[7]

Some examples of the malleability of cyberspace are the cloud environment, mobile devices, and software patches. By design, a network in the cloud can be established, expanded as demand rises, then deprovisioned when no longer needed, and the network disappears. Cell phones and laptops can move around in the physical world and, within a few minutes, join multiple logical cyber networks. A vulnerability used to penetrate an adversary's network can be closed (patched) in an instant with a simple update or administrator's action. If the network has been backed up or fully virtualized, a network administrator can simply reset the system to a previously known safe point, erasing any damage done by the attack. This difference in no way undermines the facts that actions in cyberspace can have serious consequences, even in the physical world (e.g., Stuxnet), and that activities in the physical world can create effects in cyberspace (e.g., destroying physical infrastructure). It does, however, change the way cyber operations are conducted and integrated into joint all-domain operations (JADO) and how traditional concepts such as "superiority" or "battle damage assessment" are conceptualized and performed.[8]

Low Cost of Entry

By the end of the twentieth century, the United States had largely achieved dominance in the land, sea, and air domains by spending heavily on research, development, and acquisition of technologically advanced weapons platforms. Building aircraft carriers, nuclear submarines, stealth fighter aircraft, and main battle tanks are industrial age activities. The information age presents a different range of benefits, costs, and risks.

The most particular aspect of cyber warfare is its low cost of entry. Participation in a cyber conflict often requires only a knowledgeable operator with access to a computer and an Internet connection.[9] However, the costs associated with more complex operations remain substantial. Cyber operations of consequence are not as easy as seen on TV shows such as *NCIS* or as shown in the "Fire Sale" cyberwarfare attack (an overwhelming three-stage systematic attack against the computer infrastructure of a country) in the 2007 movie *Live Free or Die Hard*. Complex operations take years to plan and significant resources to fully understand the environment and operational dependencies as well as the political and economic ramifications of any action.[10]

Unparalleled Rapidity

Actions in cyberspace happen at the speed of light. In wiring the world together, a network built to support the activities of highly trusted actors has been delivered to a far broader and less trustworthy crowd. Although law enforcement and legal systems are constrained by physical borders, adversaries in cyberspace are not. Distance does not matter; the adversary is located just on the other end of the wire. To reiterate, the preparation necessary to successfully carry out a significant attack in cyberspace remains substantial. However, once launched, a cyber operation initiated in one continent can affect a target system on another continent in milliseconds. Once the initial attack succeeds, attackers can quickly (under twenty minutes) spread beyond their initial victim in the network, achieving additional objectives or opening up new vulnerabilities to maintain their access if discovered.[11] The cyber domain's capacity to achieve results nearly instantaneously has no analogues in the land, sea, or air domains.[12]

Anonymity and Difficulties with Attribution

With actions occurring at the speed of cyber, knowing who perpetrated an attack, their motives, and their end goals in real time is essential to determine the correct defensive action or appropriate response.[13] However, cyberspace is different from the traditional domains in that it allows for an unparalleled opportunity for anonymity. Cyber operators can cover their tracks or falsely implicate others by routing their traffic through servers in other countries or launching the attack through a previously compromised machine, potentially located within the United States. Hence, the most difficult aspect of a cyber investigation after an attack is the attribution problem—namely, being able to accurately identify the "cyber-persona or action to a named individual, group, or nation-state, with sufficient confidence and verifiability to hold them accountable."[14] In large-scale combat operations, attribution is easier because the means, motive, and correlated actions in the other domains limit the possible malicious actors. However, in day-to-day competition, the Internet was set up for free and open communication, not accountability. Due to this design, combined with software applications aimed at hiding identity and the content of communications, being able to rapidly and accurately identify attribution will be the greatest challenge in this domain.

Technology and Intelligence Gain or Loss

Another challenge to the cyber domain is the idea of technology and intelligence gain or loss. Operations in cyberspace rely on the exploitation of technological vulnerabilities to achieve the intended outcomes. On the offensive side, the use of a tool may reveal the vulnerability, allowing the adversary to adjust, reducing its effectiveness for future operations. Additionally, cyber tools do not disappear upon use, as an adversary could replicate the capability. Since similar technologies are used across the world, an adversary could change its target and/or payload and use these tools against the United States and its allies. On the defensive side, if a vulnerability is discovered, releasing a patch to the world or even patching the DOD Information Network (DODIN) may limit its usefulness for offensive operations. If an adversary is discovered, actions taken to clear the adversary from the network may also tip an adversary to how it was discovered or hamper the ability of intelligence agencies to further study the adversary's actions to learn more about its capabilities and ultimate objectives.[15]

Private Industry and Public Infrastructure

America's cyber terrain is not completely owned or defended by the US military or any government entity. Power, water, communication, and financial systems are primarily owned and operated by private companies. The defense industrial base, which provides key services, research and development, and production of equipment for the DOD, are also private organizations. Adversaries target private corporations to narrow the gap in global power competition, as proven by the Chinese J-20 stealth fighter copycat of the F-22.[16] If a commercial power plant that provides electricity to a military base comes under significant cyberattack, who is responsible to defend this vital terrain? The roles and responsibilities remain unclear. Therefore, "a nation-state cyber attack on US infrastructure places private companies on the front line."[17] It is vital that federal and private roles are established, aligned, and mutually supportive. The private sector must be included in planning for offensive and defensive cyber operations.[18] This balance of honoring private industry autonomy versus defending the Western way of life is driving a continuing discussion and maturation of US and international policies surrounding military cyberspace operations.

International Norms and the Law of War

In 2011, the Pentagon announced that "when warranted, the United States will respond to hostile acts in cyberspace as we would to any other threat to our country," including "the right to use all necessary means."[19] However, retaliation in cyberspace becomes problematic when considering the law of armed conflict (LOAC), particularly its tenets of proportionality and discrimination.[20] Due to the interconnectedness of cyberspace, a small attack of benign intent can have enormous consequences. On the opposite side, a well-planned and organized attack with aggressive intent can have little to no consequences if poorly executed or properly defended. Without attribution and determination of motive, it is hard to determine the best course of action, especially responding to bits with bombs.[21] The tenet of discrimination becomes more difficult with civilian ownership of cyber terrain, and its interconnected nature increases the risk of cascading effects. NATO's *Tallinn Manual* (2013) and *Tallinn Manual 2.0* (2017) discuss the applicability of international humanitarian law and the concepts of a just war to cyber conflicts. It identified thresholds based on a cyberattack's kinetic consequences. By its definition, however, Russian attacks against Estonia, Georgia, and Ukraine would not have been considered cyberattacks because physical harm or destruction did not occur and the systems (and power in Ukraine) were reestablished after the attack was over.[22] The United States has not defined thresholds for a kinetic response either, both to avoid escalation and to retain the flexibility this uncertainty currently provides. However, adversaries are using cyberspace to hurt the West without facing retaliation, conducting lower-level attacks, with most individual attacks not rising to the level of using security agencies for countering.[23]

Discrimination can be problematic when nonstate actors use infrastructure associated with a country. For example, as part of Operation Glowing Symphony in 2016, the United States disrupted and deleted propaganda of the Islamic State of Iraq and Syria (ISIS), which was hosted on servers around the world belonging to commercial entities. While the precision operation focused solely on disrupting the ISIS propaganda, the operation caused some political friction with allies and partner nations.[24]

Deterrence

Deterrence is the act of discouraging an action or event by instilling doubt or fear of the consequences in the mind of an adversary's decision-maker. To deter effectively, the defender needs to know who is being deterred, what they want of value, and what they hold of value. The goal of deterrence is to reduce the perceived benefit or raise the perceived cost of the action(s) that is not desired. The two *means* to deter an adversary are deterrence by denial and deterrence by cost imposition.[25] The best way of denying is through good cyber hygiene, defenses, and resilience. Strong defenses can convince an adversary that the attack would most likely fail and is not worth implementing. Due to the ubiquity of cyberspace and the ease of compromise through the multiple avenues, the offense generally has the advantage, and strong defenses (e.g., firewalls, intrusion detection systems) get you only so far. The threat of retaliation or cost imposition requires credibility and will. Attribution is difficult, and a show of force in cyberspace reduces the tool's effectiveness for future operations. It is difficult to assess whether political leadership will respond to a cyberattack, at what threshold, and with what type of response (kinetic versus nonkinetic).[26] Uncertainty in these areas makes deterrence in cyberspace difficult, and adversaries leverage and exploit this ambiguity.[27]

CYBERSPACE LAYER MODEL

It is difficult to see, interact with, and comprehend the intangible, yet very real, cyberspace environment. Cyberspace can be described in terms of three interrelated layers: physical network, logical network, and cyber persona. Each layer is important to the discussion of how cyberspace operations are planned, conducted, and assessed.

Physical-Network Layer

The physical-network layer includes hardware components of the information technology (IT) devices and infrastructure that reside in the physical world and have a geographic location. When planning an operation, your information (i.e., code, attack, etc.) will need to traverse the physical mediums of the network infrastructure and the target. While national boundaries can easily be crossed in cyberspace, sovereign legal frameworks still exist.[28] Thus, cyberspace comprises physical components that are owned by governments or private entities, and each is typically capable of controlling and restricting cyber access, not to mention collecting data of activities on their components.[29]

Logical-Network Layer

The logical-network layer describes how elements of the network are related to one another and configured to operate on top of the physical layer. For instance, the Google search engine, which is hosted on multiple servers around the globe, can be accessed by a single uniform resource locator (URL) in a browser.[30] Another example is when utilizing a virtual private network (VPN) program to "dial" into the network. You could be physically located anywhere in the world, but logically your machine and its data look to be coming from the physical location of that specific VPN network. A physical computer can initiate multiple virtual machines running different operating systems and presenting multiple unique Internet protocol (IP) addresses from a single network or multiple ones.

All of these fall into the category of cloud computing. The physical masses of servers in strategic locations around the globe work together to store data and provide services to users without any obvious limits or alignment to their physical location. To conduct operations in cyberspace, planners may know one logical path to a target system or network without knowing its geographic location at all. Cyberspace is a global domain where anyone, even adversaries, can be "logical" neighbors.

Cyber-Persona Layer

This layer consists of the actors and their accounts, whether human or automated, and how they are related. A single person can have multiple cyber personas (e.g., work and personal email addresses), and multiple people can use a single cyber persona (e.g., a family sharing a Netflix username and password). Anyone is capable of creating and maintaining multiple cyber personas.[31] The use of cyber personas complicates attribution. Linking disparate, false, or duplicative personas, which are not linked to a single physical form or location, requires significant intelligence collection and analysis capabilities of digital fingerprinting to enable effective targeting or to hold an entity accountable. Like the logical layer, details in the cyber-persona layer can change quickly, causing additional uncertainty.[32]

CYBERSPACE AS A WARFIGHTING DOMAIN

Cyberspace is an emerging and ill-defined warfighting domain. The National Cyber Strategy calls out China, Russia, North Korea, and Iran for their persistent cyber campaigns as a long-term risk to US and allied interests. It tasks the DOD to take action in day-to-day competition to preserve strategic advantages, to defend forward into adversary networks, to collaborate between agencies, industry, and international partners, and to achieve and utilize offensive capabilities across the full spectrum of conflict.[33] Such a whole-of-society approach to cyber defense and offense is necessary for success as adversaries leverage every vulnerability to weaken the government, the military, and the private sector.[34]

US CYBER COMMAND AND THE CYBER MISSION FORCE

US Cyber Command (USCYBERCOM) was stood up in 2008 as a subunified command under US Strategic Command (USSTRATCOM) but with the commander of USCYBERCOM also "dual-hatted" as director of the National Security Agency (NSA). In 2018, USCYBERCOM was elevated to a functional combatant command. USCYBERCOM controls 133 teams across the services to form the Cyber Mission Force (CMF), which includes the Cyber National Mission Force (CNMF), the Cyber Protection Force (CPF), and the Cyber Combat Mission Force (CCMF).[35]

The CNMF conducts internal defense and response actions to defeat threats to the DODIN and friendly cyberspace.[36] The CPF (conducted by operational components at DODIN headquarters, combatant commands, or service cyber components) defends DODIN terrain.[37] The CCMF projects power in and through offensive cyberspace operations.[38]

WHAT ARE CYBERSPACE OPERATIONS?

Cyberspace operations are "the employment of cyberspace capabilities where the primary purpose is to achieve objectives in or through cyberspace."[39] There are four missions: offensive cyberspace operations (OCO), defensive cyberspace operations (DCO), DODIN operations (DODIN ops), and cyber intelligence, surveillance, and reconnaissance (CISR).

OCO missions are the projection of power in and through foreign cyberspace, with actions. These actions are conducted to deny, degrade, disrupt, destroy, or manipulate adversary information networks. OCO actions may exclusively target an adversary's cyberspace assets or seek to create first- or second-order effects in cyberspace to initiate effects in the physical domains. OCO missions may rise to the level of use of force, causing the physical damage or destruction of adversary systems. Therefore, each mission must be fully coordinated and issued through a military order, with the scope, rules of engagement, and measurable objectives considered by the commander and his or her legal counsel and approved at the appropriate level. Two great examples of offensive cyberspace operations include the use of the Stuxnet worm to degrade Iran's nuclear capability and Israel's cyberattack on Syria's air-defense radar in order to launch an airstrike against Syria's nuclear reactor (see learning box 11.1).[40]

DCO defends against malicious cyber threats. These actions include hunting for adversary presence, clearing an adversary from a network, hardening a network or computer system based on intelligence, and assessing a network or computer system to ensure it is hardened against specific capabilities. DCO missions often take place on the DODIN. There are two situations when DCO actions do not take place on DODIN. One is the employment of DCO forces on a hunt-forward mission to complete a forensic examination of a compromised allied computer network. This process tries to determine the tools, techniques, and procedures used by the adversary and then publish this information to the world. This outs the adversary's capability, allowing nations to better secure their systems, and also limits its future capabilities. Another example of off-DODIN operations is DCO response actions. These are cyberspace actions taken to "defend forward to disrupt malicious cyber activity at its source, including activity that falls below the level of armed conflict."[41] This mission set includes analyzing intelligence to understand adversary intent and capabilities and to limit their effectiveness.

DODIN ops build, operate, secure, and extend the network. Build and extend can be the laying of long-haul communication lines or setting up a tactical network by a deployed force to extend a capability. Security actions are part of DODIN ops as well. However, these actions are network focused and threat agnostic. An example would be proactively patching systems to address a vulnerability on the network. This is not to say actions to secure a network are not threat informed, but their goal is to reduce risk to the supported mission by mitigating vulnerabilities in a prioritized manner.[42]

LEARNING BOX 11.1. EXAMPLES OF OFFENSIVE CYBERSPACE OPERATIONS

Stuxnet

Stuxnet is a computer worm uncovered in 2010 that managed to take over physical infrastructure and disrupt Iranian nuclear ambitions. Exploiting four previously unknown flaws, the worm spread across the Internet, targeting computers running Microsoft Windows, then sought out Siemens software designed to program industrial control systems that operate computers, and then finally compromised the programmable logic units within the control systems themselves. Once this access was achieved, Stuxnet was able to speed up and slow down centrifuges used for separating nuclear material, until they tore themselves apart, while hiding these actions from the human operators at the plant. While the authors of Stuxnet have not been officially identified, its intent and sophistication have led experts to believe it was created by the United States and Israel.

Israel's Attack on Syrian Air Defenses

As part of Operation Outside the Box in 2007, Israel launched a cyberattack to enable an air strike against a strategic target: a Syrian nuclear facility. The attack utilized an advanced electronically scanned array (AESA) airborne radar to invade Syrian missile-defense system networks, monitor enemy sensors, and take control of the system to manipulate data streams introducing false targets. This enabled the hiding of Israeli aircraft that attacked Syria's nuclear facility.

CISR is an intelligence function that operates under Title 50 of the US Code to gather information from adversary networks to support military planning. CISR informs decision-makers and supports the target development process in OCO, DCO, and DODIN ops as well as other warfighting domains.

PLANNING A CYBER OPERATION

Planners must efficiently use limited cyberspace assets to effectively integrate cyberspace capabilities. Planners must identify and secure mission-critical cyberspace, understand adversary intent and capability, and coordinate access to key cyber terrain to enable maneuver in, from, and through cyberspace.

For operations in adversary cyberspace (CISR, OCO, or DCO response actions), combatant commanders, national agencies, and supporting commands submit target-development nominations for inclusion on the joint targeting list. If the targets are selected, coordination and synchronization must occur to pair operational requirements with cyberspace capabilities. Internal cyber missions (DCO or DODIN ops) receive input from the combatant commands and prioritize these inputs based on the overall risk to the mission. This includes the criticality of the cyber terrain to the mission, the vulnerability of the terrain to an adversary attack, and the threat (intent and capability) of an adversary to take advantage of a vulnerability present to affect that mission.

Planning a cyberspace operation takes time, people, and resources. Planners must match apportioned assets and capabilities with the target and effect desired. The tasked cyber operators must develop an understanding of the environment to learn unique internal attributes of the targeted system and its dependencies as well as possibly acquire a copy of the software being targeted for analysis. Intelligence professionals provide an in-depth assessment of the potential threats, including their characteristics (capabilities, intent, targeting) and behaviors (tactics, techniques, procedures, tools). This threat assessment allows cyber operators to anticipate an adversary to tailor defensive capabilities, enhance detection capabilities, and improve the ability to deliver operational effects.

Once an understanding of the environment is established, operators work to gain access to the terrain, develop a capability (weapon/payload) to achieve the objective, and gain the appropriate level of approval based on the authorities. Finally, in full coordination with operations in the other domains and at the timing and tempo desired, the operators execute the operation. This process illustrates that cyberspace operations are not what they seem in movies. Capability development can be extremely challenging and, once it has been initiated, continuous monitoring is required to ensure adversary maintenance efforts have not nullified its effects.[43]

CONCLUSION: A PREFERRED FOCUS ON CYBER?

Cyberspace operations are a potentially powerful way to achieve a wide variety of political, informational, military, and economic objectives. For DCO and DODIN, the United States is engaged in constant and daily competition. Adversaries use cyberattacks against military and private organizations to steal intellectual property, raise funds, and reduce the US overmatch in the traditional warfighting domains. To project power, the target must be present in cyberspace and vulnerable to a cyberattack. Many countries are minimally connected, such as North Korea, where a cyberattack would have a negligible effect or go completely unnoticed.[44]

Cyberspace's anonymity offers many advantages and can be used to conduct CISR and information warfare to achieve objectives across all pillars of US national power.[45] Cyberspace's pervasiveness, speed, and lack of accountability offer state and nonstate actors a degree of plausible deniability.[46] There is no need to incur the cost or political risk of transporting equipment or deploying troops. Cyberspace operations can be covert, running attacks through compromised cyber terrain that present investigators with legal complications. The speed of quick cyber tools, tactics, and procedures (TTPs) evolve often because cyber defenses, legislation, and law enforcement lag behind.[47] With this in mind, false flag operations are commonplace, disguising the actual source of responsibility to pin the blame on another entity. Even if the attacker's identity is discovered, many cyberattacks are measures short of war, and any response must account for proportionality and military distinction concerns.

In large-scale operations, offensive cyber operations are extremely effective in a combined-force environment synchronized through JADO with conventional warfare assets. Covertness allows cyber operators to maintain a foothold in a target's network for a long duration and plant persistence mechanisms, which, if properly maintained, could remain untouched and dormant for years. At the opening of conflict, the attack could be launched to disrupt the adversary's C2 infrastructure, communications capabilities, and cause confusion in the area (e.g., power outages, degraded Internet). However, once noticed, the defender will quickly move to remedy the network or shut down the system.[48] The lack of permanence of a cyberattack may be the desired effect. However, if not, the short-term effects of a cyberattack in parallel with a strategic bombing campaign could have devastating operational impacts on an adversary.

LEARNING REVIEW

- What are the key capabilities that cyber brings to the joint fight?
- Describe the advantages and disadvantages of cyber operations relative to alternative military options.
- Under what conditions would cyber warfare be the preferred focus for a military mission?

NOTES

1. Joint Chiefs of Staff (JCS), *Joint Publication 3-12: Cyberspace Operations* (hereafter *JP 3-12*) (Washington, DC: Department of Defense [DOD], 2018).
2. JCS.
3. *Summary of the 2019 National Defense Strategy of the United States of America* (Washington, DC: DOD, 2018).
4. DOD, "Summary: Department of Defense Cyber Strategy," 2018, https://media.defense.gov/2018/Sep/18/2002041658/-1/-1/1/CYBER_STRATEGY_SUMMARY_FINAL.PDF.
5. Judson Dressler, "Analyzing the Use of Cyber in Warfare at the Strategic, Operational, and Tactical Levels" (PhD diss., Rice University, 2015).
6. "Usage and Population Statistics," Internet World Stats, accessed February 18, 2021, https://www.internetworldstats.com/stats.htm.
7. Joseph S. Nye, "Nuclear Lessons for Cyber Security?," *Strategic Studies Quarterly* 5, no. 4 (2011): 18–38.
8. Dressler, "Analyzing the Use of Cyber."
9. Dressler.

10. *Annex 3-0: Operations and Planning* (Maxwell Air Force Base, AL: Curtis E. LeMay Center for Doctrine Development and Education, 2012); DOD, "Summary."

11. Andy Greenberg, "Russian Hackers Go from Foothold to Full-On Breach in 19 Minutes," *Wired*, February 19, 2019.

12. Isaac R. Porche III, "Fighting and Winning the Undeclared Cyber War," RAND Blog, June 24, 2019, https://www.rand.org/blog/2019/06/fighting-and-winning-the-undeclared-cyber-war.html.

13. Dressler, "Analyzing the Use of Cyber."

14. JCS, *JP 3-12*, I-12.

15. JCS, I-12.

16. Alex Hollings, "Counterfeit Air Power: Meet China's Copycat Air Force," *Popular Mechanics*, September 19, 2018.

17. President's National Infrastructure Advisory Council, "Securing Cyber Assets: Addressing Urgent Cyber Threats to Critical Infrastructure," 2017, https://www.cisa.gov/sites/default/files/publications/niac-securing-cyber-assets-final-report-508.pdf.

18. Herbert S. Lin, "Defining Self-Defense for the Private Sector in Cyberspace," *World Politics Review*, February 6, 2013, https://www.worldpoliticsreview.com/articles/12694/defining-self-defense-for-the-private-sector-in-cyberspace#.

19. David Alexander, "U.S. Reserves Right to Meet Cyber Attack with Force," Reuters, November 15, 2011.

20. Lawrence J. Cavaiola, David C. Gompert, and Martin Libicki, "Cyber House Rules: On War, Retaliation and Escalation," *Survival* 57, no. 1 (2015): 81–104.

21. Eric A. Heinze and Rhiannon Neilsen, "Limited Force and the Return of Reprisals in the Law of Armed Conflict," *Ethics and International Affairs* 34, no. 2 (2020): 175–88.

22. Michael Schmitt, *Tallinn Manual on the International Law Applicable to Cyber Warfare* (Cambridge: Cambridge University Press, 2013).

23. JCS, *JP 3-12*.

24. Dina Temple-Raston, "How the U.S. Hacked ISIS," National Public Radio, September 26, 2019, https://www.npr.org/2019/09/26/763545811/how-the-u-s-hacked-isis.

25. Temple-Raston.

26. Edward Geist, "Deterrence Stability in the Cyber Age," *Strategic Studies Quarterly* 9, no. 4 (2015): 44–62; Christopher Paul and Rand Waltzman, "How the Pentagon Should Deter Cyber Attacks," RAND Blog, January 20, 2018, https://www.rand.org/blog/2018/01/how-the-pentagon-should-deter-cyber-attacks.html.

27. Uri Tor, "'Cumulative Deterrence' as a New Paradigm for Cyber Deterrence," *Journal of Strategic Studies* (2017): 92–117.

28. Schmitt, *Tallinn Manual*; Lin, "Defining Self-Defense."

29. JCS, *JP 3-12*.

30. JCS.

31. JCS.

32. Dressler, "Analyzing the Use of Cyber"; Geist, "Deterrence Stability"; Martin Libicki, *Cyberdeterrence and Cyberwar* (Santa Monica, CA: RAND Corp., 2009).

33. JCS, *JP 3-12*.

34. Alexander Klimburg, "Mobilising Cyber Power," *Survival* 53, no. 1 (2011): 41–60.

35. Klimburg, 41–60.

36. JCS, *JP 3-12*.

37. JCS.

38. JCS.

39. JCS.

40. Iain Thomson, "Snowden: US and Israel Did Create Stuxnet Attack Code," *The Register* 8 (July 2013); Sharon Weinberger, "How Israel Spoofed Syria's Air Defense System," *Wired*, October 4, 2007.

41. DOD, "Summary."

42. DOD.

43. DOD.

44. Eric Lundbohm, "Understanding Nation-State Attacks," *Network Security* (2017): 5–8.

45. Jahara Matisek and Buddhika Jayamaha, *Old and New Battlespaces* (Boulder, CO: Lynne Rienner, 2021).

46. Kevin Townsend, "The Increasing Effect of Geopolitics on Cybersecurity," Security Week, October 3, 2017, https://www.securityweek.com/increasing-effect-geopolitics-cybersecurity.

47. Kenneth Geers, Darien Kindlund, Ned Moran, and Rob Rachwald, *World War C: Understanding Nation-State Motives behind Today's Advanced Cyber Attacks* (Milpitas, CA: FireEye, 2014), https://www.fireeye.com/content/dam/fireeye-www/global/en/current-threats/pdfs/fireeye-wwc-report.pdf.

48. Dressler, "Analyzing the Use of Cyber."

CHAPTER 12

Intelligence, ISR, and Strategy

Michael Fowler

The purpose of intelligence is to reduce uncertainty for a decision-maker. Of course, some level of uncertainty is always present. The fog of war prevents a decision-maker from being omniscient, particularly when dealing with human behavior. Intelligence reduces uncertainty by estimating enemy, neutral, and partner capability and intent to act and react. In this manner, intelligence shapes the decision-maker's risk assessment.

Intelligence supports decision-makers at all levels of war across all the domains of the joint fight, resulting in a wide variety of product types. Intelligence, surveillance, and reconnaissance (ISR) is a collection of *ways* and *means* to achieve the desired *end* of intelligence, a decision. It may be a decision to do something or nothing, a decision on what to effect, or a decision on the most effective or efficient means and/or ways to achieve an effect. Intelligence drives the effects-based approach to operations.[1] Contemporary military strategy is highly dependent on good intelligence, which conducts two key functions to support the joint fight: forecasting enemy actions and targeting.

FORECASTING AND TARGETING

Intelligence estimates enemy behavior—a critical step in providing attack warning, adversary and neutral courses of action, and responses to friendly courses of action. Intelligence collects on intent, objectives, locations, and capabilities to provide warning of impending or actual change in enemy capabilities, intent, or action, which drives the decision to execute (or create) a branch plan. Ideally, sufficient warning is provided to mitigate surprise attacks or crises. Of course, completely avoiding surprise is unlikely because irregular warfare and "special operations can succeed quite often despite the loss or absence of strategic surprise. . . . They succeed because of the maintenance of tactical surprise."[2]

Forecasting involves calculating opportunity costs and risk, which are "brewed from an equal dose of two ingredients—probabilities and consequences."[3] Theoretically, every potential friendly and enemy action can be plotted graphically to depict the probability of success and the estimated impact. In practice, planners often ask intelligence to focus on the two extremes: highest probability and highest impact. These are commonly referred to as the most likely and most dangerous courses of action (COAs). Once a forecast is made, collection

LEARNING BOX 12.1. CONCEPTS OF INTELLIGENCE AND INTELLIGENCE FAILURE

Intelligence, colloquially known as intel, has multiple meanings. Depending on the context, intel can refer to a process, a product, or an organization. "Go get me some intel" is a request for an intel product. Often this request is amplified as "actionable intel" referring to a product that will result in an operational decision. "Go talk to intel"—in this case, intel is the division or organization that disseminates products to the decision-maker. For the organization to create intel products, it does intel—the process. The process uses *information to reduce uncertainty for a decision-maker.*[a]

The term "intelligence failure" is a false dichotomy. "Failure" implies that there is an expectation of perfection—that uncertainty for the decision-maker can be reduced to zero. In practice, this zero-defect mentality is not achievable in any human process over the long term. Intelligence failures at the strategic level capture the headlines and the attention of the academic literature. Yet intelligence failures occur at the operational and tactical level on a daily basis: failure to detect an improvised explosive device (IED) or an ambush, failure to locate a terrorist leader, failure to track the movements of a hostage.

Intelligence failures can be categorized into three types: surprise attack (e.g., Pearl Harbor, 9/11), major event (e.g., collapse of the Soviet Union, the Arab Spring), and poor understanding (e.g., underestimation of the impact of Arab Spring on Egypt).[b] Tactical surprise is extremely common: many IED attacks against convoys in Afghanistan achieved tactical surprise. Perhaps the biggest surprise is not that intelligence failure occurs but that the complex process functions correctly most of the time. The five-phase process of the intelligence cycle has ample opportunity for human and technical error resulting in the "inability of one or more parts of the intelligence process—collection, evaluation and analysis, production, dissemination—to produce timely, accurate intelligence" products.[c]

a. See Thomas Fingar, *Reducing Uncertainty: Intelligence Analysis and National Security* (Stanford, CA: Stanford University Press, 2011); Kristan J. Wheaton and Michael T. Beerbower, "Toward a New Definition of Intelligence," *Stanford Law and Policy Review* 17, no. 1 (2006); and Richard K. Betts, "Analysis, War, and Decision: Why Intelligence Failures Are Inevitable," *World Politics* 31, no. 1 (October 1978). For other definitions of intelligence, see Michael Warner, "Wanted: A Definition of Intelligence," *Studies in Intelligence* 46, no. 3 (2002).

b. Erik Dahl, *Intelligence and Surprise Attack* (Washington, DC: Georgetown University Press, 2013).

c. Dahl, 7.

assets can be dedicated to monitor to determine if the enemy is deviating from forecast activities.

Intelligence monitors for changes in risk to forces or risk to mission, driving the decision to either accept the risk or implement modified procedures to mitigate the various types of risk. Intelligence estimates of the adversary's military capability and capacity inform risk to forces—the probability of friendly force casualties. Intelligence estimates of adversary courses of action and responses to friendly actions inform risk to mission—the probability that friendly forces will achieve the desired effect and mitigate unintended secondary effects. Finally, intelligence estimates of neutral and partner reactions inform political risk and the probability of unintended secondary effects in relations with third parties or countries.

Targeting and forecasting are interdependent processes. Intelligence determines relationships between targets; locates, tracks, and identifies targets; and assesses impacts on targets and enemy systems. At the operational level, intelligence informs the decision-maker of interrelationships in systems, suggesting optimum targets (i.e., the enemy centers of gravity [COGs]) and likely enemy targeting priorities (i.e., friendly COGs) to achieve their strategy (see chapter 21). Intelligence can support COG identification through analysis of enemy strengths, weaknesses, opportunities, and threats (SWOT analysis). Strengths and weaknesses are internal to the organization, shaping the means available to achieve strategic objectives. Organizations will seek to maintain their strengths and mitigate their weaknesses, making them both potential targets. External opportunities and threats shape national security interests and objectives. Combined, this provides potential courses of action for combined effects for each key actor being analyzed.

A key part of any campaign is assessing whether or not military power is being used effectively and efficiently. Military intelligence assesses the structural, physical, and system effects of engagements. These tactical assessments can be aggregated to assist in making operational and strategic assessments, making intelligence the primary measurement tool for measures of performance (MOPs) and measures of effect (MOE) (see chapter 22). Monitoring MOEs is key to the decision to implement a sequel plan transitioning to the next operational phase or, potentially, to redesign the current phase to improve its effectiveness.

The Intelligence Process

The intelligence process is linear in the sense that it describes the evolution of an intelligence product from the planning stage to the final decision-maker. The US intelligence community (IC) refers to the process as PCPAD: planning, collection, processing, analysis, and dissemination. Despite the linearity of the process, all phases of the cycle operate simultaneously (though not necessarily on the same product). The IC acts as a complex, adaptive system: personnel routinely interact across the cycle to optimize their portion of the process and the resulting final product. The process is cyclical or iterative: no intelligence product is ever the "final answer." Like the daily news cycle, the IC continues to react to the changing world to fine-tune its products and estimates.

The intelligence organization performs like a behind-the-scenes stage crew: a symphony of various intelligence organizations and assets working together across a spectrum of intelligence functions: planning, collecting, processing, analyzing, and disseminating. Like a symphony, each part of the intelligence process needs to do its part well and in synchronization with the other parts. Since intelligence is a team effort and is only one of several factors that impact operational success, it can be perceived as a thankless job. Sometimes bad operational decisions are made despite good intelligence.[4] Some decision-makers get bogged down in trying to eliminate all uncertainty and dissipate the fog of war.[5] Others push for oversimplification to eliminate ambiguity.[6] Even when good intelligence leads to operational success, the secretive nature of the business means that recognition may be limited to high-profile successes such as the capture of Saddam Hussein and the killing of Osama bin Laden.

For military operations, every intelligence product (e.g., a report or a briefing) begins as a requirement to support an ongoing operation or a contingency plan for a future operation. Ideally, every part of the intelligence process is designed to inform decision-makers about their strategy and key operational decision points. If key decision points and the supporting critical intelligence requirements are not adequately identified, the intelligence will lack structure and leave the warfighter wondering as to its relevance. An intelligence-operations disconnect can create a perceived "self-licking ice cream cone" in which intelligence is created for the sake of intelligence.

To properly inform the warfighter, decision points must specifically identify the anticipated change to monitor and the associated indicators of that change. The decision points and associated indicators drive the priorities and focus of the collection assets. Each combatant commander, joint task force commander, and component commander has their own set of decisions driving them to have a unique, though related, set of prioritized intelligence requirements (PIRs).

No decision-maker ever has enough intelligence to sufficiently monitor all issues simultaneously. For the commander to reassign resources to a new mission requires an intelligence signal significant enough to change the operational priorities. The intelligence process is a zero-sum game. Putting resources into a mission that might happen often takes away from a mission that is already occurring. The commander accepts the inherent risks associated with the decision to reassign intelligence resources. Accepting risk is a factor of competing priorities, probabilities, and the potential consequences.

ISR Ways and Methods

ISR collection capabilities can be loosely grouped into five categories: geospatial intelligence (GEOINT), signals intelligence (SIGINT), measurement and signatures intelligence (MASINT), human intelligence (HUMINT), and open-source intelligence (OSINT). In the ends-ways-means construct, these five types of collection represent the *ways* of ISR.

GEOINT collection primarily focuses on intelligence derived from pictures, or imagery intelligence (IMINT). Electro-optical, infrared, and radar sensors can be used to create traditional still-picture imagery and full-motion video (FMV). Using datalinks, fighter aircraft can leverage these same sensors to provide nontraditional ISR (NTISR). Ground moving-target indicator (GMTI) and airborne moving-target indicator (AMTI) collection rely on radar images to track movement.

GEOINT is ideal for locating and identifying objects, developing terrain-elevation data, and providing change detection including bomb-damage assessments. FMV is relied on to provide pattern of life (activities over time) of an individual or a location. Any country can create its own GEOINT capability using a small aircraft and a camera. Plus, commercial satellites can also provide photos, even infrared and panchromatic images.[7] On the downside, GEOINT is particularly susceptible to deception and camouflage and is severely impacted by weather, though radar does provide some all-weather capability.

SIGINT involves the interception of any type of signal, primarily communications and radar. Once intercepted, the message often requires decryption. Two of the most famous cases are from World War II: the Ultra program to decipher German messages and the Magic program to decipher Japanese communications. Even without decryption, SIGINT can assist in direction finding for geolocation and pattern analysis of military units, radars, and air-defense systems. Communications intercepts are extremely useful at monitoring intent. Adversaries can try to mitigate this by using written messages and intermittent use of communications and radars.

MASINT is a collection of capabilities that is less easy to categorize. MASINT is best known for detailed analysis of ballistic missiles and nuclear explosions. The category includes an eclectic mix of acoustic (e.g., active and passive sonar), seismic, magnetic, materials-sampling (detection of biological and chemical warfare agents), and radionuclide (e.g., Geiger counter) sensors. Navies are particularly fond of using acoustic and magnetic sensors to detect surface vessels and submarines.

In some cases, MASINT applies advanced methodological processes to traditional IMINT and SIGINT sensors. In-depth analysis of IMINT and/or SIGINT sensor-data facilitates target classification by a type of fingerprinting: "a repeatable representation of data from a given collection phenomenology that is characteristic, sometimes uniquely so, of a specific target or class of targets."[8] IMINT examples include overhead persistent infrared (OPIR) to provide missile-launch detection and multispectral imagery to detect crop failures, desertification, and camouflage. SIGINT tools include the extremely rare RC-135U Combat Sent aircraft, which is designed for extensive analysis of radar signals, and the RC-135S aircraft, which studies ballistic missile events using a combination of optical and electronic sensors.

HUMINT is the oldest of the intelligence disciplines. It has the potential to be conducted cheaply with little technology. It relies on people getting information through "direct observation, elicitation from friendly civilians, debriefing of recruited assets and interrogation of enemy personnel."[9] While it can involve the taking of photos, gathering of documents, or placement of sensors, HUMINT primarily involves people talking to people such as diplomats, travelers, defectors, or prisoners. HUMINT can be done overtly through embassies and military attachés and by walking the beat to talk to the local population. Covert HUMINT can be used to access more difficult targets but entails high risk to forces and significant political risk if detected.

HUMINT is useful for gaining insights into intentions, perceptions, and future capabilities, as well as local politics and economic conditions. HUMINT can be exciting but can be unreliable because sources may be motivated to embellish in exchange for cash, better treatment while incarcerated, or in order to shape military action. In an effort to protect sources, HUMINT reliability judgments are often far more ambiguous than those of other intelligence disciplines.

HUMINT is also the least timely of the intelligence disciplines. Unless an asset is already in place as a crisis starts, it takes time to recruit a local asset or train an operative in the local dialect and cultural nuances. Once in place, the actual collection of data typically takes considerable time. Although in some cases the information is a simple phone call away, in others the collector may need to develop a plan for how best to collect the data.

On the opposite end of the spectrum from HUMINT, OSINT's primary advantages are speed and breadth of coverage. During the 2011 Libya crisis, the Al Jazeera news network was frequently one of the first sources to indicate change in control of a town. Live video feeds showing soldiers near unique geographic markers provided convincing evidence. The breadth of coverage is a catch-22. It provides data on nearly every topic. The OSINT collector has a plethora of avenues to get information: social media, blogs, radio and television shows, public speeches, government and nongovernmental organization statistics, trade magazines, online video and meme postings, graffiti, commercial imagery, and academic literature. The challenge is filtering through it all to find something relevant.

Another challenge with OSINT is accuracy. There seems to be an inverse relationship between speed and accuracy regarding numbers, time, sequence of events, and causal arguments. Detailed, empirical academic research takes a significant amount of effort and time. Plus, like HUMINT, the source may be providing the information with the intent to influence. The bias could be from the publisher of the information or from a secondhand source. Accuracy can also be hampered by variations in local dialects and cultural nuances.

Technical intelligence (TECHINT) and counterintelligence (CI) are typically not included in collection planning because they are not "taskable" like the other disciplines. TECHINT predominantly occurs after some other event: an adversary's military pilot defects with their aircraft or a terrorist's laptop is captured. While CI might contribute to the decision-making process, CI focuses on operations to deny the adversary the ability to collect intelligence against friendly forces. CI officers use all sources of intelligence to focus their operations. Many CI officers are trained to perform a variation of HUMINT and OSINT collection to support the CI mission.

ISR MEANS ACROSS THE DOMAINS

Collection occurs on a variety of platforms that are the *means* of ISR. HUMINT and OSINT primarily reside in the land and cyber domains, respectively. Most SIGINT, GEOINT, and MASINT sensors can operate across the air, land, sea, and space domains (see table 12.1). Sensors can be placed on a variety of aircraft, ships, space vehicles, ground stations, ground vehicles, and handheld devices. Trade-offs typically include cost, endurance, flexibility, and access to the target. Aircraft often have the best flexibility and access to the target but the least endurance. Land- and sea-based assets have the best endurance but may have difficulty getting close enough to the collection target due to their limited line of sight. Air, land, and sea collection might be constrained by limited legal authority, adversary defenses, and host-nation permissions, which can be overcome by space vehicles. While space is the ultimate high ground, space vehicles are far more expensive and far less flexible than the other domains. Plus, the additional distances that the sensor must cover can result in lower quality or probability of detecting the target. Cyber ISR can also overcome traditional adversary defenses, though they are still constrained by legal authority and the complexities of targeting servers that reside outside the target country. The biggest challenge for cyber ISR is access because sensitive military systems are not accessible via the Internet (see chapter 11).

ISR requires personnel beyond the collection phase. Once data is collected, processing centers turn that data into something that analysts can use. Each collection capability has its own processing capabilities. Some collection, including SIGINT, OSINT, and HUMINT, requires translation. Ideally, translators understand local dialects, slang, idioms, historical

Table 12.1. ISR Platforms and Capabilities

Capability	Discipline/Capability	Domain	Example collection platform
IMINT (GEOINT)	Imagery intelligence	Air, land, sea, space	RQ-4 Global Hawk, U-2 Dragon Lady
FMV (GEOINT)	Full-motion video	Air, land, sea, space	MQ-1 Predator, MQ-9 Reaper, P-8 Poseidon, small UAVs
NTISR (GEOINT)	Nontraditional ISR	Air, land, sea	Aircraft with targeting pod or advanced sensor suites
GMTI	Ground moving-target indicator	Air, land, sea	E-8 JSTARS, RAF Sentinel
AMTI	Airborne moving-target indicator	Air, land, sea	E-3 AWACS, E-2 Hawkeye
SIGINT	Signals intelligence	Air, land, sea, space	RC-135 Rivet Joint, EP-3 Aries
MASINT	Measurement and signatures intelligence	Air, land, sea, space	WC-135 Constant Phoenix, ground sensors
HUMINT	Human intelligence	Human, cyber	Patrols, interviews
OSINT	Open-source intelligence	Cyber	Social media, radio, TV
TECHINT	Technical intelligence	Human	Captured equipment
CI	Counterintelligence	Human, cyber	CID, NCIS, OSI

Note: CID = Criminal Investigation Division (Army); GEOINT = geospatial intelligence; ISR = intelligence, surveillance, and reconnaissance; NCIS = Naval Criminal Investigative Service; OSI = Office of Special Investigations (Air Force); UAV = unmanned aerial vehicle.

behavior, and cultural nuances. Even with good translation, the collector must be cognizant that the source might be misinformed, exaggerating, or lying. Every "INT" is vulnerable to adversary deception.[10] To complicate the challenge, collection sensors have become so efficient in gathering data that processing centers can easily suffer data overload.[11] Computer processing helps, but that often shifts the data-overload burden to the analyst.

Data overload and conflicting and ambiguous data can lead to a "signals versus noise" problem for the analyst.[12] Analysts are susceptible to logical fallacies and cognitive errors that can lead to faulty assumptions and inaccurate conclusions.[13] Arguably, the most prominent error is confirmation bias, which reflects a "human tendency to pay attention to the signals that support current expectations."[14] In some cases, indications appear to be a repeat of a previous incident. A classic example is the Gulf of Tonkin incident. In 1964, SIGINT successfully and accurately warned of an attack by North Vietnamese torpedo boats on a US Navy destroyer off the coast of North Vietnam. A few days later, similar SIGINT indications were misinterpreted as a second attack. Instead, they were search-and-rescue operations. Confirmation bias can be created by a lack of empathy for the adversary, leading to mirror imaging, in which the analyst places their own value set or belief system on the intelligence target. Mitigating confirmation bias requires an in-depth understanding of others' (the enemy's, a neutral's, a partner's) perspective, interests, processes, values, and cultural beliefs. Culture-influence preferences can also shape strategic options and planning assumptions.[15]

Dissemination gets finished intelligence products to the decision-maker, whether that person is a pilot in the cockpit of an aircraft or the JTF commander. Intelligence products come in many oral, written, and electronic forms depending on the needs of the decision-maker. In some cases, this means an extensive PowerPoint briefing accompanied by a written report. On the opposite extreme, this might be a few lines of text chat. In rare cases, some users have the requirement to grab the raw unprocessed and unanalyzed data. Despite the seeming finality of a completed intelligence product, every analytic product is based on a partial picture. While certainly some intelligence problems get better coverage than others, no commander complains about having too many intelligence assets. There are always intelligence gaps for every military operation or defense warning problem.

CONCLUSION

Through the ends-ways-means lens, the end of intelligence is a decision. When done well, intelligence reduces uncertainty for decision-makers. At the operational level of war, intelligence reduces uncertainty about how and what to attack and protect. It also assists with decisions to modify operations or implement branch or sequel plans.

Intelligence is neither omniscient nor omnipresent. It requires trade-offs in the ways and means of intelligence. It includes decisions about personnel, platforms, and priorities of the plethora of strategic challenges for the commander. There is no perfect answer. It is one more aspect of the commander's risk management based on probabilities and the potential impact of both friendly and enemy courses of action.

LEARNING REVIEW

- Recall the purpose of intelligence.
- Recall the key capabilities intelligence brings to the joint fight.
- Identify the two ingredients of risk.

- Recall the relative advantages and disadvantages of the different types of intelligence disciplines (HUMINT, SIGINT, GEOINT, MASINT, OSINT).
- Recall the relative advantages and disadvantages of the different ISR domains (land, sea, air, space, cyber).
- Recall the impact that decision-making theory and bias in decision-making has on intelligence forecasts.
- Given a scenario, identify the optimum ISR asset to provide a specific capability.

NOTES

1. Phillip S. Meilinger, "Ten Propositions," *Airpower Journal* (Spring 1996): 2; Charles Faint and Michael Harris, "F3EAD: Ops/Intel Fusion 'Feeds' the SOF Targeting Process," *Small Wars Journal*, January 31, 2012; David Deptula, "A House Divided: The Indivisibility of Intelligence, Surveillance, and Reconnaissance," *Air and Space Power Journal* 22, no. 2 (Summer 2008): 6; Glenn W. Goodman, "ISR Now Synonymous with Operations," *Journal of Electronic Defense* 30, no. 7 (July 2007): 19.

2. John Arquilla, *From Troy to Entebbe: Special Operations in Ancient and Modern Times* (Lanham, MD: University Press of America, 1996), xx–xxi. For more on strategic warning and tactical surprise, see Erik Dahl, *Intelligence and Surprise Attack* (Washington, DC: Georgetown University Press, 2013), 159, 173.

3. Paul Slovic, "Informing and Educating the Public about Risk," *Risk Analysis* 6, no. 4 (1986): 412.

4. Loch Johnson, "Analysis for a New Age," *Intelligence and National Security* 11, no. 4 (1996): 663.

5. H. R. McMaster, "On War: Lessons to Be Learned," *Survival* 50, no. 1 (2008): 26.

6. Richard Betts, "Analysis, War, and Decision: Why Intelligence Failures Are Inevitable," *World Politics* 31, no. 1 (October 1978): 88.

7. Darryl Murdock and Robert M. Clark, "Geospatial Intelligence," in *The Five Disciplines of Intelligence Collection*, ed. Mark M. Lowenthal and Robert M. Clark (Los Angeles: SAGE, 2016), 128.

8. John L. Morris and Robert M. Clark, "Measurement and Signature Intelligence," in Lowenthal and Clark, *Five Disciplines*, 162.

9. Michael Althoff, "Human Intelligence," in Lowenthal and Clark, *Five Disciplines*, 73.

10. For more on deception, see James B. Bruce, "The Missing Link: The Analyst-Collector Relationship," in *Analyzing Intelligence: Origins, Obstacles, and Innovations*, ed. Roger Z. George and James B. Bruce (Washington, DC: Georgetown University Press, 2008), 191–210; Robert Jervis, *Why Intelligence Fails: Lessons from the Iranian Revolution and the Iraq War* (Ithaca, NY: Cornell University Press, 2010), 145–48; and Michael V. Hayden, *Playing to the Edge: American Intelligence in the Age of Terror* (New York: Penguin, 2016), 50.

11. For great insights into how the National Security Agency handled this, see Hayden, *Playing to the Edge*.

12. Roberta Wohlstetter, *Pearl Harbor: Warning and Decision* (Stanford, CA: Stanford University Press, 1962), 387.

13. See Richard Heuer, *Psychology of Intelligence Analysis* (Washington, DC: Center for the Study of Intelligence, 1999), 111–72; Robert Jervis, "Understanding Beliefs," *Political Psychology* 27, no. 5 (October 2006): 641–63; Michael Howard, "The Use and Abuse of Military History," *RUSI Journal* 107, no. 25 (1962): 4–10; and Peter Gill and Mark Phythian, "What Is Intelligence Studies?," *International Journal of Intelligence, Security, and Public Affairs* 18, no. 1 (2016): 5–19.

14. Wohlstetter, *Pearl Harbor*, 392.

15. Thomas A. Drohan, *A New Strategy for Complex Warfare* (Amherst, NY: Cambria Press, 2016), 232–33.

CHAPTER 13

The Nuclear Weapons Triad and Missile Defense

Frances V. Mercado

The United States changed the strategic landscape with the creation and use of atomic bombs in 1945 against Japan at Hiroshima and Nagasaki. The decades that followed World War II saw the US enter into an arms race with the Soviet Union, making a nuclear Armageddon a real possibility. Over time, the high-alert status of bombers, missiles, and submarines decreased through bilateral agreements that reduced the US nuclear arsenal and that of the Soviet Union (later the Russian Federation) from 60,000 to 1,550 deployed nuclear weapons per state.[1] Globally, multilateral treaties were established to prevent nuclear proliferation and testing, including the Treaty on the Non-Proliferation of Nuclear Weapons (NPT) and the Partial Test Ban Treaty (PTBT). Despite movements toward a global disarmament of all nuclear weapons, the US position remains that until that occurs the US is committed to having a nuclear force capable of defending the homeland and American allies.

The ending of the Cold War and the de-emphasis of nuclear weapons saw significant challenges to the way the US military organizes, trains, and equips its nuclear force. The years 2007 and 2008 highlighted the effects of systemic atrophy in the nuclear enterprise at the expense of conventional operations, laid bare by the unauthorized movement and misshipment of sensitive missile components. What these incidents resulted in was the resignations of the chief of staff and secretary of the Air Force due to the perception that these shortcomings of the Air Force's handling of nuclear weapons "resulted from an erosion of performance standards within the involved commands and a lack of effective Air Force leadership oversight."[2] Several studies concluded that the lack of focus on the nuclear mission resulted in a "decline in morale, cohesion, and capability."[3] The solutions included the creation of a new major command (MAJCOM), Air Force Global Strike Command (AFGSC), and a new directorate on the Air Staff, the Strategic Deterrence and Nuclear Integration Office (A10). AFGSC aligned the Air Force's two legs of the nuclear triad—strategic bombers (B-52s, B-1s, and B-2s) and intercontinental ballistic missiles (ICBMs)—under a single MAJCOM. A10 provided the management of resources and policies for Headquarters, Air Force (HAF) in the Pentagon. These new organizations reemphasized the nuclear mission and updated its integration into the national security architecture.

In 2013, an integrity issue with ICBM launch officers unfolded. These officers were found cheating on monthly proficiency tests. This incident exposed critical issues in morale within the force. Nine commanders were fired, and disciplinary action was issued to junior officers. A Department of Defense (DOD) internal nuclear enterprise review identified systemic problems and provided cultural and structural solutions summarizing that

> the bottom line is that the forces are meeting the demands of the mission with dedication and determination but with such increasing difficulty that any margin of capability to meet the demands has been consumed and the Sailors, Airmen, and Marines are paying an unsustainable price. We believe that understanding the discussion and implementing the recommendations in this report will do much to restore the essential margins to ensure that the forces can continue to successfully perform the mission with acceptable and sustainable demands on the men and women performing the mission.[4]

POST–COLD WAR TO GLOBAL POWER COMPETITION

After 9/11, the situation demanded a flexible deterrent for decision-makers. New threats came in the form of rogue states and terrorist organizations. Future problems were less predictable, with adversaries not bound to the "institutional restraints on using such weapons" like the former Soviet Union.[5] Deterrence, mostly dealing with the nuclear balance of terror, was finally reworked to reflect the reality of it being accomplished with a combination of nuclear and conventional forces. This capabilities-based approach, defined as "planning, under uncertainty, to provide capabilities suitable for a wide-range of modern-day challenges and circumstances while working within an economic framework that necessitates choice,"[6] became foundational to US nuclear posture and shaped the approach for unknown contingencies.

Since 2009, the group of official nuclear powers includes the United States, Russia, China, France, and Britain. Other nuclear nations are North Korea, India, Pakistan, and the undeclared Israel.[7] Countries like North Korea and Iran (which is unconfirmed as having established a nuclear weapons program) are willing to sacrifice isolation in order to maintain their nuclear capabilities. The 2018 Nuclear Posture Review (NPR) identified this environment as a "mix of threats, including major conventional, chemical, biological, nuclear, space, and cyber threats, and violent non-state actors."[8] Even more concerning, Russia and China are modernizing as "Russia is upgrading the capacity of its nuclear forces, especially non-strategic nuclear weapons and theater and tactical range systems meant to deter and defeat NATO [North Atlantic Treaty Organization] or China in a conflict as well as high yield and earth penetrating warheads for hardened military targets."[9] China is likely to double the size of its nuclear stockpile with a new road-mobile ICBM, a multiwarhead silo-based ICBM, a new submarine-launched ballistic missile (SLBM), and a new nuclear-capable strategic bomber, creating its own nuclear triad.[10] China is also working on fielding nuclear, theater-range precision-strike systems.

NUCLEAR TRIAD

The United States nuclear arsenal comprises a triad (i.e., three weapon systems) that are meant to provide a strategic, diverse, and flexible force for national security. It consists of ICBMs, strategic bombers, and ballistic missile submarine (SSBNs). Each leg functions as an integral piece: "ICBMs are responsive, Bombers are flexible, and SSBNs are survivable."[11] Combined, these capabilities "help ensure the enduring survivability of our deterrence capabilities against attack and our capacity to hold at risk a range of adversary targets throughout a crisis or conflict."[12] Removing a leg of the triad would limit the ability to hold adversaries at risk and weaken survivability. One leg cannot overcompensate for the overall might of all three working in concert to cover more targets against current and future threats.

Currently the ICBM force maintains four hundred Minuteman IIIs, a silo-based, three-staged, solid-fueled missile.[13] This weapon also has a multiple independent reentry vehicle (MIRV) capability.[14] The ICBM is the most responsive within the triad due to its day-to-day posture. The missile is constantly on alert, with crew members seated in launch-control centers twenty-four hours a day, seven days a week, and 365 days a year. The ICBM is always ready to launch at the president's authorization. The strategic nature of the ICBM demands adversaries to commit to a major offensive to the United States in order to eliminate it.

A key disadvantage of the American ICBM is its vulnerability to attack. The missile is immobile, and its locations are well known. Consequently, it does not have a credible second-strike capability. Despite this, nuclear planners create plans that "absorb an initial first strike and respond effectively later, or to launch ICBMs while under confirmed attack to preclude being disabled in a massive first strike."[15] The threat of a full-on nuclear conflict becomes realized in a fight with ICBMs versus any other leg of the triad, resulting in the risk of an escalated nuclear conflict. With the fear of losing a capability, decision-makers are more likely to launch their remaining ICBM forces to ensure lethality.

As of 2021, the Minuteman III missile is being replaced by the Ground Based Strategic Deterrent (GBSD), which will provide a "more survivable, cost-effective weapon system" incorporating more emerging technology to "adapt to a rapidly evolving threat environment and ensure a more maintainable weapon system into the 2070s."[16] With the new GBSD, there will be a change not just in the launch vehicle but also in all the support and command and control (C2) that are part of the ICBM structure. The modular approach to this weapon ensures that key components can be modernized while maintaining a more sustainable cost for future life-extension programs.

The second leg of the triad, the strategic bomber, has three air-based nuclear delivery systems: the B-52H, the B-2, and fighters (F-15E, F-16, F-18, and F-35). These aircraft carry various nuclear-capable weapon systems: the air-launched cruise missile (ALCM) along with the B83-1 and B61-11 gravity bombs.[17] The two bombers of the triad provide long-range capability and can employ long-range weapons, such as the ALCM, allowing them to strike from distance without sacrificing their safety. The B-52H can carry up to twenty ALCMs.[18] The B-2 is a stealth aircraft that can carry up to sixteen B83-1 gravity bombs. The fighters are typically deployed in support of US and NATO nuclear missions overseas and can carry B61-11 gravity bombs.[19]

The greatest advantage of American bombers is that they are the most flexible and visible leg of the triad. The bomber's ability to forward deploy, disperse, and be recalled once airborne provides options to decision-makers. Bombers' visible deterrent has a strong signaling capability to bolster US information operations and strategic communications. This messaging is critical in signaling to adversaries and allies the US resolve and intent to escalate or de-escalate if needed.

The strategic environment that has evolved in the post–Cold War, 9/11 era and now back to an age of strategic competition has driven the DOD to reevaluate current delivery and weapon systems that air-based nuclear weapons can provide in future conflicts. Two major modernization projects, the B-21 Raider and the Long-Range Standoff Weapon (LRSO), are meant to provide decision-makers with the ability to have effective weapons for the most contested and unpredictable environments. The B-21 is the new stealth bomber slated to replace the B-2 in the late 2020s and should be capable of overcoming future air defenses.[20] The LRSO is the cruise missile slated to replace the ALCM. It is not only meant to maintain the long-range capability achieved by the ALCM but will also "reduce over-flight concerns [in countries' airspaces] and provide the most visible and responsive extended deterrent to our allies and partners, supporting the well-established United States counter-proliferation policy. . . . The LRSO missile will ensure the bomber force continues to hold high-value targets at risk . . . , including targets deep within an advanced integrated air defense system."[21]

The final leg of the nuclear triad is the SSBN. The *Ohio*-class SSBN has been deployed since 1997. It carries twenty Trident II D5 SLBMs.[22] The SSBN is the most survivable leg of the triad, able to operate undetected during long deterrent patrols.[23] The submarine can stay at sea on a continuous basis for months at a time in order to provide a reliable and responsive asset.[24] Its low-yield SLBM provides a "prompt and survivable capability—a deterrent against any adversary's potential misperception regarding the possible gains from a limited or regional nuclear strike."[25] SSBNs survivability provide a valuable second-strike capability due to the difficulty to locate them, which increases the likelihood of surviving a first strike. As a result, the SSBN has "guaranteed the stability of the balance in the international system."[26]

Where this weapon system provides the US with a survivable and scaled response to escalating threats, it carries one limitation: communication structure. The submarines rely on naval aircraft to enable communication to national command authorities, which is further discussed later in the chapter. The E-6 Mercury TACAMO (Take Charge and Move Out) aircraft ensures survivable communication between the *Ohio*-class submarines and US decision-makers by using very low frequency (VLF) radios and a long trailing-wire antenna, but they force SSBNs to rise to a few hundred feet below sea level to receive transmission.[27] As a result, the decision to launch has to be quick and definitive because once the SSBN submerges below that threshold, communications cease, making it virtually impossible to recall.

The *Ohio*-class SSBN is being replaced with the new *Columbia* class, which introduces new technologies, including a stealthier all-electric propulsion system and a life-of-the-ship nuclear reactor.[28] The Navy is also working on upgrading the SLBNs' warheads to incorporate low-yield capability as well as create a nuclear-armed sea-launched cruise missile (SLCM-N).[29] These modernization programs provide deterrence and assurance platforms for future conflicts.

STRATEGIC VERSUS TACTICAL NUCLEAR WEAPONS

At the height of the Cold War, in 1965, the United States had a maximum of 31,255 nuclear warheads, which turned into a steady decline by the 1980s.[30] The American goal was no longer to make more nuclear weapons than the Soviet Union but to maintain a credible, flexible, and resilient deterrent.

In the 1960s, US forces operated with tactical (often called nonstrategic) and strategic nuclear delivery systems both in the continental United States (CONUS) and Europe, such as the tactical Nike Hercules. Type of nuclear weapons, tactical or strategic, refers to the range of the weapon. For example, tactical weapons include land-, air- and sea-launched weapons with ranges of less than six hundred kilometers.[31] The 1991 Presidential Nuclear Initiatives eliminated all tactical nuclear weapons from surface ships, attack submarines, and naval aircraft as well as all ground-launched short-range missile that carried nuclear warheads.[32] But the US still operates tactical nuclear weapons through its partnerships with NATO, like the B61 bomb, carried by dual-capable aircraft. For most countries, tactical nuclear weapons make up the majority of their arsenal. For Russia and the US, about 30 to 40 percent of their arsenal is tactical.[33]

The nuclear weapons of other countries are almost all nonstrategic nuclear weapons, in Pakistan's case due to India's Cold Start doctrine (i.e., its capability to rapidly launch retaliatory, large-scale conventional strikes on Pakistan).[34] Nonstrategic nuclear weapons are a controversial topic, with several countries, including Russia, increasing their tactical nuclear capabilities while the US adheres to its informal 1991 agreement. Russia plans on developing its missiles, including short-range ballistic missiles and ground-launched cruise missiles, which the US claims is a violation of the Intermediate-Range Nuclear Forces Treaty (INF Treaty).[35] Though the emphasis and speed of their modernization is concerning, Russian doctrine dictates that these weapons would be used only if conventional forces are preforming poorly or if national survival depends on it.[36]

The benefit or advantage of a tactical nuclear weapon is that it is a rapid and visible deterrent in a battlespace. The mobility of the weapons provides security and presents a risk of detonation if an adversary decides to attack. The nature of a nonstrategic nuclear weapon is that it is deployed in theater (or even closer to the fight) in order to be used. Such shorter ranges bring the concern that a country might be more willing to use the weapons in a conflict, which would possibly escalate it into a nuclear confrontation.

Despite the growing number of countries acquiring nonstrategic nuclear weapons, the United States started to reduce its nonstrategic arsenal. During the George W. Bush and Barack Obama administrations, the plan was to utilize conventional forces to fill the gap left from tactical nuclear weapons. The 2018 NPR expressed the need to develop two new types of nonstrategic nuclear weapons: the low-yield warhead for the Trident D5 and the SLCM-N.[37] The major reluctance and disadvantage of the US reinitiating its tactical nuclear weapons programs are the safety and security risks of these weapons. There are reports claiming that Russia does not have a full grasp of where all of its weapons are and as a result has a higher risk of being lost, stolen, or sold to other countries.[38] It is debated whether, under the Joe Biden administration, the Department of the Navy will develop the nuclear-armed cruise missile.[39] Regardless, the more countries decided to invest in nonstrategic weapons, the more the presumed threshold of usability decreases, making the idea of a limited nuclear conflict with shorter-range weapons a very real possibility.

COMMAND AND CONTROL

The president of the United States, as commander in chief, is the sole authority for the use of nuclear weapons. That responsibility requires a C2 structure that enables rapid and secure communication between the national authority and operators. The Nuclear Command and Control System (NCCS) is a survivable, reliable, and secure network of communication and warning systems that maintains a relay line to the president at all times. The NCCS is divided into two main components: nuclear command, control, and communications (NC3) and nuclear weapons safety, security, and incident response.[40] NC3 performs five critical functions:

- detection, warning, and attack characterization
- nuclear planning

- decision-making conferencing
- receiving presidential orders
- enabling the management and direction of forces[41]

The NC3 apparatus comprises ground and airborne facilities: the National Military Command Center (NMCC); the Global Operations Center (GOC); the National Airborne Operations Center (NAOC), an E-4B aircraft; and the Airborne Command Post, an E-6B TACAMO aircraft. The ground facilities (NMCC and GOC) provide command, control, and communications to national authorities and US Strategic Command (USSTRATCOM). The NMCC monitors nuclear forces and ongoing conventional military operations for national authorities, while the GOC provides C2, daily management of forces, and emerging threats for USSTRATCOM.

The two airborne command centers, the NAOC and the TACAMO Airborne Command Post, are the survivable alternatives to the ground stations. The NAOC provides national-level C2 for the president, and the E-4B can take off within minutes from random locations in order to maintain its survivability for the president.[42] The E-6B, on the other hand, serves as a backup to the GOC and acts as the airborne launch-control system for the Minuteman III and serves the TACAMO mission of relaying presidential nuclear orders to the triad.[43]

The president is the sole authority for the use of nuclear weapons, and the NCCS was built in order to meet that demand at a moment's notice within any contested environment. AFGSC acts as the joint force air component commander (JFACC) for USSTRATCOM. The responsibilities for air, space, and naval strategic missions, which were once spread over several lines of authority, are under the Joint-Global Strike Operations Center (J-GSOC). The J-GSOC is divided into the Joint Air Operations Center (JAOC) and the Joint Nuclear Operations Center (JNOC), which separates conventional and nuclear missions. For the Navy, the Cruise Missile Support Activity Atlantic (CMSALANT) and the Cruise Missile Support Activity Pacific (CMSAPAC) aligned under the Navy's fleet forces support to J-GSOC.[44]

The US membership in NATO results in a unique C2 structure, where US nonstrategic weapons reside in Europe for NATO missions. Due to their flexible-response policy, all NATO member states require a vote in the use of nuclear weapons. Debates revolve around the need for NATO to remain a nuclear alliance, with claims that "the supreme security guarantee is provided by U.S. strategic nuclear forces." The official NATO stance claims that as long as there are nuclear weapons, NATO will maintain its status as a nuclear alliance. The United States maintains control and custody of nuclear weapons deployed in Europe, and its allies provide aircraft capable of employing these weapons. Use would require the US national command authority to authorize the transfer of these weapons to the air force of a NATO member (where the missiles are located). A problem with the extended-deterrence policy with NATO is that it is challenging to deter threats to both US allies and the homeland—in other words, what happens when you have to risk losing either Boston or Berlin? The United States attempts to minimize that risk through a combination of a strong conventional deterrent capability to its strategic nuclear arsenal in order to supplement this potential gap.

Currently the US has nuclear weapons deployed to two US Air Force bases and five host-nation bases in Europe (Belgium, Germany, Italy, Netherlands, and Turkey).[45] NATO's Nuclear Planning Group (NPG) deals with nuclear matters and policy issues, while the North Atlantic Council (NAC) is its political decision-making body. The NAC ultimately makes defense and political decisions within the alliance, but NPG authorities complement NAC.

The supreme commander Europe (SACEUR), an American flag officer, is part of the NATO Military Committee, the senior military authority for both the NAC and NPG. A major political limitation with these bases results in stability of the nation vis-à-vis the security of the nuclear weapons. Examples like the political crisis in Turkey in 2016 show the risk of theft or sabotage and raise the concern about overall security and stability of the weapons on foreign soil.[46] The goal of these weapons is to support NATO and extended deterrence missions while also preventing nations from wanting to pursue their own nuclear programs.

BALLISTIC MISSILE DEFENSE

In the era of nuclear and conventional ballistic missiles, defense systems are needed to protect against such threats. The United States has been active in improving missile defenses since the end of World War II. From the Nike programs in the 1950s to a space-based ballistic missile intercept layer in the 2010s, missile defense evolved with the growing threat of countries increasing their capabilities, requiring a comprehensive approach to defense that "integrates offensive and defense capabilities for deterrence, passive defense to mitigate the effects of missile attack, and attack operations during a conflict to neutralize offensive missile threats prior to launch."[47] The idea of missile defense was counter to several theories on the use of nuclear weapons and poised a risk that the increase in missile defense would further the arms race. Treaties such as the Strategic Arms Limitation Treaty (SALT I) and the Anti-Ballistic Missile Treaty (ABM Treaty) were seen to "lead to a decrease in risk of outbreak of war involving nuclear weapons."[48] By 1983, President Ronald Reagan had called on the scientific community to "turn their great talents now to the cause of mankind and world peace, to give us the means of rendering nuclear weapons impotent and obsolete," adding that he would direct "a long term research and development program to begin to achieve our ultimate goal of eliminating the threat."[49] The Strategic Defense Initiative (SDI), known also as Star Wars, was the major project that tried to neutralize that threat from space. The major concern with SDI was that it countered the established American and Soviet deterrence policy of mutually assured destruction (MAD). MAD stated that both countries agreed not to attack the other because of the strong probability that both sides would be annihilated.[50] In the end, SDI afforded the Reagan administration a bargaining chip to negotiate more treaties, such as the INF Treaty and the Strategic Arms Reduction Treaty (START).[51]

Nuclear threats to the global order emanate from China and Russia as well as Iran and North Korea. While large numbers of Chinese and Russian ICBMs pose a significant threat to the United States and its allies, short- and medium-range ballistic missiles (SRBMs and MRBMs) are also being honed by China, Iran, and North Korea.[52] North Korea is likely to have several SRBMs that are a threat to South Korea and some MRBMs that could strike Japan and US bases in the region. North Korea is also in the process of developing an ICBM capable of hitting CONUS. Iran has the most ballistic missiles in the Middle East, with the majority being SRBMs and MRBMs.[53] Two major adversaries, Russia and China, are developing technologies that pose a significant threat to US forces and homeland defense.

China's SRBMs, among its other ballistic missiles (MRBMs and ICBMs), are all pointed at Taiwan, and China is also developing ballistic missile defense (BMD) systems.[54] China also leverages electromagnetic pulse (EMP) weapons to disrupt electrical networks, posing a fear that they, combined with kinetic and cyber weapons, could pose a significant risk to the homeland. The Chinese are willing to use these weapons as part of a first strike, defeating US aircraft carriers and achieving a surprise attack on US soil.[55]

Russia is pushing on its technology as well in order to challenge current defenses. The hypersonic Kinzhal air-defense missile system on its *Peter the Great* heavy nuclear-powered missile cruiser can use nuclear or conventional warheads and has a range of 1,250 miles.[56] Also, the Russians are investing in hypersonic missiles, carried by their Tu-22M3 bombers and Su-34 fighter-bombers, that they claim can "break through any modern air defense system."[57] Finally, Russia is producing the Poseidon drone, a robotic nuclear-capable mini-submarine with a miniature nuclear reactor that is capable of carrying nuclear warheads.[58]

BMD systems are meant to detect and intercept missiles of all ranges in multiple flight phases: boost (ascent), midcourse, and terminal. The boost or ascent phase is from the initial launch of the missile until booster burnout. The midcourse phase begins when the booster burns out and the missile begins coasting in outer space toward a target. The terminal phase begins on a missile's reentry into the atmosphere and is the last opportunity for a defense system to intercept the warhead.[59] American BMD systems are deployed in a network of ground-, sea-, and space-based sensors for target detection and tracking as well as ground- and sea-based hit-to-kill and blast-fragmentation warhead interceptors. These systems are housed under an integrated C2, battle management, and communications system. Testing of these systems provides assurance of their predictive capabilities against attack. According to latest reports, Ground-Based Midcourse Defense (GMD) is the sole US missile-defense system against ICBMs.[60] It features a hit-to-kill interceptor that intercepts a missile during the midcourse phase. The system has forty-four interceptors deployed in Alaska and California and is meant to protect the United States from ICBMs coming from Iran and North Korea.[61] Although GMD test interceptors have shown a 50 percent success rate, the Missile Defense Agency (MDA) classifies this as a success.[62]

Aegis is the US sea-based BMD system. Deployed on the Navy's Aegis cruisers and destroyers for regional defense against short- to intermediate-range ballistic missiles, it employs Standard Missile-3 interceptor missiles. Finally, BMD systems also support NATO defense with Aegis Ashore (land based) in Romania and Poland. In tests, Aegis BMD has had a success rate of 82 percent, establishing it as having reliable performance.[63]

Terminal High Altitude Area Defense (THAAD) is one of two mobile defense systems that is rapidly deployed to shoot down short- and medium-range missiles during the terminal phase of flight. The second mobile defense system, the Patriot Advanced Capability-3 (PAC-3), is the newest BMD in the US defense portfolio. It is a deployable system meant to defend area targets, such as bases, ports, and airfields. It can integrate into the THAAD system to provide an overlapping defense. There are seven active THAAD batteries deployed around the world, including South Korea and Guam. The US has six PAC-3 batteries, about half of which are deployed. Each battery has up to sixteen launchers, and each launcher has sixteen missiles.[64]

C2 for ballistic missile defense is managed by the Command and Control, Battle Management and Communications (C2BMC) system. This system integrates multiple BMD systems, including GMD and THAAD, and is fielded in multiple combatant commands. It provides C2 capabilities and integrates multiple BMD systems from CONUS and in theater to ensure continuous communication and planning. It also allows for this system to provide data to Aegis BMD and C2BMC-networked systems as well as coordinate weapon system engagements of multiple targets simultaneously.[65] These systems ensure interoperability of multiple systems and security against ballistic missiles.

The area air-defense commander (AADC), designated by the joint force commander (JFC), is responsible for defensive counterair (DCA), including missile defense (MD). This individual is normally the commander with the preponderance of MD capability. The USSTRATCOM commander coordinates the overall collaborative MD planning process across multiple areas. The AADC is responsible for integrating defense capabilities into a C2 structure. BMD capabilities are meant to provide "surveillance, detection, tracking, and lower- and upper-tier intercept capabilities to counter BMs of all ranges. The objective of BMD is an integrated, layered architecture with overlapping sensors and weapons to enable multiple engagement opportunities."[66] The BMD is typically integrated into the area air-defense plan (AADP).

CONCLUSION

Several presidents have spoken of a world without nuclear weapons and of a resolve to reach that end state. However, they all reaffirmed that until that day comes, the United States remains committed to having a nuclear force capable of defending the homeland and US allies. The nuclear triad is the means by which the US can ensure a flexible, reliable, and secure deterrent that assures allies of protection and signals swift lethality to adversaries. In 2020, the AFGSC commander, Gen. Timothy M. Ray, described the situation: "We have multi-polarity with competitors like China, Russia, North Korea, Iran, violent extremist organization challenges; they are now part of the equation. That's a very different game when you start to understand what's really going on out there."[67] While the US operated with a different mind-set during the Cold War, the new threat environment of today means the methods of the past will not sustain American nuclear deterrence success.

Remaining competitive in the face of this new threat requires a flexible, effective, and reliable deterrent. This includes not only the weapon systems but also the command, control, and communications platforms, the missile-defense systems, and the personnel who operate these systems. The United States relies on the nuclear enterprise to ensure the ability to operate with a strategic advantage and to set the pace of conflict. According to the chairman of the Joint Chiefs of Staff, Gen. Mark Milley, "The nuclear Triad has kept the peace since nuclear weapons were introduced and has sustained the test of time."[68] There is no security equation for the US that exists without the potential threat of nuclear escalation. While adversaries continue to modernize and prioritize nuclear weapons, it is vital for the United States to guarantee that it is staying competitive for its own protection in the era of great-power competition.

LEARNING REVIEW

- Describe the nuclear triad and the advantages and disadvantages of each leg.
- Describe the conditions under which nuclear weapons would be the preferred focus for a military mission.
- Given a scenario, identify the appropriate nuclear C2 capability.
- Describe the capabilities and limitations of the BMD system and the elements that support it.
- Explain how deterrence and assurance might play out in a possible nuclear conflict against a nuclear adversary and a nonnuclear one.

NOTES

1. Federation of American Scientists, "Nuclear Weapons: UNODA," United Nations, n.d., accessed July 14, 2021, https://www.un.org/disarmament/wmd/nuclear/.

2. "Nuclear Lapses Trigger Ouster of Top U.S. Air Force Officials," Nuclear Threat Initiative, June 6, 2008, https://www.nti.org/gsn/article/nuclear-lapses-trigger-ouster-of-top-us-air-force-officials/.

3. Air Force Nuclear Task Force, *Reinvigorating the Air Force Nuclear Enterprise* (Washington, DC: Headquarters USAF, 2008), https://fas.org/irp/doddir/usaf/nuclear.pdf. See also, *Report of the Secretary of Defense Task Force on DOD Nuclear Weapons Management* [the Schlesinger Commission report]: *Phase I; The Air Force's Nuclear Mission* (Washington, DC: Office of the Secretary of Defense [OSD], 2008), http://www.defenselink.mil/pubs/ Phase_I_Report_Sept_10.pdf.

4. Department of Defense (DOD), *Independent Review of the Department of Defense Nuclear Enterprise* (Washington, DC: DOD, 2014), ii.

5. Donald H. Rumsfeld, *Annual Report to the President and the Congress: 2002*, www.hsdl.org/?view&did=851.

6. National Research Council, *Naval Analytical Capabilities: Improving Capabilities-Based Planning* (Washington, DC: National Academies Press, 2005), https://doi.org/10.17226/11455.

7. Reuters Staff, "FACTBOX: Who Are the World's Nuclear Powers?," Reuters, May 18, 2009, https://www.reuters.com/article/us-russia-usa-nuclear-powers-factbox-sb/factbox-who-are-the-worlds-nuclear-powers-idUSTRE54H35T20090518.

8. OSD, "Nuclear Posture Review Executive Summary," February 2018, https://media.defense.gov/2018/Feb/02/2001872877/-1/-1/1/EXECUTIVE-SUMMARY.PDF.

9. Robert Ashely Jr., "Russian and Chinese Nuclear Modernization Trends: Remarks at the Hudson Institute," Defense Intelligence Agency, May 29, 2019, https://www.dia.mil/News/Speeches-and-Testimonies/Article-View/Article/1859890/russian-and-chinese-nuclear-modernization-trends/.

10. John Grady, "Russian and Chinese Nuclear Threats Pose Problem for U.S. Deterrence, Experts Say," USNI News, April 8, 2021, https://news.usni.org/2021/04/08/russian-and-chinese-nuclear-threats-pose-problem-for-u-s-deterrence-experts-say.

11. OSD Nuclear and Missile Defense Policy, "The Importance of the Nuclear Triad," November 2020, https://media.defense.gov/2020/Nov/24/2002541293/-1/-1/1/FACTSHEET-THE-IMPORTANCE-OF-MODERNIZING-THE-NUCLEAR-TRIAD.PDF.

12. OSD, "Nuclear Posture Review Executive Summary."

13. Missile Defense Project, "Minuteman III," Missile Threat, Center for Strategic and International Studies (CSIS), accessed July 13, 2021, https://missilethreat.csis.org/missile/minuteman-iii/.

14. A MIRV weapon system has the capacity to add multiple reentry vehicles to a single missile. Originally the Minuteman III had three reentry vehicles. Due to the 2001 Strategic Arms Reduction Treaty (START Treaty) and 2014's new START requirements, all Minuteman III missiles are equipped with a single warhead.

15. OSD Nuclear and Missile Defense Policy, "Importance of the Nuclear Triad."

16. OSD Nuclear and Missile Defense Policy.

17. OSD Nuclear and Missile Defense Policy.

18. Missile Defense Project, "AGM-86 Air-Launched Cruise Missile (ALCM)," Missile Threat, CSIS, accessed July 13, 2021, https://missilethreat.csis.org/missile/alcm/.

19. Joseph Trevithick, "Get to Know America's Long Serving B61 Family of Nuclear Bombs," The Drive (blog), March 15, 2018, https://www.thedrive.com/the-war-zone/19263/get-to-know-americas-long-serving-b61-family-of-nuclear-bombs.

20. OSD Nuclear and Missile Defense Policy, "Importance of the Nuclear Triad."

21. Timothy Ray, "FY20 Posture for Department of Defense Nuclear Forces," Senate Armed Services Committee, https://www.armed-services.senate.gov/imo/media/doc/Ray_05-01-19.pdf.

22. Congressional Research Service (CRS), "A Low-Yield, Submarine-Launched Nuclear Warhead: Overview of the Expert Debate," January 5, 2021, https://fas.org/sgp/crs/nuke/IF11143.pdf.

23. OSD Nuclear and Missile Defense Policy, "Importance of the Nuclear Triad."

24. OSD Nuclear and Missile Defense Policy.

25. OSD Nuclear and Missile Defense Policy.

26. Isaac Jenkins, Isaac, "The Future of Submarine Second Strike and the Balance of Stability," Next Generation Nuclear Network, May 7, 2017, https://nuclearnetwork.csis.org/the-future-of-submarine-second-strike-and-the-balance-of-stability/.

27. "The E-6 TACAMO Enables America's Nuclear Deterrent," Lexington Institute (blog), April 8, 2014, https://www.lexingtoninstitute.org/the-e-6-tacamo-enables-americas-nuclear-deterrent/.

28. Jon Harper, "Columbia-Class Program Must Navigate Sea of Risks," *National Defense Magazine*, November 5, 2018, https://www.nationaldefensemagazine.org/articles/2018/11/5/columbia-class-program-must-navigate-sea-of-risks.

29. OSD Nuclear and Missile Defense Policy, "Importance of the Nuclear Triad."

30. For an illustration, see Office of the Deputy Secretary of Defense for Nuclear Matters, *Nuclear Matters Handbook: 2020* (Washington, DC: DOD, 2020), 6, https://fas.org/man/eprint/nmhb2020.pdf.

31. Nikolai Sokov, "Tactical Nuclear Weapons (TNW)," NTI, May 1, 2002, https://www.nti.org/analysis/articles/tactical-nuclear-weapons/.

32. Sokov.

33. Sokov.

34. Hans M. Kristensen and Matt Korda, "Tactical Nuclear Weapons, 2019," *Bulletin of the Atomic Scientists*, August 30, 2019, 259–60, https://www.tandfonline.com/doi/pdf/10.1080/00963402.2019.1654273?needAccess=true.

35. Sokov, "Tactical Nuclear Weapons (TNW)." Cruise missiles follow a flight path similar to aircraft and can be shot down by traditional air defenses. Ballistic missiles use an arc trajectory that temporarily transits through space. Their steep angle of attack and high speeds make them more difficult to intercept.

36. Kristensen and Korda, "Tactical Nuclear Weapons, 2019," 259–60.

37. Amy F. Woolf, *Nonstrategic Nuclear Weapons* (Washington, DC: CRS, 2021), https://fas.org/sgp/crs/nuke/RL32572.pdf.

38. William C. Potter and Nikolai Sokov, "Nuclear Weapons That People Forget," *International Herald Tribune*, May 31, 2000.

39. Bryan Bender, "Navy Eyes Canceling Nuclear Missile," *Politico*, June 9, 2021, https://www.politico.com/newsletters/morning-defense/2021/06/09/navy-eyes-canceling-nuclear-missile-795839.

40. Bender, 14.

41. Bender, 14.

42. Bender, 24.

43. Bender, 25.

44. Bender, 25.

45. "Nuclear Disarmament NATO," NTI, June 28, 2019, https://www.nti.org/analysis/articles/nato-nuclear-disarmament/.

46. "Can the U.S. Protect Its Nuclear Weapons in Turkey?," *Washington Post*, October 18, 2019, https://www.washingtonpost.com/politics/2019/10/18/can-us-protect-its-nuclear-weapons-turkey/.

47. DOD, "Missile Defense Review," https://www.defense.gov/Portals/1/Interactive/2018/11-2019-Missile-Defense-Review/The%202019%20MDR_Executive%20Summary.pdf.

48. Joseph Cirincione, "Brief History of Ballistic Missile Defense and Current Programs in the United States," Carnegie Endowment for International Peace, February 1, 2000, https://carnegieendowment.org/2000/02/01/brief-history-of-ballistic-missile-defense-and-current-programs-in-united-states-pub-133.

49. Cirincione.

50. Rob Herber, "Strategic Defense Initiative (SDI)," in Rob Herber, *Nico Bloembergen: Master of Light*, Springer Biographies (Cham, Switzerland: Springer International Publishing, 2019), 319–48.

51. Herber, 319–48.

52. CRS, "Defense Primer: Ballistic Missile Defense," https://fas.org/sgp/crs/natsec/IF10541.pdf.

53. CRS.

54. CRS.

55. James Conca, "China Has 'First-Strike' Capability to Melt U.S. Power Grid with Electromagnetic Pulse Weapon," *Forbes*, June 25, 2020, https://www.forbes.com/sites/jamesconca/2020/06/25/china-develops-first-strike-capability-with-electromagnetic-pulse/.

56. Will Stewart, "Putin Showcases Russia's 'Dagger' Hypersonic Missile Ahead of Summit with Joe Biden," *Mirror*, June 15, 2021, https://www.mirror.co.uk/news/world-news/putin-showcases-russias-dagger-hypersonic-24320667.

57. Will Stewart, "Russia Reportedly Developing New Hypersonic Missile 'to Break through Any Modern Air Defence System,'" *Daily Mail*, May 21, 2021, https://www.dailymail.co.uk/news/article-9603651/Russia-reportedly-developing-new-hypersonic-missile-break-modern-air-defence-system.html.

58. "Weapons of the Future," *Russian Times*, May 21, 2021, https://www.rt.com/russia/524496-autonomous-war-robots-mass-production/.

59. "The Ballistic Missile Defense System" Missile Defense Review, DOD, 2019, https://www.defense.gov/Portals/1/Interactive/2018/11-2019-Missile-Defense-Review/MDR-BMDS-Factsheet-UPDATED.pdf.

60. For an illustration, see "Ground-Based Midcourse Defense (GMD) System," CSIS, June 14, 2018, https://missilethreat.csis.org/system/gmd/.

61. CRS, "Defense Primer."

62. George N. Lewis, "Ballistic Missile Defense Effectiveness," AIP Conference Proceedings, November 15, 2017, https://doi.org/10.1063/1.5009222.

63. Lewis.

64. For an illustration, see Kohei Sakai, "Japan to Deploy New Land-Based Missile Defense System," *Nikkei Asia*, August 17, 2017, https://asia.nikkei.com/Politics/Japan-to-deploy-new-land-based-missile-defense-system.

65. "Command and Control, Battle Management and Communications (C2BMC)," Missile Defense Advocacy Alliance, December 2016, https://missiledefenseadvocacy.org/defense-systems/command-and-control-battle-management-and-communications-system-c2bmc/.

66. Joint Chiefs of Staff, *Joint Publication 3-01: Countering Air and Missile Threats* (Washington, DC: Department of Defense, 2017), https://irp.fas.org/doddir/dod/jp3_01.pdf, V-3.

67. Greg Biondo, "Sustainable Competition," interview with Gen. Timothy M. Ray, *Airman Magazine*, March 3, 2020, https://www.airmanmagazine.af.mil/Features/Display/Article/2603235/sustainable-competition/.

68. OSD Nuclear and Missile Defense Policy, "Importance of the Nuclear Triad."

PART IV

MILITARY THEORY AND OPERATIONS

CHAPTER 14

Theory, Doctrine, and Application of Strategic Air War

John T. Farquhar

In the eyes of many of the first air theorists, airpower revolutionized the conduct of warfare. The speed, range, altitude, and flexibility provided by aircraft transformed not only war's character but also its nature. Thus, aerial operations not only enabled traditional armies and navies to fight better but also to fight differently: to bypass fielded forces and strike enemy nations directly. Airpower enabled the third dimension (air domain) to be exploited for military purposes. Early airpower thinkers were influenced by the Wright Brothers' first flight in 1903, the first military use of aircraft in 1911 by the Italians dropping bombs on Turkish troops in Libya, and aviation's rapid evolution as an instrument of war during World War I.

Early theorists experienced the carnage and despair created by World War I trench warfare that scarred a generation. With airpower's early context in mind, this chapter introduces Giulio Douhet and William "Billy" Mitchell and their ideas on strategic air war as the foundation for an independent air force; the US Army Air Corps Tactical School, which created an air war doctrine for World War II; and the application of both theory and doctrine in two World War II strategic air campaigns, the European theater's Combined Bomber Offensive (CBO) and the strategic bombing of Japan. The convergence of lessons learned from the theory, doctrine, and application of strategic airpower shaped the first decades of the United States Air Force.

EARLY AIRPOWER THINKING

Giulio Douhet (1869–1930), an Italian general, gained recognition as the first theorist to write seriously about the use of the airplane in war.[1] He noted the potential of military aviation as early as 1909 and urged Italians to support its rapid development. His most famous work, *The Command of the Air* (1921), was the first to state a comprehensive theory of airpower. Douhet proposed an air force be used for two key purposes: gaining command of the air and shattering the enemy's will to fight by attacking population centers. His vision of airpower as a war-winning weapon and alternative to the meat-grinder tactics of World War I appealed to airmen and some political leaders.[2] For airmen, Douhet's arguments constituted a starting point for justifying autonomous air forces that would be coequal to armies and navies. His major points are as follows:

- Airpower is inherently offensive, and command of the air is essential for success.
- There is no adequate defense against air attack; enemy air forces must be destroyed on the ground, preferably in a surprise attack.
- Future wars will be total wars between entire peoples demanding destruction of vital centers essential to a state's function. In turn, air attacks should focus on destroying the enemy population's will to fight.
- The psychological effects of aerial bombardment are greater than physical destruction. By using a combination of high-explosive, incendiary, and poison gas bombs, aerial bombardment would cause panic, and in turn a terrorized population would demand a swift end to the war.
- Airpower constitutes a revolutionary weapon and requires air leaders commanding an independent air force to exploit its capabilities.[3]

From today's perspective, Douhet exaggerated many of his claims, and subsequent events proved some of his ideas wrong. Douhet ignored the potential of tactical aviation, dismissed challenges inherent in target selection, assumed aircraft could always hit their targets, vastly overestimated the physical destructiveness of bombardment, and greatly underestimated both civilian resilience and air-defense capabilities to defeat attacking air forces. Douhet never considered that the same impressive science and engineering that could produce "battleplanes" might also produce equally impressive defensive systems—interceptors, effective antiaircraft guns, surface-to-air missiles, and radar. Douhet assumed that all future wars would be total wars fought between modern industrial nations with large cities and fixed targets vulnerable to bombardment. His emphasis on destroying population centers shocked most people and violated traditional moral standards regarding noncombatants but formed the heart of World War II strategic bombing and early Cold War nuclear deterrence theories.

In many ways, nuclear weapons validated many of Douhet's ideas, whether for good or evil. On the other hand, Douhet's theory had little to no use in guerrilla wars (e.g., Vietnam) or for conflicts involving agrarian societies that lack easily identifiable vital centers (e.g., Afghanistan). Douhet did correctly identify some key principals. Defending against all possible avenues of air attack would require enormous resources without assurance of success: airpower is inherently offensive, providing strategic effect. Few would deny the validity of his central premise: command of the air is crucial to success in war.[4] Strategic thinker Bernard Brodie noted that Douhet's "essential, correct, and enduring contribution" was to recognize that the existence of the airplane "must revolutionize the whole strategy of war."[5]

Like Douhet, Billy Mitchell (1879–1936) began his military career before the invention of the airplane.[6] The son of a US senator from Wisconsin, Mitchell enlisted in the Wisconsin Volunteer Infantry at the outset of the Spanish-American War. Thanks to his political influence, charisma, ambition, confidence, and competence, Mitchell advanced rapidly through US military ranks. On the eve of America's entry into World War I, Mitchell emerged as the ideal candidate to serve as the US Army Air Service observer of French air operations. Fluent in French, a trained pilot, and possessing unmatched social connections, Mitchell proved adept.[7]

Named commander of Air Service units assigned to Gen. John J. Pershing's American Expeditionary Force, Mitchell earned respect as an able tactical and operational leader while infuriating his superiors with his habit of ignoring the military chain of command. In September

1918, Mitchell gained fame for the largest single aerial force used in the war, commanding 1,481 American, French, British, and Italian aircraft to support General Pershing's Saint-Mihiel offensive. The planning and preparation of Mitchell's staff for Saint-Mihiel foreshadowed the functions of today's joint force air component commander (JFACC), although primitive World War I communication technology limited tactical control of air operations. Mitchell refined both aerial tactics and operations planning during the Meuse-Argonne offensive, the most ambitious campaign in American military history up to that point, where six hundred thousand American ground troops and four thousand artillery pieces massed against German defenses. In 1918, from September 26 until the Armistice on November 11, seven hundred American aircraft faced five hundred German planes. American aircraft and observation balloons provided vital air-to-ground support functions, including day, night, visual, and photographic reconnaissance, artillery spotting, close air support (CAS), interdiction, and limited "strategic" attacks against enemy railroad marshaling yards and supply centers.[8]

Flamboyant, photogenic, and media savvy, Mitchell emerged from the war as the most renowned American air commander. Convinced of airpower's potential as the primary component of national defense and a revolutionary war-winning weapon, Mitchell aggressively promoted his cause. In the 1921 *Ostfriesland* bombing trials, Mitchell's airmen "sank a battleship." He escalated his cause through rhetorical attacks on the Department of War and the Department of the Navy for "gross negligence" in the 1925 crash of the dirigible USS *Shenandoah*. Mitchell seized newspaper headlines and sparked public debate.[9] His incendiary remarks led to a highly publicized court-martial that Mitchell attempted to transform into a public hearing on airpower. Found guilty of "conduct of a nature to bring discredit upon the military service," the court sentenced Mitchell to a five-year suspension from service without pay. On February 1, 1926, he resigned from the Air Service but continued to fight tenaciously for an independent air force.[10]

More a propagandist than a theorist, Mitchell targeted the American public and pressured Congress for an independent air force. In *Winged Defense* (1925), Mitchell presented four major points that mirrored themes of Douhet and of Britain's Hugh Trenchard:

- "Airpower may be defined as the ability to do something in the air" and includes civilian commercial and cultural dimensions as well as the military function.
- "Neither armies nor navies can exist unless the air is controlled over them." Airpower is no longer an auxiliary to land or naval forces.
- "No longer will the tedious and expensive processes of wearing down the enemy's land forces by continuous attacks be resorted to. The air forces will strike immediately at the enemy's manufacturing and food centers, railways, bridges, canals and harbors [vital centers]. The saving of lives, man power and expenditures will be tremendous to the winning side. The losing side will have to accept without question the dominating conditions of its adversary."
- "Surface navies have entirely lost their mission of defending a coast because aircraft can destroy or sink any seacraft coming within their radius of operation. In fact, aircraft today are the only effective means of coast protection. . . . The surface ship as an element of war is disappearing. Today the principal weapon in the sea is the submarine."[11]

Given the isolationist, antiwar atmosphere of the 1920s, Mitchell couched his early airpower arguments in defensive terms, but frustration over lack of progress with Congress prompted him to become more strident. In *Skyways: A Book on Modern Aeronautics* (1930), Mitchell repeated his revolutionary airpower themes and upped his rhetoric:

- War is the attempt of one nation to impress its will on another nation by force after all other means of arriving at an adjustment of a dispute have failed. The attempt of one combatant, therefore, is to so control the vital centers of the other that it will be powerless to defend itself. The vital centers consist of cities where the people live, areas where their food and supplies are produced and the transportation lines that carry these supplies from place to place.
- The result of warfare by air will be to bring about quick decisions. Superior airpower will cause such havoc, or the threat of such havoc, in the opposing country that a long drawn out campaign will be impossible.
- The conceptions we have always had that wars must be waged by armies and navies must be revised, as these two branches of the military service will take a position second to that of airpower, and will act principally as aids to it. Armies will hold the land. Navies will no longer be able to remain on top of the water where they are a sure prey to aircraft, but will have to act in submarines beneath the surface.
- What will future war hold for us? Undoubtedly an attack on the great centers of population. If a European country attacks the United States, New York, Chicago, Detroit, Pittsburgh and Washington will be the first targets. It is unnecessary that these cities be destroyed in the sense that every house be leveled with the ground. It will be sufficient to have the civilian population driven out of them so that they cannot carry on their usual vocations. A few [poison] gas bombs will do that.[12]

Although his plea for air force autonomy and expanded military aviation largely failed, Mitchell inspired a generation of American airmen who later fought World War II and established the foundation for today's US Air Force.

Although airpower's technological advances and public relations forays continued into the 1930s, the Great Depression dominated a volatile decade. The technological promise of all-metal construction, monoplane design, and advanced power plants met the harsh realities of shrinking budgets. Toward the latter half of the decade, powerful totalitarian states, represented by Fascist Italy, Nazi Germany, Imperial Japan, and Communist Soviet Union, threatened Western democracies, but powerful isolationist sentiment limited the US military response.

DEVELOPING AIRPOWER DOCTRINE: THE AIR CORPS TACTICAL SCHOOL

The Air Corps emphasized doctrinal development through the Air Corps Tactical School (ACTS). "Doctrine" is the thinking behind how best to fight. It provides the intellectual and conceptual foundation for the optimum use of military force. From doctrine evolved ideas for technological requirements, aircraft procurement, strategy, and tactics. The ACTS attracted the best and brightest airmen as its faculty, including George C. Kenney and Haywood S. Hansell. Influenced by Mitchell, the ACTS faculty developed an air war theory that emphasized long-range strategic bombardment.[13]

According to ACTS, massed bombers would penetrate enemy defenses, bypass armies and navies, and strike enemy "vital centers," key industrial nodes whose destruction would collapse the enemy's economy. Proper target selection would destroy both an enemy's capability and will to fight. Selective, precision bombardment ensured economy of force and minimized civilian casualties. In an era before radar, airpower theorists believed effective air defense would be impossible. They looked to high altitude, speed, and internal armament for defense. Eventually the ACTS idea became known as the "industrial web" theory, or the acronym HAPDB (high-altitude precision daylight bombardment).[14] Brig. Gen. Donald Wilson captured the essence of the "industrial web theory" based on his 1933–34 ACTS lectures:

> Future wars of survival would be between industrial nations; continuation of the war would depend on maintaining intact a closely-knit and interdependent industrial fabric. . . . Precision bombing gave us an instrument which could cause collapse of this industrial fabric by depriving the web of certain essential elements—few as three main systems such as transportation, electric power and steel manufacture would suffice. . . . Modern industrial nations are susceptible to defeat by interruption of this web. . . . This interruption is the primary objective of an air force.[15]

The American aviation industry in the 1930s introduced a series of advanced bombers that encouraged airpower advocates, most notable the four-engine Boeing B-17 Flying Fortress. In August 1935, the aircraft flew 2,100 miles nonstop from Seattle to Dayton, Ohio, at an average speed of 232 mph. Paired with the highly accurate Norden bombsight, the B-17 revolutionized bombardment aviation with its size, range, speed, and precision, just as winds of war stirred in Europe.[16] US Army Air Corps leaders viewed the bomber as the instrument to achieve their theories of strategic air warfare pursued by means of HAPDB.

APPLYING AIRPOWER THEORY AND DOCTRINE: THE CBO AND STRATEGIC BOMBARDMENT OF JAPAN

With America's entry into the war in December 1941, British military leaders in the Royal Air Force (RAF) attempted to persuade leaders in the US Army Air Forces (USAAF) to switch to night operations. Under Air Marshal Arthur Harris, RAF bombing evolved to night area bombing of German cities using incendiary bombs. USAAF leaders rejected RAF arguments, convinced that the superior range, ceiling, and defensive firepower of the B-17 would overcome the defenses. To the USAAF, night area bombing would be ineffective, inefficient, and indiscriminate, resulting in excessive civilian casualties. After a series of negotiations, the January 1943 Casablanca Directive inaugurated the CBO, marked by American precision daylight bombing and British night area bombing. Code-named Operation Pointblank, the CBO threatened the Germans with "round-the-clock" bombing that would overwhelm their defenses.

However, as the air forces suffered heavy casualties in 1943–44, American and British air leaders learned tough lessons regarding the effectiveness of integrated air defenses that combined day and night fighters, radar, and ground-controlled intercept networks. Three disastrous missions, Ploesti, Schweinfurt-Regensburg, and Schweinfurt, in the late summer and fall of 1943 demonstrated flaws in USAAF theory and doctrine, especially its belief in the B-17's self-protection. Undaunted, Allied perseverance, increased numbers, and technological advances increased the accuracy and lethality of bombing. In late February 1944, P-51 Mustang and P-47 Thunderbolt long-range escort fighters broke the Luftwaffe's back in Operation Argument, better known as "Big Week," which gained Allied air superiority. Although the CBO never stopped German industrial production, American and British bombing disrupted the Axis economy and led to shortages of fuel, munitions, food, and war matériel. Operationally, Allied bombing forced the Germans to convert their air forces from offense to defense and denied the German army the benefits of close air support that it enjoyed earlier in the war. Psychologically, Allied bombing denied the Axis populations sanctuary from the war by destroying German cities and revealing the lies of Nazi propaganda.[17]

The CBO constituted the longest, bloodiest, and greatest sustained air campaign in history. From 1942 to 1945, the British lost twenty-two thousand aircraft and over seventy-nine thousand airmen, and the Americans lost eighteen thousand planes and another seventy-nine thousand men killed. The Allies flew nearly 1.7 million combat sorties and dropped over 1.5 million tons of bombs, which killed an estimated 300,000 Germans, wounded 780,000, and destroyed 3.6 million buildings, 20 percent of the nation's total. Although horrible in its destruction and lamentable in its many civilian casualties, airpower emerged as the dominant weapon in Western Europe.[18]

In the Pacific, the Japanese attack at Pearl Harbor and the loss of the Philippines, Malaysia, Singapore, the Dutch East Indies (Indonesia), and vast expanses of China staggered the Allies. For six months, Japanese land, air, and naval forces won every battle and inflicted severe losses. With the August 1942 Guadalcanal campaign, Allied soldiers, sailors, and marines slowly pushed back the borders of the Japanese empire. As Allied industrial production turned the tide, Gen. Henry H. "Hap" Arnold and American airmen hoped to avoid a costly land invasion of Japan and clinch victory through strategic bombardment.

The Boeing B-29 Superfortress served as the primary instrument of the USAAF strategic air war against Japan. With a pressurized crew compartment, remotely controlled guns, and new radial engines, the B-29 proved a revolutionary aircraft of unprecedented size, range, and payload capacity. The USAAF ordered 1,664 before the prototype had even flown, and by April 1944, B-29s appeared in the Pacific Theater.[19]

At first, USAAF leaders attempted to reproduce the HAPDB but saw disappointing results. Flying from primitive bases in China with logistic staging from India, bomber crews faced significant B-29 engine problems amplified by distance and weather (including two-hundred-knot headwinds later known as a jet stream). By October 1944, B-29 operations shifted to Saipan, which reduced supply lines. General Hansell renewed efforts for a daylight precision-bombing campaign but faced problems due to a lack of intelligence on Japanese industry. Impatient, in January 1945, General Arnold replaced Hansell with Maj. Gen. Curtis E. LeMay, a proven commander from Europe.[20]

By March 1945, LeMay altered B-29 tactics. To avoid jet stream winds and high-altitude engine problems, LeMay ordered low-altitude night attacks with bombers stripped of defensive machine guns; he reduced fuel loads and increased bomb loads. Like in RAF night area bombing, LeMay's B-29s relied on darkness for protection and pummeled enemy cities with incendiary bombs. From March to August 1945, American fire-bomb raids destroyed sixty-six Japanese cities and burned 178 square miles of urban landscape. Civilian casualties were severe; in one raid against Tokyo, eighty thousand people perished.[21]

With a successful atomic test in July 1945, the Allies issued an ultimatum calling for the Japanese to surrender or suffer "prompt and utter destruction." On August 6, 1945, Col. Paul W. Tibbets piloted the *Enola Gay*, which dropped a uranium device, known as "Little Boy," over Hiroshima. Nearly five square miles of the city were destroyed, and eighty thousand people died, yet no surrender immediately resulted. On August 9, another B-29, *Bock's Car*, commanded by Maj. Charles W. Sweeney, released a plutonium bomb known as "Fat Man" over Nagasaki. With the city partially protected by hilly terrain, the second bomb devastated 1.5 square miles, killed thirty-five thousand people, and injured sixty thousand. Faced with a defeated army, a decimated navy and air force, devastated cities, a Soviet declaration of war, and terrible atomic weapons, the Japanese government surrendered on August 14, 1945.[22]

The Pacific air campaign combined efforts of Navy, Marine, and Army air forces in both carrier- and land-based forms. US industrial might overwhelmed Japanese forces in both technology and numbers. The geographic circumstances and immense distances involved made aircraft the preeminent weapon but did not negate the essential contributions of land and naval forces.

In the last weeks of the war, General Arnold commissioned the United States Strategic Bombing Survey (USSBS) to assess the impact of strategic air war in both Europe and the Pacific. The report's summary of the European War included these findings:

- The German experience suggests that even a first class military power—rugged and resilient as Germany was—cannot live long under full-scale and free exploitation of air weapons over the heart of its territory.
- As the air offensive gained in tempo, the Germans were unable to prevent the decline and eventual collapse of their economy. Nevertheless, the recuperative and defensive powers of Germany were immense; the speed and ingenuity with which they rebuilt and maintained essential war industries in operation clearly surpassed Allied expectations.
- The mental reaction of the German people to air attack is significant. Under ruthless Nazi control they showed surprising resistance to the terror and hardships of repeated air attack, to the destruction of their homes and belongings. . . . The power of a police state over its people cannot be underestimated.[23]

The Pacific War Summary Report added five "signposts":

- Control of the air was essential to the success of every major military operation.
- Control of the air was not easily achieved, and involved the coordinated application of all the resources of the nation.
- The limitations of air control deserve special mention. It was never completely possible to deny the air to the enemy.
- Given air control, there were also limitations as to the specific results which could be achieved . . . by aircraft carrying conventional high-explosive bombs.
- The experience of the Pacific war supports the findings of the Survey in Europe that heavy, sustained and accurate attack against carefully selected targets is required to produce decisive results when attacking an enemy's sustaining resources. It further supports the findings in Germany that no nation can long survive the free exploitation of air weapons over its homeland.[24]

Although intended to demonstrate the decisiveness of strategic air war, the USSBS presented nuanced evidence and analysis. Allied strategic bombing proved vital to the war effort, especially in the early stages when Allied land forces were beaten and could not engage directly. Both the CBO and strategic air campaign against Japan reinforced the economic and psychological aspects of total war. But civilian resilience to air attack proved Douhet, Mitchell, and other early air theorists wrong. Strategic bombing never totally destroyed the enemy's economy, although against Japan it did come close. The early air theorists were also proved wrong regarding air warfare as a means to achieve quick victory at little cost.

While air advocates exclaimed airpower's role in avoiding trench warfare, opponents countered by observing that a bloody war of attrition took place in the skies. Regardless of strategic air war's effectiveness in World War II, the undeniable impact of air operations propelled the creation of an independent air force. The advent of the atomic bomb signaled a new era of conflict where technology provided unmatched lethality and airpower emerged as a uniquely suited means of delivery.

LEARNING REVIEW

- Recall the technological advancements (e.g., speed, overflight/altitude, range) and planning assumptions that facilitated the creation of new military strategies leading up to World War II.
- Review the purpose of military theory.
- Describe the relevance of "vital centers" and the industrial web theory to contemporary military strategy.
- Describe how Douhet's argument that defense is inefficient can be applied to contemporary military operations.
- Debate the utility of targeting civilian morale as a military operation.
- Debate the utility of targeting a country's war-supporting industries.

NOTES

1. This introduction of Giulio Douhet pays tribute to Dr. Jim Titus, whose distinguished career at the Air Force Academy and Air University spanned nearly four decades. He based his writing on "Air Warfare by General Gulio [*sic*] Douhet," an Air Corps Tactical School publication signed by Brig. Gen. Oscar Westover, December 12, 1933, file U-1078, Air University Library, Maxwell Air Force Base (AFB), AL.

2. The best work on Douhet is Phillip S. Meilinger, "Giulio Douhet and the Origins of Airpower Theory," in *Paths of Heaven: The Evolution of Airpower Theory*, ed. Phillip S. Meilinger (Maxwell AFB, AL: Air University Press, 1997), 1–40. See also Phillip S. Meilinger, *Airmen and Air Theory: A Review of the Sources* (Maxwell AFB, AL: Air University Press, 2001), 103–6; Edward Warner, "Douhet, Mitchell, Seversky: Theories of Air Warfare," in *Makers of Modern Strategy: Military Thought from Machiavelli to Hitler*, ed. Edward Mead Earle (Princeton, NJ: Princeton University Press, 1971), 484–503; David MacIsaac, "Voices from the Central Blue: The Airpower Theorists," in *Makers of Modern Strategy from Machiavelli to the Nuclear Age*, ed. Peter Paret (Princeton, NJ: Princeton University Press, 1986), 624–47; and Bernard Brodie, "The Heritage of Douhet," in *Strategy in the Missile Age* (Princeton, NJ: Princeton University Press, 1965). For the original, see Giulio Douhet, *The Command of the Air*, trans. Dino Ferrari (Washington, DC: Office of Air Force History, repr. 1998). For Douhet's influence, see Frank P. Donnini, "Douhet, Caproni and Early Airpower," *Air Power History* (Summer 1990): 45–52; and Claudia Segrè, "Giulio Douhet: Strategist, Theorist, Prophet?," *Journal of Strategic Studies* 15, no. 3 (September 1992): 351–66.

3. Meilinger, *Airmen*, 103–5; Meilinger, "Giulio Douhet," 8–4.

4. Meilinger, *Airmen*, 103–5; Meilinger, "Giulio Douhet," 8–34.

5. Brodie, "Heritage of Douhet," 22.

6. The best sources on Mitchell are Mark Clodfelter's "Molding Airpower Convictions: Development and Legacy of William Mitchell's Thoughts," in Meilinger, *Paths of Heaven*, 79–114; and Alfred F. Hurley, *Billy Mitchell: Crusader for Airpower* (Bloomington: Indiana University Press, 1975). Readers will also benefit from Phillip S. Meilinger's biography of Mitchell in *Airmen and Air Theory*, 7–13, 107–8.

7. Clodfelter, "Molding Airpower Convictions," 82; Hurley, *Billy Mitchell*, 14.

8. Clodfelter, "Molding Airpower Convictions," 82–83; Hurley, *Billy Mitchell*, 22, 35–36. For details of the US Army Air Service planning, preparation, execution, and after-action assessments, see Mauer Mauer, ed., *The U.S. Air Service in World War I*, 4 vols. (Washington, DC: Office of Air Force History, 1978).

9. For accounts of the post–World War I Army Air Service, see Ron Dick, *Reach and Power: The Heritage of the United States Air Force in Pictures and Artifacts* (Washington, DC: Air Force History and Museums Program, 1997), 82–86; Alfred Goldberg, ed., *A History of the United States Air Force, 1907–1957* (Princeton, NJ: D. Van Nostrand, 1957), 29–31; John F. Shiner, "From Air Service to Air Corps: The Era of Billy Mitchell," in *Winged Shield, Winged Sword: A History of the United States Air Force*, ed. Bernard C. Nalty (Washington, DC: Air Force History and Museums Program, 1997), 93–95; Robert Frank Futrell, *Ideas, Concepts, Doctrine: Basic Thinking in the United States Air Force*, vol. 1, *1907–1960* (Maxwell AFB, AL: Air University Press, 1989), 32–33, 37; and Hurley, *Billy Mitchell*, 64–68.

10. Hurley, *Billy Mitchell*, 90–109; Dick, *Reach and Power*, 89; Shiner, "From Air Service to Air Corps," 98–100; Goldberg, *History of the United States Air Force*, 31–32; Futrell, *Ideas, Concepts, Doctrine*, 46–47.

11. William Mitchell, *Winged Defense: The Development and Possibilities of Modern Airpower—Economic and Military* (New York: G. P. Putnam's Sons, 1925; repr., Mineola, NY: Dover, 2006), xi–xvi.

12. William Mitchell, *Skyways: A Book on Modern Aeronautics* (Philadelphia: J. B. Lippincott, 1930), 253, 256, 262.

13. Peter R. Faber, "Interwar US Army Aviation and the Air Corps Tactical School: Incubators of American Airpower," in Meilinger, *Paths of Heaven*, 183–238; Thomas H. Greer, *The Development of Air Doctrine in the Army Air Arm, 1917–1941* (Washington, DC: Office of Air Force History, 1955; repr. 1985), 47–67; Meilinger, *Airmen*, 109–13; Futrell, *Ideas, Concepts, Doctrine*, 62–65.

14. Faber, "Interwar US Army Aviation," 186, 216–19; Meilinger, *Airmen*, 109–10; Futrell, *Ideas, Concepts, Doctrine*, 80; Shiner, "From Air Service to Air Corps," 113.

15. Donald Wilson, "Origin of a Theory for Air Strategy," *Aerospace Historian* 18, no. 1 (Spring 1971): 19–21.

16. Dick, *Reach and Power*, 121–24; Shiner, "From Air Service to Air Corps," 144; Futrell, *Ideas, Concepts, Doctrine*, 81; Goldberg, *History of the United States Air Force*, 41–42; Greer, *Development of Air Doctrine*, 46–47; DeWitt S. Copp, "Frank M. Andrews: Marshall's Airman," in *Makers of the United States Air Force*, ed. John L. Frisbee (Washington, DC: Office of Air Force History, 1987), 55–57.

17. William R. Emerson, "Operation POINTBLANK: A Tale of Bombers and Fighters," in *The Harmon Memorial Lectures in Military History, 1959–1987*, ed. Harry R. Borowski (Washington, DC: Office of Air Force History, 1988), 441–72; Dick, *Reach and Power*, 194–95; Bernard C. Nalty, "The Defeat of Italy and Germany," in Nalty, *Winged Shield, Winged Sword*, 275, 281; Futrell, *Ideas, Concepts, Doctrine*, 149–50; Goldberg, *History of the United States Air Force*, 57, 60; Stephen L. McFarland and Wesley Phillips Newton, "The American Strategic Air Offensive against Germany in World War II," in *Case Studies in Strategic Bombardment*, ed. R. Cargill Hall (Washington, DC: Air Force History and Museums Program, 1998), 188–93.

18. "The United States Strategic Bombing Survey: Summary Report (European War)," September 30, 1945, in *The United States Strategic Bombing Surveys (European War) (Pacific War)* (1945; repr., Maxwell AFB, AL: Air University Press, 1987), 5–6; Dick, *Reach and Power*, 238.

19. Dick, *Reach and Power*, 270–71; Bernard C. Nalty, "Victory over Japan," in Nalty, *Winged Shield, Winged Sword*, 341–42; Goldberg, *History of the United States Air Force*, 83–84; Richard R. Mueller, "Air War in the Pacific," in *A History of Air Warfare*, ed. John Andreas Olsen (Washington, DC: Potomac Books, 2010), 73–74; Alvin D. Coox, "Strategic Bombing in the Pacific," in Hall, *Case Studies in Strategic Bombardment*, 273–75; "Strategic Air Offensives," in *Oxford Companion to World War II*, gen. ed. I. C. B. Dear (Oxford: Oxford University Press, 1995), 1076; Daniel L. Haulman, *Hitting Home: The Air Offensive against Japan* (Washington, DC: Air Force History and Museums Program, 1999), 5–7.

20. Dick, *Reach and Power*, 271–74; Nalty, "Victory over Japan," 342–44, 350–52; Goldberg, *History of the United States Air Force*, 84–85; Mueller, "Air War in the Pacific," 74–75; Coox, "Strategic

Bombing in the Pacific," 275–93; Haulman, *Hitting Home*, 8–11. See also Haywood S. Hansell Jr., *The Strategic Air War against Germany and Japan* (Washington, DC: Office of Air Force History, 1986).

21. Dick, *Reach and Power*, 274–79; Nalty, "Victory over Japan," 356–59; Goldberg, *History of the United States Air Force*, 86–87; Mueller, "Air War in the Pacific," 75–76; Coox, "Strategic Bombing in the Pacific," 311–26, 330–43; Ronald H. Spector, *Eagle against the Sun: The American War with Japan* (New York: Free Press, 1985), 493–94, 503–5; "The United States Strategic Bombing Survey: Summary Report (Pacific War)," September 30, 1945, in *United States Strategic Bombing Surveys*, 83–96; Edward Jablonski, *Airwar*, vol. 4 (Garden City, NY: Doubleday, 1971), 160–73; Haulman, *Hitting Home*, 18–23.

22. Dick, *Reach and Power*, 279–87; Nalty, "Victory over Japan," 360–64; Goldberg, *History of the United States Air Force*, 87; Mueller, "Air War in the Pacific," 76–77; Coox, "Strategic Bombing in the Pacific," 351–60; "United States Strategic Bombing Survey: Summary Report (Pacific War)," 96–103; Jablonski, *Airwar*, 209–12; Haulman, *Hitting Home*, 32–37. Note: The sources disagree on the spelling of "Bock's Car" (Nalty and Coox) versus "Bockscar" (Dick, Mueller, Haulman). I selected the former based on Edward Jablonski's reference to the airplane being named by Capt. Frederick C. Bock, who had switched planes with Major Sweeney. Jablonski, *Airwar*, 212.

23. *United States Strategic Bombing Surveys (European War) (Pacific War)*, 37–40.

24. "The United States Strategic Bombing Survey: Summary Report (Pacific War)," 108–10.

CHAPTER 15

Contemporary Air Theory Strives for Strategic Effect

John T. Farquhar

The initial decades of the independent US Air Force (USAF) adhered to the doctrine of strategic air war shaped by classic airpower theorists (Giulio Douhet, Billy Mitchell, and the Air Corps Tactical School) and honed by technological advancements represented by long-range, jet-engined bombers (Boeing's B-47 and B-52), intercontinental ballistic missiles (ICBMs), and nuclear weapons. The theories of strategic air war and capabilities of nuclear-armed bombers provided the retaliatory fist to nuclear deterrence theory, but the challenges of limited, nonnuclear war in Korea and Vietnam forced USAF leaders to revise and rethink doctrine. At the heart of the revision were three thinkers: British military theorist Basil Henry Liddell Hart, who introduced modern strategic concepts (grand strategy, combined-arms operations, and strategic dislocation), and two USAF colonels, John Boyd and John Warden, who honed airpower's potential for strategic effect through the concept of strategic paralysis. Instead of devastating the enemy's economic and population centers by mass conventional or nuclear bombardment, contemporary theorists sought to stun enemy leadership and command centers to achieve strategic effect. Thus, Liddell Hart, Boyd, and Warden formed the basis for contemporary airpower theory.

LIDDELL HART: INDIRECT APPROACH, GRAND STRATEGY, AND STRATEGIC DISLOCATION

Building on the classic strategic works of Carl von Clausewitz and Sun Tzu, Basil Henry Liddell Hart (usually called B. H. Liddell Hart) bridged the gap between historic and contemporary views of strategy. Renowned as a journalist and historian, Liddell Hart emerged as arguably the most significant British military theorist of the twentieth century. During World War I, he fought at the Battle of the Somme, where he became a casualty of poison gas. During the 1920s and 1930s, Liddell Hart gained fame as the military correspondent of major London newspapers, including the *Daily Telegraph* and *The Times*. Liddell Hart published thirty major books and articles dedicated to preventing a reoccurrence of trench warfare.[1]

An early advocate of mobile offensive tactics and tank warfare, Liddell Hart introduced the concept of "expanding torrent," a combined-arms approach using mechanized infantry, tanks, and aircraft to penetrate enemy lines and strike enemy command and control facilities in the rear.[2] Liddell Hart also argued for an "indirect approach" in both strategy and tactics. On the battlefield, mechanized forces would maneuver to avoid enemy strength, while strategists would use emerging land, air, and sea technologies to strike enemy flanks. In both tactics and strategy, headfirst attacks into enemy defenses would be avoided at all costs. Combining these ideas, many considered Liddell Hart to be the intellectual father of "blitzkrieg," although contemporary scholarship diminishes this reputation.[3] Nevertheless, Liddell Hart's work inspired contemporary American airpower theorists John Warden and John Boyd.

Liddell Hart was one of the first theorists to introduce the concept of "grand strategy," expanding on Clausewitz's original ideas from *On War* (1832). He examined Clausewitz's definition of strategy: "the art of the employment of battles as a means to gain the object of war. In other words strategy forms the plan of the war, maps out the proposed course of the different campaigns which compose the war, and regulates the battles to be fought in each."[4] Then he analyzed the elder Helmuth von Moltke's version: "the practical adaptation of the means placed at a general's disposal to the attainment of the object in view."[5] Liddell Hart viewed both definitions as too narrow and overly focused on the military. He proposed a shorter definition: "the art of distributing and applying military means to fulfill the ends of policy." Liddell Hart elaborated, "For strategy is concerned not merely with the movement of forces—as its role is often defined—but with the effect."[6] Fighting power is only one aspect of grand strategy whose primary function is to coordinate and direct a nation's resources toward attaining a political object. Liddell Hart concludes: "Moreover, fighting power is but one of the instruments of grand strategy—which should take account of and apply the power of financial pressure, of diplomatic pressure, of commercial pressure, and, not least of ethical pressure, to weaken the opponent's will. A good cause is a sword as well as armor."[7] Thus, Liddell Hart established contemporary ideas of "instruments of national power," often described as DIME: diplomatic, informational, military, and economic. His final conception of grand strategy: "While the horizon of strategy is bounded by the war, grand strategy looks beyond the war to the subsequent peace. It should not only combine the various instruments, but so regulate their use as to avoid damage to the future state of peace—for its security and prosperity."[8] Liddell Hart's ideas significantly shaped and influenced post–World War II and post-Vietnam air thinkers who recognize the need to use airpower to achieve strategic effect in concert with overall national policy.

Finally, Liddell Hart argued that the aim of strategy is not to annihilate the enemy but to produce strategic dislocation. Ideally, the "true aim is not so much to seek battle as to seek a strategic situation so advantageous that if it does not of itself produce the decision, its continuation by a battle is sure to achieve this."[9] Strategic dislocation consists of two spheres: the physical and the psychological. In the physical sphere, Liddell Hart advocated maneuver to upset the enemy's dispositions, separate his forces, endanger his supplies, and/or threaten his lines of retreat. In the psychological sphere, dislocation affects the enemy's mind, especially if the maneuvers are sudden or unexpected. For emphasis, Liddell Hart quoted Thomas "Stonewall" Jackson's motto: "Mystify, mislead, and surprise."[10] If executed correctly, "Psychological dislocation fundamentally springs from this sense of being trapped."[11]

AIRPOWER THINKING EVOLVES WITH TECHNOLOGY: JOHN BOYD AND JOHN WARDEN

An eclectic thinker and reader inspired by Liddell Hart, Col. John Boyd energized airpower thinking and symbolized a new breed of "outside-the-box" thinkers. A Korean War fighter pilot and pioneer of the Air Force Weapons School, Boyd studied American F-86 vs. Soviet MiG-15 fighter tactics and observed that the F-86's hydraulically operated flight controls gave it a significant advantage over the mechanical flight controls of the MiG-15. He used this realization to influence the design and procurement of both the McDonnell Douglas F-15 and the General Dynamics F-16, stressing the need for "fast transient maneuvers."[12] Later in his career, Boyd broadened his observations to both operational and strategic levels, emphasizing the need to think and act more quickly than the opponent. His extensive briefing variously titled "Patterns of Conflict" and "A Discourse on Winning and Losing" assumed nearly legendary status within the US armed forces in the 1970s and 1980s.[13] Unfortunately, Boyd never published his theories. Instead, a number of sources published copies of the briefing, and scholars interpreted his work, most notably a Dutch air theorist, Frans Osinga.[14] In many ways, John Boyd continued an intellectual theme initiated by Sun Tzu and developed by B. H. Liddell Hart: to avoid enemy strength and strike weakness. In further refining the theme, airman-scholar David S. Fadok described Boyd's work as a "quest for strategic paralysis." Similar to Liddell Hart's strategic dislocation, Boyd's strategic paralysis concept was defined by Fadok as "a military option with physical, mental, and moral dimensions that intends to disable rather than destroy the enemy. It seeks maximum possible political effect or benefit with minimum necessary military effort or cost. Further, it aims at rapid decision through a maneuver battle directed against an adversary's physical and mental capability to sustain and control his war effort in order to diminish his moral will to resist."[15]

Boyd's "Patterns of Conflict" represented a living document and tool for thinking. He engaged his audience in a conceptual forum, and no presentations were the same. Boyd proposed a fourfold mission with the intent of revealing the character of conflict, survival, and conquest (with all emphasis in the original):

- To make manifest the nature of *moral-mental-physical conflict*
- To discern a *pattern for successful operations*
- To help *generalize tactics and strategy*
- To find a basis for *grand strategy*[16]

Early in the briefing, Boyd proposed an idea linked to "fast transient" maneuver (i.e., the ability to accelerate, decelerate, climb, dive, and turn rapidly): "in order to win, we should operate at a faster tempo or rhythm than our adversaries—or, better yet, get inside adversary's observation-orientation-decision-action time cycle or loop."[17] In air-to-air combat, pilots must first see the enemy (observe), maneuver to a position of advantage (orient), decide whether to engage (decide), and then act. Thus, Boyd's fast transient maneuver ideas morphed into the famed observe-orient-decide-act (OODA) loop. He explained:

- Why? Such activity will make us appear *ambiguous* (unpredictable) thereby generate [*sic*] *confusion* and *disorder* among our adversaries—since our adversaries will be *unable* to generate mental images or pictures that agree with the *menacing* as well as *faster* transient rhythm or patterns they are competing against.
- [The central idea is to] simultaneously compress own time and stretch-out adversary time to generate a *favorable mismatch in time/ability* to shape and adapt to change.
- [Thus, the goal is to] collapse adversary's system into *confusion* and *disorder* causing him to over and under react to activity that appears simultaneously *menacing* as well as *ambiguous*, *chaotic*, or *misleading*.[18]

In surveying a variety of wide-ranging, but selective, examples from history, Boyd observed successful patterns of response:

- He who is willing and able to take the *initiative* to exploit *variety*, *rapidity*, and *harmony*—as the basis to create as well as adapt to the more indistinct—more irregular—quicker changes of rhythm and pattern, yet shape the focus and direction of effort—survives and dominates.
- He who is unwilling to take the *initiative* to exploit *variety*, *rapidity*, and *harmony* . . . goes under or survives to be dominated.[19]

Boyd readily admitted to drawing ideas from Clausewitz, Sun Tzu, and Liddell Hart and urged his audience to think deeply and read widely. Boyd inspired, influenced, and inculcated across all military branches.

If Boyd's thinking was heavily influenced by his experience flying fighters in the Korean War, Col. John Warden's Vietnam combat experience shaped his airpower concepts. To Warden, Vietnam air campaigns, especially Operation Rolling Thunder, represented a misapplication of airpower. Graduated, limited, and diluted application of air assets against inappropriate targets failed to exploit the inherent strengths of the air weapon. As a student at the National War College in 1986, Warden revamped airpower's use as a strategic instrument by focusing on enemy leadership. Assigned to the Air Staff at the Pentagon, Warden headed the team responsible for producing an air-attack plan, called Instant Thunder, in response to Saddam Hussein's 1990 invasion of Kuwait. Warden aimed to produce strategic paralysis by targeting enemy leadership through his five-ring and parallel attack (often called parallel warfare) theories. He called for attacking the enemy's command and control network as a priority, with simultaneous, overwhelming air attacks to achieve synergistic effects. Following the Gulf War, Warden gained acclaim and doctrinal influence within the US armed forces, but his intellectualism, confidence, and outspoken manner also led to disputes with senior Air Force leaders. Arguably one of the best-known airmen of his generation, Warden never achieved the rank of general.[20]

Warden's 1995 *Airpower Journal* article "The Enemy as a System" called for deductive, strategic thinking versus inductive, tactical thought. He argued for focusing "on the totality of our enemy, then on our objectives, and next on what must happen to the enemy before our objectives become his objectives," adding the need to understand "how we are going to produce the desired effect on the enemy—the weapons, the delivery systems, and other means we will use."[21] Warden contended that technology alters the traditional relationship between morale and the physical: "The advent of airpower and accurate weapons [i.e., precision-guided munitions] has made it possible to destroy the physical side of the enemy. This is not to say that morale, friction, and fog have all disappeared. It is to say, however, that we can now put them in a distinct category, separate from the physical. As a consequence, we can think broadly about war in the form of an equation: (Physical) x (Morale) = Outcome."[22] Warden believed military planners must consider the enemy as a strategic entity and as a system composed of subsystems. Before operations, military and political leaders must focus on objectives:

> At the strategic level, we attain our objectives by causing such changes to one or more parts of the enemy's physical system that the enemy decides to adopt our objectives,

> or we make it physically impossible for him to oppose us. The latter we call strategic paralysis. Which parts of the enemy system we attack (with a variety of weapons ranging from explosives to nonlethal computer viruses) will depend on what our objectives are, how much the enemy wants to resist us, how capable he is, and how much effort we are physically, morally, and politically capable of exercising.[23]

To simplify, Warden's "Five Rings Model" draws an analogy to the human body. At the center, the brain serves as the body's strategic center, the organ responsible for making it a strategic entity providing leadership and direction. Vital organs, such as the heart, lungs, and liver, necessary for converting food and air into energy, constitute the second ring. Without organic essentials, the brain could not perform its strategic function. Next, an infrastructure of bones, blood vessels, and muscles provide the body's third ring, responsible for mobility and movement. Warden then lists the millions of cells that populate the body carrying nutrients and sustaining the whole. Finally, the fifth ring consists of the body's defenses: white blood cells and other elements that protect the other rings. In total, the system consists of four basic components: central leadership or direction, organic essentials, infrastructure, and population, protected by a fifth.[24]

In explaining his model, Warden emphasized the need for conceptual, strategic thinking and repeated his theme of the enemy as a system: "Strategic war is war to force the enemy state or organization to do what you want it to do. In the extreme, it may even be war to destroy the state or organization. It is, however, the whole system that is our target, not its military forces. If we address the system properly, its military forces will be left as a useless appendage, no longer supported by its leadership, organic essentials, infrastructure, or population."[25] He admitted that despite the model's simplicity, it would be difficult to execute. Each ring possesses more than one center of gravity with varying degrees of vulnerability. Nevertheless, Warden stressed the importance of striking the enemy's command ring as a priority, the key to strategic functioning and the first place to attack. He added a nuance missed by later critics:

> The most critical ring is the command ring because it is the enemy command structure . . . the only element of the enemy that can make concessions, that can make the very complex decisions that are necessary to keep a country on a particular course, or that can direct a country at war. . . . Capturing or killing the state's leader has frequently been decisive. In modern times, however, it has become more difficult—but not impossible—to capture or kill the command element. At the same time, command communications have become more important than ever, and these are vulnerable to attack.[26]

He also noted the difficulty of attacking an enemy's population ring directly. In addition to moral concerns, "there are too many targets, and, in many cases, especially in a police state, the population may be willing to suffer grievously before it will turn on its own government." Warden acknowledged that the model might be "somewhat diminished" in guerrilla or irregular warfare, where the people may be motivated to fight for extended periods of time against an invader.[27]

Warden concluded his argument in "The Enemy as a System" with a concept of parallel attack made possible by technological advances in precision, range, speed, and lethality.

In the past, armies fought sequentially since a commander had to concentrate resources to prevail against a single vulnerability of the enemy. In the modern era, technology permits "the near simultaneous attack on every strategic- and operational-level vulnerability of the enemy. This parallel process of war, as opposed to the old serial form, makes very real what Clausewitz called the ideal form of war, the striking of blows everywhere at the same time."[28] Warden stressed airpower's role in strategic warfare and the need to understand the enemy's objectives. He also emphasized thinking deductively, from big to small, focusing on enemy systems comprising subsystems and, in turn, avoiding the urge to concentrate on the tools of war—enemy weapons. Warden clinched his argument with the following reflection: "Fighting is not the essence of war, nor even a desirable part of it. The real essence is doing what is necessary to make the enemy accept our objectives as his objectives."[29]

CONCLUSION

B. H. Liddell Hart, John Boyd, and John Warden transitioned earlier classic airpower theories into contemporary airpower doctrine. Liddell Hart opened military theorists to the concept of grand strategy, where the combined diplomatic, financial, economic, ethical, and military instruments of power are used to achieve policy objectives. He sought to avoid the carnage of head-to-head trials of strength by the Sun Tzu–like "indirect approach," where forces maneuver to strike enemy weakness. Along the same lines, Liddell Hart explored combined-arms warfare, an operational approach utilizing armor, mechanized infantry, and air forces to bypass enemy strongholds and strike vulnerable rear areas. Ideally, skillful maneuver achieves strategic dislocation, a physical and psychological state where enemy forces feel panicked and trapped.

Inspired by Liddell Hart's "strategic dislocation," Warden joined Boyd as an important air theorist who bridged classical airpower theory with modern doctrinal ideas. While both aimed to achieve strategic paralysis through aerial warfare, Boyd emphasized the mind of the enemy, while Warden sought to destroy leadership structure. Warden's Five Rings Model appeals to military leaders as a simple, coherent, conceptual template, but the model assumes a centralized state with a defined or authoritarian leader. Likewise, parallel attack (or parallel warfare) assumes both command of the air and overwhelming numbers. It does not account for an enemy of near equal or superior strength. Like earlier airpower theorists, Warden lacked precision with some terms. For example, Warden used "centers of gravity" like Mitchell used "vital centers" but not like Clausewitz's concept of a single "center of gravity." Despite flaws in some aspects of their respective theories, both Warden and Boyd joined classic airpower theorists in envisioning airpower's strategic effect. They modified, but did not challenge, airpower as an inherently strategic entity. They sought Liddell Hart's strategic dislocation through strategic paralysis—in other words to stun, not annihilate the enemy. Thus, airpower theorists bridged the gap between past and present, laying the foundation for today's effects-based operations.

LEARNING REVIEW

- Recall the technological advancements (e.g., PGMs, ISR) that facilitated the creation of the concept of parallel warfare.
- Describe the relevance of the OODA loop to the operational level of war to induce strategic paralysis.

- Describe how Warden's Five Rings Model can be used to induce strategic paralysis.
- Given a strategic problem, justify an indirect approach.

NOTES

1. Tim Travers, "Liddell Hart, B. H.," in *The Officer's Companion to Military History*, ed. Paul E. Bauman (New York: Houghton Mifflin, 1999), 265.

2. British military thinker J. F. C. Fuller is also credited with this. See Travers, 265; Alex Danchev, "Liddell Hart, Capt Sir Basil Henry," in *The Oxford Companion to Military History*, ed. Richard Holmes (Oxford: Oxford University Press, 2001), 505–6.

3. Some view Erwin Rommel and George S. Patton as students of Liddell Hart, but many military thinkers developed similar ideas about armored warfare in the 1930s. See Dennis E. Showalter, *Patton and Rommel: Men of War in the Twentieth Century* (New York: Berkley Caliber, 2005); and James S. Corum, *The Roots of Blitzkrieg: Hans von Seeckt and German Military Reform* (Lawrence: University Press of Kansas, 1992).

4. B. H. Liddell Hart, *Strategy*, 2nd rev. ed. (New York: Frederick A. Praeger, 1967), 333.

5. Helmuth von Moltke (the elder) was a noted nineteenth-century military theorist who served as chief of staff of the Prussian Army during the Wars of German Unification (1864–71). He should not be confused with his nephew, Helmuth von Moltke (the younger), who served as chief of the German General Staff from 1906 to 1914 and is associated with the Schlieffen Plan of World War I. Caleb Carr, "Moltke, Helmuth Karl von," and Daniel Moran, "Moltke, Helmuth von (the Younger)," in Bauman, *Officer's Companion to Military History*, 306–8; Liddell Hart, *Strategy*, 334.

6. Liddell Hart, *Strategy*, 335.

7. Liddell Hart, 336.

8. Liddell Hart, 336.

9. Liddell Hart, 339.

10. Liddell Hart, 341.

11. Liddell Hart, 340.

12. Phillip S. Meilinger, *Airmen and Air Theory: A Review of the Sources* (Maxwell Air Force Base [AFB], AL: Air University Press, 2001), 141–42; David S. Fadok, "John Boyd and John Warden: Airpower's Quest for Strategic Paralysis," in *The Paths of Heaven: The Evolution of Airpower Theory*, ed. Phillip S. Meilinger (Maxwell AFB, AL: Air University Press, 1997), 363; Grant T. Hammond, *The Mind of War: John Boyd and American Security* (Washington, DC: Smithsonian Books, 2001), 91–98.

13. On February 2, 1978, Colonel Boyd presented "Warp XII: Patterns of Conflict" to a class at the US Air Force Academy with the author in attendance. For academic year 2005/6, Air University's School of Advanced Air and Space Studies published Boyd's "A Discourse on Winning and Losing," dated August 1987, as a course reader. In January 2007, Chet Richards and Chuck Spinney edited Boyd's "Patterns of Conflict" as a PowerPoint presentation based on a 1986 version. It is available through the Air University Library at http://www.ausairpower.net/APA-Boyd-Papwers.html (accessed January 18, 2021). The last slide of "Patterns of Conflict" (197) explains the PowerPoint's presentation's lineage.

14. Fadok, "John Boyd and John Warden," 357–98; Meilinger, *Airmen and Air Theory*, 141–43; Frans P. B. Osinga, *Science, Strategy and War: The Strategic Theory of John Boyd* (New York: Routledge, 2007).

15. Fadok, "John Boyd and John Warden," 361.

16. John R. Boyd, "Patterns of Conflict," PowerPoint briefing, ed. Chet Richards and Chuck Spinney, January 2007, http://www.ausairpower.net/APA-Boyd-Papers.html, slide 2.

17. Boyd, slide 5.

18. Boyd, slides 5, 7.

19. Boyd, slide 174.

20. For a short, but incisive, account, see Meilinger, *Airmen and Air Theory*, 141–44. For more detail, see Fadok, "John Boyd and John Warden," 357–98.

21. John A. Warden III, "The Enemy as a System," *Airpower Journal* 9, no. 1 (Spring 1995): 42.

22. Warden, 43.

23. Warden, 43.
24. Warden, 49–51.
25. Warden, 47.
26. Warden, 49.
27. Warden, 53.
28. Warden, 54.
29. Warden, 55.

CHAPTER 16

Constructing a Compellence Strategy

Michael Fowler

It is easy to overlook Sun Tzu's maxim that "what is of supreme importance in war is to attack the enemy's strategy."[1] This understanding requires in-depth research to "know the enemy."[2] Along with force location, capability, and intent, strategists require knowledge of the driving political and socioeconomic factors. With that knowledge, they can estimate the adversary's strategy and construct a counterstrategy. This chapter presents a framework to characterize military strategies through a paradigm of target sets and intended effects.[3] The framework captures the options of military force using the six ways of compellence: annihilate, exhaust, deny, decapitate, intimidate, and subvert. For each of the six ways, the framework provides a logical alignment of ways, effects, and centers of gravity (i.e., impacting this target set leads to the direct effect). From this, analysts should be able to assess the ways-ends logic of any military operation—and its relationship to strategy.

INFLUENCE AND STRATEGY

The essence of strategy is influencing the behavior of others. Strategies are created to align the appropriate ways (methods) with means (resources) to achieve a desired end state or objective. It involves opportunity costs and risk-management calculations to come to a decision. Regardless of the mission, foreign policy decisions are usually designed to influence others.[4] From a national security perspective, achieving the desired end state almost always requires another party (e.g., enemy, ally, partner, third-party country, or nonstate actor) to do something that it otherwise would not do (e.g., surrender, give up territory, cooperate in a partnership, sign an international convention, not invade a neighbor). For military strategy, in particular, there is invariably a competing strategy that should be taken into account. The essence of military strategy is to get that other party to modify its behavior in a manner that helps achieve objectives.

The purpose of military strategy is not to destroy. However, wars include destruction, and the pursuit of destruction is one of many different tasks—along the spectrum of violence—given to a military. When destruction is pursued, it is a means to some end. Regardless of the physical effect, all forms of military action intend to influence the adversary psychologically. In some cases, military action against one group may be intended to influence a third party:

partners, neutral countries, the international community, the domestic population, or the domestic government or military.

In a broad sense, influence can be simplified into two categories: coercion and cooperation. Coercion is the threat or use of force to shape behavior. Cooperation is the use of rewards and incentives to shape behavior (usually of a friendly country). Table 16.1 further breaks down coercion and cooperation by the primary focus of the method: preventive or causative. Therefore, attempts at coercion can be further refined into deterrence and compellence (though sometimes they are used simultaneously). Similarly, cooperation is refined into assurance and persuasion.[5]

For complex problems, actors may employ coercion and cooperation simultaneously. For example, US troops in South Korea are intended to *deter* North Korean aggression and *assure* allies of US commitment. Allied shipments of rice to North Korea and the cancellation of military exercises were (failed) attempts to *persuade* North Korea to halt its nuclear program. Periodically, US threats of air strikes are intended to *compel* North Korea to halt aggressive behavior such as long-range ballistic missile testing. The synchronized, complementary employment of these influence methods (deter, assure, persuade, compel) does not necessarily lead to success, because the fear of US strikes actually increases North Korea's perceived need for nuclear weapons.

Prevention strategies are designed to maintain the status quo. Change to the strategic status quo can come in many forms: formation of alliances or coalitions, geographic ownership, and technological advances in weaponry (e.g., nuclear weapons). While alliances often pursue a prevention approach, alliance formation is inherently disruptive. Security concerns about the status quo are driven by perceptions of changes in adversary capability and/or intent.[6] As the alliance grows, it increases the potential threat to those outside of the alliance, sometimes referred to as a security dilemma.[7]

Deterrence increases the perceived costs of war for the opponent. Specific threats or general fear of retribution are intended to prevent the adversary from attempting to change the status quo.[8] Ideally, the calculated costs of war are raised sufficiently so that they outweigh any potential benefits of using force. Assurance, on the other hand, focuses on reducing the costs of the status quo, primarily for allies.[9] Assurance is used to maintain alliances or to convince a country that weapons development is unnecessary. High-level visits, defense cooperation, intelligence sharing, security force assistance, shows of force (e.g., B-52 flyovers in the region), and prepositioning of forces can be used to assure allies against potential threats, mitigating their perceived costs of maintaining the status quo.

Poor communication can result in ambiguous or contradictory signals. For instance, US warnings to Saddam Hussein in 1990 were somewhat ambiguous and did not deter Iraq

Table 16.1. Influence Methods

	Prevent action	**Cause action**
Coercion (threats or destructive effects)	Deterrence	Compellence
Cooperation (rewards or constructive effects)	Dissuasion or assurance	Persuasion

Note: While "dissuasion" is more accurate linguistically, "assurance" is more common in the literature. For this chapter, the terms should be considered interchangeable.

from invading Kuwait.[10] Even if Saddam understood the threat and power of the US military, American messaging about removing dictatorships and perception of a US-supported regional conspiracy against him led Saddam to calculate that an invasion of Kuwait might improve his odds of regime survival.[11]

Prevention can send conflicting signals as it typically involves the development of a strong defense either to deter the potential aggressor or reassure the potential defender. However, it is difficult to develop defensive capabilities that do not also provide additional offensive capabilities, potentially complicating the problem. For example, joining the nuclear club can be the ultimate trump card to deter stronger opponents. But nuclear proliferation is perceived by many as an escalatory action (with significant offensive capabilities) that should be prevented.

While deterrence and assurance are types of preventive methods, compellence and persuasion seek to encourage action. Whereas compellence uses or threatens force, persuasion offers rewards to change or entice actor behavior. The spectrum of rewards is diverse and includes high-level visits, training, funds, and military equipment. Large states will often reward developing states in exchange for joining a coalition or for providing basing rights, overflight permissions, rhetorical or military support to an operation, or political support for a United Nations vote or trade negotiation.[12] If the desired end state is an improved image or a specific quid pro quo, it is irrelevant how the partner uses the reward. The measure of success is the change in international image or the delivery of the quid pro quo.

Rewards as a quid pro quo can be somewhat problematic as the recipient may not fully follow through after the delivery of the reward. Known as the principal-agent problem, the donor (principal) and recipient (agent) may have conflicting interests in this quid pro quo relationship. The recipient state may attempt to maximize benefits and aid from the donor while minimizing the costs associated with what the donor state wants it to do.[13] To ensure that a country does not shirk, the donor state may intentionally design the reward so that it can be withdrawn. For example, a single cash donation is difficult to take back. On the other hand, providing a country with aircraft and support and logistics (e.g., spare parts, maintenance) is more flexible. The donor can stop providing supplies, reducing the utility of the donation (or increasing the cost of shirking). Persuading adversaries typically involves the halting of an undesired activity. For example, granting rewards to an adversary in exchange for halting a major, covert weapon of mass destruction (WMD) program requires additional donor resources to detect shirking. Disarmament programs during insurgencies can have a similar result because civilians can turn in old, obsolete, or inoperable firearms for cash and, in turn, use that cash to purchase better weapons.

Compellence increases the cost of noncompliance, while persuasion provides benefits for compliance. In contrast to deterrence and assurance, compellence and persuasion are used to *cause* a change in behavior. This change focuses on one of two outcomes. Some countries desire to change the status quo to create some type of power differential in their favor. Others use these techniques in a reactionary way to attempt to return to the status quo ante (e.g., get Iraq to leave Kuwait).

METHODS OF COMPELLENCE

While military campaigns are complex and involve multiple methods of influence, planning for combat operations focuses on the art of compellence. This often gives outsiders the

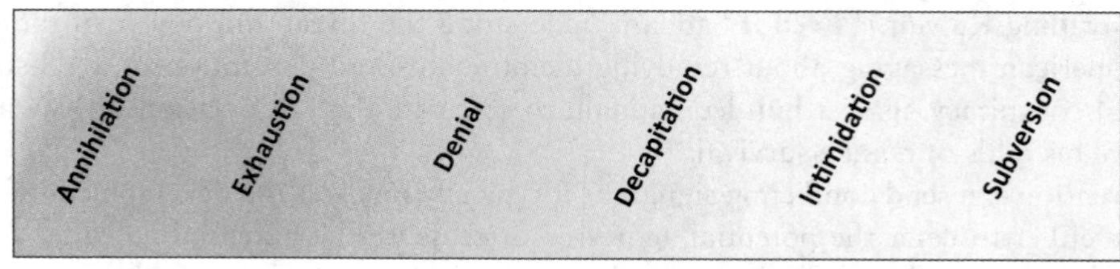

Figure 16.1. The Compellence Spectrum

perception that military members are warmongers. In reality, the use of military force means that the other methods of influence (i.e., deterrence, persuasion, and assurance) have failed or are perceived as ineffective. While there are seemingly infinite ways to use military force, an effects approach to the means-to-ends chain condenses decision-making into a handful of strategic options.[14] Terms such as "degrade," "diminish," "dislocate," "negate," "neutralize," "paralyze," and "suppress" might be useful for tactical planning.[15] However, at the operational level, this lengthy lexicon of terms is insufficiently differentiated to provide any value to a military planner. Figure 16.1 depicts compellence options along a spectrum, from direct physical effects to psychological effects (see this chapter's appendix).[16] The physical effect is important only if it causes a functional or behavioral effect.

The use of military force rarely achieves the intended effect directly. Direct effects are interim objectives to a cumulative effect—a specific change in behavior. Force is designed to facilitate "an outcome with significant consequences for nonmilitary matters."[17] The desired behavior might be for the adversary to surrender, pay financial reparations, give up some territory, make changes in its government, or dismantle an advanced weapon program. When trying to identify the desired behavior, it is important to consider that organizations may choose to ignore the underlying causes of a strategic problem in favor of focusing resources on the near-term resolution of symptoms. This "plug-the-wound" mentality—focusing on tactics at the expense of strategy—may prevent the crisis from getting worse but is unlikely to prevent the problem from recurring.

The probability that military action will result in the desired cumulative effect is not easy to predict. Tactical effects (e.g., bridge is out) may or may not achieve the operational effect (e.g., enemy forces unable to move to their objective). This is because there can be externalities, such as inconveniencing civilians whom you may want on your side, and/or the adversary will adapt and find a way to move its military forces covertly. In turn, operational effects may not achieve the strategic effect. This can become more complex when this cumulative effect is an interim objective to an information operations campaign against a third party. For example, Argentina attacked the British-owned Falkland Islands to improve its image with its domestic constituents.[18]

Military theory is critical for providing the logical bridge that links centers of gravity, direct effects, and the intended cumulative effect. Table 16.2 depicts the six ways or methods of compellence. Despite the evolution of joint operations, airpower advocates and surface warfare strategists have divergent opinions on preferred options and the preferred target sets within an option.

Table 16.2. Ways of Compellence

Way	Annihilate		Exhaust		Deny			Decapitate	Intimidate	Subvert
Target set COG	Military forces	War-related industry	Military forces	Civilian targets	Military forces	Transportation nodes	Key offensive capability	Headquarters or communications	Decision-makers	Disgruntled military/society
Intended direct effect	Forces not combat-capable		Military loses will to fight	Revolt or change in government	Physically unable to hold territory, maneuver forces, and/or attack.			Unable to make or send orders	Perceives costs as too high	Coup, civil war, or revolt
Intended cumulative effect	**Desired behavior change in target (e.g., surrender, retreat, regime change, reduced aggression)**									

Note: See this chapter's appendix for a typology clarification that includes the rationale for excluding "extermination."

Annihilate

Annihilation is intended to be quick and decisive. There are two variants, both of which seek to negate the combat capability of adversary forces.[19] The first focuses on destroying the enemy's military forces to physically or mentally break the units' ability to function. The second targets war-related industries to indirectly wear down military forces by virtue of starving them of sustainment.

Annihilation of military forces seeks a decisive battle to destroy the enemy's strong point (a method the US Marine Corps refers to as attrition). Once the strong point is destroyed, the enemy will fall apart. For example, Gen. Douglas MacArthur's amphibious landing at Inchon during the Korean War caused the North Korean force to collapse.

Air Force doctrine favors annihilation through an indirect approach by "going directly to the heart of an enemy . . . [to] achieve strategy objectives without necessarily having to achieve operational objectives . . . [, which produces] the greatest effect for the least cost."[20]

This can be achieved by targeting war-sustaining industry (e.g., ammunition, fuel, parts, production of military aircraft, vehicles, and ships) and war-supporting industry (concrete, steel, power, materials-handling equipment, and interindustry transportation).[21] In theory, this degradation would make military forces combat-ineffective. In practice, the impacts of targeting industry have been mixed. During World War II, Allied attacks against ball-bearing plants had a negligible impact on military forces. The targeting of German oil and aviation fuel severely degraded the Luftwaffe but only after a long period of sustained bombing (i.e., exhaustion).[22]

In practice, militaries and industry maintain stockpiles of vital components, creating a significant delay between disruption and impact. Industrial equipment is rugged and difficult to destroy. Governments dedicate repair crews to important industries and find alternative sources (e.g., the black market). Industry can complicate targeting by dispersing, developing backup or alternative systems, relocating near entities protected by international conventions (e.g., hospitals, religious sites), or innovating new solutions, routes, methods, and sources. Deliberate, consistent targeting must occur to use up the existing stockpile and prevent replenishment of stockpiles.

Time is both the advantage and bane of the annihilation method. Designed for rapid results, annihilation is intended to knock the opponent off balance and finish it off before it is able to recover and adjust. Conceptually, this can be achieved through parallel attack—simultaneous attacks across multiple target systems. In practice, conducting parallel attack and achieving rapid results requires an overwhelming advantage.

If it fails to work quickly, annihilation often unintentionally devolves into exhaustion. World War II is replete with examples of theater maneuver designed to create a decisive battle that turned into exhaustion: North Africa, Italy, Yugoslavia, D-Day, the Battle of Britain, the Combined Bomber Offensive, the Battle of the Atlantic, and Pacific island hopping. In comparison, the Germans were extremely successful until their advantages in the ground domain were nullified by the English Channel and, later, the vast expanse of Russia and its crushing winter.

This miscalculation can be fueled by unrealistic expectations of what is possible with available resources or by gross underestimations of enemy resolve. Over time, resources must be dedicated to repair and replace absorbing manpower and matériel. It is a twofold cost because not only must those be purchased but those resources are also no longer participating in the growth of the country's civil economy. Unfortunately, it may not be obvious that the strategy has devolved into exhaustion until many years into the war or even afterward.

Exhaustion

Sometimes referred to as the strategy of the weak, exhaustion targets morale through a combination of kinetic attacks and information operations against either military forces or civilian targets. Exhaustion creates in the adversary's mind the perception of "the improbability of victory or the unacceptable cost" of continuing the war, wearing down the enemy's resolve over time.[23] This strategy is useful when there is a major difference in the cost of forces (e.g., irregular versus conventional forces) or when a country can trade space for time. Because exhaustion takes time, it is selected by those with long time horizons who can essentially wait out a victory in pursuit of their objectives.

When targeting military forces, the intent is to destroy equipment and people faster than the adversary's ability to reconstitute, which eventually leads to combat ineffectiveness. A good example of this was the Luftwaffe in World War II. While the Combined Bomber Offensive pursued a combination of destruction that would deliver a knockout blow, bombers and fighter escorts wore down the Luftwaffe to the point that it relied on inexperienced pilots and had insufficient numbers.

When exhaustion is employed against civilian targets, the objective is to get the population to stop supporting the government, perhaps even taking steps to install a more compliant government. German and British attacks against civilians during World War II failed to achieve the desired effect. The firebombing of Hamburg and Dresden did not have a decisive impact on national morale. An arguable exception was the nuclear attack on Japan. Even that case did not follow the causal chain, because the government sought peace without significant pressure from the population.

LEARNING BOX 16.1: EXAMPLES OF SUCCESSFUL COMPELLENCE METHODS

Annihilate:

- The Germans used maneuver warfare during World War II to capture most of Europe.
- The US "shock and awe" campaign quickly deposed Saddam Hussein.
- The Islamic State used conventional forces to capture northern Iraq.

Exhaust:

- The Taliban fought as an insurgency during the US occupation of Afghanistan.
- The Soviet Union traded space for time to wear down Germany during World War II.

Deny:

- British control of Gibraltar and the Suez Canal denied the German navy access to the Mediterranean Sea during World War II.
- The 1981 Israeli bombing of an Iraqi nuclear reactor delayed nuclear weapons development.
- The Japanese attack on Pearl Harbor, Singapore, and the Philippines delayed Allied responses while Japan secured desired natural resources and established a defensive perimeter.

Decapitate:

- Coalition attacks on command centers isolated Saddam Hussein from his commanders during Desert Storm.
- The death of Osama Bin Laden led to the Islamic State splintering off from al-Qaeda.

Intimidate:

- Spain withdrew forces from Iraq after al-Qaeda attacks on Spanish commuter trains in 2004.

Subvert:

- Russian information operations and support to irregulars destabilized Ukraine, facilitating the Russian takeover of Crimea and undermining Ukraine's opportunity to join the North Atlantic Treaty Organization (NATO).
- Islamic State social media motivated "homegrown" terrorist attacks in Western countries.

Deny

There are three types of denial. The first type focuses on enemy frontline forces, denying their ability to control key terrain. Key terrain can be a choke point, such as the Sinai Desert. Key terrain may provide access to natural resources (e.g., oil, fishing rights, diamonds, water, and land for grazing livestock). Attempts to treat entire borders as key terrain have been less successful. The French Maginot Line and the German Atlantic Wall were both classic, though failed, World War II attempts to deny access to key terrain. A contemporary variant is China's antiaccess/area-denial concept, which envisions long-range cruise missiles, antiship missiles, and antiaircraft missiles to deny US maritime access and use of nearby air bases.[24]

The second type of denial focuses on key transportation nodes or choke points to prevent reinforcements and movement of second-echelon forces. In some cases, these will increase the adversary's vulnerability to direct attacks. During Operation Desert Storm, coalition forces destroyed key bridges to delay the deployment of Saddam's premier Republican Guard armor forces. On the other hand, bombing the Ho Chi Minh Trail was only marginally effective in reducing the movement of troops and supplies into South Vietnam.

The third type denies the enemy's employment of some key offensive capability. Whether the threat is a weapon such as a WMD, an improvised explosive device (IED), a delivery platform such as a ballistic missile or a bomber, or a computer network attack, each of these methods seeks to deny the enemy the ability to employ the weapon. Early World War II British plans intended to target Luftwaffe forces on the ground to "blunt the much-feared knockout blow."[25] Of course, denial of an offensive capability is simpler when there is a single key target such as a nuclear enrichment facility. Destroying every enemy airfield and aircraft often requires an unrealistic amount of resources. While conceptually the British were seeking denial, in practice the amount of resources they could dedicate resulted in an exhaustion approach.

Decapitation

Decapitation disables the ability to make and/or distribute decisions. For ground forces, decapitation is achieved by capturing the enemy capital, the hub of political and economic power, which is often associated with the enemy's surrender.[26] However, industrialization and globalization distributed power nodes across countries, making the capture of a capital in modern warfare a dubious metric for success.

For airpower, decapitation focuses on command. Decapitation is often oversimplified as killing the enemy leader. While this can disrupt the enemy in the short term, the long-term effect is often negligible because it can find a replacement leader.[27] For example, the death of Osama bin Laden disrupted al-Qaeda, but the externality of his death was the split-off of the Islamic State. Hence, his death did not result in organizational collapse but instead fragmentation and adaptation. Besides killing leaders, destroying command centers and communications nodes are alternative methods to disrupting command and control. Nonkinetic means such as electronic warfare and computer network attack can be equally effective, though the effects are typically of shorter duration.

Intimidation

The decision-making of enemy leaders can be manipulated without decapitation. While intimidation may involve destruction, its purpose is psychological targeting of the enemy mind. It is meant to alter the strategic decision-making process of leaders or the support of the population, elites, or external patron/donor. Efforts at intimidation vary from dramatic air shows to destroying the ruler's summer palace. Ideally, the action threatens something the leader values.

Insurgents frequently use intimidation to get support from the local population and to establish safe havens. Of course, counterinsurgents attempt their own variation of intimidation through foot patrols, checkpoints, raids, and air strikes.[28] For example, anecdotal evidence indicates that attacks by unmanned aerial vehicles created fear in Waziristan, which may have reduced cross-border activity into Afghanistan.[29] In some cases, intimidation can influence state behavior. In 2004, al-Qaeda successfully intimidated Spain by causing mass casualties on commuter trains, leading to a quick withdrawal of its forces from Iraq.

In some cases, planners will develop a show-of-force option to intimidate the enemy. These can be ineffective for several reasons. First, such actions rarely threaten anything specific. Second, a physical presence may not be sufficient to convince the adversary. In fact, the enemy may perceive the use of force as unlikely due to a lack of threat credibility, based on a combination of past behavior, feasibility, and relative importance of the issue to the intimidator.[30] In the case of Bashar al-Assad's use of chemical weapons in the Syrian Civil War, United Nations intervention was never credible since the Russians would veto any measure that hurt Assad's regime. Even cases of specific threats and overwhelming presence may still be insufficient. Three days before the bombing of Hiroshima, leaflets threatened impending destruction, which was insufficient to convince all of the civilians to evacuate.

Subversion

Typically done using nonkinetic information operations, subversion intends to get the enemy to turn on itself. Whether it results in a coup, a civil war, or a popular uprising, subversion can be used to disrupt the enemy or to facilitate regime change. Subversion often targets disgruntled members of the military or a segment of the population. In autocracies, some segment of the population is underrepresented in the country's political, economic, or military power structures, usually based on an identity cleavage (e.g., ethnicity, tribe, or religion). Subversion is a key part of any insurgency, creating weapons caches, human intelligence networks, and recruitment pools.

At the interstate level, subversion can exploit legal and political loopholes to reduce the potential for a response. Unlike a military invasion, the use of irregular warfare, cyberattacks, and covert operations provides a semblance of plausible denial. For example, Russian subversion was effective in Eastern Ukraine, leading to the bloodless capture and annexation of Crimea in 2014. Leveraging the perceived disenfranchisement of Russian-speaking Ukrainians living far from the capital, the Russians created an uprising that destabilized Ukraine for years and derailed Ukraine's potential induction into NATO and the European Union.[31]

CONCLUSION

Using the vocabulary of the six compellence methods provides intellectual clarity and rigor to strategic thinking. It facilitates standardization among planners and solidifies the logical connections between the selection of targets and desired effects. Through a framework of the ways of compellence, center of gravity, direct effects, and desired behavior, a rudimentary version of a strategy can be constructed or deconstructed. Understanding the adversary's strategy is an integral part to creating the friendly strategy, not to mention understanding how the enemy will evolve and adapt its strategy in reaction to your strategic efforts. It is foundational for understanding the problem, forming military objectives, and identifying both friendly and adversary centers of gravity.

LEARNING REVIEW

- Define deterrence, compellence, and cooperation.
- Distinguish between different methods of compellence by their target set and intended direct effect.
- Match the appropriate compellence method to the appropriate intended direct effect and cumulative effect.

APPENDIX: TYPOLOGY CLARIFICATION

This typology excludes several concepts to maximize clarity and minimize redundancy.

Extermination

Pure physical destruction and death with no intent to influence. The goal is for the adversary to be nonexistent. The use of extermination is rare and typically limited to intrastate violence (e.g., Rwanda in 1994, Bosnia in 1992–95, the Rohingya genocide in Myanmar in 2016–20). Even the infamous Mongols gave their adversaries an opportunity to capitulate before destroying a city.

Brute Force

Closely associated with extermination, the term is frequently misunderstood by students because it encourages them to focus on destruction without fully understanding the purpose of using force.

Punishment

The intentional targeting of civilians to affect their morale. On paper, bombing civilians was designed to shorten a war. In practice, targeting civilian morale via bombardment requires an exhaustion of morale, which proves elusive. The term fell out of use, to be replaced by the more accurate "exhaustion."

Risk

A gradual escalation variant of punishment. It is not a distinct strategy but a phased approach of exhaustion.

Attrition

The term lacks definitional rigidity in the military lexicon. In some circles, it has a pejorative connotation referring to high casualties for limited gains (e.g., trench warfare in World War I). J. Boone Bartholomees argues that attrition and exhaustion are interchangeable. The

US Marine Corps warfighting manual describes attrition as a direct attack lacking maneuver. Due to the lack of standardization and the readiness of alternatives, attrition was excluded from figure 16.1.

Total War

A major commitment of civic and economic resources to the war effort, which leads to targeting of war-supporting industries and society's morale.

Defense

Compellence methods are used both offensively and defensively. Defense land operations might be designed to deny key terrain or to exhaust the adversary by trading ground for time (e.g., like Russia did in the Napoleonic Wars and World War II). In the air, maritime, and information domains, offensive and defensive operations overlap. Countries on the strategic, conventional defensive will typically employ some type of offensive method, such as information operations to subvert the enemy's populace and troops, ballistic missiles for denial or intimidation, or terrorist attacks to exhaust the country's will.

NOTES

1. Sun Tzu, *The Art of War*, trans. Samuel B. Griffith (New York: Oxford University Press, 1971), 77.
2. Sun Tzu, 84.
3. In line with the thinking of Colin Gray, *Strategy and Defence Planning* (Oxford: Oxford University Press, 2014), 99. Gray's categorization of strategies is based on predicted future utility.
4. Valerie M. Hudson and Benjamin S. Day, *Foreign Policy Analysis: Classic and Contemporary Theory*, 3rd ed. (Lanham, MD: Rowman & Littlefield, 2020), 4.
5. Typology derived from Thomas Schelling, *Arms and Influence* (New Haven, CT: Yale University Press, 1966), 71; Edward Luttwak, *Strategy: The Logic of War and Peace* (Cambridge, MA: Belknap Press of Harvard University Press, 2001), 218; and Thomas Drohan, *A New Strategy for Complex Warfare: Combined Effects in East Asia* (Amherst, NY: Cambria Press, 2016).
6. Stephen Walt, *The Origins of Alliances* (Ithaca, NY: Cornell University Press, 1987).
7. Glenn H. Snyder, "The Security Dilemma in Alliance Politics," *World Politics* 36, no. 4 (1984): 461–95.
8. See Schelling, *Arms and Influence.*
9. See Jeffrey W. Knopf, "Varieties of Assurance," *Journal of Strategic Studies* 35, no. 3 (2012): 375–99.
10. John Mearsheimer, "An Unnecessary War," *Foreign Policy* 134 (January/February 2003): 50–59.
11. F. Gregory Gause III, "Iraq's Decisions to Go to War, 1980 and 1990," *Middle East Journal* 56, no. 1 (Winter 2002): 49; Janice Gross Stein, "Deterrence and Compellence in the Gulf, 1990–1991: A Failed or Impossible Task?," *International Security* 17, no. 2 (Fall 1992): 162.
12. Michael Fowler, "Constructing Effects: A Strategic Theory of Security Cooperation," in *Military Strategy, Joint Operations, and Airpower*, ed. Ryan Burke, Michael W. Fowler, and Kevin McCaskey (Washington, DC: Georgetown University Press, 2018).
13. Stephen Biddle, "Building Security Forces and Stabilizing Nations: The Problem of Agency," *Daedalus* 146, no. 4 (2017): 126–38.
14. See Barry R. Posen, *The Sources of Military Doctrine: France, Britain, and Germany between the World Wars* (Ithaca, NY: Cornell University Press), 13; and Robert Pape, *Bombing to Win: Airpower and Coercion in War* (Ithaca, NY: Cornell University Press, 1996), 56–57.
15. Patrick D. Allen, *Information Operations Planning* (Boston: Artech House, 2007), 39.

16. Randall Bowdish, "Military Strategy: Theory and Concepts" (doctoral diss., University of Nebraska–Lincoln, 2013), http://digitalcommons.unl.edu/cgi/viewcontent.cgi?article=1026&context=poliscitheses.

17. Robert Art, "The Fungibility of Force," in *The Use of Force: Military Power and International Politics*, ed. Robert Art and Kelly Greenhill (Lanham, MD: Rowman & Littlefield, 2015), 12.

18. Greg Cashman and Leonard C. Robinson, *An Introduction to the Causes of War: Patterns of Interstate Conflict from World War I to Iraq* (Lanham, MD: Rowman & Littlefield, 2007), 10.

19. See J. Boone Bartholomees, "The Issue of Attrition," *Parameters* 40, no. 1 (Spring 2010): 5–19.

20. "Introduction to Strategic Attack," in US Air Force, *Air Force Doctrine: Annex 3-70 Strategic Attack* (Maxwell Air Force Base, AL: Curtis E. LeMay Center for Doctrine Development and Education, 2017).

21. Interindustry transportation is the shipment of raw materials to and finished products from factories.

22. Tami Davis Biddle, *Rhetoric and Reality in Air Warfare: The Evolution of British and American Ideas about Strategic Bombing, 1914–1945* (Princeton, NJ: Princeton University Press, 2009).

23. Bartholomees, "Issue of Attrition," 9.

24. Stephen Biddle and Ivan Oelrich, "Future Warfare in the Western Pacific: Chinese Antiaccess/Area Denial, US AirSea Battle, and Command of the Commons in East Asia," *International Security* 41, no. 1 (2016): 7–48.

25. W. A. Jacobs, "The British Strategic Air Offensive against Germany in World War II," in *Case Studies in Strategic Bombardment*, ed. R. Cargill Hall (Washington, DC: Air Force Historical Studies Office, 1998), 108.

26. Stephen L. Quackenbush, "Centers of Gravity and War Outcomes," *Conflict Management and Peace Science* 33, no. 4 (2016): 364–65.

27. Patrick B. Johnston, "Does Decapitation Work? Assessing the Effectiveness of Leadership Targeting in Counterinsurgency Campaigns," *International Security* 36, no. 4 (2012): 47–49.

28. Stathis N. Kalyvas, *The Logic of Violence in Civil War* (New York: Cambridge University Press, 2006).

29. Peter Bergen and Katherine Tiedemann, "Washington's Phantom War: The Effects of the U.S. Drone Program in Pakistan," *Foreign Affairs*, July/August 2011, 17; Alex S. Wilner, "Targeted Killings in Afghanistan: Measuring Coercion and Deterrence in Counterterrorism and Counterinsurgency," *Studies in Conflict and Terrorism* 33, no. 4 (2010): 307–29.

30. Schelling, *Arms and Influence*, 74–75; Daniel Byman and Matthew Waxman, *The Dynamics of Coercion: American Foreign Policy and the Limits of Military Might* (Cambridge: Cambridge University Press, 2002); Daryl Press, *Calculating Credibility: How Leaders Assess Military Threats* (Ithaca, NY: Cornell University Press, 2005).

31. Michael Kofman, Katya Migacheva, Brian Nichiporuk, Andrew Radin, and Jenny Oberholtzer, *Lessons from Russia's Operations in Crimea and Eastern Ukraine* (Santa Monica, CA: RAND Corp., 2017).

CHAPTER 17

The Paradox of Irregular Warfare

John T. Farquhar

Irregular warfare challenges armed forces across a broad spectrum, from concepts to application, from doctrine to training, and even in terminology. What is now commonly referred to as irregular warfare (IW) used to be called unconventional warfare, guerrilla warfare, revolutionary warfare, small wars, asymmetrical warfare, and others. Each term reflects similarities but also the zeitgeist of differences based on author or institution. *Joint Publication 1: Basic Doctrine for the Armed Forces of the United States* (JP 1), establishes common terminology and outlines appropriate theory for joint warfighters. JP 1 confronts the reality of the post-9/11 world: the "regular" wars since 2001 have been "irregular" by previous definitions. JP 1 clarifies the terms, which I paraphrase:

- War: Socially sanctioned violence to achieve a political purpose.
- Warfare: The mechanism, method, or modality of armed conflict against an enemy. It is the "how" of waging war. Warfare continues to change and be transformed by society, diplomacy, politics, and technology.[1]
- Traditional warfare: A violent struggle for domination between nation-states or coalitions or alliances of nation-states (often described in other publications as conventional or regular warfare).
- IW: A violent struggle among state or nonstate actors for legitimacy and influence over the relevant population(s). In IW, a less powerful adversary seeks to disrupt or negate the military capabilities and advantages of a more powerful military force, which usually serves that nation's established government.[2]

Related terms appear in *Joint Publication 3-23: Counterinsurgency*:

- Insurgency: The organized use of subversion and violence to seize, nullify, or challenge political control of a region. Insurgency can also refer to the group itself.
- Counterinsurgency (COIN): Comprehensive civilian and military efforts designed to simultaneously defeat and contain insurgency and address its root causes.[3]

JP 1 explains that "warfare is a unified whole, incorporating all of its aspects together, traditional and irregular."[4] The doctrine acknowledges that common symmetries of language—

conventional/unconventional, traditional/nontraditional, regular/irregular—no longer work.[5] Since 9/11, IW has become the norm. Making matters worse, many respected, older works use a variety of terms to describe aspects of IW: guerrilla warfare, insurgency, revolutionary warfare, asymmetrical warfare, small wars, often paired with civil war. Some describe terrorism and guerrilla warfare as tactics to achieve the political objectives of IW. The confusion generated by complex, overlapping terms mirrors the challenges of waging irregular war. Despite its quest for clarity, standardization, and common language, joint doctrine faces a paradox where IW is inherently messy, amorphous, and confusing; IW defies convention and precise definition. For joint teamwork and communication, learn the JP 1 terms, but be aware that reality will mock you.

To best comprehend IW, students should explore the ideas of four theorists: T. E. Lawrence, Mao Zedong, David Galula, and David Kilcullen. Lawrence and Mao articulate concepts associated with insurgency, revolutionary war, and guerrilla war, while Galula and Kilcullen examine COIN and counterterrorism (CT). Each theorist emphasizes the political, psychological, and social dimensions of war. All would agree with a theme: IW is a battle of ideas, a struggle for the hearts, minds, and aspirations of the population. Furthermore, IW reinforces Carl von Clausewitz's observation that war is politics by other means.[6] The four theorists form the bedrock of contemporary IW doctrine and insist that comprehending political objectives and the political acts to achieve them is paramount.

T. E. LAWRENCE

Thomas Edward Lawrence (T. E. Lawrence) (1888–1935), also known as Lawrence of Arabia, stands as one of the most fascinating military figures of the twentieth century. Oxford University–educated in literature and the classics, he mastered several Arabic dialects in his travels across Palestine, Lebanon, Syria, Egypt, and Turkey in the five years before World War I. After volunteering to serve the British Army as an intelligence officer, Lawrence received the task of inciting an Arab revolt against Turkish forces in the Arabian Peninsula (mostly modern-day Saudi Arabia). He proved astute as an "outside the box" thinker who captured his insights in a literary classic, *The Seven Pillars of Wisdom* (1922), and a condensed article, "The Science of Guerrilla Warfare," known for its conciseness and originality.

Lawrence adapts strategy and tactics to match the cultural, geographic, and political realities of the Arabian Desert. He recognizes that Arab Bedouin tribesmen were different from a conventional army and fought as families, not as disciplined soldiers. Hence, Bedouins could not afford casualties and needed to avoid battles, but instead they could excel at raiding enemy supply lines. Lawrence raises the question of how the Turks could defend against a nomadic, undisciplined, irregular Arab army hidden by the desert and appearing at will: "Suppose they were an influence, a thing invulnerable, intangible, without front or back, drifting about like a gas? Armies were like plants, immobile as a whole, firm-rooted, nourished through long stems to the head. The Arabs might be a vapor, blowing where they listed. It seemed that a regular soldier might be helpless without a target. He would own the ground he sat on, and what he could poke his rifle at?"[7]

Lawrence describes the "algebraic, biological, and psychological" elements of IW:

- Algebraic: Those elements that can be measured: physical size and space, numbers of troops and population.

- Biological: Thinking of the enemy as a biological organism, understanding the actions of humanity in battle, comprehending the Arabs not as an army but as individuals and families, and avoiding casualties by never giving the enemy a target.
- Psychological: Comprehending the power of ideas and the value of propaganda; preparing combatant's minds for battle as more important than arranging their bodies in formation.[8]

Lawrence considers his amateur, civilian mind-set an asset that provides a fresh perspective untainted by military discipline and dogma. He considers the IW fought on the Arabian Peninsula as an experiment, although not complete, of the scientific principles of guerrilla warfare. The final page of "The Science of Guerrilla Warfare" proves a masterpiece, capturing succinctly the essence of IW:

> Here is the thesis: Rebellion must have an unassailable base, something guarded not merely from attack, but from the fear of it: such a base as the Arab revolt had in the Red Sea ports, the desert, or in the minds of men converted to its creed. It must have a sophisticated alien enemy, in the form of a disciplined army of occupation too small to fulfill the doctrine of acreage: too few to adjust number to space, in order to dominate the whole area effectively from fortified posts. It must have a friendly population, not actively friendly, but sympathetic to the point of not betraying rebel movements to the enemy. Rebellions can be made by 2% active in a striking force, and 98% passively sympathetic. The few active rebels must have the qualities of speed and endurance, ubiquity and independence of arteries of supply. They must have the technical equipment to destroy or paralyze the enemy's organized communications, for irregular war is . . . in its extreme degree, of attack where the enemy is not. In 50 words: Granted mobility, security (in the form of denying targets to the enemy), time, and doctrine (the idea to convert every subject to friendliness), victory will rest with the insurgents, for the algebraical factors are in the end decisive, and against them perfections of means and spirit struggle quite in vain.[9]

MAO ZEDONG

Like T. E. Lawrence, Chinese leader Mao Zedong (1893–1976) gained international fame for his ideas on guerrilla war, political mobilization, and protracted war. In terms of sheer numbers, Mao influenced more people than all other military theorists combined. Today's Chinese Communist Party and military leadership continue to extol Mao's writings.

Born to a prosperous peasant family, Mao exploits a period of revolutionary turmoil to lead the communist Red Army to victory in the Chinese Civil War (1927–49) and then to rule the People's Republic of China as a totalitarian communist state. Mao's military writings emphasize five key ideas:

- The political nature of war—Mao links war and politics.
- The role of the military as a political instrument in revolutionary war—the Red Army *is* the Chinese Communist Party during the Chinese Civil War.
- The advantages of protracted war for revolutionaries—wear out and demoralize the enemy over years of struggle.

- Mao's three stages of protracted war—a systematic process to transition from insurgent, guerrilla warfare to traditional (or conventional) warfare. Mao believed IW could not win final victory on its own.
- The primacy of ideas over weapons—political indoctrination to weaponize the people's aspirations mattered more than military victories; ideas over technology.[10]

"Winning the hearts and minds of the people" emerges as a primary theme of Mao's writing as well as "time is on the side of Communism." Many specialists note similarities between Mao and Carl von Clausewitz and between Mao and Sun Tzu. For example, in "On Protracted War" (1938), Mao writes, "War is a continuation of politics," "In a word, war cannot for a single moment be separated from politics," and "It can therefore be said that politics is war without bloodshed while war is politics with bloodshed." Consequently, Mao emphasizes the overwhelming priority of political mobilization of the masses.[11]

Mao's theory of protracted war provides a blueprint for insurgency in some ways similar to Lawrence's "fifty words." Like Lawrence, Mao believes that time and space favored the insurgent. In contrast to Sun Tzu, Mao believes that a protracted war favored the militarily weak and drained the resources and the will of the strong (i.e., the government). Mao describes three stages of protracted war:

- Strategic defensive: Where the enemy was on the offensive and the revolutionary Red Army must adopt the strategic defensive, avoiding battle, defending no territory, surviving, and building base camps in isolated, rural, rugged terrain in order to politicize the masses.
- Strategic stalemate: Where the insurgent expands his base areas through guerrilla war, conducts hit-and-run raids, denies targets to the enemy by blending into the population, infiltrating rear areas, and increases political work with the population. In stage 2, the revolutionaries begin to build a regular army, form a shadow government, and expand their rural base camps.
- Strategic counteroffensive: When strong enough, in stage 3 revolutionary forces transition to traditional (or conventional) war. Mao's Red Army did fight battles, take cities, and destroy enemy military forces. Stage 3 is crucial for victory, but if defeated by enemy forces, the insurgent simply returns to stage 2 or stage 1 since time is on the side of the revolutionary.[12]

Mao's theory of protracted war proved successful in the largest civil war in history and inspired a generation of anticolonialist, nationalist, and communist revolutionaries around the world. Mao provided the weak a method for victory against more powerful and technologically advanced armies, as shown by revolutionary victories against the French in Indochina (1945–54) and Algeria (1954–62) and in the Vietnam War against the South Vietnamese and the Americans (1961–75).

DAVID GALULA

Confronted by a tide of people's wars in the mid-twentieth century, French army officer David Galula (1919–67) devised a counter to Mao's revolutionary method. In *Counterinsurgency Warfare: Theory and Practice* (1964), he provided an intellectual foundation for IW and practical, actionable steps for combating insurgency. Although intended to help American forces in Vietnam, Galula's thoughts also profoundly influenced Gen. David Petraeus and US Army leadership battling Islamist insurgents in Afghanistan (2001–21) and Iraq (2003–present). Galula's emphasis on security for the population emerged as a key theme of contemporary COIN doctrine, best codified in the US Army's *Field Manual 3-24: Counterinsurgency* (2006).

Born in French Tunisia, Galula formed a unique perspective on IW based on his personal experience fighting with the Free French forces in North Africa, Italy, and France in World War II. He also served as a military observer of the Chinese Civil War, the failed communist revolution in Greece, and the successful Philippine repulse of the communist Hukbalahap movement in the late 1940s. Although he did not fight in French Indochina, Galula commanded a company of French colonial infantry in a successful pacification campaign in Algeria (1956–58). After retiring from the French army in 1962, Galula wrote *Counterinsurgency Warfare* as a research fellow at Harvard University. Before his death in 1967, Galula earned respect as a leading expert in COIN theory.[13]

Galula's *Counterinsurgency Warfare* appeals to COIN practitioners. He emphasizes that insurgents are materially weak but possess the strategic initiative. They not only determine when an insurgency begins but also the timing and pace of the campaign. At the outset, counterinsurgents possess all the tangible advantages: an established government, diplomatic recognition, political legitimacy, administrative and police control, and financial, industrial, and agricultural resources. In contrast, the insurgent possesses few tangible means but vital intangible assets: the ideas of a cause and the grievances of the people. Additionally, the counterinsurgent faces a huge liability: the responsibility for maintaining order and stability throughout the country. These opposites result in a truism: insurgency is cheap; COIN is costly.[14] Galula insists that the objective for both the insurgent and counterinsurgent is the population: "If the insurgent manages to dissociate the population from the counterinsurgency, to control it physically, to get its active support, he will win the war because, in the final analysis, the exercise of political power depends on the tacit or explicit agreement of the population or, at worst, on its submissiveness."[15] Clear, concise, and logical, Galula's ideas offer practical suggestions for those "on the ground" confronted with overwhelming political and military problems. What does a junior officer do to confront a nameless, faceless foe? Galula provides a start. For example, he presents a number of short, useful concepts:

- Revolutionary war: Consists of "cold revolutionary war" (insurgents remain legal and nonviolent) and "hot revolutionary war" (insurgents become openly illegal and violent).[16]
- Four conditions for a successful insurgency: (1) a cause, (2) a police and administrative weakness in the counterinsurgent, (3) a not-too-hostile geographic environment, and (4) outside support in the middle- and later-stages of the insurgency.[17]
- In cold revolutionary war, the counterinsurgent should be open to four general courses of action: (1) acting directly against insurgent leaders, (2) acting indirectly against the conditions driving an insurgency, (3) infiltrating the insurgent movement, and (4) building up or reinforcing his political machine.[18]
- Four laws of counterinsurgency in "hot revolutionary war": (1) support of the population is as necessary for the counterinsurgent as the insurgent, (2) support is gained through an active minority, (3) support from the population is conditional, and (4) intensity of efforts and vastness of means are essential.[19]

- A step-by-step counterinsurgency procedure (strategy):
    - Concentrate enough armed force to destroy or to expel the main body of armed insurgents.
    - Detach sufficient troops to oppose an insurgent's comeback.
    - Establish contact with the population and control its movements.
    - Destroy the local insurgent political organizations.
    - Set up, by elections, new provisional local authorities.
    - Test these authorities and replace the soft and incompetent ones.
    - Group and educate the leaders in a national political movement.
    - Win over or suppress the last insurgent remnants.[20]

Although there is no evidence that Galula read T. E. Lawrence, his ideas reflect serious study of Mao's theory of protracted war and other writings on guerrilla warfare.[21] For those confronting the daunting challenge of insurgency, Galula provides a way to start and a strategy to follow. Despite his expertise and valuable insights, warnings should sound in a reader's mind. Remember Clausewitz's observation "Everything in strategy is very simple, but the simplest thing is difficult"?[22] And Sun Tzu's famous line "Therefore, it can be said that, one may know how to win, but cannot necessarily do so"?[23] Thus, the budding student of war should remain cautious regarding Galula's sage advice. Fog, friction, and chance will always remain in play, and population support can be fickle.

DAVID KILCULLEN

A studied reader of T. E. Lawrence, Mao Zedong, David Galula, and other classic theorists of insurgency and COIN, former Australian lieutenant colonel David Kilcullen, PhD, is one of the leading contemporary thinkers on modern strategy. Kilcullen served with Australian COIN forces in East Timor and later with the US Army in Iraq and Afghanistan, most notably as the commanding general's senior COIN adviser. Kilcullen played a major role in contributing to the US Army and US Marine Corps doctrine that resulted in the acclaimed joint service *Field Manual 3-24*, which integrated classical insurgency and COIN theories in a comprehensive COIN campaign planning guide. Additionally, Kilcullen has published a number of books and articles, including *The Accidental Guerrilla: Fighting Small Wars in the Midst of a Big One* and "Twenty-Eight Articles: Fundamentals of Company-Level Counterinsurgency."

In *The Accidental Guerrilla*, David Kilcullen adapts COIN concepts into an adaptive hybrid warfare model, transforming classic IW ideas to meet contemporary challenges in an era of globalization. He theorizes that America's global war on terrorism (GWOT) consists of a global insurgency with a "vanguard of hypermodern" international terrorists associated with al-Qaeda and its affiliates, paired with local, traditional Muslim tribal groups. The al-Qaeda vanguard exploits modern tools of globalization and applies a transnational guerrilla warfare strategy. It inspires, organizes, funds, and accelerates long-standing local grievances. Often, traditional, nonstate Muslim tribes and other social groups reject Western values and intrusion. They view Westerners as invaders of their space and a threat to their religion and way of life.[24]

In "Twenty-Eight Articles," Kilcullen contributes to the population control theories that marked the 2007–8 "surge" in Iraq and the 2009–11 strategy in Afghanistan. He introduces concise, practical measures reminiscent of Galula but oriented to junior, tactical-level leaders. Among his precepts, Kilcullen communicates some nontraditional gems of thought:

- Diagnose the problem. Once you know your area and its people, you can begin to diagnose the problem. Who are the insurgents? What drives them? What makes local leaders tick? . . . This means you need to know your real enemy, not a cardboard cut-out. The enemy is adaptive, resourceful and probably grew up in the region where you will operate. The locals have known him since he was a boy—how long have they known you? Your worst opponent is not the psychopathic terrorist of Hollywood, it is the charismatic follow-me warrior who would make your best platoon leader.
- Rank is nothing: Talent is everything. Not everyone is good at counterinsurgency. Many people don't understand the concept, and some who do can't execute it. It is difficult, and in a conventional force only a few people will master it. Anyone can learn the basics, but a few "naturals" do exist. Learn how to spot these people and put them into positions where they can make a difference.
- Be there. The most fundamental rule of counterinsurgency is to be there. You can almost never outrun the enemy. If you are not present when an incident happens, there is usually little you can do about it. So your first order of business is to establish presence. . . . This demands a residential approach—living in your sector, in close proximity to the population, rather than raiding into the area from remote, secure bases. Movement on foot, sleeping in local villages, night patrolling: All these seem more dangerous than they are. They establish links with the locals, who see you as real people they can trust and do business with, not as aliens who descend from an armored box. Driving around in an armored convoy—day-tripping like a tourist in hell—degrades situational awareness, makes you a target and is ultimately more dangerous.[25]

In sum, David Kilcullen argues that protecting the people and winning their respect in a practical sense are more important than killing insurgents. He defines COIN as "a competition with the insurgent for the right and the ability to win the hearts, minds and acquiescence of the population."[26] He emphasizes that the enemy is smart and adaptive. Not blind to the drawbacks of population-centric COIN, Kilcullen states that successful counterinsurgencies take time: ten years is the norm; difficult ones take a generation. Finally, students should remember that Kilcullen's "Twenty-Eight Articles" contains nuggets of practical truth that, like other military theories, are easy to state but difficult to do.

CONCLUSION

At its core, IW is political warfare. Current joint doctrine builds on the wisdom of T. E. Lawrence and Mao Zedong as they expressed ideas related to insurgency and revolutionary war. Lawrence's fifty words provide a blueprint to the insurgent given mobility, security, time, and doctrine, while Mao's ideas on mass political mobilization and three stages of protracted war inspire the weak against the strong. On the other hand, Galula captures the priority of protecting and controlling the population versus killing terrorists. He provides simple, practical steps for the counterinsurgent who faces the vast resource burden of maintaining order and stability over decades. Kilcullen advances COIN to the twenty-first century with both practical tactics and strategic insights into modern challenges. He links modern transnational, global terrorist networks utilizing high-tech communications and weaponry with local, traditional tribal groups who reject Western globalization and values. Hence, IW presents a paradox in terminology (IW is now the norm) and practice (terrorists reject globalism and Western values but use its freedoms, transportation, and technology to fight against Western militaries).

LEARNING REVIEW

- Describe how IW differs from conventional land warfare.
- Recall the key concepts of insurgency theory and COIN theory.
- Evaluate the utility of the concepts of hybrid warfare and unconventional war.
- Describe the conditions under which IW would be the preferred military option.
- Evaluate military options to counter IW.

NOTES

1. Joint Chiefs of Staff (JCS), *Joint Publication 1: Basic Doctrine for the US Armed Forces, Incorporating Change 1, July 12, 2017* (hereafter *JP 1*) (Washington, DC: Department of Defense, March 25, 2013), ix, I-4, https://www.jcs.mil/Portals/36/Documents/Doctrine/pubs/jp1_ch1.pdf?ver=2019-02-11-174350-967.
2. JCS, *JP 1*, x, I-6.
3. JCS, *Joint Publication 3-24: Counterinsurgency* (Washington, DC: April 28, 2018; validated April 4, 2020), 51, 106, https://www.jcs.mil/Portals/36/Documents/Doctrine/pubs/jp3_24pa.pdf.
4. JCS, *JP 1*, I-5.
5. JCS, I-5.
6. Carl von Clausewitz, *On War*, ed. and trans. Michael Howard and Peter Paret (Princeton, NJ: Princeton University Press, 1989), 87–88, 605–7.
7. T. E. Lawrence, "Guerrilla Warfare" (originally "The Science of Guerrilla Warfare"), Encyclopedia Britannica, accessed April 13, 2021, https://www.britannica.com/topic/T-E-Lawrence-on-guerrilla-warfare-1984900.
8. Lawrence.
9. Lawrence.
10. Mao Tse-tung, "On Protracted War" and "Problems of Strategy in Guerrilla War," in *Selected Military Writings of Mao Tsetung* (Peking: Foreign Languages Press, 1972), 155–56, 167–68, 208–19, 226–29.
11. Mao Tse-tung, 226–27.
12. Mao Tse-tung, "The Three Stages of Protracted War," in *Selected Military Writings of Mao Tsetung*, 210–19.
13. For an insightful, detailed biography, see Ann Marlowe, *David Galula: His Life and Intellectual Context* (Carlisle, PA: Strategic Studies Institute, US Army War College, 2010).
14. David Galula, *Counterinsurgency Warfare: Theory and Practice* (Westport, CT: Praeger Security International, 2006), 3–5.
15. Galula, 4.
16. Galula, 43.
17. Galula, 28.
18. Galula, 44.
19. Galula, 52–55.
20. Galula, 55–56.
21. See especially chap. 3, "The Insurgency Doctrine," in Galula, *Counterinsurgency Warfare*, 29–39.
22. Clausewitz, *On War*, 119.

23. Tao Hanzhang, *Sun Tzu's Art of War: The Modern Chinese Interpretation*, trans. Yuan Shibing (New York: Sterling Innovation, 2007), 39.

24. David Kilcullen, *The Accidental Guerrilla: Fighting Small Wars in the Midst of a Big One* (Oxford: Oxford University Press, 2009); David Kilcullen, "Twenty-Eight Articles: Fundamentals of Company-Level Counterinsurgency," *Military Review* (May/June 2006): 103–8.

25. Kilcullen, "Twenty-Eight Articles," 103, 105.

26. Kilcullen, 103.

CHAPTER 18

Airpower's Unconventional Irregular Warfare Challenge

John T. Farquhar

In a 2015 *Wall Street Journal* article, "Why Air Power Alone Won't Beat ISIS," military analyst Max Boot presents a clear thesis: anti-ISIS coalition airpower efforts will fail if not combined with ground forces.[1] He describes early airpower theories and their limitations confronting irregular warfare (IW).[2] He looks at the airpower doctrine devoted to strategic air war for an industrial age but neglects more contemporary thinking. His critique appears on the mark and is largely unchallenged by many contemporary airmen, but Boot's article misses an even more important question, given public opposition to committing large numbers of ground forces in Syria and Iraq: What can airpower do to confront the Islamic State and counter IW?

A survey of the relatively limited contemporary literature devoted to airpower and IW reveals a focus on kinetic effects (e.g., bombing and targets) and overlooking the political nature of IW. For airmen confronting IW, three ideas by Prussian theorist Carl von Clausewitz set the stage:

- War is an instrument of politics.
- The first, the supreme, the most far-reaching act of judgment that the statesman and commander have to discern and agree on is the kind of war they are facing.
- Everything in strategy is very simple, but that does not mean that everything is very easy. Great strength of character, clarity, and firmness of mind are needed to follow through and not be distracted by thousands of diversions.[3]

With these thoughts in mind, airmen should consider the following thesis: In IW, first and foremost airpower is an instrument of politics. No matter how spectacular its technological potential in the air, space, and cyberspace domains, airpower is simply a means to achieve a political end. Current IW doctrine captures effective ideas to exploit airpower's many attributes that enhance other instruments of power, but airpower must be used within a comprehensive political strategy. Airpower alone, especially kinetic air strikes, cannot substitute for sound policy.

AIRPOWER: USEFUL FOR IRREGULAR WARFARE?

At its core, IW is conceptual, a battle of ideas. Considering the 1916 Arab Revolt, T. E. Lawrence observed the difficulty posed for a conventional army confronting an idea: "How would the Turks defend . . . [against] an influence, a thing invulnerable, intangible, without front or back, drifting about like a gas?"[4] Writing of the Chinese Revolution, Mao Zedong talked of winning the hearts and minds of the people and described a process of using an ideologically trained army to not only fight but also to persuade the people through word (propaganda, education, and indoctrination) and deed (moral example, civic actions, and coercion). Along the same lines, contemporary Australian counterinsurgency (COIN) expert David Kilcullen defines COIN as "a competition with the insurgent for the right and the ability to win the hearts, minds and acquiescence of the population."[5] For success, the counterinsurgent must use combat power carefully, indeed even sparingly, because misapplied firepower

> creates blood feuds, homeless people and societal disruption that fuels and perpetuates the insurgency. . . . The most beneficial actions are often local politics, civic action, and beat-cop behaviors. For your side to win, the people do not have to like you but they must respect you, accept that your actions benefit them, and trust your integrity and ability to deliver on promises, particularly regarding their security. In this battlefield popular perceptions and rumor are more influential than the facts and more powerful than a hundred tanks.[6]

The difficulty of IW lies not in theory but in practice. "Winning hearts and minds" seems intuitively obvious but proves exceedingly hard to do. How do you convince a population of your righteous view when you are an outsider and do not speak the language or know the culture? IW theory evokes Sun Tzu's famous line "Know the enemy and know yourself; in a hundred battles, you will never be defeated."[7] This certainly is a wise observation, but how can you "know your enemy" in a single short deployment? Additionally, do external political constraints prevent the targeting of the enemy's protected sanctuaries? Thus, the airman's conundrum is to use airpower as an instrument to advance the overall political objective without damaging the cause through excessive force.

IW poses a particularly tough challenge for airpower and airmen. For its first fifty years as a service, critics observed that the US Air Force (USAF) "has not effectively accounted for the realities" of IW in its airpower theory and instead preferred to think of it as "little more than a small version of conventional war."[8] Five differences between irregular and traditional (or conventional) wars prove vexing for applying airpower:

- Time: Classic insurgencies were protracted struggles intended to frustrate the Western concept of short, decisive wars.
- Dual military and political strategy: IW features both a military and a political strategy intended to harass and frustrate a government by showing its inability to cope. After wearing down the government's resources and morale, the insurgents harness the masses to overwhelm government forces in a conventional campaign. Airmen cannot directly influence a government's policies, and when airpower is called for in direct combat, it is too late.

- Insurgents use guerrilla tactics to negate superior government firepower by blending insurgents into the civilian population—to deny airpower targets.
- Insurgent/guerrilla logistics are largely immune from classic airpower interdiction and strategic attack, being too small, too dispersed, and too blended into the populace for attack.
- The center of gravity is the same for both the government and the insurgents: the people. "Putting fire and steel on target" may backfire by alienating this center of gravity.[9]

Critics caution that American airmen tend to be "doers" rather than "thinkers" and value technology and mental toughness over devotion to academic study and conceptual inquiry. During the first five decades of USAF doctrinal development, well-reasoned thinking on the application of airpower appeared occasionally, but basic USAF doctrine was "unaffected at best and contradictory at worst" in its treatment of IW.[10]

Seeking to establish airpower's role in IW, James S. Corum and Wray Johnson argue that airpower is an "indispensable tool" for militaries confronting terrorists, guerrillas, insurgents, or other irregular forces. They emphasize that all forms of aviation constitute airpower, including army, navy, and air force aircraft, plus civilian, police, unmanned, space, and other nontraditional aviation sources. Presenting a series of cases ranging from the 1916 Mexican punitive expedition against Pancho Villa to Israeli air strikes against Hezbollah in the early 2000s, Corum and Johnson conclude with eleven lessons:

1. A comprehensive strategy is essential. Military, political, economic, social, and other resources must be coordinated to attain a political goal.
2. The support role of airpower (e.g., intelligence, surveillance, and reconnaissance [ISR]; transport; medical evacuation; supply) is usually the most important and effective mission in a guerrilla war.
3. The ground-attack role of airpower becomes more important when the war becomes conventional (Mao's protracted war stage 3).
4. Bombing civilians is ineffective and counterproductive. Campaigns to punish can backfire and create insurgents.
5. There is an important role for the high-technology aspect of airpower in small wars. Smart bombs, space and cyber operations, and remotely piloted aircraft (RPA) provide information and precision.
6. There is an important role for the low-technology aspect of airpower in small wars. Simple, old aircraft can still do the job and may be more cost-effective for host nations.
7. Effective joint operations are essential for the effective use of airpower.
8. Small wars are intelligence-intensive.
9. Airpower provides the flexibility and initiative that is normally the advantage of the guerrilla.
10. Small wars are long wars.
11. The United States and its allies must put more effort into small-wars training. Irregular wars are not simply smaller versions of conventional war; similarly, building host-nation airpower capacity is an effective force multiplier.[11]

The writings of Corum and Johnson complement the important 2006 *Counterinsurgency* manual (Army FM 3-24 / Marine Corps MCWP 3-33.5) signed by lieutenant generals

David H. Petraeus and James N. Mattis. In this first new COIN manual in twenty years, a celebrated writing team captures classic ideas of how to defeat insurgency through protecting the population: "The government normally has an initial advantage in resources; however, that edge is counterbalanced by the requirement to maintain order and protect the population and critical resources. Insurgents succeed by sowing chaos and disorder anywhere; the government fails unless it maintains a degree of order everywhere."[12] In FM 3-24, "Appendix E: Airpower in Counterinsurgency" recognizes airpower's asymmetrical advantage and echoes Corum and Johnson. It emphasizes airpower's supporting role in most counterinsurgencies. It acknowledges airpower's importance in direct strike, intelligence collection, transport, airlift, close air support, reconnaissance, and surveillance and the need to develop a host nation's airpower capability. Still, with the manual's population-protection emphasis, the appendix cautions: "Precision air attacks can be of enormous value in COIN operations: however, commanders [must] exercise exceptional care. Bombing, even with the most precise weapons, can cause unintended civilian casualties. Effective leaders weigh the benefits of every air strike against its risks. An air strike can cause collateral damage that turns the people against the host-nation (HN) government and provides insurgents with a major propaganda victory."[13] Succinct, insightful, and conceptually sound, FM 3-24's airpower annex represents an important step forward in doctrinal thinking regarding airpower in IW. Furthermore, it demonstrates the value of applying academic thought to warfighting challenges.[14]

Despite the doctrinal advance, USAF major general Charles J. Dunlap Jr. claims that FM 3-24 failed to go far enough. He acknowledges the manual's skillful statement of classic, population-centric COIN doctrine but points out the document's failure to exploit contemporary airpower's potential made possible by advanced technology. More important, Dunlap argues, "the value of an Airman's contribution to the counterinsurgency . . . is not limited to airpower capabilities," but "equally—or more—important is the Airman's unique *way of thinking*." A joint doctrine, including an *air-minded* perspective, must emerge to fight unconventional war.[15]

Dunlap proposes changing FM 3-24's troop-heavy, close-engagement approach because airpower is an asymmetrical advantage for the United States. Airpower can replace American "boots on the ground," more likely to stir local resentment of foreign occupiers, with technology-enhanced capabilities of air, space, and cyberspace.[16] Dunlap reasons that due to domestic political constraints, "masses of ground forces, especially American troops, simply is not *sustainable* strategy."[17] Public aversion to US casualties and long-term, costly employment of American ground troops weakens FM 3-24's case. Instead of "clear-hold-build," airpower could provide an alternative "hold-build-populate," where airpower could help create havens, making it easier to rehabilitate, protect, and repopulate.[18] Dunlap fuses FM 3-24 COIN theories with contemporary precision, high-technology capabilities and thinking: "The challenge for military strategists is to devise *pragmatic* options within the resources realistically available to political leaders."[19]

Phillip S. Meilinger also critiques the boots-on-the-ground approach of American COIN doctrine. Even with the relative success of the 2007–8 "surge" in Iraq, Meilinger considers the presence of thousands of American ground troops dangerous and deadly for both US forces and for Iraq's civilian population. He suggests the US should study the British Royal Air Force's "air control" operations in the Middle East during the 1920s and 1930s and also the cases of Bosnia and Kosovo (1990s), Afghanistan (2001-2), and Iraq (2003), where airpower, special operations forces (SOF), and indigenous ground forces succeeded.[20] Meilinger reinforces Dunlap's argument and calls for a joint, air-centric COIN to build on American strengths and avoid political weaknesses. In other words, precision airpower plus SOF plus ISR plus indigenous troops is the key.[21]

In "Preparing for Irregular Warfare: The Future Ain't What It Used to Be," retired Air Force colonel John Jogerst lauds the USAF's superb tactical capabilities but proclaims these skills "irrelevant" strategically. In COIN, "the critical capability involves building the partner nation's airpower—an essential distinction."[22] In a war for political legitimacy, the USAF must understand the difference between "doing COIN (the job of the local authorities) and enabling COIN (the role of external actors)," including the United States.[23] Agreeing with FM 3-24, Jogerst emphasizes assisting the host nation by enhancing its local presence and enabling small-unit tactical prowess through "immediate, precise, and scalable firepower."[24] But unlike Dunlap or Meilinger, Jogerst emphasizes foreign internal defense (FID), building partner capability, and training host-nation air forces to do the job themselves.[25]

Jogerst proposes creating a permanent USAF Irregular Warfare Wing staffed by COIN experts to avoid the usual American tendency to provide overwhelming force independent of local control. Since IW and COIN are inherently political wars, host nations must be trained to function independently and reinforce the government's legitimacy.[26] Hence, a USAF IW wing would provide a long-term, sustainable organization with a COIN group to teach airpower employment and provide initial capability while integrating an FID group to develop host-nation capacity. Jogerst stresses that the wing must prepare a small number of personnel with intensive cultural and language skills to build useful personal relationships with the partner nations.[27]

Sanu Kainikara's *The Bolt from the Blue: Air Power in the Cycle of Strategies* (2013) presents fresh, air-minded perspectives useful for IW at the conceptual, strategic level. A former Indian Air Force wing commander and currently an air theorist at Australia's Air Power Development Centre, Kainikara argues that airpower planners must reject the concept of a linear end state.[28] Airpower represents an instrument in a cycle of strategies that include influence and shape, deterrence, coercion, and punishment. In other words, the spectrum of violence is not a line as often depicted, with humanitarian assistance on one end and total war on the other, but a circle (or cycle) with war termination immediately linked to postconflict stabilization. In this, Kainikara evokes Clausewitz's famous aphorism "In War the Result is Never Final."[29] Just as classic insurgency theory often talked of stages of guerrilla or IW, Kainikara suggests applying COIN air strategies as a cyclical process.

Kainikara emphasizes the correct calculation of ends and means and airpower's inherent flexibility. For example, in the strategy of influence and shape, Kainikara describes distinct airpower contributions to monitor, assist, intervene, police, and stabilize in an effort to avoid conflict.[30] Highlighting airpower's strategic contribution, Kainikara explores airpower's ability to apply nonlethal force through precision ISR. Like General Dunlap, Kainikara articulates four airpower advantages applicable to IW:

- It carries comparatively low operational risk with respect to one's own casualties.
- Since operational risk is low, it is easier to obtain political support for action.
- Airpower is scalable. It is relatively easy to ramp up or down the intensity and tempo of operations.
- Airpower responds rapidly to evolving threats.[31]

Western policymakers may be unable to resist applying limited airpower even when airpower alone may not win an IW. The need to "do something" will trump military planners' understanding of airpower's limits in fighting insurgencies.

The thinking on airpower's role in IW significantly advanced over the past decade. Airpower, combined with advanced ISR and SOF, generates unparalleled precision strikes and greatly enhances local forces. Operations in Afghanistan, Iraq, and Syria have demonstrated the value of airborne ISR in providing persistent overwatch for ground operations, convoy protection, and guarding forward outposts. Despite airpower's important technological contribution, airmen must resist the lure of technological determinism. Technology is vital and should not be minimized, but it is not a silver bullet.

Recent insurgencies present a twist for IW: insurgent airpower. For instance, the Liberation Tigers of Tamil Eelam (LTTE, aka the Tamil Tigers) fought a long insurgency (1976–2009) against the government of Sri Lanka that showcased the emergence of an insurgent Tamil Tigers air force.[32] The Islamic State of Syria and Iraq (ISIS) began using low-cost, commercial drone technology in 2014, proving innovative and adaptive in developing surveillance, reconnaissance, and limited strike capabilities. Exploiting gaps and seams in drone countermeasures, ISIS challenged counterinsurgent air superiority in specific areas in 2016 and 2017, as evidenced by the description of ISIS drones by the commander of US Special Operations Command as "the most daunting threat" for personnel in 2016. In a single day, as many as seventy insurgent drones flew underneath friendly air cover to achieve physical and psychological effects. Although no evidence showed autonomous or preprogrammed swarm capability, the ISIS drones achieved surprise and media sensation.[33] The drones thus achieved a political goal: validating ISIS's claims of sovereignty and legitimacy. ISIS airpower also served as an example for other insurgents. Beginning in 2019, Iranian-backed Houthi rebels in Yemen and Shia militias in Iraq began attacking Saudi Arabia. Both groups conducted a form of strategic air war with drone attacks, and the Houthis used Quds-2 short-range ballistic missiles against Saudi towns, airfields, and oil facilities.[34] Thus, technological diffusion opens another dimension of airpower potential for IW.

CONCLUSION

Context matters, history matters, and a government's political ends must be understood and acceptable to the populations involved. COIN and IW are inherently political. Outsiders will inevitably face frustration when local domestic politics and internal dysfunction take their toll. Airpower may provide enhanced capabilities to a host nation but cannot substitute for competent government. Therefore, an observation from T. E. Lawrence complements irregular airpower ideas and should not be ignored: "In 50 words: Granted mobility, security (in the form of denying targets to the enemy), time, and doctrine (the idea to convert every subject to friendliness), victory will rest with the insurgents, for the algebraical factors are in the end decisive, and against them perfections of means and spirit struggle quite in vain."[35]

Lawrence's ideas provide a blueprint to the insurgent (achieve mobility, security, time, and doctrine; create an unassailable base) but also to the counterinsurgent—deny these elements to the enemy. Lawrence's phrase of "algebraic factors" translates into land area, population size, government fiscal constraints, and other elements that can be counted. Airmen must contribute in the battle for ideas for IW through creative thinking—how to employ the many unique, force-multiplying attributes of airpower to the comprehensive political strategy. As technology advances, airmen must take steps to deny the enemy airpower's attributes as well. IW air theorists provide many of the tactical, operational, and strategic ideas needed to enhance local forces and avoid large numbers of American boots on the ground. However, used in political isolation, or without strategic thought, airpower simply illustrates the truth of Lawrence's fifty words: "for the algebraic factors are in the end decisive, and against them perfections of means and spirit struggle quite in vain." Airpower represents a perfection of means but in itself cannot negate the algebraic factors.

LEARNING REVIEW

- Describe the four advantages of airpower for IW: low operational risk, fewer obstacles for domestic political support, scalable intensity, and rapid response.
- Recall the primary air missions conducted in support of COIN.
- Debate airpower's role in IW.
- Describe why some see airpower as the political "easy button" in IW.

NOTES

1. Max Boot, "Why Air Power Alone Won't Beat ISIS," *Wall Street Journal*, December 2015. The author thanks Phillip S. Meilinger, Jim Titus, Wray Johnson, and two anonymous *Air and Space Power Journal* referees for insightful comments that improved this work.

2. Although specialists will debate the nuances and differences between terms, this article will use "irregular warfare," "small wars," "guerrilla war," and "counterinsurgency" interchangeably. Additionally, it substitutes "irregular warfare" for "low-intensity conflict" (LIC) for Dennis Drew's observations. For astute commentary on the problem of terminology in irregular warfare / counterinsurgency / small wars, see Colin S. Gray, "Irregular Warfare: One Nature, Many Characters," *Strategic Studies Quarterly* (Winter 2007): 37.

3. These famous passages have been paraphrased. Carl von Clausewitz, *On War*, ed. and trans. Michael Howard and Peter Paret (Princeton, NJ: Princeton University Press, 1984), 87, 88, 178.

4. T. E. Lawrence, "The Science of Guerrilla Warfare," in *Encyclopedia Britannica*, 14th ed. (1929), accessed April 13, 2021, https://www.britannica.com/topic/T-E-Lawrence-on-guerrilla-warfare-1984900.

5. David Kilcullen, "Twenty-Eight Articles: Fundamentals of Company-Level Counterinsurgency," *Military Review* (May/June 2006): 103.

6. Kilcullen, 103.

7. As famous as this line is, consider carefully the rest of the quote: "When you are ignorant of the enemy but know yourself, your chances of winning or losing are equal. If ignorant both of your enemy and of yourself, you are sure to be defeated in every battle." Tao Hanzhang, *Sun Tzu's Art of War: The Modern Chinese Interpretation* (New York: Sterling Innovation, 2007), 36.

8. Dennis M. Drew, "Air Theory, Air Force, and Low Intensity Conflict: A Short Journey to Confusion," in *The Paths of Heaven: The Evolution of Airpower Theory*, ed. Phillip S. Meilinger (Maxwell Air Force Base, AL: Air University Press, 1997), 321.

9. Drew, 323–25.

10. Drew, 347.

11. James S. Corum and Wray R. Johnson, *Airpower in Small Wars: Fighting Insurgents and Terrorists* (Lawrence: University Press of Kansas, 2003), 425–37.

12. Headquarters, Department of the Army, and Headquarters, Marine Corps Combat Development Command, Department of the Navy, Headquarters United States Marine Corps, *Field Manual 3-24 Marine Corps Warfighting Publication No. 3-30.5: Counterinsurgency* (respectively; hereafter FM 3-24) (Washington, DC, December 2006), 1–2. Although the manual has both Army and Marine Corps numerical designations, this chapter will simply refer to it in the text as FM 3-24. In *The Gamble: General Petraeus and the American Military Adventure in Iraq* (New York: Penguin Press, 2009), Thomas E. Ricks describes the writing of FM 3-24 as an intellectual, policy, and leadership tour de force. Ricks details General Petraeus's role in assembling a diverse team of practitioners and academics, both military and civilian, to produce a groundbreaking, insightful, focused attack on the challenge of counterinsurgency. FM 3-24 features the writings of David Galula, Charles Calwell, David Kilcullen, Roger Trinquier, and others, in addition to excerpts from famed guerrilla-warfare classics, including

works by Sun Tzu, T. E. Lawrence, and Mao Zedong. The field manual's annotated bibliography is impressive and worth professional study.

13. FM 3-24, E-1. The similarities between FM 3-24's airpower annex and Corum and Johnson are intentional: Jim Corum largely authored the document, with coordination in the early stage with Conrad Crane and Wray Johnson. Wray R. Johnson, telephone call with author, November 18, 2016.

14. A 2006 RAND Project Air Force monograph that provides a valuable primer on airpower's role in counterinsurgency and advocates for expanding the resources and scope of Air Force Special Operations Command's 6th Special Operations Squadron. In a thorough, perceptive analysis, the RAND team ably articulates four COIN principles: (1) understand the adversary, (2) build state capacity and presence, (3) control the population, and (4) keep the use of force to a minimum. The RAND study joins Drew's, Corum's, Johnson's, and others' ideas expressed in this article in reinforcing the theme that airpower provides a vital, cost-effective COIN enabler for a host nation's political strategy. Alan J. Vick, Adam Grissom, William Rosenau, Beth Grill, and Karl P. Mueller, *Air Power in the New Counterinsurgency Era: The Strategic Importance of USAF Advisory and Assistance Missions* (Santa Monica, CA: RAND Project Air Force, 2006).

15. Charles J. Dunlap Jr., *Shortchanging the Joint Fight: An Airman's Assessment of FM 3-24 and the Case for Developing Truly Joint Doctrine* (Maxwell Air Force Base, AL: Air University Press, 2008), 7–8. Note: General Dunlap's observations made an impact. The current COIN manual is now a joint publication, Joint Chiefs of Staff (JCS), *Joint Publication 3-24: Counterinsurgency* (Washington, DC: Department of Defense, April 24, 2018).

16. Dunlap, 13.

17. Dunlap, 33.

18. Dunlap, 43.

19. Dunlap, 64.

20. It should be mentioned that British air-control practices lacked many of today's ethical concerns and were not subject to global media scrutiny common to current operations. Phillip S. Meilinger, "Counterinsurgency from Above," *Air Force Magazine* 91, no. 7 (July 2008): 39, https://www.airforcemag.com/issue/2008-07/. Another well-written article reinforced the precision airpower plus SOF theme: John James Patterson VI, "A Long-Term Counterinsurgency Strategy," *Parameters* 40, no. 3 (Autumn 2010): 118–31.

21. Note that Dunlap and Meilinger do not say "airpower alone" but instead American airpower to augment host-nation forces—in other words, American air in lieu of American "boots." Phillip S. Meilinger, email message to author, May 12, 2016.

22. John D. Jogerst, "Preparing for Irregular Warfare: The Future Ain't What It Used to Be," *Air and Space Power Journal* 23, no. 4 (Winter 2009): 68.

23. Jogerst, 68.

24. Jogerst, 72.

25. Jogerst, 75.

26. Jogerst, 74.

27. Jogerst, 76. Complementing Colonel Jogerst's work, a 2010 RAND study, *Courses of Action for Enhancing U.S. Air Force "Irregular Warfare" Capabilities: A Functional Solutions Analysis*, systematically articulates four courses of action to build an IW mind-set and build capacity within the institutional Air Force. It reinforces Jogerst's emphasis on building partner capacity through FID and insists that many essential COIN tasks could not be done without the Air Force. Richard Mesic, David E. Thaler, David Ochmanek, and Leon Goodson, *Courses of Action for Enhancing U.S. Air Force "Irregular Warfare" Capabilities: A Functional Solutions Analysis* (Santa Monica, CA: RAND Project Air Force, 2010), xi, xix.

28. This refers to *Joint Publication 5-0*, which outlines an operational design process envisioning an initial state, identifying friendly centers of gravity, tangible "lines of effort" for focus, intermediate objectives for measured progress, and enemy centers of gravity, to achieve a desired end state linking military and political objectives. JCS, *Joint Publication 5-0: Joint Planning* (Washington, DC: December 1, 2020).

29. Carl von Clausewitz, *On War*, ed. and trans. Michael Howard and Peter Paret (Princeton, NJ: Princeton University Press, 1984), 80.

30. Sanu Kainikara, *The Bolt from the Blue: Air Power in the Cycle of Strategies* (Canberra, Australia: Air Power Development Centre, 2013), 35.

31. Paraphrased from Kainikara, 74–75.

32. Paige Ziegler, "Learning from the Liberation Tigers of Tamil Eelam," Strategy Bridge, April 13, 2017, https://thestrategybridge.org/the-bridge/2017/4/13/learning-from-the-liberation-tigers-of-tamil-eelam.

33. Don Rassler, *The Islamic State and Drones: Supply, Scale, and Future Threats* (West Point, NY: Combatting Terrorism Center, US Military Academy, 2018), v, 1–2, 23.

34. Emil Archambault and Yannick Veilleux-Lepage, " Drone Imagery in Islamic State Propaganda: Flying like a State," *International Affairs* 96, no. 4 (July 2020): 955–73, https://academic.oup.com/ia/article/96/4/955/5813533; "Yemen's Houthi Rebels Claim Attacks on Saudi Oil Facilities," Al Jazeera, April 12, 2021, https://www.aljazeera.com/news/2021/4/12/yemens-houthi-rebels-claim-strikes-on-saudi-oil-plants; "Yemen's Houthis Say They Launched Drone Attacks on Saudi Capital," Al Jazeera, April 1, 2021, https://www.aljazeera.com/news/2021/4/1/yemens-houthis-say-attacked-saudi-capital-riyadh-with-four-drone.

35. Lawrence described the "algebraic" factor as those things that could be measured: size of territory, number of troops, population size, and miles of roads and railroads, noting that in Arabia the Turks simply did not have enough troops for the land mass. Lawrence, "Science of Guerrilla Warfare."

PART V

PLANNING AND DESIGN IN THE CONTEMPORARY ENVIRONMENT

CHAPTER 19

Operational Design as a Framework for Strategic Understanding and Agility

Ryan Burke and Rob Grant

At the strategic and operational levels of war, military commanders and their staff study and use operational design. Operational design is a methodology and tool to understand the operational environment, understand the relevant problems underlying national security challenges, and communicate a conceptual approach—through *visualizing* and *describing*—to transform the environment into desired conditions.[1] As a practice, operational design is applicable across all security contexts, forms of warfare, and levels of leadership. Richard Swain, a former US Army colonel and an early developer of operational design, observed that not only senior military leaders can use design methodology but "design principles and practices are useful to all leaders contending with complex problems and situations"[2] as well. The strategic and operational levels of war can be characterized as complex phenomena. According to former secretary of defense and US Marine Corps general James Mattis, "*design does not replace planning, but planning is incomplete without design.* The balance between the two varies from operation to operation as well as within each operation. Design helps the commander provide enough structure to an ill-structured problem so that planning can lead to effective action toward strategic objectives."[3]

As aspiring future leaders, cadets who learn and practice operational design fundamentals—while appreciating the limitations and criticisms of design—gain early advantages over their peers. National security professionals will gain insight to the systemic challenges of developing and adapting military effects over time; grasp how tactical resources, missions, and tasks are determined for operational use; and be in an advanced position to not only solve complex, ill-defined problems but also be able to appraise how their own tactical operations promote (or counteract) strategic aims. Plus, learning the lexicon of design enables officers to engage in commanders' business and international security discourse earlier in their career.

This chapter introduces operational design as a tool for military strategy, presents the elementary foundations of design, and provides an overview of operational design practices. It explains how to accomplish the first major step in the design process: strategic guidance and strategic environment. It concludes by offering critiques, dangers, and limitations of using design methodologies.

DESIGN AND STRATEGY

Operational design has evolved since it emerged in the early 2000s. Design refers to creative and critical thinking to solve ill-structured problems.[4] It is a method to bring clarity from complexity by leveraging a variety of tools and perspectives to facilitate thinking, generate understanding, and communicate solutions.[5] Design is "'a method of problem solving that utilizes learning and rigorous dialectic to derive sound appreciation of the problem and the best options available for managing and treating' the underlying causes of complex transformative situations."[6] *Operational* design combines that creative and critical approach with elements of military planning.[7] Operational design is a multidisciplinary practice driven by critical and creative thinking through structured discourse among commanders and staff to create a deep understanding of ourselves in relation to an adversary and the environment, to create a logic for action through the arrangement of *ends*, *ways*, *means*, and *risk* and to transform complex security environments to maintain a position of advantage.[8]

Ill-structured contexts can be thought of as open systems where the relationship among parts do not produce linear, predictive outputs like a machine. Rather, the system is characterized by probabilities and tendencies, emergent properties, multidimensional relationships,[9] and hard-to-determine reactions to inputs. Examples include human economies, ant colonies, climate, and ecosystems. War and conflict are typically ill-structured systems.

There are three Clausewitzian concepts (see chapter 1) that inform the view that *war is a complex phenomenon*: war is a clash of wills, war is based on probabilities, and war is subject to fog and friction.[10] War is a human endeavor not governed by purely scientific laws or perfect political objectives but by the ever-shifting and imperfect human will and moral forces.[11] In other words, "rational political objectives can become skewed"[12] and even turn irrational due to the human conditions of fear, honor, and interests, as observed by Thucydides. Clausewitz alludes that the nature of war is one of probabilities and chance,[13] not replicable calculations. The trinity analogy evokes the notion that war "behaves in a non-linear manner—it never establishes a repeating pattern."[14] Clausewitz tells us that war is unpredictable due to fog and friction. Unpredictable systems tend toward complexity at best and chaos at worst. These concepts tell us we can treat war as a complex system and as ill-defined/ill-structured problems; therefore, we benefit from applying a conceptual approach (operational design) to planning. Concrete thinking, linear arguments, and rules in general do strategists little good, at least initially, in the broader joint planning process (JPP).

Military commanders throughout history have intuitively applied design concepts and principles in their thinking about campaigns and operations, though only recently have militaries codified design into a lexicon and framework for planning. While the US Army and US Marine Corps experimented with elements of design in the 1990s, the Joint Staff officially adopted operational design as a term/concept in 2002.[15] By the end of the decade, all services embraced operational design and incorporated it into doctrine and professional scholarship. Initial design thinking built on systemic operational design, or SOD, introduced by the Israeli military in the mid-to-late 1990s.[16] Some services embraced design, such as the Army and Marine Corps, while the Air Force and Navy had a more tepid response. Even with almost twenty years of refinement, the core idea behind operational design remains: a framework from which to *conceptualize* (i.e., understand, visualize, and describe that which is abstract) both ill-defined problems and approaches for "effective action towards strategic objectives."[17] The US military still defines operational design as the "analytical framework that underpins planning."[18] The goal of this and subsequent chapters is to introduce the basics of an "analytical framework," how to employ it, and what products result from such work.

Finally, a note on the relationship among the concepts of operational design, operational art, and the operational level of war. Just because the word "operational" modifies the word "design," operational design should not be confused with the operational level of war or operational art. Operational art is a "cognitive activity," while the operational level can be thought of as a "location where discrete activities take place."[19] Operational art is the broad cognitive "skill, knowledge, experience, creativity, and judgment" that commanders and their staff apply to operational design and planning.[20] Like operational art, operational design can also be thought of as a cognitive activity, and as such, operational art and design are mutually supportive activities. For simplicity, our focus remains on operational design as a part of the greater art of strategy. The operational level of war is typically synonymous with major campaigns and operations at the theater level of war—the bridge between strategic logic and tactical action. The methodologies and elements of operational design are easily applicable at the strategic and operational levels of war.

FOUNDATIONS OF DESIGN THINKING

There are a host of theoretical perspectives that design thinking and practice draw on. Operational design is a creative art that doctrine alone cannot teach but simply guides.[21] This section explores the elementary aspects of design thinking and theory; subsequent sections explore the doctrinal scaffolding through which to execute operational design and apply judgment.

Learning to think as an operational designer is a multidisciplinary endeavor, drawing from history, theory, doctrine, philosophy, and practice.[22] History provides perspective and scale as well as a place to gain experience by learning to think in time and about continuity versus contingency and generalities versus particulars—to see not just resemblances but also differences.[23] Leveraging theories and perspectives from political science, sociology, anthropology, organizational theory, psychology, and military theory helps the practitioner draw from a deep well when faced with ill-defined problems. Doctrine provides institutionally sanctioned principles for planning and executing military force. It is a guide that need not stifle creativity. It provides a common starting place and, more important, a common language through which to enter planning and design. Crisis situations rarely afford military planners much time to spend resolving vocabulary issues or getting lost in arguments over principles, concepts, and best practices. Doctrine is authoritative but requires judgment and assessment against the given context and situation.[24] Philosophical theories help planners to ask hard, meta-analysis questions about sociocultural contexts and meaning; philosophy provides a solid place from which to engage in critical, logical thinking while challenging cognitive biases. To excel at design, one must practice design. Practice encompasses learning theories, organizational learning constructs, and reflection during the execution to develop the skills and markers of adaptability.

Of all the various theories, systems theory is one of the chief constructs. A systems approach is *the* interdisciplinary theory for thinking about complex systems. Peter Singe states that "systems thinking is a discipline for seeing wholes. It is a framework for seeing interrelationships rather than things, for seeing patterns of change."[25] It is about "synthesizing and organizing complex and often contradictory information."[26] Typically, the word "system" evokes thoughts of traditional closed systems (such as a thermostat, a car, or a jet engine).

Such systems can be thought of as *complicated*, and for a given input to such systems, the output is known and calculable even if difficult to determine. In the case of design theory, systems are characterized as an open system where the boundaries are not always clear or are at least semipermeable to outside forces; the best we can do is find the most relevant actors/components and suborganizations of the system, knowing that the system will likely be in flux. There are multidimensional relationships and feedback loops inside such systems, making an output for a given input all but impossible to determine precisely. Such systems are *complex* systems: adaptable, self-organizing, nonlinear in its interactions, and with emergent properties. Design is a way of dealing with such systems.

Normally, the only way to deal with complex systems and design solutions to change such systems is through "simultaneous, rather than sequential actions."[27] This means doing many things at once, even if small. As one executes design, particularly in the development of an operational approach, it will become clear why lines of effort and simultaneity are key concepts of operational design.

Operational design thinking must remain wedded to military theory in order to be effective for security contexts. Clausewitzian theory emphasizes the interactive nature of actors and forces of war as a violent phenomenon; by nature, war is a complex system. The practitioner of operational design also draws on Sun Tzu's admonition to know oneself and know the enemy, and by doing so, one will never lose a war.[28] Here, it is not hard to imagine that Sun Tzu was thinking in terms of complex systems, philosophy, and history pushing the strategist to consider deep interdependent sociocultural systems: knowing oneself in relation to one's enemy in holistic terms. Design is a reflective practice similar to John Boyd's observe-orient-decide-act (OODA) loop (see chapter 15). The concepts of the OODA loop can be seen in the steps of design and planning: observe (frame the environment), orient (frame the problem, develop an approach), decide (conduct detailed planning), act (execute through military operations). The often forgotten or missed step in Boyd's OODA loop is that after an action, the underlying conditions of the system have changed, requiring one to iteratively return to the observe step since there are now fresh initial conditions that characterize the system. Military theory and design thinking go hand in hand, and the military strategist must incorporate such conceptual thinking into a part of operational planning.

OPERATIONAL DESIGN AND THE JOINT PLANNING PROCESS

Design and planning are two sides of the same coin, each imbued with its own logic, yet both originate when leaders *initiate* a mission to achieve a strategic- or operational-level objective. Upon initiation, both design and planning begin a symbiotic relationship. Design is about conceptual development; planning is about detailed, concrete development. Design assumes an ill-structured environment of probabilities; planning assumes a complicated environment of causal effects. Design logic is critical, creative, continuous, and circular, while planning logic is rational, rigorous, reductive, and repeatable.[29] Neither is wrong, and both are required to create real change when faced with holistic, complex systems that are not beholden to linear rules. Circumstances determine the weight of effort between design and planning, and neither is sufficient alone to solve strategic and operational objectives. Because ill-structured problems violate the assumptions required for conventional planning (e.g., planning for complicated problems), launching into detailed planning without first doing design will generate counterproductive, unintended consequences.[30]

To simplify this symbiotic relationship between design and planning, it is helpful to know the seven steps of the JPP and then situate operational design in relation to those steps. Design and the JPP are used by all combatant commanders, joint force commanders, and their staffs. In a cascading effect, the services conduct their own versions of the planning process and embed operational design in the same fashion. The services create supporting designs and plans, which are nested to fit and support the joint higher headquarters' planning, analysis, and directives. Design and planning between joint headquarters and the supporting service / functional component commanders is an iterative and collaborate process, with the commander as the central figure of the process. The staff executes design and planning processes as a collaborative effort. This is frequently initiated by specifying a cross-organizational operational planning team (OPT) for either deliberate planning or crisis-response planning.[31]

Operational design coincides with JPP steps 1 and 2 (see below). Much of the operational design process can be thought of as step "1.5" of JPP. After mission initiation (JPP step 1) and initial commanders' guidance, operational design processes focus on a few key elements that constitute the practice of design.

THE PROCESS OF OPERATIONAL DESIGN TO SUPPORT PLANNING FUNCTIONS

There are four major steps in the process of operational design, with each step resulting in a major product at the end. The steps are done in an iterative fashion, feeding back into one another as understanding of the complex system evolves, because "design is not a *sequential* methodology or a simplistic checklist. It is a foundational part of operational art that provides the crucial elements of structure."[32] The four steps are (1) strategic guidance and the strategic environment, (2) the environment frame, (3) the problem frame, and (4) the operational approach. The first step is reviewed in this chapter, while the other three are covered in subsequent chapters.

The first practice of design "step 1" is describing "strategic guidance" and "the strategic environment." Operational design uses a backward-planning approach. Backward planning starts with the end state first. While it might imply a finiteness in military planning that does not exist, "end state" is a common term used to indicate a strategic goal.

Strategic Guidance: National End States

The first step is defining the national end state, or the broad goal(s) and condition(s) or advancement of national interests to be attained. The end state establishes the required conditions that will be met through the achievement of strategic objectives. It represents vision and intent. The national end state encompasses diplomatic, information, military, and economic (DIME) interests. In this DIME-wide analysis, the national end state must be conditional—that is, it must describe a state of affairs, circumstance, or situation that can be objectively assessed, measured, or determined to be present at a concluding point. The end state should be unambiguous, specific, and prescriptive.

The national end state relative to a given situation is interpreted and derived from primary source documents such as the US National Security Strategy (NSS). Unfortunately, many national strategy documents do not define specific goals for a given region or scenario. In other cases, strategic documents use ambiguous, subjective goals such as stability. Stability, absent qualifying indicators, is ambiguous. At what point can the commander look at the facts on the ground and say, "We have achieved stability. Mission accomplished"? For an end state to truly meet its intent, it must be definable. In meeting this requirement, a well-developed national end state provides the commander with a clearly defined goal by which to focus the application of military power and resources.

To mitigate absent or ambiguous directions, military planners interpret strategic guidance to formulate goals. This part of the design process is arguably the most critical step. Defining the end state, or what must be achieved, sets in motion the rest of the operational design process and its related analysis and planning efforts. Everything that occurs after defining the national end state does so with this goal in mind. Careful and thoughtful consideration of strategic guidance is necessary to inform the development of attainable end states.

As an example, say the NSS contains verbiage outlining that national security interests rest on a certain country's inability to obtain, develop, and use nuclear weapons. The NSS may or may not say that the US goal is to prevent Country X from possessing nuclear weapons. Sometimes the NSS guidance is clear and obvious; other times is it far more subtle. It is the job of planners and strategists to interpret this guidance and formulate goals deemed consistent with higher-level guidance. In this case, a suitable and relevant national end state—derived from the NSS—might be to ensure Country X does not become a nuclear weapons state. It sounds simplistic and elementary, but this is the point. The end state should be objective and unambiguous. In this case, and assuming sufficient intelligence, achievement of this end state can be assessed in a binary manner: either Country X is a nuclear weapons state or it is not. This national end state can then form the basis for the remaining development of and progression through the operational design process.

Strategic Guidance: National Objectives

National objectives describe what must be achieved to reach the national end state. National objectives can be thought of as subsets to the national end states—specific goals that, when met, contribute to achieving or arriving at the condition prescribed in the national end state. At the national-strategic and theater-strategic levels, objectives must be "defined, decisive, and attainable goals toward which all operations, not just military operations, and activities are directed."[33] These national objectives establish the criteria that must be met to arrive at the desired conditions. The national objective must be directly linked to the national end state such that achieving the objective(s) should be a requirement for achieving the national end state.

For example, if the national end state above is to ensure Country X does not become a nuclear weapons state, planners need to determine what is required for this to happen and then define objectives to contribute to preventing it. Becoming a nuclear weapons state implies that a country must both possess viable nuclear weapons *and* functioning delivery mechanisms. These requirements form the basis for the objectives. Whereas weapons delivery mechanisms tend toward military platforms and thus present a military challenge, actions to prevent a country from developing viable nuclear weapons may rely on multiple instruments of national power.

This objective is written as a tasking: prevent Country X from doing Y. It is subordinate and linked to the national end state of ensuring Country X does not possess nuclear weapons. One or more instruments of national power (i.e., diplomatic, information, military, or economic) can be used to prevent X from weaponizing uranium. This ensures Country X does not possess nuclear weapons (because it cannot achieve nuclear weapons status without an ability to weaponize the element required). For those situations in which force is considered, planners craft military end states and objectives to support the national end state and objectives.

The operational designer should be able to describe the strategic environment in broad terms, leveraging concepts such as DIME. While not experts in the *D*, *I*, and *E* facets of national security, military operational designers and planners must comprehend how they inform, shape, constrain, or otherwise impact their military approach. Further, planners and designers should consider how their approach and solutions impact the other aspects of DIME and whether military actions might help or hinder other instruments of national power.

Military End States

Commanders determine the military end states and objectives based on the national end states and objectives. Higher-level guidance such as the National Defense Strategy (NDS), the National Military Strategy (NMS), and Combatant Commander Posture Statements provide useful insight into developing specific military end states and objectives for theater campaign planning. While the military end state may be redundant or similar to the national end states and objectives, it establishes the specific condition(s) to achieve relative to the military's role in the operation. US doctrine defines the military end state as "the set of required conditions that defines achievement of all military objectives."[34] The military end state is conditional, requiring it to be unambiguous and objectively definable but specific to something that can be achieved through the application of military power.

A military end state to the above national end state and objective could be that Country X does not have functioning nuclear weapons delivery mechanisms. Neutralizing potential nuclear weapons delivery platforms is something that can be achieved using force. This military end state is clearly derived from and linked to the preceding national end states and objectives and thus contributes to ensuring Country X is not a nuclear weapons state, as having functional delivery mechanisms is a requirement to achieve nuclear weapons state status.

Military Objectives

Military objectives are "clearly defined, decisive, and attainable goals toward which every military operation should be directed."[35] This is different from the national objectives in that it is specific to military operations. Military objectives describe what must be achieved to reach the military end state. Objectives are not written as task statements in that they do not infer the use of specific means and ways. Rather, objectives prescribe what must be accomplished to reach the end state—not how to accomplish it (the *how* is what the rest of operational design is for).

Continuing the example, the military end state is to ensure Country X does not have functioning nuclear weapons delivery mechanisms. Following that logic, the objective must prescribe what must be done to ensure Country X does not possess weapons delivery platforms. If, through the analysis of Country X's capabilities, its only viable nuclear weapons delivery platform is the heavy bomber, then a clear and obvious military objective linked to ensuring Country X's inability to delivery nuclear weapons would be to neutralize Country X's bomber fleet.

The linkages to each of the elements discussed above, from the national end state and objective to the military end state and objective, are clear. The derivative nature of one to the next is plainly visible. The national objective forms the basis for subsequent planning efforts ultimately leading to the achievement of the originally established national end state—which was derived from the national security strategy. In total, the end states and objectives combination forms the basis of strategic guidance within the operational design framework that serves as the foundation for the subsequent progression through the rest of the design process. This foundation is a perquisite to the rest of the framework but is especially important for guiding the analysis of the operational environment and framing the specific problem, which will be covered in the next chapter. From that, planners derive centers of gravity (chapter 21) and develop lines of effort (chapter 22) to achieve desired objectives.

OPERATIONAL DESIGN METHODOLOGY SHORTCOMINGS

Operation design is critiqued for having an imprecise lexicon that is "unintelligible" and for theoretical underpinnings of design that are too broad—basically on the cusp of being a pseudoscience at best.[36] There is no empirical evidence of successful outcomes when design thinking and process have been applied. It is difficult for commanders to know how to assess whether their plans are being effective since "despite the fact that design emphasizes iterative learning, it leaves the development of measures of effectiveness and assessment to the individual command and provides no methods with which to guide the collection of evidence or the interpretation of results."[37]

Good operational design can be time- and resource-intensive, and that comes at an opportunity cost for detailed planning. However, detailed planning without some design development could result in the employment of the wrong means, in wrong ways, that will not achieve the desired ends. Political factors can force quick decisions, leaving no time to do effective operational design.

Operational design processes could become unending—always looking for one more piece of evidence, pattern, or idea that will produce further understanding and learning. The operational designer could be accused of "navel gazing"—contemplating the meaning of everything associated with the problem and solving nothing. The operational designer could miss the boat for actually contributing to the planning process by virtue of the design being cumbersome. Last, operational designers could lose the opportunity to contribute in meaningful and important ways if they rely on an unwieldy and unfamiliar lexicon or an "academic-ese" that loses people in the process. It is important to know the doctrinally accepted lexicon and processes while remaining sensitive to new and creative synthesis throughout the process.

In the end, we do design because we are interested in solving the right problem, not just solving problems right. We do design because it generates deeper meaning, adaptability, and understanding, even if through inefficient methods.[38] Regardless of the amount of time afforded due to political or other constraints, a commander should always devote some portion of precious time to operational design processes in parallel with joint planning processes. Design done right will aid military organizations in dealing with "complexity over time," "promote adaptation to dynamic conditions, and strengthen the link between strategy and tactics."[39] Budding operational artists, practitioners, and warfighters advance our nation's common defense by learning and employing operational design.

LEARNING REVIEW

- State the purpose of the operational design construct.
- Identify the component parts of the operational design construct.

- Describe what makes a problem "complex."
- Identify systems theory as a component to operational design.
- Synthesize strategic guidance from primary source documents into strategic and military end states and objectives for a given military problem.
- Evaluate the importance of well-defined objectives.

NOTES

1. Joint Chiefs of Staff (JCS), *Joint Publication 5: Joint Planning* (hereafter *JP 5-0*) (Washington, DC: Department of Defense, December 1, 2020).

2. Richard M. Swain, "Commander's Business: Learning to Practice Operational Design," *Joint Forces Quarterly*, no. 53 (2nd Quarter 2009): 61.

3. Joint Staff, J7, *Planner's Handbook for Operational Design* (Washington, DC: Joint Staff, October 7, 2011) (emphasis added). General Mattis wrote this in the October 6, 2009, release of "Vision for a Joint Approach to Operational Design," memorandum for US Joint Forces Command.

4. Joint Staff, J7, I-2.

5. Jeffrey M. Reilly, *Operational Design: Distilling Clarity from Complexity for Decisive Action* (Maxwell Air Force Base, AL: Air University Press, 2012), 1.

6. Swain, "Commander's Business," 62.

7. Joint Staff, J7, *Planner's Handbook for Operational Design*, I-2.

8. Everett Carl Dolman, *Pure Strategy: Power and Principle in the Space and Information Age* (New York: Frank Cass, 2005), 12.

9. Jamshid Gharajedaghi, *Systems Thinking: Managing Chaos and Complexity; A Platform for Designing Business Architecture*, 3rd ed. (Amsterdam: Morgan Kaufmann, 2011), 38–39.

10. Carl von Clausewitz, *On War*, ed. and trans. Michael Howard and Peter Paret (Princeton, NJ: Princeton University Press, 1976), 75.

11. Jasmin Čajić, "The Relevance of Clausewitz's Theory to Contemporary Conflict Resolution," *Connections* 15, no. 1 (Winter 2016): 74.

12. Mark Gilchrist, "Why Thucydides Still Matters," Strategy Bridge, November 30, 2016, https://thestrategybridge.org/the-bridge/2016/11/30/why-thucydides-still-matters.

13. Clausewitz, *On War*, 89.

14. Edward J. Villacres and Christopher Bassford, "Reclaiming the Clauswitzian Trinity," *Parameters* (Autumn 1995): 14.

15. Joint Staff, J7, *Planner's Handbook for Operational Design*, I-2.

16. Milan N. Vego, "A Case against Systemic Operational Design," *Joint Forces Quarterly*, no. 53 (2nd Quarter 2009): 69–70.

17. Joint Staff, J7, *Planner's Handbook for Operational Design*, I-1.

18. JCS, *JP 5-0*.

19. Dale Eikmeier, *Small Wars Journal*, comment thread, July 1, 2011, https://smallwarsjournal.com/jrnl/art/operational-art-is-not-a-level-of-war. See also Huba Wass de Czega, "Thinking and Acting like an Explorer: Operational Art Is Not a Level of War," *Small Wars Journal*, March 14, 2011, https://smallwarsjournal.com/jrnl/art/operational-art-is-not-a-level-of-war.

20. JCS, *JP 5-0*, xii.

21. *Art of Design*, student text version 2.0 (Fort Leavenworth, KS: School of Advanced Military Studies, 2011), 9.

22. *Art of Design*, 28.

23. *Art of Design*, 28. Quoting Julian Corbett: "The value of history in the art of war is not only to elucidate the resemblances of the past and present, but also their essential differences."

24. Joint Staff, *DoD Dictionary of Military and Associated Terms* (Washington, DC: Joint Staff, January 2021).

25. Peter M. Senge, *The Fifth Discipline: The Art and Practice of the Learning Organization* (New York: Doubleday, 2006), 68.

26. *Art of Design*, 52.

27. *Art of Design*, 72. See also Dietrich Dörner, *The Logic of Failure: Recognizing and Avoiding Error in Complex Situations* (Cambridge, MA: Perseus Books, 1997).

28. Sun Tzu, *The Art of War*, trans. Samuel Griffith (Oxford: Oxford University Press, 1984).

29. *Art of Design*, 120.

30. *Art of Design*, 25.

31. The Air Force also uses the term "air planning group" (APG) when the effort is led by the air operations center or at the behest of the joint forces air component commander. Deliberate planning is based on potential scenarios. "Crisis action planning" (CAP) is in response to an emerging threat or opportunity.

32. Reilly, *Operational Design*, xi–xii (emphasis added).

33. JCS, *JP 5-0*, III-20.

34. JCS, III-19.

35. JCS, III-20.

36. Vego, "Case against Systemic Operational Design," 70, 75.

37. William J. Gregor, "Military Planning Systems and Stability Operations," *Prism* 1, no. 3 (2010): 109.

38. *Art of Design*, 21–22.

39. *Art of Design*, 17.

CHAPTER 20

Framing Wicked Problems to Analyze the Operational Environment

James Davitch and Michael Fowler

With an understanding of how we define and develop national and military end states and objectives, we next progress into assessing the operational environment to inform our eventual operational approach. Understanding the operational environment puts the situation into context, which assists commanders to "better identify the problem; anticipate potential outcomes; and understand the results of various friendly, adversary, enemy, and neutral actions" and how each can help or inhibit forces from achieving the military end state.[1] The environment shapes actors' intent, capabilities, and the potential to project military force, which determines potential threats and lays the groundwork for predicting enemy courses of action. Poor understanding of the environment can result in plans that solve the wrong problems.

The complexity of the environment can be overwhelming because a variety of factors might be relevant to a particular security problem. Unfocused research results in a plethora of data that is not useful to a decision-maker. Novices struggle to filter the wheat from the chaff to identify what is relevant in a given scenario. Complex problems are rarely one-dimensional but instead include a collection of subproblems.[2] To make the process manageable, it is critical to determine the time available (i.e., the deadline), the required product format, and the necessary level of detail. Sometimes, the time-detail trade-off requires a negotiation because a decision-maker may want the maximum level of detail in the minimum amount of time. When time is available, analysts do a two-step process: a broad analysis followed by an in-depth analysis.

INTRODUCTION TO CONDITION ANALYSIS

Condition analysis identifies the *problematic conditions*, *contributing factors*, and *desired conditions*.[3] Identifying the problematic conditions and the relevant contributing factors is a necessary prerequisite to determining the desired conditions. Without proper framing, it is easy for the analyst to get lost in the details or the crisis du jour and lose sight of the problem.

The analyst should *frame the problem using strategic guidance*, which provides long-term objectives and should answer the question, What does success look like? The problem and guidance are interdependent and iterative; as one changes, the other adjusts. In essence, a problem is any condition that does not align with national security objectives or those of the joint force commander. In some cases, resolving the problem is the objective, while in others the problem is an obstacle that is preventing achievement of an objective. The problem is exacerbated by contributing factors. Complex problems do not have a single cause but can be narrowed down to a few major factors often called "root causes."[4]

Ideally the guidance will identify a specific problem, such as a country's program to develop nuclear weapons and/or ballistic missiles. Just as often, strategic guidance will use an ambiguous label such as "regional stability." While the term is politically popular, "instability" might mean coups, economic crises, terrorism, protests, crime, environmental degradation, or human rights abuses. In those cases, *the problem needs refinement to focus only on those conditions necessary to achieve the strategic objectives that are achievable via military power.*

The same analyst(s) who identified the problem should be part of the team to select the desired conditions. Desired conditions overlap between the problematic conditions and strategic guidance. The desired condition may be the antithesis of the problematic condition. Many plans are built because the current situation has the potential to lead to some suboptimal future situation. For example, in deterrence operations, the objective may be to maintain the status quo, but the desired condition would highlight the action that the plan is intended to prevent (e.g., prevent a ballistic missile attack on a partner country). The conditions may not be related to military force. For example, other conditions worthy of avoidance include famines, public health catastrophes, and mass refugees. Historical trends or patterns can be used to project scenarios, though history rarely repeats in precisely the same manner.[5]

The desired condition should not be a "dream" state in which everything turns out perfect. It should be logically achievable based on theories of cause-effect relationships, available resources and capabilities, and forecast adversary actions. It should not be a Band-Aid that solves symptoms but leaves root causes to fester until a later crisis. It should anticipate secondary effects. When conditions within a complex system change, there will be a reaction as the various actors (e.g., competing sides, the population, a third country, international organizations) will adapt to mitigate the change, potentially creating undesired conditions.[6] It is a type of victory condition that can be measured to determine operational success and the conclusion of military operations. However, it is rarely a permanent solution, as it merely proceeds "to the next stage rather than some ultimate destination."[7]

ORGANIZING THE CONDITION ANALYSIS

To deal with complexity, analytic frameworks make the process manageable and organize the data.[8] Frameworks are garbage-in, garbage-out constructs; they will not fix sloppy research. They should not be used as a linear checklist, which would result in oversimplistic analysis that ignores fog, friction, and the human dimension by turning the study of war into datasets and mathematical equations.[9] The analysis must blend art and science to grapple with personal, social, and ethical phenomena.[10]

The most common military framework is political, military, economic, social, information, and infrastructure (PMESII) analysis. PMESII is optimum for conventional, country-level analysis. For other missions such as irregular warfare and humanitarian operations, a PMESII-ASCOPE (areas, structures, capabilities, organizations, people, and events) matrix provides a substructure to ensure relevant data is captured (see table 20.1).

Table 20.1. Example of an ASCOPE Matrix

	Political	Military	Economic	Social	Infrastructure	Information
Areas	Political boundaries	Areas of responsibility, historic	Grazing areas, water holes, marketplaces	Picnic areas, stadiums, arenas, religious districts	LOCs, irrigation networks, areas with medical services	Radio/TV coverage, gathering points
Structures	Government buildings, polling sites, police stations	HQs, training facilities, storage areas	Factories, warehouses, banks	Places of worship, popular restaurants	Bridges, railyards, dams	Cell, radio, and TV towers; printing shops; Internet cafés
Capabilities	Justice system, dispute-resolution services	Security, long-range strike weapons, IEDs	Finance, crop care, manufacturing, smuggling	Cultural norms	Build, maintain, inspect	Literacy rate, availability of media and phone service
Organization	Political parties, NGOs, IO	Command and control	Banks, corporations, criminal organizations	Tribes, clans, classes, families, diasporas, sports clubs	Construction companies, government ministries	Media, mosques, churches
People	President, legislature, governors, council members	Coalition, host country, insurgent groups	Bankers, landholders, merchants, moneylenders	Influential families, church leaders	Contractors	Media owners, elders, heads of families
Events	Elections, council meetings, speeches	Attacks	Drought, harvest, business openings or closures	Ceremonies, holidays, prayer gatherings, market days	Construction	Collateral-damage incidents, ceremonies

Note: IEDs = improvised explosive devices; IO = information operations; LOCs = lines of communication; NGOs = nongovernmental organizations.

Source: Derived from Natalie R. Meyers et al., *Understanding the Effects of Infrastructure Changes on Subpopulations: Survey of Current Methods, Models, and Tools* (Champaign, IL: Army Engineer Research and Development Center, 2016), 28.

MAKING PMESII RELEVANT

Systems analysis is a problem-solving technique that deconstructs a system into its component pieces to study how well the components work (or not) and how they interact.[11] Since every subsystem is made up of more systems and every model can be clarified with a supporting model, systems analysis can lead to a "paralysis by analysis" since there is always more things to research. Despite a commander's desire for omnipotence, no amount of time will facilitate the complete elimination of the fog of war.[12] If used improperly, systems analysis can lead to *stovepiping*, which is the failure to identify interactions between systems. This is problematic during oral presentations that use PMESII in a linear fashion, giving equal time to each section and distorting their relative importance. To mitigate stovepiping, a more natural intersystem analysis can combine the systems into three groups: political-information, socioeconomic, and military-infrastructure.

Political and Information

Instead of political parties and government organizational hierarchies, planners are interested in four key research areas:

- Reason: What are their strategic goals and values?
- Reason: Who are their friends? Who are their potential friends? How do their goals and values align (or not)?
- Chance: What is the probability of an internal change in leadership?
- Passion: How does the organization use information to influence the values and behaviors of others toward the above goals?

Political objectives drive military strategy. Understanding a country's political goals is a key step in determining how to influence friends, adversaries, and neutrals. Some countries publicly release their national security goals. For others, several think tanks analyze national security objectives.[13] When required, intelligence collection can be leverage to discern more sensitive objectives. For situations that are less widely followed by either the think tanks or the US intelligence community, a country's political security objectives can be derived from an analysis of its information operations, socioeconomic factors, and its military power-projection capabilities.

While country partnerships can be kept secret, they are more often publicly proclaimed. Government websites, including that of the US Department of State, often provide the status of bilateral relations.[14] These relations vary from trade agreements to rhetorical support to formal mutual-defense agreements. Partner countries do not necessarily have overlapping goals, and times of crisis and changes in leadership can fracture these agreements. These diplomatic relationships factor into arms sales and partner willingness to allow access, basing, or overflight.

A change in government leadership can have a serious impact on foreign relations, changing friends to adversaries or vice versa. While the final decision-maker may be the head of government, head of state, or organizational leader, every decision-maker has a group of key supporters whose cooperation is necessary to facilitate the decision-maker's ability to stay in power. To some extent, the process, key supporters, and relevance of domestic politics can be estimated from the country's political system and its associated transfer-of-power rules. Intelligence collection can monitor for specific indicators for a potential change in government. At a more macro level, the Fragile States Index and the State Fragility Index use a variety of political, security, and socioeconomic factors to provide warning of a state's potential to collapse.[15]

Most countries work to shape their internal politics and foreign relations through the information domain. The country's information infrastructure enables distribution of messages on a massive scale, leveraging ambiguities in ethics, law, and state-influenced media to shape the perceptions of both domestic and foreign audiences. From a security perspective, strategic communication can be used for three purposes: legitimization, securitization, and influence. Legitimization is a strategic communication method to convince audiences that the regime is (or is not) the legitimate ruler of the country. Securitization promotes an issue to garner public support for a national security issue (e.g., China's "nine-dash line" to bolster territorial claims to the South China Sea). Finally, strategic communication can be used to send a message of coercion or cooperation. For instance, both the United States and Iran used social media to influence the European Union's support for the Iran nuclear deal.[16]

Political goals and strategic communication campaigns are not created in a vacuum. To get a more nuanced picture of the situation, political and information factors should be viewed through the prism of the local socioeconomic context. While socioeconomic factors are rarely determinative in themselves, political leaders leverage these factors to justify their internal and external security goals.

Socioeconomic Factors

Socioeconomic data is plentiful but is less easy to put into context to answer the question "So what?" It is critical to frame the analysis around planner requirements, such as

- Reason: How do economic interests contribute to the problem?
- Passion: How are values and fears reflected in the perception of other key actors?
- Chance: What is the potential for domestic economic or social crisis?

Easy-to-find metrics such as gross domestic product (GDP), GDP growth, and GDP per capita are not helpful in explaining foreign national security objectives. For example, Malaysia's GDP at $1 trillion is less than US GDP of $20 trillion but higher than neighboring Indonesia's $300 billion. While a larger GDP implies the potential to spend more on a military, it tells little about relative capability or goals.

More important than GDP comparisons are territorial disputes over economic resources, such as the rights for natural resources: oil and natural gas, fishing, and water. The significance of each resource is relative to each country's economy. For example, do Vietnam's oil claims in the South China Sea represent 1 percent or 50 percent of its oil reserves? Would successful exploitation be a major impact on the Vietnamese economy or a drop in the bucket?

International trade is another area that is often misunderstood. Analysts often overestimate the impact that trade has on a country's decision to coerce its trading partner. Trade relations did little to prevent conflict throughout the nineteenth and early twentieth centuries.[17] Since many goods (e.g., oil) are fungible, aggressors may assume that they can shift their trade elsewhere. Similarly, analysts overemphasize control of maritime trade routes as a potential source of conflict. In theory, total control of a trade route could be used for pure profit or to close trade to opponents. A country could charge a fee for transit through a maritime choke point.

In reality, this is somewhat rare and might be difficult to enforce in areas of overlapping claims. While a country could stop the use of a trade route, closing it does not actually stop trade in most cases. It simply makes it less efficient because shipments find an alternative, longer route.

For national security, the domestic economy is often of little import but can be useful for analyzing internal conflicts and for target selection. A country's economy is often vital to support a war effort with electric power; petroleum, oil, and lubricants (POL); ammunition, armaments, and explosives; military vehicles, aircraft, and maritime vessels; civil trucks and materials-handling equipment (MHE), such as cranes and forklifts; and basic industry for construction and repair, such as cement and steel. Attacking economic targets assumes a protracted war and requires detailed understanding of a country's economic production, consumption, and alternatives.[18] In many developing countries, variations in the domestic economy are often linked to social identity.

Socioeconomic divisions can be exploited for political gain and are a popular tool for insurgent recruitment.[19] Examples:

- ethnicity
- linguistic
- religion
- dominant professions (e.g., farmer, herder, rancher, miner)
- tribes or clans
- ideological factions
- regionalism
- age (e.g., youth bulge)
- urbanization
- education and literacy levels
- income inequality
- displaced people

These factors create different subcultures. Analysts must be careful to avoid both treating an entire society as homogeneous and mirror-imaging (projecting their values onto others). Plus, these factors are not static. Over time, these demographics can change, leading to shifts in identity, creating new divisions or easing long-held grievances. Long-term changes also impact birth and death rates, which eventually impact population size and density, potential indicators of foreign policy proclivity. For instance, a country with declining birth rates may not be economically sustainable, which would impact foreign relations and limit the instruments available. Like all of the other factors, though, demography is only a piece of the puzzle. For example, a declining Russian population since the end of the Cold War implies that Russia would be less relevant on the world stage, yet it presently executes an aggressive foreign policy despite domestic challenges.[20]

The potential for social-identity divisions can be exacerbated by domestic economic crisis because it creates social unrest at a time when the government can least afford to spend additional funds on internal security or social projects. Factors that increase the probability of an economic crisis include

- Overreliance on a single commodity (e.g., oil, sugar, coffee) as a percentage of GDP or as a percentage of government tax revenues. An unexpected commodity glut, global recession, or crop failure can precipitate an economic crisis.

- Resource exhaustion from nonsustainable activities that lead to desertification, deforestation, soil depletion, overfishing, overhunting, and competition over water rights. This can be exacerbated by a natural disaster such as flood, drought, or disease that destroys the resource or halts extraction.
- Serious infrastructure flaws. Similar to resource exhaustion, long-term negligence of infrastructure inhibits economic growth and increases the severity of economic crises.
- A major portion of GDP comes from aid: foreign aid, international aid, the International Monetary Fund, the World Bank, nongovernmental organizations, and diaspora donations. A sudden reduction in aid (e.g., world financial crisis, evidence of human rights abuses, diversion of funds due to a major crisis elsewhere) can leave this country vulnerable.

Economic crisis can cause a downward spiral. For example, some countries subsidize basic staples such as flour or fuel. During times of economic trouble, the country may have to slash the subsidy. This cut typically comes at a time of overall economic downturn, when people can least afford the price increase in items required for basic sustenance. Economic collapse can be especially dangerous in countries with sizable lootable natural resources. Commodities such as oil, gold, timber, and diamonds are easily exploited by nonstate actors to fund warlords and insurgent operations.[21]

Military and Infrastructure Analysis

Whether using classified or publicly available information, the process for analyzing military capability is the same, as analysts focus on three research questions:

- What is their ability to defend against their likely adversary (internal and/or external)?
- What is their ability to project military power (external)?
- How does the infrastructure facilitate the projection of power (internal/external)?

Estimating the ability to defend or project power begins with an order of battle. Lists of the quantities, variants, and location of military equipment are available in databases such as Janes IHS, Military Periscope, *The Military Balance*, and Gladius Defense and Security. Think tanks publish specialty orders of battle, such as the Asia Maritime Transparency Initiative of the Center for Strategic and International Studies. Databases provide rough planning factors for missile-engagement ranges and aircraft-combat radii.[22] While tactical planners want classified data on tactics, precise parameters of weapon-engagement zones, and jamming/antijamming capabilities, that level of detail is not required to estimate military capability. For operational planning, scale is more important than precision. For example, for a tactical planner, the difference between forty and forty-five MiG-29 fighters is significant. But the operational planner is more interested in scale (tens, hundreds) and the ability of an adversary to sustain combat operations over time.

Estimating capabilities is not simply about counting equipment. While quantities are relevant to provide a sense of scale, estimates should consider range, quality (or threat level), and the capability it provides. As discussed earlier in this chapter, military equipment provides one or more capabilities (see table 20.2) to achieve military objectives. As a general rule, newer weapon systems are of higher quality and represent a more significant threat. For example, an air-defense system designed in the 1960s may pose little threat to advanced

Table 20.2. Key Capabilities

	Task	Type of force (means)				
		Maritime	Air	Land	Special operations	Information[1]
Main effort	Control the domain	Sea-surface control	Air superiority, offensive counterair	Infantry: seize or hold territory	FID, UW	Information operations, space control
Main effort	Disrupt	Cruise missiles	Strategic attack	Rockets, artillery	DA, counterterrorism	Network attack
Support	Enable control of the domain	Submarine warfare, antisubmarine warfare, mine warfare	ISR, airlift, air refueling	Antiarmor, airborne, armor	Reconnaissance	Deception, space access
Support	Support control of another domain	Amphibious assault	Close air support, interdiction	Anti-irregular or urban warfare	Search and rescue, psyops	Secure data, bandwidth, electronic attack
Defend	Protect friendly COG	AAW	DCA	Air defense, missile defense	Hostage rescue	Network defense

Note: AAW = antiair warfare; DA = direct action; DCA = defensive counterair; FID = foreign internal defense; ISR = intelligence, surveillance, and reconnaissance; UW = unconventional warfare.

[1] While space and cyber require different infrastructure, they have overlapping capabilities: to gather, transmit, and/or disrupt information.

fighter aircraft though may still be capable against slow-moving cargo or civil aircraft. An important but often overlooked consideration that can help estimate warfighting capability is the degree to which an adversary trains. Just as it is ineffective to count individual pieces of equipment, it is likewise inappropriate to view equipment capabilities in isolation. Rather, it is necessary to view them as a whole to determine whether they are effective as a cohesive military capability. During the Cold War, analysis of this type of military activity was typically restricted to classified channels, but today there is an abundance of publicly available information discussing bilateral and multilateral training events, which analysts can use to explore foreign military capabilities.

Infrastructure Analysis

Every piece of military equipment has some ability to project power. For example, missile ranges and an aircraft's combat radius represent estimates of power projection. To project power beyond these normal distances, a country must have the supporting logistics, infrastructure, airlift, sealift, and replenishment. For example, a six-hundred-person US Army Airborne battalion requires twelve C-17s (half for troops, half for heavy equipment).[23] Air refueling extends an aircraft's combat radius, while at-sea replenishment extends the patrol range of maritime forces and enables longer duration patrols.

Effective logistics requires reliable infrastructure, including roads (bridges, junctions, and truck stops), mass transit and rail (bridges, yards), water (locks, ports), airports, and communications nodes. Key port data can be used to determine utility for military vessels based on vessel size, water depth, lifts and cranes, and available supplies (e.g., fuel).[24] Key airfield data such as runway length (e.g., combat aircraft typically need ten-thousand-foot runways) helps determine which fields could potentially be used for military aircraft. For nonstate actors, the concept of infrastructure is slightly different because difficult terrain and political boundaries can provide a haven. Plus, even the smallest of actors can project power through the information domain.

MITIGATING BIASES

Sun Tzu's advice that "If you know the enemy and know yourself, you need not fear the result of a hundred battles" can be profoundly difficult to follow. To know ourselves, we should be aware of our own thought processes. Our minds regularly execute mental shortcuts that attempt to make routine decision-making easier. For procedural tasks (e.g., your morning routine), these intuitive, gut choices work. During military planning, stress and fatigue encourage the mind to draw on evidence that supports our predetermined conclusions (confirmation bias). Or we quickly recall examples of similar events despite their incongruities (the availability heuristic). Or we privilege the initial information we encounter when making subsequent judgments (the anchoring effect).[25]

There is no one solution that will mitigate our mind's cognitive traps. It is important to first know that these biases and heuristics exist and, second, deliberately slow down our decision-making to avoid the allure of easy answers. Intentionally seeking "disconfirming evidence" or considering the opposite of your first instinct can slow your judgment down enough to allow your mind to consider alternatives. Challenging your mind to think through problems in conditions of uncertainty is thus an important part of understanding and correctly characterizing the operational environment.[26]

CONCLUSION

Frameworks are merely tools to help shape a problem by identifying the problematic condition, contributing factors, and desired condition. Understanding the problem is critical to any attempts to solve the problem. Although these tools are not a panacea, when they are used correctly they help analysts organize their thoughts to make them more efficient and communicate their findings more effectively. A great analysis will simplify the planners' job to develop strategic objectives and identify enemy strengths to mitigate and vulnerabilities to exploit. Like all intelligence, the final product must be useful to the customer, not just interesting to the analyst.

LEARNING REVIEW

- Recall the purpose of defining the operational environment.
- Describe the relationship between desired conditions and problem conditions.
- Describe the elements of PMESII analysis.

- Recall the advantages and disadvantages of systems analysis.
- For each system, identify likely sources to conduct PMESII analysis for a national security issue.

NOTES

1. Joint Chiefs of Staff, *Joint Publication 5-0: Joint Planning* (Washington, DC: Department of Defense, December 1, 2020), IV-6.

2. Paul Hanstedt, *Creating Wicked Students: Designing Courses for a Complex World* (Sterling, VA: Stylus, 2018), 86.

3. Robert M. Clark, *Intelligence Analysis: A Target-Centric Approach* (Washington, DC: CQ Press, 2004), 166.

4. Morgan D. Jones, *The Thinker's Toolkit: 14 Powerful Techniques for Problem Solving* (New York: Three Rivers Press, 1998), 47.

5. Horst Rittel and Melvin Webber, "Dilemmas in a General Theory of Planning," *Policy Sciences* 4, no. 2 (1973): 155–59; Ernest May and Richard Neustadt, *Thinking in Time: The Uses of History for Decision Makers* (New York: Free Press, 1986).

6. Dietrich Dörner, *The Logic of Failure: Recognizing and Avoiding Error in Complex Situations* (New York: Metropolitan Books, 1996), 21.

7. Lawrence Freedman, *Strategy: A History* (Oxford: Oxford University Press, 2013), 628.

8. Richard Buchanan, "Wicked Problems in Design Thinking," *Design Issues* 8, no. 2 (1992): 5–21; Peter Checkland and Jim Scholes, *Soft Systems Methodology in Action* (New York: John Wiley & Sons, 1999); Martin Reynolds and Sue Holwell, eds., *Systems Approaches to Managing Change: A Practical Guide* (London: Springer, 2010); Robert Farrell and Cliff Hooker, "Design, Science, and Wicked Problems," *Design Studies* 34, no. 6 (November 2013): 681–705; Brian W. Head and John Alford, "Wicked Problems: Implications for Public Policy and Management," *Administration and Society* 47, no. 6 (March 2013).

9. Milan Vego, "Systems versus Classical Approach to Warfare," *Joint Force Quarterly* 52 (First Quarter 2009): 40–47.

10. Nigel Cross, "Designerly Ways of Knowing: Design Discipline versus Design Science," *Design Issues* 17, no. 3 (Summer 2001): 49–55.

11. Lonnie Bentley, *Systems Analysis and Design for the Global Enterprise* (New York: McGraw Hill, 2007), 160.

12. H. R. McMaster, "On War: Lessons to Be Learned," *Survival* 50, no. 1 (2008): 26.

13. E.g., the Carnegie Endowment for International Peace, the Center for New American Security, the Center for Strategic and International Studies, the Council on Foreign Relations, the International Crisis Group, the International Institute for Strategic Studies, and the Institute for the Study of War.

14. E.g., "U.S. Relations with Brunei," US Department of State, https://www.state.gov/u-s-relations-with-brunei/.

15. Both quantitative databases track vulnerabilities that might lead to internal conflict. The Fragile States Index is privately funded. The State Fragility Index was primarily funded by the US government, which suspended funding in 2020.

16. Kulsoom Belal, "Uncertainty over the Joint Comprehensive Plan of Action: Iran, the European Union and the United States," *Policy Perspectives* 16, no. 1 (2019): 23–39.

17. Katherine Barbieri, *The Liberal Illusion: Does Trade Promote Peace?* (Ann Arbor: University of Michigan Press, 2002). For the counterargument, see Quan Li and Rafael Reuveny, "Does Trade Prevent or Promote Interstate Conflict Initiation," *Journal of Peace Research* 48, no. 4 (2011): 437–53; and Havard Hegre, John R. Oneal, and Bruce Russett, "Trade Does Promote Peace: New Simultaneous Estimates of the Reciprocal Effects of Trade and Conflict," *Journal of Peace Research* 47, no. 6 (2010): 763–74.

18. Thomas E. Griffith, "Strategic Attack of National Electrical Systems" (postgraduate thesis, 1994, School of Advanced Airpower Studies), 45.

19. Ann Hironaka, *Neverending Wars: The International Community, Weak States, and the Perpetuation of Civil War* (Cambridge, MA: Harvard University Press, 2005), 81–96; Jack Snyder, *Myths of Empire: Domestic Politics and International Ambition* (Ithaca, NY: Cornell University Press, 1991).

20. Michael Kofman, "Russian Demographics and Power: Does the Kremlin Have a Long Game?," War on the Rocks, February 4, 2020, https://warontherocks.com/2020/02/russian-demographics-and-power-does-the-kremlin-have-a-long-game/.

21. Philippe Le Billon, *Wars of Plunder: Conflicts, Profits and the Politics of Resources* (New York: Columbia University Press, 2012).

22. Combat radius is a planned round-trip with weapons. Aircraft range is a one-way trip, typically calculated without weapons.

23. Stanley McChrystal, *Team of Teams: New Rules of Engagement for a Complex World* (New York: Penguin, 2015), 33.

24. See World Port Source, http://www.worldportsource.com/. Draft (the required water depth) for military vessels is available through Wikipedia and military equipment databases.

25. Daniel Kahneman, *Thinking, Fast and Slow* (New York: Farrar, Straus & Giroux, 2011).

26. Philip E. Tetlock and Dan Gardner, *Superforecasting: The Art and Science of Prediction* (New York: Crown, 2016).

CHAPTER 21

Analyzing Centers of Gravity

Ryan Burke and Michael Fowler

Within the operational design construct, center of gravity (COG) analysis is arguably one of the most difficult analytic concepts to apply. While they can easily memorize the various definitions, novice planners struggle to describe potential centers of gravity when given real-world situations. This leads to reliance on overly simplistic rules of thumb or clichés to identify COGs, which, in turn, jeopardizes operational planning. Because COG analysis is one of the most critical functions to informing a sound operational approach, it is critical to understand its utility for effective line-of-effort design and execution. This chapter synthesizes COG analysis, design thinking, and systems analysis to create a framework for context analysis to facilitate accurate COG identification.

Planners use COG analysis to identify their own strengths and weaknesses relative to those of the enemy. Knowing where one is both strong and weak promotes planning and action toward leveraging strengths and defending weaknesses. This same knowledge also allows military planners to assess, by way of defined processes and tools, the enemy's system, its points of strength, and its areas of vulnerability for exploitation. COG analysis is, in many ways, the defining process to operational execution leading to achieving the desired conditions. It is a multistep process requiring planners to assess both the friendly and enemy systems relative to each other.

Identifying and analyzing friendly and adversarial COGs is a critical step within operational design.[1] Carl von Clausewitz defines a COG as "the hub of all power and movement, on which everything depends. . . . [It is] the point at which all our energies should be directed."[2] The COG is a moral or physical point of leverage one possesses that must be considered when developing an operational approach. It can be a strength that provides a critical capability to facilitate an operational approach. It can also be conceptualized as a vulnerability—a key requirement without which the intended operational approach cannot be executed. Regardless, the entire operational plan should hinge on the COG. If planners misidentify the COG or select something ambiguous, the logic of the plan to achieve the desired conditions is flawed. On the other hand, correctly identifying the COG does not guarantee victory. However, it should enable the planner to logically justify the actions that are intended to transform the problem conditions into the desired conditions. *The COG should be the logical lynchpin that synergizes the problem conditions, desired conditions, and associated lines of effort into a coherent idea.*

CONTEXT OF COG ANALYSIS

Traditionalists argue that Clausewitz's definition implied that the COG should be the enemy army or the capital.[3] While this might be accurate, telling a military planner to focus on the enemy army is not particularly useful. During the conventional conflicts of the twentieth century, capturing a capital was closely associated with military victory.[4] Arguably, the evolving character of war has made the capture of a capital less desirable. The proliferation of nuclear weapons as well as international responses to conventional conflict encouraged limited conflicts, proxy wars, and irregular warfare. In these cases, the COG might be the common interests of partnerships, leadership, or public opinion.[5] During the 1980s, the popularity of maneuver warfare led to arguments that the COG was some geographic feature such as a line of communication.[6] While certainly still important, the relative growth in power of nonstate actors such as insurgents, terrorist groups, and transnational criminal organizations obfuscates the nature of control of geography while emphasizing the temporality of victory.

In a counterargument to the traditionalists, John Warden argued that cities and military forces were actually the least efficient path to victory. Instead, the COG should be the leadership or some other key aspect of the decision-making or command and control process or structure. Removing enemy decision-makers is not a proven method of victory, though it can be disruptive.[7] Targeting the leadership would be most effective when applied to a rigid hierarchy like North Korea's. Striking rigid hierarchies that lack a clear line of succession can lead to internal power struggles, temporarily disrupting the organization's ability to function. Targeting leaders is less useful when considering a flatter, distributed decision-making organization such as al-Qaeda. While still disruptive, removing leaders in flat organizations has a less visible operational impact. Warden recognized the difficulty of targeting enemy decision-makers and proposed targeting "organic essentials" as a second priority. Organic essentials are critical to the organization's survival. Unfortunately, determining what is critical to the enemy is not always easy. It might be money or ideology or a highly trained presidential guard, depending on the context. Warden's concept of organic essentials is interesting but not sufficiently different from Clausewitz's "hub of all power and movement." While the narrative description is compelling, it fails to provide useful guidance to the military planner on what is essential. Emphasis should be on connectivity and disproportionate impact on the rest of the system, which when targeted would "throw an enemy off balance or even cause the entire system (or structure) to collapse."[8]

Despite the evolution of the COG concept over the last two centuries, the classic writings of Sun Tzu provide a more detailed road map to identifying COGs. Sun Tzu argued that to win you needed to know the enemy, know yourself, and know the conflict environment. From this understanding, you should attack the enemy's strategy. Estimating the enemy's strategy requires a detailed understanding of the adversary, friendly forces, potential partners for both sides, and the conflict environment. *In order to identify a COG, the analyst must first understand the complex problem from multiple perspectives.* Only from this detailed understanding can an analyst attempt to estimate a COG.

COGs are neither eternal nor static. They are relative to the specific context in time and vary based on the problem that is being solved. For national security challenges, these problems tend to be complex since competing (and often cooperating) states have diverging perceptions of both the problem and the desired end state.

Unfortunately, it is not unusual for planners to skip detailed analysis since it can be time-consuming. Some planners will use COG methodologies as rules of thumb without delving into specific, detailed contextual analysis. This shortcut process typically leads to the identification of generic COGs that are not particularly helpful in refining operational efforts: enemy forces, the leader, weapons of mass destruction (WMDs), or support of the population. Targeting the enemy's military is the default position for any use of force. To highlight it as the COG does nothing to refine the planning effort. Targeting the adversary's leader or WMDs might be counterproductive because it could lead to escalation. Attacking a country's WMD capability could be the catalyst that sparks them to use that capability. Finally, influencing the support of the population toward or away from the government is overly simplistic because it assumes a homogeneous population that rarely exists in practice. To identify a useful COG for planning, a detailed systems analysis is vital.

The challenge of a systems analysis approach is that every organization, process, and facility is a system or a subset of systems. Every element of a system can be broken down into its own set of systems. A leading thinker in operational design, Jeffrey M. Reilly, captured the complexity and scope of the process: "The environment is a multifarious, interactive, and constantly evolving series of systems. It encompasses not only the immediate area of operations, but also all areas, actors, and factors that either influence or have the potential to influence the area of operations."[9] Of course, that is a lot of systems to analyze. To minimize the analytic burden and avoid paralysis by analysis, systems analysis requires a disciplined approach to determine which systems should be analyzed and to what level of detail.

Not all systems and subsystems are of equal importance. At some point in the process, most analysts will need to focus their research on those subsystems that matter most. Some planners refer to this step as COG identification. COG analysis justifies actions and targets. *Focusing on a single COG can be a useful tool to depict a rough sketch of the strategic approach to a problem.* This can be helpful in explaining the commander's intent to higher headquarters, supporting forces, subordinate units, and the general population. Strategic COG analysis tends to focus on identifying the key strength.[10] Arguably, the strategic COG should be bound to decision-makers and their will to fight.[11]

The challenge with a single COG is that in order for it to act as a justification mechanism for the broad spectrum of planned actions, it will be too general or ambiguous to provide sufficient guidance for operational planning. For example, telling a counterinsurgency planner that the COG is the population may be accurate, but it is not useful. To support planning, it is necessary to also identify operational COGs. *At the operational level, affecting a single COG will rarely, by itself, transform the problem conditions into the desired conditions.* Most systems are complex and adaptive. The purpose of COG identification at the operational and tactical levels is to identify those portions of the system that will have a disproportionately large impact toward the desired effect. COG identification is really about finding ways to make operations more efficient (typical clichés include "higher return on investment" and "bigger bang for the buck"). Analysts and planners who immerse themselves in finding that one perfect target that will force the enemy to capitulate are likely to be disappointed. Ideally, *operational COG analysis results in multiple operational COGs—one for each friendly and adversary objective.* Dale Eikmeier, a retired Army colonel and prolific author on COGs, presents a method that is a good example of this level of analysis that focuses on deconstructing the strategy and operational approach.[12] At the operational level, COGs tend to be a combination of strengths and vulnerabilities.

For example, as Japan's War Ministry prepared for war against the United States, it recognized that it could not match US industrial capacity for production over time. With no suitable methods to attack that strategic COG, Japanese planning focused on the US operational

COG: maritime power-projection capabilities in the Pacific. From a targeting perspective, this translated into battleships, aircraft carriers, and oil storage. The planners recognized that the effects of their attack on Pearl Harbor would be time limited. Ideally, the attack would deny US power-projection capabilities in the Pacific for six months, which would enable the Japanese to conquer the majority of Southeast Asia without US interference. While the attack missed the US aircraft carriers and the oil storage, Japan's six-month goal was largely achieved. At the five-month point, the United States was able to conduct its first power-projection capability, with the Doolittle Raid. The first attempt at interfering with Japanese expansion, the Battle of the Coral Sea, was at almost exactly the six-month point. The Japanese thus were tactically and operationally successful in the six-month campaign, but without degrading the US will to fight or its military production capabilities, Japanese victories would be short-lived.

At the tactical level of war, every target system and subsystem has a COG. Once an operational COG is identified, vulnerability analysis techniques can be used for tactical-level target systems analysis, which results in a list of individual targets. Methods such as the critical factors analysis (CFA) method (championed by Joseph Strange of the US Marine Corps War College and also known as the Strange Model or the Marine Corps Model) and CARVER (criticality, accessibility, recuperability, vulnerability, effect, and recognizability) can be used to identify the "best" target—those critical vulnerabilities that will prevent the COG from functioning or achieving objectives.[13]

APPLYING COG ANALYSIS

Performing a COG analysis requires planners to first identify both friendly and enemy COGs and then determine how they can best be attacked or defended in an effort to reach the desired end state. Dozens of models within military strategy literature present alternative methods to identify and assess COGs and associated factors. Thus, scholars and strategists continue to engage in academic discourse concerning the validity, applicability, and effectiveness of various models. While acknowledging the existence of numerous methods to approach COG analysis, this chapter adopts the joint doctrine approach and emphasizes CFA. Regardless of the chosen approach, it is important to remember that while dealing with the inherent complexities of COG analysis, the intent is to discern foundational sources of power (friendly and enemy) and how they are vulnerable. Determining what is vulnerable and how it is vulnerable ultimately influences how military forces attempt to exploit the identified weaknesses in an enemy system. Because of this, the COG analysis process is critical to the operational design.

COG Identification

COG analysis and identification occurs within each level of war (strategic, operational, tactical). Generally speaking, COGs exist in an adversarial context established from the relationships between adversaries' capabilities, intent, and interests. The adversarial nature of an operational environment creates the structure for framing and assessing the COGs due to the perceived threats presented by each force in context. Each military force within the operational environment assesses the adversary's strengths and weaknesses relative to its own. This assessment is critical in guiding military actions toward developing and maintaining power aimed at achieving military objectives while also protecting vulnerabilities that, through exploitation, may hinder operational performance and the achievement of objectives.[14]

COGs at the tactical and operational levels are nested in and contribute to COGs at the operational and strategic levels, respectively. The level of war in which the COG is identified does not change the definitional nature of the COG—it is still a source of power. The level does, however, influence what the COG can be. Military forces, alliances, political or military leaders, or even national will, among other things, can be COGs at the strategic level. Military capabilities are generally associated with operational- and tactical-level COGs, though not exclusively.[15] And while COG identification is influenced by the level of war, so too is it influenced by the type of conflict. COGs in a traditional warfare context often emphasize industrial capabilities, terrain, position, or even a fielded force. COGs in irregular warfare environments may be different altogether (e.g., the population or neutral actors).[16]

COG Analysis Process

After identifying COGs—whether at the strategic, operational, or tactical level—planners can use CFA to analyze the key components inherent in both the enemy and friendly COG system. The CFA allows planners to consider effective ways to influence the enemy COGs while determining ways to protect friendly COGs. Following the identification of both friendly and enemy COGs, the CFA method involves discerning and prioritizing decisive points, which can be "a geographic place, specific key event, critical factor, or function that, when acted upon, allows a commander to gain a marked advantage over an adversary or contributes materially to achieving success (e.g., creating a desired effect, achieving an objective)."[17] Plus, it identifies critical capabilities (CCs), critical requirements (CRs), and critical vulnerabilities (CVs). The key for planners is to identify each of these elements as a system, both interconnected and interdependent. In assessing the interdependencies of the elements of a COG analysis, planners can better understand and then "determine which of these elements offer the best opportunity to influence the adversary's COGs (through direct or indirect approaches), extend friendly operational reach, and enable the application of friendly forces and capabilities."[18]

Critical Factors

The CFA begins with the identification of a COG, which Strange contextualizes as "they don't just contribute to strength; they ARE the strength."[19] This is followed by the identification of three additional critical factors (see figure 21.1):

- CCs are those that are considered crucial enablers for a COG to function as such and are essential to the accomplishment of the adversary's assumed objective(s).[20]
- CRs are the conditions, resources, and means that enable a critical capability to become fully operational.[21]
- CVs are those aspects or components of critical requirements that are deficient or vulnerable to direct or indirect attack in a manner achieving decisive or significant results.[22]

In essence, what evolves from this CFA is an interconnected representation of elements critical to the functioning of an enemy system. The COG, CC, CR, and CV maintain clearly established linkages and interconnectivity such that all elements within the system support each other and enable the functioning of the system as a whole. When assessing the

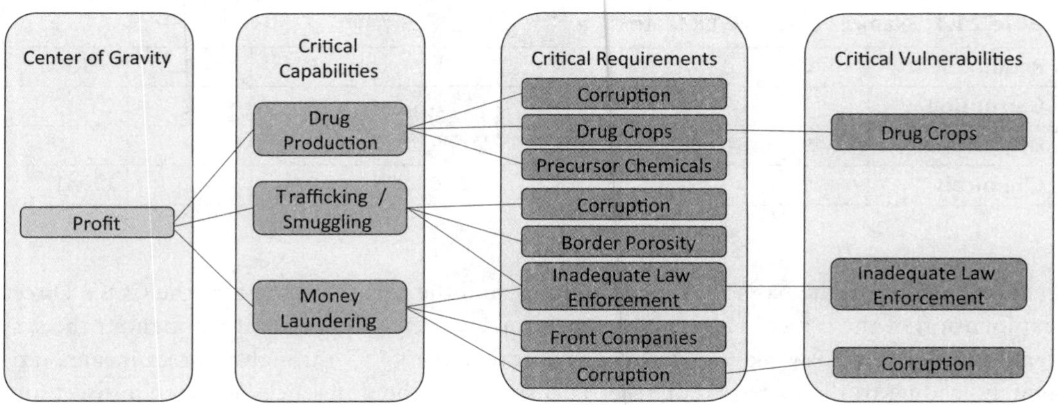

Figure 21.1. COG Analysis Example

enemy system, planners focus on assessing critical requirements and determining which of these requirements also constitute critical vulnerabilities. To discern which of the critical requirements are most vulnerable and therefore create the most ideal points of exploitation, planners employ the CARVER assessment. CARVER assesses each of the system's critical requirements in terms of their perceived criticality, accessibility, recuperability, vulnerability, effect, and recognizability:[23]

- Criticality: How essential is this element to the successful functioning of its parent component, complex, or system?
- Accessibility: How susceptible is this element to attack, given its defenses and friendly offensive capabilities?
- Recuperability: How quickly and easily can this element recover from inflicted damage or destruction?
- Vulnerability: How susceptible is this element to neutralization, damage, or destruction, given friendly offensive capabilities?
- Effect: What is the confidence that successfully prosecuting this element as planned will create the overall desired effect of the mission?
- Recognizability: How easily recognizable is this element (i.e., differentiated from surrounding nodes), considering sensor capabilities, employment conditions (weather, etc.), and time available to analyze the situation and take action?

Planners assess requirements using CARVER in terms of relative value. In other words, what is the criticality of one requirement as compared to the other? Typically, a numeric scale is applied (1–5, 1–10, etc.) for each element, with requirements assigned a relative value for each. The requirement receiving the greatest point value in the CARVER matrix is designated as the critical vulnerability (see table 21.1).

Using this assessment mechanism, planners can—with some degree of confidence and consistency—identify the most critically vulnerable elements within the system that should be the focus of force application aimed at neutralizing the enemy's strength. When the critical vulnerability is affected, exploited, or attacked, this, in theory, creates a systemic failure in the remaining system because the vulnerability is one of the system's requirements; the

Table 21.1. Example of a CARVER Matrix

Requirement	C	A	R	V	E	R	Total
Corruption	7	2	6	5	8	2	30
Drug crops	9	8	8	9	8	8	50
Chemicals	9	7	8	6	9	2	41

requirements form the basis for the capabilities, and the capabilities enable the COG. Direct exploitation of the critical vulnerability, therefore, causes a ripple effect throughout the system, which serves to weaken, destroy, or neutralize the COG through indirect means, ultimately leading to the system's collapse. This speaks to the differences between a direct and indirect approach and the necessity to perform a detailed COG analysis that will ultimately inform the operational approach or "the manner in which a commander contends with a COG."[24] Whereas exploiting a critical vulnerability constitutes an indirect approach, commanders can choose, instead, to perform a direct approach targeted at the enemy's strength. In a direct approach, commanders leverage friendly strengths (COGs) and concentrate combat power directly against an enemy's COG. However, COGs—given that they are the source of strength and power for an adversary—tend to be well protected and difficult to exploit. In this case, an indirect approach—one where the commander applies force to defeat the COG while avoiding the enemy's strength—focuses on the direct exploitation of the critical vulnerability in an attempt to indirectly influence the COG (see figure 21.2).[25]

This logic—whether direct or indirect—forms the basis of planning efforts and provides planners with obvious targets or points of exploitation for which they attempt to concentrate the application of military force within the operational approach. This same logic and process, when mirrored to reflect a self-assessment of the friendly system, informs planners and commanders of their perceived COGs, CCs, CRs, and CVs. Just as commanders attempt to exploit the enemy's critical vulnerabilities in an indirect approach, they seek to protect their own vulnerabilities from the perceived enemy strength, or COG. "In other words, the JFC seeks to undermine the adversary's strength by exploiting adversary vulnerabilities while protecting friendly vulnerabilities from adversaries attempting to do the same."[26]

Whether it informs the commander of a particular target within an enemy system or helps to call attention to a self-identified vulnerability, COG analysis has utility in the joint operations planning process. And while some question the placement of COG analysis within the operation design, it is largely believed to be a necessary component to inform the operational approach.[27] Joint doctrine emphasizes that COG analysis should be approached seriously as a valued form of operational assessment. It further suggests that failure to correctly apply the construct through hasty analysis can generate flawed conclusions leading to grave consequences, including "the inability to achieve strategic and operational objectives at an acceptable cost.[28] For these reasons, COG analysis using the critical factors method, or the Marine Corps Model, is a critically important step in assessing the operational environment and building the foundation for further development of the operational approach.

From assessing general context and political, military, economic, social, information, and infrastructure (PMESII) factors to performing COG analysis and everything in between, it is important to recall that analysis of the operational environment is an iterative process. Understanding of the operational environment should be refined whenever objectives change, conditions change, or new information becomes available. Iterative assessments enable the

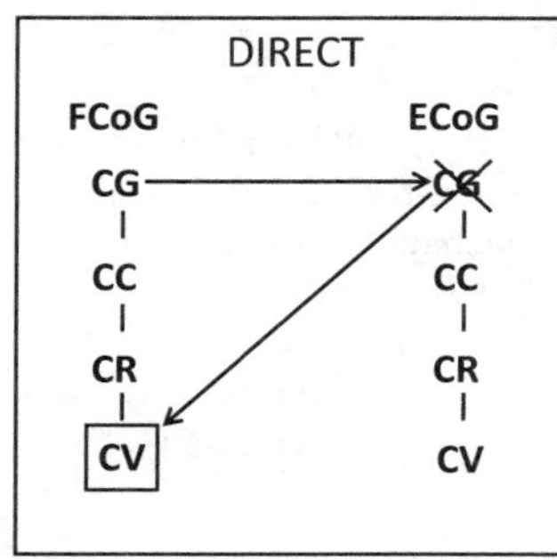

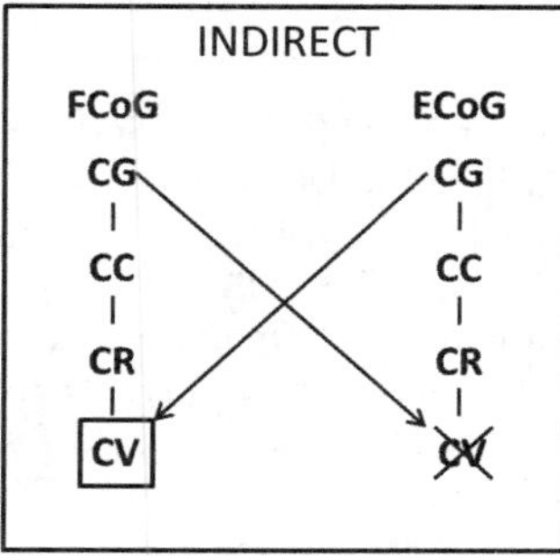

Figure 21.2. Direct and Indirect Approaches

commander to refine the plan with the consideration of new and evolving information. Iterations also help to mitigate potential undesired effects of a planned approach through identification of strategic and operational risks that may not have been present at the onset of the analysis.[29] These are important points of emphasis and underline the significance of a sound assessment of the operational environment. Developing a firm understanding of the relevant factors in the operational environment ensures—at the very least—an informed operational approach planning process. This process provides the basis for a well-developed and logical approach aimed at achieving both the military and national end states and objectives.

CONCLUSION

COG analysis is not simply about picking a single target or vulnerability to exploit. A single COG may be useful for strategic communications and projecting the commander's vision. But more detailed analysis is necessary to facilitate operational planning. To improve the quality of a COG analysis, it is vital to have a good understanding of the environment framed within the context of the problem. Understanding the environment includes estimating the current conditions, likely contributing factors, and projecting future conditions.

While there are a variety of systems models to evaluate an organization, the PMESII model provides a basic framework that is sufficiently flexible to use in a variety of situations. Regardless of the model chosen, the key to a successful analysis is to constrain the project in time and scope. The analysis must meet the needs and timelines of the planners. That analysis should include COG recommendations and detailed analysis of, and linkages to, preceding elements of the operational design model. COG analysis is inherently imperfect, but if done deliberately and methodically it should provide the 80 percent solution that enables line-of-effort design planning to occur.

LEARNING REVIEW

- Recall the purpose of COG analysis.
- Recall Clausewitz's concept of COG.
- Evaluate the utility of Joseph Strange's CFA and the CARVER matrix.
- Evaluate the rules of thumb for COG to identify a set of COGs for a complex national security issue.
- Explain the challenges of applying CFA and the CARVER matrix to a COG.

NOTES

1. Chairman of the Joint Chiefs of Staff (hereafter CJCS) *Joint Publication 5-0: Joint Planning* (hereafter *JP 5-0*) (Washington, DC: Government Printing Office, 2011), III-22.

2. Carl von Clausewitz, *On War*, ed. and trans. Michael Howard and Peter Paret (Princeton, NJ: Princeton University Press, 1976), 703.

3. Michael Matheny, *Carrying the War to the Enemy: American Operational Art to 1945* (Norman: University of Oklahoma Press, 2011), 51; Stephen L. Quackenbush, "Centers of Gravity and War Outcomes," *Conflict Management and Peace Science* 33, no. 4 (2016): 364–65.

4. Quackenbush, "Centers of Gravity."

5. Clausewitz, *On War*, 596.

6. Antulio Echevarria II, "Clausewitz's Center of Gravity Legacy," *Infinity Journal* (February 2012): 5.

7. John A. Warden, "The Enemy as a System," *Airpower Journal* 9, no. 1 (Spring 1995); Robert Pape, *Bombing to Win: Airpower and Coercion in War* (Ithaca, NY: Cornell University Press, 1996).

8. Antulio J. Echevarria, "Clausewitz's Center of Gravity: It's *Not* What We Thought," *Naval War College Review* 56, no. 1 (Winter 2003).

9. Jeffrey M. Reilly, *Operational Design: Distilling Clarity from Complexity for Decisive Action* (Maxwell Air Force Base [AFB], AL: Air University Press, 2012): 5–6.

10. James P. Butler, "Godzilla Methodology: Means for Determining Centers of Gravity," *Joint Force Quarterly* (2014).

11. Jacob Baroed, "The COG Strikes Back: Why a 200 Year Old Analogy Still Has a Central Place in the Theory and Practice of Strategy," *Baltic Security and Defence Review* 17, no. 2 (2014): 15.

12. Dale C. Eikmeier, "Redefining the Center of Gravity," *Joint Force Quarterly* (2010): 156–58.

13. Joe Strange and Richard Iron, "Understanding Centers of Gravity and Critical Vulnerabilities," Air University Press, November 4, 2016, AFD Annex 3-0, Appendix A: Center of Gravity Analysis Methods, https://www.doctrine.af.mil/Portals/61/documents/AFDP_3-0/3-0-D30-Appendix-1-COG-Analysis.pdf.

14. CJCS, *JP 5-0*, III-22–III-23.

15. CJCS, III-22.

16. CJCS, III-22.

17. CJCS, III-26.

18. CJCS, III-26.

19. Strange and Iron, "Understanding Centers of Gravity," 7.

20. CJCS, *JP 5-0*, III-24.

21. CJCS, III-24.

22. CJCS, III-24.

23. Curtis E. LeMay Center for Doctrine Development and Education, *Annex 3-0: Operations and Planning* (Maxwell AFB, AL: LeMay Center, 2016), appendix A, 6, https://www.doctrine.af.mil/Portals/61/documents/AFDP_3-0/3-0-D30-Appendix-1-COG-Analysis.pdf.

24. CJCS, *JP 5-0*, III-31.

25. Baroed, "COG Strikes Back," 8.

26. CJCS, *JP 5-0*, III-24.

27. Dale Eikmeier's article "Operational Design and the Center of Gravity" criticizes the placement of COG analysis within the operational environment section of operational design as premature. He contends that COG analysis should instead be left to be conducted within the operational approach phase of the design process, as it should more directly inform and influence the commander's operational approach. See Dale C. Eikmeier, "Operational Design and the Center of Gravity: Two Steps Forward, One Step Back," *Joint Forces Quarterly* 68, no. 1 (1st Quarter 2013): 108–12.

28. CJCS, *JP 5-0*, III-23.

29. CJCS, III-16.

CHAPTER 22

Building Lines of Effort to Link Ends, Ways, and Means

Ryan Burke

Upon completing a center of gravity (COG) analysis for both friendly and enemy systems, the planner's next step is to develop lines of effort (LOEs) that apply military power against an adversarial system.

OPERATIONAL APPROACH AND EFFORT FRAMING

In the operational approach, planners seek to combine *means* (military assets) with *ways* (asset capabilities with task orientation) to achieve desired military *ends* (conditions and end states).[1] The combination of this means, ways, and ends construct forms the basis of what joint doctrine describes as LOEs. These LOEs establish the structure for complementary military force application across multiple operational domains to transition from the problematic condition to the desired condition. LOEs concentrate military power (either directly or indirectly) on the adversary's COG in an attempt to defeat it.[2] Before linking ends, ways, and means to form an LOE, commanders must answer the following questions:

- What is the military end state that must be achieved, how is it related to the strategic end state, and what objectives must be achieved to enable that end state? (Ends)
- What sequence of actions is most likely to achieve those objectives and the end state? (Ways)
- What resources are required to accomplish that sequence of actions within given or requested resources? (Means)
- What is the chance of failure or unacceptable consequences in performing that sequence of actions? (Risk)[3]

LINES OF EFFORT

The answers to these questions are found in LOEs linking means and ways in an attempt to achieve the desired conditions linked to military and national end states. As shown in figure 22.1, LOEs specify the linkages between (1) the assets to be employed (means), (2) the

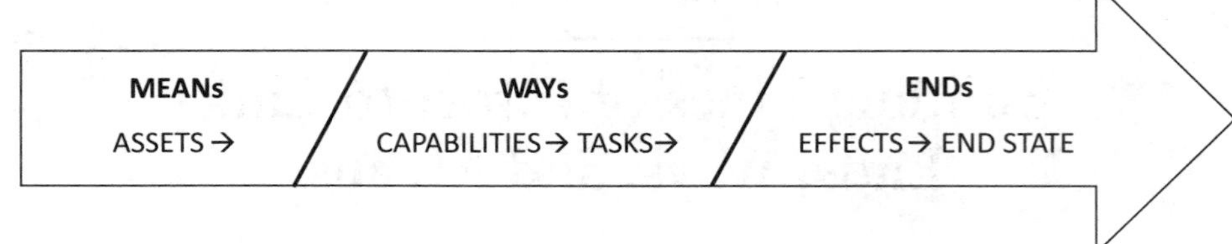

Figure 22.1. LOE Construct

capabilities those assets provide and the tasks they will perform (ways), and (3) the effects created from the resulting actions and the end state produced from the aforementioned effects (ends).

The linkages depicted above form the basic structure of an LOE within the operational approach portion of the operational design framework. This simplified representation provides a linear construct commanders can use to design and visualize an LOE.[4] LOEs attempt to "link multiple tasks and missions using the logic of purpose—cause and effect—to focus efforts toward establishing operational and strategic conditions."[5] This is not to say that an LOE is only used in smaller-scale efforts; rather, it suggests that an LOE tends to emphasize the accomplishment of specific tasks and missions within the operational environment on a path toward achieving the end state.[6] In order to reach the end state established in the operational design, the LOE—through the linking of means and ways—should concentrate military power on the enemy COG using either a direct approach aimed at attacking the COG or an indirect approach aimed at exploiting the critical vulnerability and neutralizing the COG in effect. This point cannot be overemphasized. To remain consistent with the operational design construct and give the commander the best chance of reaching the desired end state, the LOE's primary objective should be focused on attacking, neutralizing, or destroying the enemy's COG through direct or indirect approaches. LOEs provide commanders with a structured approach to reconciling means and ways to achieve desired ends. By linking assets and capabilities with specific tasks, commanders can anticipate and direct the achievement of effects leading to desired conditions and end states, all while remaining consistent with the broader planning process and operational design.[7]

Elements of the LOE Construct

To form a complete LOE, link assets, capabilities, tasks, intermediate objectives, measures of effect and performance, effects, ends, and risks in the means-to-end chain. The means-to-end chain creates a logical connection to bring the problematic condition to the desired condition through the application of military power. The first step in LOE creation—once the desired conditions have been established—is to determine the required capabilities needed to achieve the desired effect and which assets provide the requisite capabilities.

Assets

Assets, in this case, are broadly defined. Personnel, equipment, weapon systems, and so forth that make up the elements of the force structure that a commander has available for employment—otherwise referred to as means. A simple example of an asset is an F-22. A commander must also consider which capabilities are required for achieving a desired effect relative to available assets.

CAPABILITIES

Military capabilities, for our purposes, refer to skills or abilities inherent to a single war-fighter or unit, piece of equipment, or weapon system (broadly defined) that the commander can use to perform a specific or designated function—otherwise referred to as *ways*. Capabilities link means to tasks and produce effects. In the example above, I identified an F-22 as an asset, or means. Using the linear construct, the commander must also determine what capabilities this asset provides in the operational context and in what *way* this asset and its associated capabilities should be employed. The F-22 generally has both an air-to-air (A2A) and an air-to-ground (A2G) capability. With this information, the commander knows what *ways* this asset can employ. With an understanding of the asset/capability links available, the commander can then progress to tasking available means with specific ways.

TASKS

Tasks, according to *Joint Publication 5-0*, "describe friendly actions to create desired effects or preclude undesired effects."[8] However, for the purposes of this chapter, I define a task as commander guidance specifying the use of military assets with unique capabilities to achieve effects. Progressing through the LOE construct, the available assets (means) provide capabilities (ways). The commander must determine what tasks must be accomplished to achieve desired effects. For example, a task for the aforementioned F-22 (means) with A2G capability (way) can be to destroy a command and control node (building) in a particular enemy haven. This is a simple task statement linking an asset with its capability. Thus far, the LOE is vague. To help guide the specific task performance, planners sometimes establish intermediate military objectives (IMOs) along the LOE that closely link to the tasks.

INTERMEDIATE OBJECTIVES

Objectives exist on every level of war and along a broad continuum of significance. As discussed earlier, the operational design framework establishes both national and military objectives linked to the national and military end states, respectively. Whereas these objectives connect to military and national strategic interests on the broader level, objectives can—and should—be included within the LOE planning structure on the operational level to further specify and define the goals for conducting military operations. To give the commander a firm sense of what is to be done and an ability to assess whether the objective has been achieved, intermediate objectives along the LOE spectrum should—without ambiguity or question—meet the SMART (specific, measurable, attainable, relevant, time-bound) criteria.[9] Establishing SMART criteria for intermediate objectives ensures substance and clarity for the basis of task orientation. It enhances the ability to assess performance relative to the achievement of the desired effect if the task accomplishes the objective consistent with the SMART criteria.

Using the F-22 example: an intermediate task objective in this case is that a specific building known to be a key C2 node for enemy fighters is destroyed. Notice this objective is not written as a task statement—that is, it did not say *to destroy the building* (because this is written as a task or action). Rather, it said that the *building is destroyed* (conditional). However, simply saying whether the building is destroyed does not meet the SMART criteria noted above and therefore leaves a great deal of ambiguity for the commander in terms of the operational plan. To meet these criteria, the intermediate objective must go beyond whether the building is destroyed. A better, SMART objective in this example is "100 percent of building X is destroyed before 1600 Zulu, resulting in no observable movement in or out of the location for twelve hours." This objective is specific (building X), measurable (100 percent destroyed; no movement for twelve hours), attainable (the capability [F-22 A2G] to destroy the building), relevant (destroying the targeted building furthers the task of destroying the C2 network broadly), and time-bound (before 1600 Zulu). But is it necessary to destroy 100 percent of the building? Or does it have to be destroyed by 1600 Zulu? Or what is significant about twelve hours of no observable activity at the site? Why not six hours of no activity? Or twenty-four hours? All of these measures are linked to the achievement of an objective that leads to a desired effect.

EFFECTS

Effects are the observable results of a preceding action—or, as doctrine defines it, "the physical or behavioral state of a system that results from an action, set of actions, or another effect."[10] In this way, effects are the direct and observable results of tasks aimed at accomplishing SMART objectives. For instance, our F-22's task was to destroy the enemy C2 building, leading to its destruction within a specific time frame (intermediate objective). The effect of this task and achieved objective is the disruption and subsequent degradation of enemy C2 capabilities within the affected network. This effect is then directly linked to our end state. However, how do we know we have achieved this effect? How do we measure degraded enemy C2 capabilities? How do we determine, with observable indicators, whether we have succeeded? To assess whether the tasks have achieved the desired effect, planners must use deliberate assessment mechanisms to aid their analysis. Here, it is imperative to understand the differences between and utility of measures of effect and measures of performance.

MEASURES OF EFFECT AND MEASURES OF PERFORMANCE

Measuring or assessing performance relative to task achievement and effects accomplishment requires specific understanding of the task being performed, the associated intermediate objective(s) for that task, and the desired effects of the task performance. Military planners develop measures of effect and measures of performance that establish criteria for assessing task accomplishment as well as changes in system behavior or the observable effects of military action.[11] Doctrine defines a measure of effect (MOE) as "a criterion used to assess changes in system behavior, capability, or operational environment that is tied to measuring the attainment of an end state, an objective, or the creation of an effect. It measures the relevance of actions being performed."[12] A measure of performance (MOP), by contrast, is defined as "a criterion used to assess friendly actions that are tied to measuring task accomplishment."[13] Both MOPs and MOEs are used throughout the strategic, operational, and tactical levels of war and can be simplified into two questions:

- MOPs pose the question, Are we doing things right?[14]
- MOEs pose the question, Are we doing the right things?

The above questions imply a linkage between MOPs and MOEs, with MOEs serving as subordinate assessment mechanisms to MOPs. In our example above, the task was to destroy a building housing the enemy C2 node. The intermediate objective for the task was that the enemy C2 node is destroyed. The effect of this sequence was the degradation of enemy C2 capabilities. To assess whether the military action has resulted in the desired effect—or are we doing things right?—the planner establishes success indicators. In this case, an MOP "confirms or denies that a task has been properly performed."[15] MOPs provide direct—usually *yes* or *no*—assessment mechanisms to evaluate task accomplishment. Our task above was to destroy an enemy C2 node with intended effect of degrading enemy C2 capabilities, so to confirm that the task was properly performed, our MOP to assess this is "percentage of the building destroyed." In determining the percentage of the building destroyed, planners can assess whether the task (to destroy the building) was performed right. Was 100 percent of the targeted building destroyed? If so, the task was performed properly. But determining whether the task alone was (or was not) properly performed is only part of the assessment equation. Remember, we are ultimately seeking to determine whether we achieved the desired effect of degrading the enemy's C2 capabilities. If we assume that 100 percent of the targeted enemy C2 node was destroyed and that we did something right, our next step is to determine whether we did the right thing. Perhaps we targeted the wrong building. We may have performed the task properly, but if the task was based on poor intelligence, then we have failed to also achieve our desired effect. Therefore, an MOE (did we do the right thing relative to this task and objective?) is necessary as a complement to our measure of performance. In this context, MOEs emphasize "observable and collectable indicators . . . [that] provide evidence that a certain condition exists or certain results have or have not been attained."[16] If we use the previously stated intermediate objective of "enemy C2 node—building X is destroyed," an example MOE is "increase/decrease in number of C2 orders emanating from the targeted C2 node." The MOE helps us assess whether we notice an increase or decrease in the number of orders leaving the C2 node. If we notice a decrease in C2 orders as a result of destroying the building we believed to harbor enemy leadership, we can logically make the assumption that not only did we do things right but also that this was also the *right* thing to do. In affirming both that we did things right and it was the right thing to do, we can further determine with a greater degree of accuracy that we have successfully degraded the enemy C2 capabilities and thus achieved the desired effect of our LOE.

The literature on performance measures and metrics is vast; so, too, is the doctrine concerning applications and uses of MOEs and MOPs in the military context. For the purposes of this chapter, the reader must simply understand the relationship between MOPs and MOEs and how they are used to assess performance relative to tasks and objectives. Additionally, it is necessary to understand that simply developing MOPs and MOEs in the proper context and relationship is insufficient. A planner must not only develop these measures as mechanisms to assess performance and effectiveness; he or she must also establish the relevance of said measures to the operational environment. As discussed earlier, what is the relevance or significance of accomplishing a task by a certain time? What logic, reasoning, rationale, or basis do we have for establishing, say, a twelve-hour window of inactivity as a performance requirement? Planners must be able to develop MOPs and MOEs that are relevant and also justifiable to the commander. In this context, planners should avoid establishing "numbers for the sake of numbers." With properly developed measures specific and relevant to both the task and objectives, we can better assess our performance and effectiveness toward achieving SMART objectives. And with well-developed SMART objectives, we can say our objectives appropriately link a particular asset and capability package to a specific task that, when performed, will achieve effects consistent with our desired conditions and linked to our broader end state.

ENDS

The final element of the LOE construct is the end state. However, unlike the effects previously mentioned, the end state differs in that it offers some level of finality, whereas effects present steps in a progression to a final point. Doctrine refers to the end state as "how the operational environment should look when operations conclude."[17] In the example, the effect is the degradation of enemy C2 capabilities. This, however, does not imply finality in the broader operational environment. In the operational context, there will be other complementary LOEs occurring simultaneously with their own tasks and intermediate objectives. Through the application and execution of multiple contributing LOEs, a suitable end state for our example of degrading the enemy's C2 can be no further enemy activity in the defined area. In this way, this end state is consistent with the doctrinal definition and gives us a specific "picture" of how the operational environment should look at the conclusion of operations. We can see, both literally and figuratively, whether any further enemy operations occur in the area served by the notional C2 node that we set out to destroy.

RISKS

Assessing operational risk is critical within the LOE planning process. There is a vast body of literature discussing operational risk and risk management, both in and out of the military context. Risk can be thought of in multiple ways, including risk to mission, risk to forces, and even political risk.

A commander must determine the level of risk to mission and forces and whether such risk is deemed acceptable when considering whether to pursue a particular LOE.[18] Determining acceptable operational risk requires planners and commanders to both identify and assess hazards, among other steps of the risk-management process. A hazard is "a condition with the potential to cause injury, illness, or death of personnel; damage to or loss of equipment or property; or mission degradation."[19] Military planners must first identify the potential hazards to a military operation, with the first point of emphasis on identifying hazards most likely to threaten mission accomplishment.[20] Once hazards have been identified, planners must assess them in terms of their probability or likelihood of occurrence as well as the severity of the hazard should it occur.[21]

Assessing probability and severity within the risk context is an inexact science, as it is largely dependent on subjective assessment of known and unknown hazards. However, once risks to mission accomplishment have been identified, planners and commanders can use matrices like figure 22.2 to assess the probability and severity of those risk(s). For example, if a task, activity, mission, or operation carries a perceived severity rating of I (death) but a probability rating of D (unlikely), the risk-assessment code (RAC) given to that particular effort is an I/D 3 (moderate risk). Using this assessment process, the planner can provide the commander with a risk assessment. The commander then uses this information to determine whether the potential risk is acceptable or not and makes recommendations to mitigate risk accordingly.

RISK MATRIX					
		PROBABILITY			
		A LIKELY	B PROBABLY	C MAYBE	D UNLIKELY
SEVERITY	I - DEATH	1	1	2	3
	II - SEVERE INJURY	1	2	3	4
	III - MINOR INJURY	2	3	4	5
	IV - MINIMAL THREAT	3	4	5	5

RISK ASSESSMENT CODE	
1	Critical Risk
2	Serious Risk
3	Moderate Risk
4	Minor Risk
5	Negligible Risk

Figure 22.2. Assessing Risk

LOE SUMMARY

Commanders use the LOE construct to simplify and guide the application of military power toward the achievement of effects that will produce the desired ends. Using this linear construct allows commanders to evaluate various LOE proposals and better determine the best courses of action to accomplish the operational mission. The operational approach construct within the operational design framework provides commanders the visualization tools necessary to develop asset, capability, and task packages aimed at achieving specific effects and ends. In an otherwise complex environment, this simplified linear construct offers commanders clarity, at least in terms of framing the problem and designing the approach prior to execution.

LEARNING REVIEW

- Recall the purpose of the operational approach.
- Describe the relevance of the spectrum of military theory to the development of an operational approach.
- Given a scenario, estimate the level of risk. (Note: When estimating risk, planners must clearly differentiate risk to mission [opportunity cost] and risk to force [death/injury/damage].)
- Describe the challenge of creating useful MOEs.

NOTES

1. Chiefs of Staff (JCS), *Joint Publication 5-0: Joint Planning* (hereafter JP 5-0) (Washington, DC: Department of Defense, 2020), IV-14, describes operational approach as a commander's description of the broad actions the force must take to achieve the desired military end state.
2. JCS, III-1–III-2.

3. JCS, III-1–III-2.

4. Commanders develop lines of operation (LOOs) for larger-scale efforts such as major combat operations that require linking offensive, defensive, and stability operations needed to achieve the desired end state.

5. JCS, *JP 5-0*, III-28.

6. JCS, III-28.

7. JCS, III-28.

8. JCS, III-21, fig. III-10.

9. George Doran is credited with developing the SMART objective framework in a 1981 *Management Review* article, "There's a S.M.A.R.T. Way to Write Management's Goals and Objectives," *Management Review*, November 1981, 35–36. The concept is loosely based on the "management by objectives" (MBO) concept championed by Peter Drucker—that is, "what gets measured gets managed." Peter F. Drucker, *The Practice of Management* (New York: Harper & Row, 1954). There are several different interpretations of SMART within business and management literature, leaving the user to take some liberties to fit the needs of the work.

10. JCS, *JP 5-0*, III-20.

11. JCS, III-45.

12. JCS, III-45.

13. JCS, III-45.

14. "Assessment Measures," in *Air Force Doctrinal Publication 3-0: Operations and Planning* (Maxwell Air Force Base, AL: Curtis E. LeMay Center for Doctrine Development and Education, November 4, 2016), https://www.doctrine.af.mil/Portals/61/documents/AFDP_3-0/3-0-AFDP-OPERATIONS-PLANNING.pdf.

15. "Assessment Measures," D-4.

16. JCS, *JP 5-0*, D-3–D-4.

17. JCS, III-8.

18. JCS, III-17.

19. JCS, GL-7.

20. For more on hazard identification in the military context, review the mission, enemy, terrain, troops, time, civilians (METT-TC) framework found in numerous service and joint publications.

21. JCS, *JP 5-0*, IV-11.

Conclusion

Ryan Burke

What is contemporary military strategy? How do we combine military means and ways to achieve desired ends? What are the most appropriate strategies for addressing the military and national security concerns of today? These are just some of the questions policymakers, strategists, and scholars squabble over in the current threat environment, and with good reason. If these questions elicited simple answers and those simple answers resulted in swift, efficient, and effective execution of those solutions, the contemporary "problems" of today would not be problems at all. However, both state and nonstate actors present threats in the contemporary environment. And whether today's challenges are the same as tomorrow's, one thing is for certain: we need a military capable of both analytic thought and deliberate action. Now, more than ever, the US military must be able to understand threats and develop courses of action to meet these challenges and overcome them, both in thought and in practice. We need officers, therefore, who understand the *context* of the situation, the *theory* that informs it, and can devise sound approaches to the *application* of military power toward solving these ever-growing, complex challenges. It is this *context-theory-application* paradigm that informs our book and its approach to educating our readers.

As we conclude this second edition of *Military Strategy, Joint Operations, and Airpower*, we emphasize—again—that it is not the intent of this book to be an exhaustive discussion of military strategy, nor is it to offer a how-to manual. The intent is to educate the reader on the complexities of the contemporary military environment and to better understand how we reconcile military means and ways to achieve desired ends, with particular emphasis on the operational level of war. In its second edition, the textbook evolved from our first and presents a continually competing interpretation of contemporary military strategy while also offering an overview of the ways we approach planning for—and executing—military operations. Having read the new edition, our audience will have a foundational understanding of contemporary military strategy and how the US military goes about achieving desired effects relative to its strategic aims. The book provides current and future officers with knowledge—both in depth and breadth—of contemporary military strategy within the profession of arms. Officers equipped with this knowledge will be better positioned in the future to consider the relevant context and theories of a situation before determining the proper application of military capabilities to achieve desired effects. This warrior-scholar mind-set is something we strive to instill in our future leaders and something every future officer should aspire to embrace. To quote Sir William Francis Butler, "The nation that will insist on drawing a broad line of demarcation between the fighting man and the thinking man is liable to find its fighting done by fools and its thinking done by cowards."[1]

We must not allow fools guided by cowardly philosophies to fight. The officer who is both a warrior and a scholar, who understands not only the application of military force but also the context and theory that informs it, is the more valuable asset. Ignorance compounds complexity, and in the military context complexity breeds fog and friction. Military leaders need to understand the environments they face before wading into the fray and making decisions of consequence. Given this charge, officers must embrace the warrior-scholar mentality. Our intent with this latest iteration is to continue our contribution to enhancing the warrior-scholar mind-set of current and future officers interested in contemporary military strategy, specifically in the air, space, and cyber domains.

Other books have addressed military strategy in both historical and modern contexts. Some are intended for consumption by undergraduates, most for the graduate level and beyond. This book continues to be the first of its kind to emphasize strategic studies education focused on the context, theory, and application of air, space, and cyber power at the operational level of war and specifically targeting the undergraduate reader. With such a focus, the reader gains a greater understanding of the contemporary military environment and the role of airpower in producing desired effects in a joint context. To do this, we again segmented the book into five sections as with the first edition.

A SHORT REVIEW

In part I, we offered the keystone concepts inherent in the curriculum of the Department of Military and Strategic Studies (MSS) at the US Air Force Academy. In a departure from the first edition, we opened this latest edition with John Farquhar's discussion of the foundations of US military strategy and its link to national security interests. From there, Paul Bezerra, Mark Grotelueschen, and Marybeth Ulrich discussed the intricacies of and decisions informing uses of the diplomatic, information, military, and economic instruments of power, with particular emphasis on the military instrument's use and utility for achieving desired national ends. With that understanding, Danielle Gilbert and Kyleanne Hunter took us through their discussion of the spectrum of conflict and how and why the United States chooses the military instrument of power for particular missions extending from conventional war to peacekeeping and stability operations. In these three opening chapters, the reader gained a foundational understanding of the defense environment and the military's utility within it.

Having provided the reader the groundwork for how to think about the military broadly, part II overviewed the joint force structure and each military service's respective roles within it. Buddhika Jayamaha opened the section with his overview of the joint force, offering an analysis of the structure's evolution and value in achieving national ends in an increasingly complex and interconnected environment. Brian Drohan then discussed the US Army's role as a land force before James Holmes outlined how and why the US Navy projects power in the maritime domain. Ryan Burke and Kyleanne Hunter expanded the discussion to outline the role of the US Marine Corps and the service's unique ability to conduct expeditionary power-projection operations in both contested and cooperative locales. Heather Venable offered a thorough discussion of the US Air Force's role in the joint force, emphasizing its ability to shape battlespaces through airpower. Finally, Michael Martindale tackled the newest challenge—and perhaps most significant addition to this section—through his discussion of the US Space Force and its future attempts to operate in and influence the space domain.

After discussing the joint force concept and the military service roles, part III emphasized functional capabilities across the joint force. Specifically, Jon McPhilamy outlined the dynamic tool that is special operations forces and the missions these elite operators and units execute toward national ends. Judson C. Dressler then walked us through the nature of cyber power as an increasingly relevant and consequential approach to military power application in the twenty-first century. Michael Fowler evolved the discussion next, emphasizing the value of intelligence, surveillance, and reconnaissance in the joint force and how we use these tools to inform the application of particular military means and ways toward desired ends. Rounding out the section, Frances V. Mercado discussed the historical significance and evolving role of weapons of mass destruction and missile defense systems in an increasingly interconnected and compressed military environment.

Now that readers have broad exposure to the defense environment and the pieces within it, or the context for discussion, part IV engaged them with the theory derived from the preceding content. John T. Farquhar started the section by repurposing his chapters from the first edition, modernizing his discussion of both the classic and contemporary airpower theorists and the theories they developed. From there, Michael Fowler retooled his previous "Ways of War" chapter to offer the reader a frame of analysis for determining desired effects. Farquhar then expanded from Fowler's chapter to revisit the topic of irregular warfare in the contemporary environment, which again provided the natural transition to Farquhar's closing chapter in this section outlining the utility and application of airpower in the same context of today's irregular warfare challenges.

Finally, part V concluded with a dedicated focus on the third pillar of the MSS paradigm: application. Repurposing some of the first edition's chapter 3, Ryan Burke and Rob Grant opened the final section's discussion with an overview of operational design and the necessity of developing sound national end states and objectives informing subsequent military planning considerations. From this overview, James Davitch and Michael Fowler detailed how military planners frame problems and analyze the operational environment to sift through information and derive relevance informing a commander's problematic and desired conditions. With an understanding of how such conditions are created, readers were walked through the center-of-gravity analysis process by Mike Fowler and Ryan Burke, who described the military planner's approach to systems analysis and determining how and where to apply military power to cripple adversarial systems. Finally, Burke outlined the process and elements involved in developing military lines of effort aimed at exploiting enemy critical vulnerabilities noted in the previous chapter. In sum, part V discussed how military planners use the operational design process, informed by the context and theories of military strategy, to facilitate analysis and apply military power to achieve effects through a methodologically robust process.

PARTING SHOT

Throughout the five sections of this new edition, we offered both a broad and at times focused assessment of contemporary military strategy and an emphasis on airpower within the profession of arms. Following our context-theory-application paradigm, we maintained consistency with the first edition and designed this book to remain theoretically substantive and practically relevant. The reader has, at this point, gained insight, knowledge, and understanding of some of the most significant elements of the contemporary military environment and the context and theories informing the application of various strategies intended to achieve our national and military ends. The reader now understands the strategic theories and planning frameworks underpinning and guiding the application of military force at the operational level, with additional knowledge regarding the decision points at the strategic and tactical levels as well. The reader also now better understands how airpower is used to achieve effects across the multidomain spectrum encompassing the air, land, maritime, space, and cyber domains. Finally, the reader is familiar with the basic structure and organization of the Department of Defense and the contemporary challenges the military faces in today's interconnected global setting.

With its continued emphasis on airpower and operational strategy in the contemporary military context while specifically targeting an undergraduate audience of future officers, this book again situates itself within an obvious literature gap and consolidates knowledge into a readable, relevant, and substantive assessment that contributes to the continued education of our current and future military leaders.

Finally, we must, as we did before, consider the future of the contemporary military environment. We ask the same questions: In what ways will military strategy change? Will we develop new and better approaches to address contemporary challenges? What will the role of the US military be in the evolving global environment? And how can we best prepare our current and future leaders to serve as warrior-scholars ready to meet these challenges and contribute to the achievement of our national and military end states? These and other questions will continually challenge policymakers, strategists, and scholars alike. And while the answers may not always be apparent, we can, most certainly, offer mechanisms to guide the way—hence the utility and motivation for continued editions of this book.

If we are to adopt Clausewitz's oft-quoted interpretation that "War Is Merely the Continuation of Policy by Other Means,"[2] then we should also adopt the paradigm that our warriors must be scholars and strategists fluent in not only the nuances of contemporary challenges but also in the context and theory that ultimately informs future application of military force intended to achieve desired ends. Knowledge helps guide future action, and officers who understand contemporary military strategy will one day be better prepared to contribute to our profession of arms. As Sun Tzu famously wrote, "If ignorant both of your enemy and of yourself, you are sure to be defeated in every battle."[3] Through efforts like more iterations of this book, we can contribute, in continued ways, to the advancement of military thought and knowledge, the reduction or avoidance of ignorance, and—by extension—success in future battles. With continued discourse and dialogue such as that presented here, we can educate current and future military leaders in the relevant military context, theory, and application considerations present in the contemporary operational military environment. Instilling this paradigm throughout the developing officer corps will generate warrior-scholars better prepared to adapt to the complexities of contemporary military strategy while reconciling means and ways to create effects and achieve desired ends.

NOTES

1. William Francis Butler, *Charles George Gordon* (London: Macmillan, 1889), 85.
2. Carl von Clausewitz, *On War*, ed. and trans. Michael Howard and Peter Paret (Princeton, NJ: Princeton University Press, 1976), 87.
3. Tao Hanzhang, *Sun Tzu's Art of War: The Modern Chinese Translation*, trans. Yuan Shibing (New York: Sterling, 2007), 36.

CONTRIBUTORS

Dr. Paul Bezerra is an assistant professor of military and strategic studies at the US Air Force Academy (USAFA) and previously worked as the National Security Affairs Postdoctoral Fellow at the US Naval War College (2018). His research focuses on economic statecraft and corresponding patterns of political resistance and cooperation.

Dr. Ryan Burke is professor of military and strategic studies at USAFA. A veteran US Marine Corps officer, Dr. Burke teaches courses in joint operations strategy, military logistics, and power projection. He earned his PhD from the School of Public Policy and Administration at the University of Delaware. He writes widely on military affairs and defense policy issues.

Lt. Col. James Davitch is a US Air Force intelligence officer pursuing a PhD. He is a graduate of the US Air Force Weapons School, where he was also an instructor. Colonel Davitch was commissioned from Penn State University ROTC and earned master's degrees from the University of Oklahoma and the Air University.

Lt. Col. Judson C. Dressler is the director of the Academy Center for Cyberspace Research and is an experienced cyber officer who has commanded twice. He holds a PhD in computer science from Rice University and was an assistant professor in the Department of Computer Science at USAFA.

LTC Brian Drohan is a US Army strategist. He led an armor platoon in Iraq, served at the US embassy to Sri Lanka and the Maldives, taught history at the US Military Academy, and worked as a plans officer in South Korea. Colonel Drohan holds BA and MA degrees in history from the University of Pennsylvania and a PhD in history from the University of North Carolina at Chapel Hill. He is also the author of *Brutality in an Age of Human Rights: Activism and Counterinsurgency at the End of the British Empire.*

Dr. John T. Farquhar graduated from USAFA and flew as a navigator in the RC-135 reconnaissance aircraft with the Strategic Air Command and Air Combat Command. With an MA in US diplomatic history from Creighton University and a PhD in American military history from Ohio State University, Dr. Farquhar has taught courses in military history, airpower, strategy, and military innovation at USAFA, where he serves as an associate professor of military and strategic studies.

Dr. Michael Fowler is an associate professor of military and strategic studies at USAFA. He served over twenty-four years in the Air Force in operations, intelligence, and headquarters staff positions. He earned his PhD in national security studies from the Naval Postgraduate School. His research focuses on overlaps between military strategy, security cooperation, and military intelligence. His book *Democratic Equilibrium: The Supply and Demand of Democratic Change* explores the relationships between internal violence, economics, and political change.

Dr. Danielle Gilbert is an assistant professor of military and strategic studies at USAFA. She previously has held fellowships with the United States Institute of Peace, the Minerva Research Initiative, the Institute for Security and Conflict Studies at George Washington University, and the Bridging the Gap Project. Before entering academia, Dr. Gilbert served four years on Capitol Hill, including as a senior legislative assistant and an appropriations associate to the State, Foreign Operations, and Related Programs Subcommittee. She holds a PhD in political science from George Washington University.

Col. Rob Grant is an assistant professor in the Department of Military and Strategic Studies at USAFA. He is a senior air battle manager with over 1,800 flying hours and 240 combat hours in US and NATO E-3 Airborne Warning and Control System (AWACS) aircraft. He is a graduate of the US Air Force Weapons School and the US Army's School of Advanced Military Studies. He earned his PhD in security studies from the Naval Postgraduate School. His research areas of interest include airpower; operational art and design; strategy, leadership, and innovation; and European security issues.

Dr. Mark E. Grotelueschen is an associate professor in the Department of Military and Strategic Studies at USAFA. He is the author of *The AEF Way of War: The American Army and Combat in World War I* and, most recently, the editor of *The Harmon Memorial Lectures in Military History, 1988–2017*.

Dr. James Holmes holds the J. C. Wylie Chair of Maritime Strategy at the US Naval War College and served on the faculty of the University of Georgia School of Public and International Affairs.

Dr. Kyleanne Hunter is an assistant professor of military and strategic studies at USAFA and director of the Strategy and Warfare Center. She holds a PhD in international studies from the Josef Korbel School of International Studies at the University of Denver. Dr. Hunter is a Marine Corps combat veteran.

Dr. Buddhika Jayamaha is an assistant professor of military and strategies studies at USAFA. Formerly a US Army infantryman, he earned his PhD at Northwestern University.

Dr. Michael Martindale is a retired US Air Force lieutenant colonel and the director of the Space Education Committee for the Space Force Association. He served in a variety of space and nuclear operations positions, including the US Air Force Weapons School, the Checkmate Division on the Air Staff, and on the Joint Staff. Dr. Martindale is also a group analyst with Frontier Technology Inc., delivering decision analysis technologies to Department of Defense customers. He holds master's degrees in space studies from the University of North Dakota and in logistics management from the Air Force Institute of Technology and a PhD in political science from the University of South Carolina.

Lt. Col. Jahara Matisek, USAF, earned his PhD in political science (comparative politics) at Northwestern University. He is a former instructor pilot with over three thousand flight hours on the C-17 and T-6, including over seven hundred hours of combat flight time. He has a BS in behavioral science from USAFA, a master's in public administration from the University of Oklahoma and an MS in international relations from Troy University.

Lt. Col. Jon McPhilamy is a PhD candidate at the University of Notre Dame. He earned a master's in international Affairs at the Bush School of Government and Public Service at Texas A&M and earned a masters of business administration from Mississippi State University. He is a prior special operations pilot with over 800 hours of combat time in Iraq, Afghanistan, and Africa. He has commanded a special operations training unit. In the academic year 2019–20, he was the course director for Military and Strategic Studies 251—the course for which this textbook is designed.

Lt. Col. Frances V. Mercado is an instructor in the Department of Military and Strategic Studies at USAFA. She is a space and missile officer. Her most recent assignment was with Air Force Global Strike Command. She has a master's in strategic studies from the Naval Postgraduate School and a master's in international relations from St. Mary's University.

Col. Thomas T. Swaim is permanent professor and head of the Department of Military and Strategic Studies at USAFA. He is an AWACS air battle manager and a former USAF Weapons School instructor. He has a diverse background of operational and tactical command and control duty experiences in the United States, Pacific, and European/NATO theaters of operation. He holds a PhD in educational leadership, research, and policy, with research focused on airpower education and teacher development.

Dr. Marybeth Ulrich is a professor of government at the US Army War College and is currently the distinguished visiting professor of political science at USAFA. Her research interests include strategic studies, with an emphasis on civil–military relations, international security, and national security democratization issues.

Dr. Heather Venable is an assistant professor of military and security studies in the Department of Airpower at the US Air Force's Air Command and Staff College. As a visiting professor at the US Naval Academy, she taught naval and Marine Corps history. She received her PhD in military history from Duke University.

INDEX

Note: Information in figures and tables is indicated by page numbers in *f* and *t*, respectively.